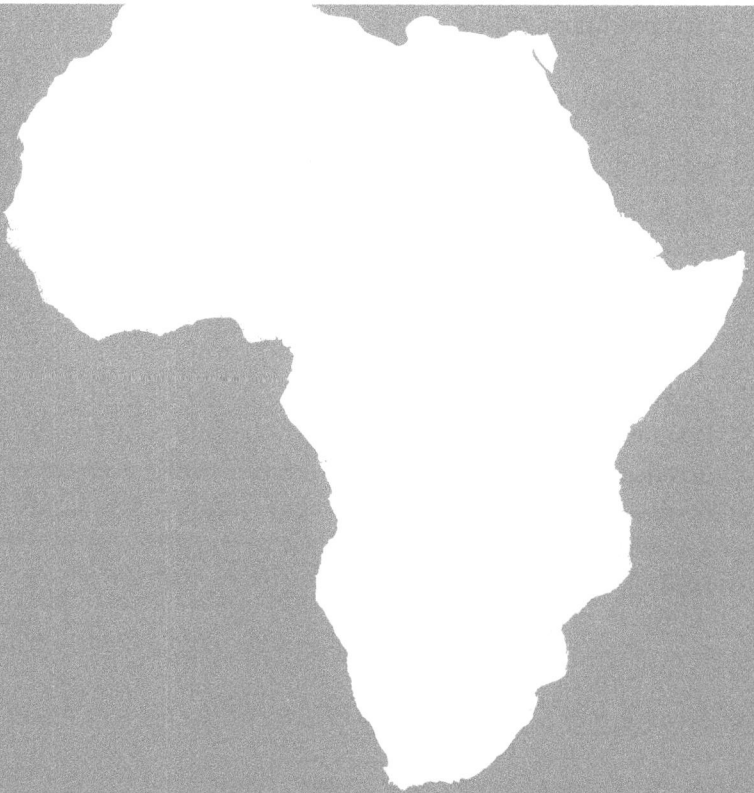

CLEAR DIRECTION

DRIVE THE RIGHT CHANGE IN THE RIGHT WAY

Rose Heathcote

HEATHCOTE
H&A
ASSOCIATES

Published in 2014 by Heathcote & Associates
© 2014 Rose Heathcote

First published 2014

ISBN: 978-0-620-62252-3

Editor: Jennifer Saunderson
Book Design by: Bluewire Design
Cover Design by: Bluewire Design
Typesetting and Layout by: Bluewire Design
Images sourced from: Shutterstock

Heathcote & Associates
Postnet Suite 749
Private Bag X153
Bryanston
Republic of South Africa
2021

CONTENTS

DETAILED CONTENTS

2

3

ABOUT THE AUTHOR

As an improvement enthusiast, author and consultant, Rose Heathcote has focused on raising the performance of enterprises through the principles of Lean Thinking, Advanced Problem Solving and Best Practice in most industry sectors in Africa, the Middle East, the United Kingdom and Indian subcontinent. During her 17-year career, Rose has been privileged to work with more than 100 organisations, from micro enterprises to large multinationals, bringing to them expertise in the strategy, execution methodologies and learning of Operational Excellence.

As a proud South African, Rose's philosophy on improvement has always been centred around keeping it simple. She understands that problems faced by organisations are complicated enough and that the methods to address them, need to be presented in a way that can be used in the most challenging of settings. Rose has spent years testing a multitude of philosphies, methods, tools and techniques in a variety of environments, to consolidate a proven and successful approach that can be effectively used in emerging and developing economies, particularly in Africa.

Rose is the founder of Thinking People South Africa, a consultancy that specialises in delivering an integrated approach to Operational Excellence. She has a background in industrial engineering and business management, where she continues to research new ways of achieving excellence through first principles. Rose is mother to a beautiful daughter and wife to a supportive husband.

ACKNOWLEDGEMENTS

Rose's own personal journey in Operational Excellence began at the age of eighteen as an aspiring student of industrial engineering. It was while reading a prescribed book by John Bicheno (Bicheno, J, 1994, Cause and Effect JIT), that she realised that she, too, wanted to commit her own ideas in operational improvement to publication. Over the years, the more knowledge she absorbed on continuous improvement, the more passionate she became about the topic and the more certain she became of following through on her dream.

Through the years there were a number of defining experiences that helped foster her love and respect for Operational Excellence, including a mentorship with Nissan and the UK Society for Motor Manufacturers and Traders. In 2003, Rose met Deputy Director General at the Confederation for Indian Industry, Dr Sarita Nagpal. Dr Nagpal mentored Rose both in South Africa and India (Delhi, Pune and Chennai Automotive Sector), and demonstrated to her the true potential that organisations can achieve through dedication and a structured improvement approach. Dr Nagpal opened up a world of possibilities for Rose to explore, and this greatly improved her ability to assist South African automotive suppliers to raise competitiveness.

In 2005, Rose was introduced to Prof. Norman Faull from the Graduate School of Business in Cape Town (currently chairman for the Lean Institute Africa). One of the first questions Prof. Faull asked Rose when they met was, 'What do you understand by Lean Thinking?' Without hesitation, but with a hint of discomfort and embarrassment as a proclaimed Lean consultant, she answered that she was not quite sure! Much to Rose's surprise, Prof. Faull seemed to agree with this answer and a relationship formed that day, which would shape her own personal ideology and tenets of Operational Excellence for the duration of her career. Prof. Faull shared his view on the meaning of Lean Thinking and explained that it is a system to create Thinking People. It is also a system for built-in reliability and quality, and should be seen as a holistic management system. Rose took this to heart and spent the next few years trying to define what this system should look like. Thus the 5P Model (Purpose, Process, People, Problem Solving and Planet) was evolved for developing Thinking People, which comprises the contents for the series of books to follow.

Rose was fortunate to meet Michael Ballé in 2009, co-founder of the Projet Lean Entreprise, co-author to a series of books on Lean turnaround (Ballé, F, Ballé, M, 2005, The Goldmine; Ballé, M, Ballé, F, 2009, The Lean Manager; Ballé, M, Ballé, F, 2014, Leading with Respect). Engaged, intrigued and inspired by Michael and his understanding of how a Lean Culture is truly created, and the concept of building people before parts and services, Rose set out to find ways of connecting Purpose, People and Process in her own approach to bring respect for people to the forefront of Operational Excellence. Michael helped her realise the importance of developing a book for Operational Excellence focused on Africa and other emerging economies, which is the strong theme throughout the series of work she has launched.

Rose is grateful to each of these extraordinary individuals who have, in their own way, contributed to her values, beliefs, understanding and execution of Operational Excellence. People don't always realise the positive influence they emanate, and for the person who is willing to listen, wonderful results become possible.

Finally, Rose must give credit to all the clients shes has worked with. Every question asked that she did not know the answer to, formed a baseline from which to continuously improve from, for which she is grateful.

WHAT MAKES THIS BOOK DIFFERENT

The chapters included in this book cover similar topics to many of the books available on the subject of Operational Excellence. The principles are not new, and the author fervently believes in going back to basics and respecting first principles provided by the thought leaders of today and past generations.

The key differentiator of this book, however, is how these existing philosophies, systems, tools, techniques and methods have been packaged into a management system and presented as a 'how-to guide' for you, the reader. It is a time-consuming process to digest the plethora of material out there in Operational Excellence, in order to define your own 'road map', and it is the goal of this series to demystify this process for you, by clearly and concisely offering the following:

1. An illustrated path to Operational Excellence that has been tried and tested in developing and emerging markets. Although the book was completed in 2010, the author has spent the past four years (and several years prior to this) successfully testing the approach in Africa and the Middle East to prove it worthy of publication and appropriate to developing or newly industrialised nations.

2. Many of the books available on the subject, document tools, methods, case studies and even diagnostic assessments, which although enlightening, still leave the reader unsatisfied as they do not necessarily provide the structured guidance that many organisations are looking for. The 5P series takes the reader much further, offering sequence, content, purpose, examples and guided steps to follow, steering clear of a one-size-fits-all approach. The books provide specific information to create your own customised, standardised road map to excellence, by homing in on those techniques that will make a significant impact to the business. Very few consultants share the subtle tricks of the trade. Follow the steps and you will see an immediate outcome.

3. Many improvement publications tend to specialise to one particular approach or philosophy. Admittedly, the author has traditionally been 'Lean-heavy' in her own approach, however, in this series, she deliberately focuses on creating a well-balanced style that integrates using the right tool for the job, depending on the particular problem being tackled. The theme of the series of books falls under the banner of Operational Excellence and uses the principles of Lean Thinking coupled with important concepts from Six Sigma, Theory of Constraints and Best Practice that cannot be ignored.

This book is the first of five in the series, focusing on the following preliminary steps:

○ What problem are you really trying to solve, and in what way?

○ How will you articulate the problem, gain consensus and engage the organisation to join you in solving it?

○ How will you drive the outcome to meet the target condition and then start all over again?

By adding the rest of the series to your collection, you start to see the Management System for Operational Excellence emerge. Browse through the content, and start creating your own structured improvement journey.

WHO SHOULD READ THE SERIES

Anyone trying to understand or execute structured change in an organisation. More specifically, the following audience has been the primary motive for developing the series:

- Leaders and Department Heads in Manufacturing, Service and Government
- Government Agencies mandated to serve the advancement of competitive capability in SMME's from developing and emerging economies
- Business Improvement Specialists, Change Agents and Consultants
- Students from Engineering and Business Management disciplines

HOW THIS BOOK GUIDES YOU

PART I CONDUCT A BUSINESS DIAGNOSTIC						PART II DEVELOP A CHANGE PLAN			PART III DEPLOY THE CHANGE PLAN	
THE NORTH STAR	BEST PRACTICE EVALUATION	VALUE STREAM EVALUATION	BASIC CASH LOSS EVALUATION	FUTURE STATE CONSOLIDATION	IMPROVEMENT STRATEGY	CHANGE MANAGEMENT STRATEGY	LEARNING STRATEGY	ENABLERS FOR SUCCESS	EXECUTION THROUGH PDCA CYCLE

THE LEARNING ROAD MAP
Understand the thought-process

? **WHAT IS THIS?**
Understand the purpose

? **WHY IS THIS HELPFUL?**
Understand the benefits

? **HOW TO DO IT**
Understand the process

✓ **NOW YOU TRY**
Execute your own path

YOUR JOURNEY TO OPERATIONAL EXCELLENCE

To Maria,
for helping me find my strength.

To Sean,
for helping me shape my dreams.

To Eden,
may you always find the strength to follow your dreams.

To simplify you first have
to delve into the devillish detail

AUTHOR'S NOTE

PART I: CONDUCT A BUSINESS DIAGNOSTIC
Discover the Current Performance and True Potential

Embarking on an improvement journey can be overwhelming. Of course, if it was easy, everyone would be doing it and it would not be a competitive advantage. So rest assured, this process is meant to be challenging and take you out of your comfort zone.

PART I of this book is designed to give you a comprehensive guideline to understanding your current business and how to recognise opportunity aligned to your business goals. It covers tools, techniques and principles from Lean Thinking, and important concepts from Constraint Management, Six Sigma and Best Practice. The use of this material requires the support of a sensei and should be tackled by a multi-disciplinary group to ensure system's thinking drives the improvement logic.

The book begins with an evaluation of the North Star and how to set clear direction for the assessments that follow. By starting with this section, you will uncover potential that is important to your business and its customers. Thereafter, we take you through a comprehensive Best Practice Evaluation, which will help define the Current State and target condition for each of the 5P people practices. Best Practice is as important as achieving results, and it will help you define the changes in habit that will create the right culture for continuous improvement in your business.

Understanding the key business processes, using the Value Stream Evaluation follows, and from this, you can map and visualise your current state of flow and develop a Future State condition to meet speed, flexibility and flow requirements.

The next step is linking improvements to the bottom line and this is critical for leadership buy-in and ensuring a positive impact on the profitability of your business. The Basic Cash Loss Evaluation will help you assess the cost drivers in your business and leverage points to tackle in the roll-out.

The final step in PART I is consolidation. Results from each of the evaluations are merged to create a road map for change. The objective is to develop an integrated and clear Future State Road Map with metrics to track performance. The road map will form a major input to the Change Plan in Part II.

PART II: DEVELOP A CHANGE PLAN
A Clear, Compelling Plan to Raise Performance

Equipped with clear direction and the gaps identified in best practice and performance, you will now be able to develop a plan that will steer the leadership of your company and its employees through the journey of improved performance.

PART II of this book is designed to give you a practical guideline to the critical elements your change effort must consider before proceeding. It binds this information into one manageable pack to be used as the guiding star and with this in hand, you and the rest of the senior team, will provide clear direction to the employees impacted by the change. More notably, you will be better prepared for the challenges that lie ahead by the questions you will need to answer.

This section of the book begins by summarising the Improvement Strategy. Improvement Strategy will help you conclude the business Purpose and why the change is necessary. It will also confirm the direction that needs to be taken to meet the objectives and it will define how success is tracked and measured throughout the process, at various levels in the business.

Thereafter, you can consider important factors of the Change Management Strategy, how to develop, enthuse and engage employees to support the change effort, and how to maintain it along the way.

Developing a learning strategy relevant to your improvement objectives follows. This helps quality assure all the time, money and effort spent on learning and development, resulting in true benefit to the business and the achievement of goals.

Finally, we introduce the principles of execution required to turn your strategy into results, although these will be covered in more detail in PART III. We summarise the Future Project Plan and milestones and discuss the benefits of creating A3 one-page summaries to concisely depict how the strategy has been formulated and will be deployed.

PART III: DEPLOY THE CHANGE PLAN

Channel Activities towards Effective Execution

With a comprehensive Change Plan in hand, you are ready to design how the goals will be cascaded through the layers of management and the improvements will be executed in a structured, sustainable way. Perfect goals do not make deployment happen, however, a system designed to maintain focus and direction in times of chaos or uncertainty, will.

PART III provides practical guidelines to implement the Change Plan. It begins by addressing the deployment enablers required for execution. We revisit Clear Direction and the management system to ensure direction is set and agreed habits of best practice lay a foundation for the journey. From there, we look at leadership styles, review current mental models in play and plan how leadership should progress to support the new way of doing business.

Once enablers for success have been attended to, the book focuses on the execution system and developing structures to drive a culture of Plan, Do, Check and Adjust (PDCA). We commence with a clear idea on what is to be done, how, by whom and when. This guides the activities taking place in implementation and maintains alignment to the North Star. It is captured on one page according to the principles of A3 Thinking, and the implementation plan is visualised. We then cascade the high-level plan down to each level, developing subsequent A3 summaries to provide clarity in priorities and responsibilities through the ranks.

With sufficient progress in planning and how the work will be deployed, the attention shifts to verifying results from the action. You will develop review cycles and structures to ensure that what was agreed is achieved, and appropriate action is taken when issues arise and successes are achieved.

This part of the book encourages shared decision making and consensus building. We believe a collaborative approach will bring you closer to creating thinking people who can continue to drive improvement forward. Aim to achieve 80 percent implementation supported and driven by the majority of employees, rather than 100 percent actioned by a select few. Supporting this thinking with organisation-wide PDCA, as a scientific structure for follow-through, is therefore a primary goal in execution. PDCA is a powerful mental model that can set the scene for collaborative problem solving and execution through the organisation, regardless of the nature of the improvement.

Finally, we remind you that delivering value to the customer remains at the heart of Operational Excellence and is the ultimate objective. If deployment of value is initiated from the highest level in the organisation, it will succeed and be sustained. If it is driven only by the lower levels, you will see benefits but they may have a limited life span.

This book cannot give you all the answers but it can send you on a journey of discovery. If you are brave enough to ask the tough questions, you will be rewarded with a new perspective in the way you do business.

Rose Heathcote

OVERVIEW OF OPERATIONAL EXCELLENCE

A STRATEGY TO RAISE PERFORMANCE

Operational Excellence means many things to different people and could appear to be a runaway train of models, philosophies, principles, methods, tools, terms and acronyms. Depending on whom you have asked, they may place emphasis on different elements, perhaps because there is no international common approach. However, there is a need to customise its meaning for each business environment. Interpretations vary, implementation varies and of course, results vary too.

Operational Excellence implies being great at how you go about satisfiying customers, being the best in class and being the one to which other organisations compare themselves. Making it more tangible to digest, Operational Excellence can be viewed as a system where the key elements are important to any organisation but the detailed content of the implementation is customised to suit the business strategy and particular problems faced.

There is, however, an added challenge. To take your operations to new levels of performance means taking your people and processes to places they may not have been before. The critical factor here is people because real change will involve adjustments to the habits of those who drive the processes. Without involvement and an emotional connection to the change, they remain content and secure in how things work today and invariably migrate to old, comfortable practices – a frustrating outcome to those who are already onboard!

We encourage you to view Operational Excellence as a system that nurtures the growth of people throughout the change effort. It is a system that respects all five elements (Purpose, Process, People, Problem Solving and Planet) that collectively drive the right balance of changes. Finally, Operational Excellence is a system that creates thinking people, who significantly contribute to the sustainability of the business and who discover innovative ways to provide more value to the customer.

Creating the system starts with a clear understanding of why you are in business, where the business is prospering and what true value means in the eyes of the customer, shareholder, environment and employee. This is often referred to as the 'North Star' and will provide direction to the improvement strategy and help define problems on which the organisation will need to spend time on.

Progressing from a grand vision for change to something more practical, we take a look at the previous year's goals and objectives to see exactly how well the business performed, and where it failed to meet expectation. A comprehensive diagnostic exposes the current performance to the North Star, the potential for future performance and the road map to achieve the improvement strategy. **PURPOSE** (Book 1 of the 5P Series) is made clear and through planning for change and strategy deployment efforts, the goals for change become a reality.

Armed with clarity in direction, and a system with which to deploy this, it is possible to delve into the nuts and bolts, thereby identifying where the **PROCESS** (Book 2 of the 5P Series) can be better designed and managed to expose problems effectively and achieve the goals for Operational Excellence. Due to the fact that activities are focused, only leverage points to the improvement strategy are assigned scarce resources and this in turn, breeds a culture of continuous improvement in the areas that matter. Customisation of what is to change in the processes, begins its journey.

Having a plan, knowing what problems to fix and where, is only the start. Aligning **PEOPLE** (Book 3 of the 5P Series) to understand their role in the process and helping them to achieve the improvement strategy is a critical cog in the works. This involves everyone, not just the leaders and not just the front-line. It requires creating an environment of teamwork, collaboration, problem solving and learning, coupled with the strength of leadership skills to guide the right behaviour and to drive results. The outcome is a change in the daily, weekly and monthly habits to kindle a culture of continuous improvement and sustainability.

Experience tells us that improvement soon declines if it is not suitably sustained. This not only applies to the systems we put in place after a change event but also how we worked through the improvement phases from the start. Each phase in the change is critical and will ultimately determine whether or not the improvement will last. **PROBLEM SOLVING** (Book 4 of the 5P Series) best practices assist in reaching effective counter-measures and structuring the outcomes to preserve the changes.

A big part of the change effort involves banishing wasteful activites that do not bring value to the customer or business. An organisation accomplishes more efficient processes that perform to customer needs, made possible through people involvement. This improvement directly influences how the organisation contributes to environmental sustainability, but to bring more focus to this strategy for change, we include specific tools and methods to manage environmental impact. **PLANET** (Book 5 of the 5P Series) completes the model with a robust appproach to cleaner, more responsible, environmentally sustainable processing.

In conclusion, developing each element of the 5P Model to support the level of business improvement required, will create a fit-for-purpose management system to create **THINKING PEOPLE** who deliver value to the triple bottom line.

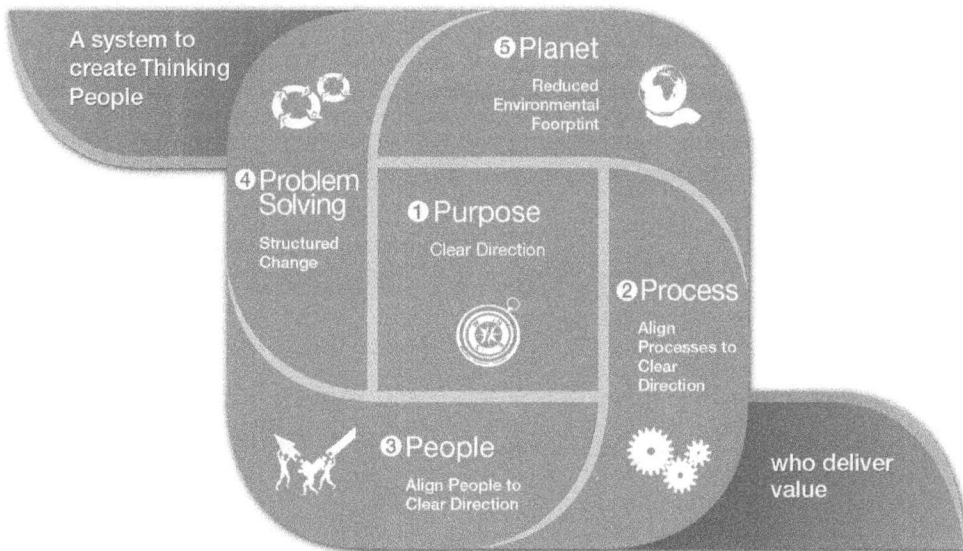

The 5P Model represents the system to create *Thinking People*

PART I
CONDUCT A BUSINESS DIAGNOSTIC

Discover the Current Performance and True Potential

DIAGNOSTIC LEARNING ROADMAP

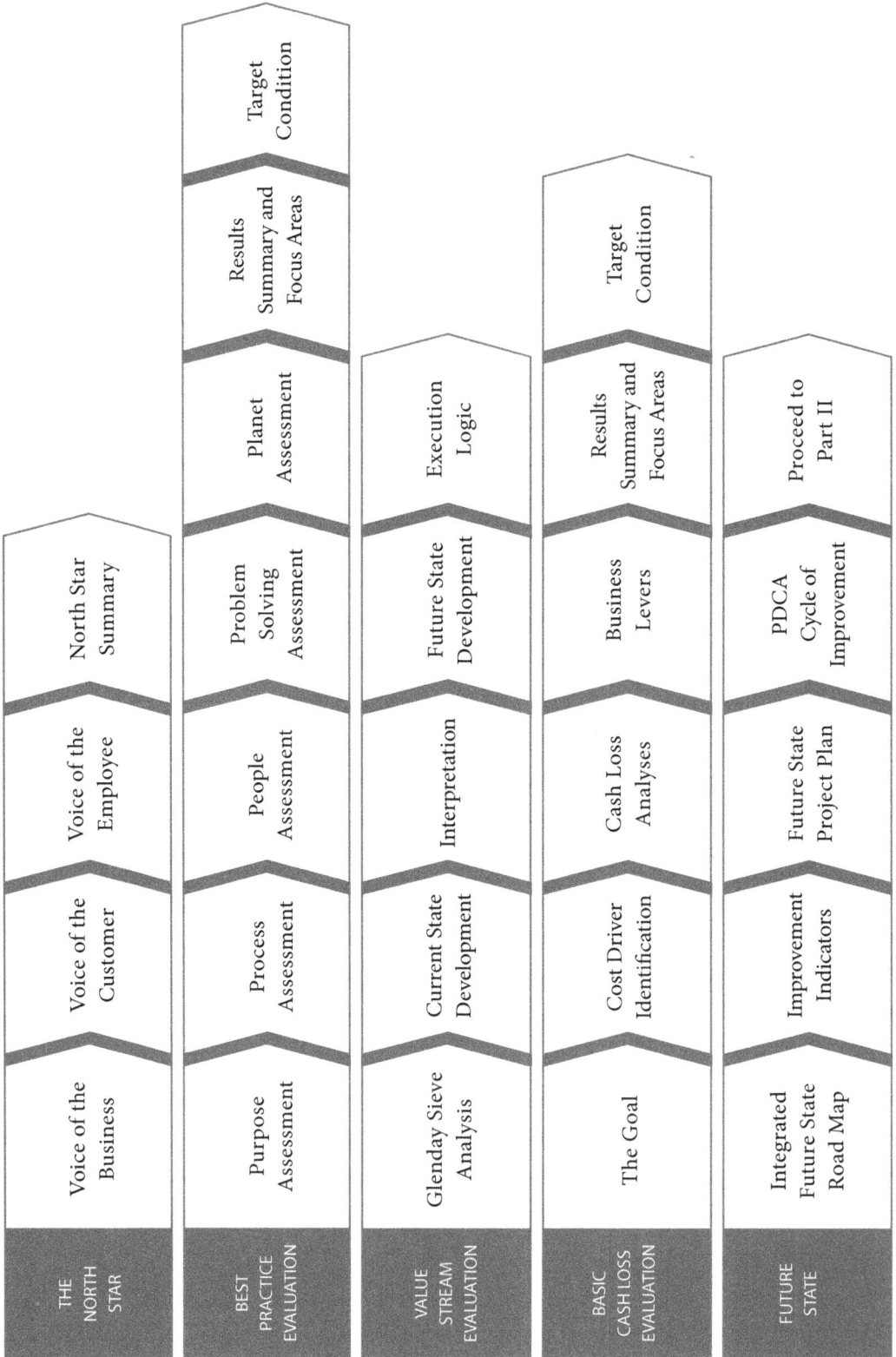

THE NORTH STAR	Voice of the Business	Voice of the Customer	Voice of the Employee	North Star Summary		
BEST PRACTICE EVALUATION	Purpose Assessment	Process Assessment	People Assessment	Problem Solving Assessment	Planet Assessment	Results Summary and Focus Areas	Target Condition
VALUE STREAM EVALUATION	Glenday Sieve Analysis	Current State Development	Interpretation	Future State Development	Execution Logic	
BASIC CASH LOSS EVALUATION	The Goal	Cost Driver Identification	Cash Loss Analyses	Business Levers	Results Summary and Focus Areas	Target Condition
FUTURE STATE	Integrated Future State Road Map	Improvement Indicators	Future State Project Plan	PDCA Cycle of Improvement	Proceed to Part II	

1 THE NORTH STAR
THE VOICE OF THE BUSINESS

❓ WHAT IS THIS?

Voice of the Business relates to the strategic intent of the business for future prosperity and defines a plan of action to raise the current performance towards a goal. This plan is usually a three to five-year focus and based on rigorous analysis such as Strengths, Weaknesses, Opportunities and Threats Analysis (SWOT), Competitor Analysis and Market Trend Analysis. Developing the business strategy is beyond the scope of this book but understanding the Voice of the Business is a necessary input to the diagnostic.

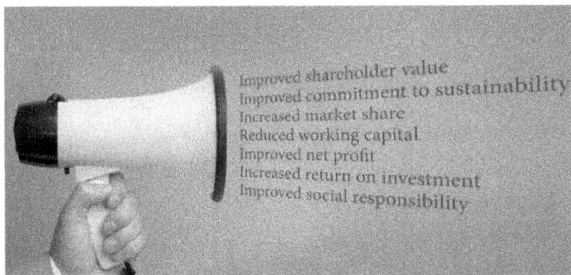

In short, we seek to understand the goals, objectives and any key initiatives already identified to take the business forward and the current performance to those goals set. This will inform where we go looking and what impact we strive for in the diagnostic results.

❓ WHY IS THIS HELPFUL?

o We cannot define our problems until we know what constitutes a problem. By comparing our current performance to the goals and objectives, the shortfalls become clearer and the diagnostic takes on a strategic focus.

o The improvement strategy is closely connected to the business strategy and so leaders are able to provide clear direction to focus their people on the right activities.

o Employees develop faith that the leadership team is aligned and maintains a constancy of purpose.

o Performance improvement efforts can be measured for their impact on the bigger picture.

o More focus leads to better use of scarce resources.

o The improvement strategy is not deemed a 'stand-alone' exercise by a 'stand-alone' department but a critical component in the achievement of the business strategy.

❓ HOW TO DO IT

Clarify the Business Goals, Objectives and Planned Initiatives

Depending on the availability of a strategic plan and defined goals and objectives, capture the key components of the improvement focus using Table 1.1 as a guideline:

VOICE OF THE BUSINESS			Example
Business Goal (Mar 2015)	Business Objective	Existing Key Initiatives	Current Performance (Feb 2014)
Grow market share by 25%	Secure existing customer base	**Superior Service** ○ Service 80% of clients in fewer than 10 days ○ Achieve zero customer complaints	○ Lead time ranges from 10 to 60 days ○ 15 complaints received per annum
	Increase market penetration in existing markets	**Responsible Company** ○ Reduce tons of hazardous waste by 50% ○ Improve packaging recycling by 100% **Entry Incentives** ○ Service 100% of clients in fewer than 14 days ○ Implement loyalty plans with incentive ○ Offer hassle-free application process	○ Hazardous waste averages at 3 tons per month ○ 100% of packaging discarded after single use ○ Lead time ranges from 10 to 60 days ○ No loyalty plan in place ○ Complex application process
Reduce working capital by 18%	Reduce Inventory Holding by R20m		○ R120m inventory holding
	Reduce Cash-to-Cash Cycle to 45 days	*Undefined, awaiting diagnostic results*	○ 79 days financing time (cash-cash)
	Reduce capital expenditure by 25%		○ Planned capital expenditure is R50m
Reduce environmental impact on energy and water by 30%	Reduce water consumption by 30%	○ Improve cleaning process to reduce 70% water consumption ○ Reduce need for cleaning through scheduling changes	○ 150 000 m³ groundwater per
	Reduce energy consumption by 30%	○ Convert all lighting to low energy ○ Implement office auto-lighting system	○ 2500 GWh per annum
Increase net profit by 5%	Reduce operating expenses by 17%	*Undefined, awaiting diagnostic results*	○ R47m operating expenses

Table 1.1

VOICE OF THE BUSINESS			
Business Goal	Business Objective	Key Initiatives	Current Performance

Capture the critical areas of focus from the Strategic Plan.
If initiatives have been identified, include them or make a comment.

✓ FOR YOU TO TRY

- Review the available strategic plan.
- Capture the focus areas including:
    - Business goals
    - Business objectives
    - Key initiatives identified to date
    - Current performance in these goals.

THE VOICE OF THE CUSTOMER

❓ WHAT IS THIS?

Before commencing with any improvement initiative, it is critical to understand the needs of the customer to ensure the changes made bring real benefit to the customer.

> *'Customer requirements, as expressed in the customer's own terms, are called the voice of the customer. However the customer's meaning is the crucial part of the message.'*

(Evans and Lindsay 1996: p161)

You may have heard the expression: 'don't improve the business until your doors close'. This is a profound statement but it makes sense when you think about it. If we are constantly throwing our efforts into activities that have no impact on the customer, then surely this is just exploiting resources unnecessarily and increasing costs? Surely this is 'improvement' without real benefit? We call this 'improvement noise'.

We therefore encourage you not to proceed without giving careful consideration to the customer's meaning of 'requirement', and if at the end of the section, you can answer the following questions, you are one step closer to understanding the Voice of the Customer:

WHO	are the customers?
WHAT	do they want?
WHY	do they want it?
WHERE	do they want it?
WHEN	do they want it?
HOW	do they want it[6]?

❓ WHY IS THIS HELPFUL?

Conducting this exercise will help you:

- Figure out what your customers care about.
- Set your priorities and goals consistent with the customer needs.
- Determine what customer needs you can profitably meet (George 2005).

❓ HOW TO DO IT

Depending on the nature of the business, there are several tools available to better understand the Voice of the Customer. You may need to come up with your own creative variations but what follows are a few examples that other organisations have found particularly useful.

Step 1: Group your Customers

Customers may have different needs or requirements, and customer service suffers when we try to put every customer into the same pot. If you have a reasonably large customer base, it is useful to first group your customers and then proceed to develop the Voice of the Customer.

Quality guru, Joseph Juran suggested classifying customers into two main groups: 'the vital few' and 'useful many' (Juran 1992: ch 3). You could segment your customers by:

- Geographical location
- Products or how they use them
- Cost of doing business with them
- Volumes (figure 1.1)
- Revenue they generate
- Loyalty
- How often they purchase
- Strategic goals

CUSTOMER CLASSIFICATION — Example AT DECEMBER 2013

CUSTOMER	VOLUME	REVENUE	LOCATION
A	45 000	R2 000,000.00	Gauteng
B	35 000	R1 600,000.00	Gauteng
C	30 000	R1 200,000.00	Durban
D	8 000	R450 000.00	Durban
E	7 000	R100 000.00	Durban
F	6 500	R80 000.00	Durban
G	2,000	R50 000.00	Cape Town
H	500	R20 000.00	Cape Town

Try not over-complicate the analysis. You want to understand the needs of the customers and to start, you may want to understand the needs of the vital few.

Once you have completed the grouping, visualise the findings using table 1.2. We will build on the content throughout this section:

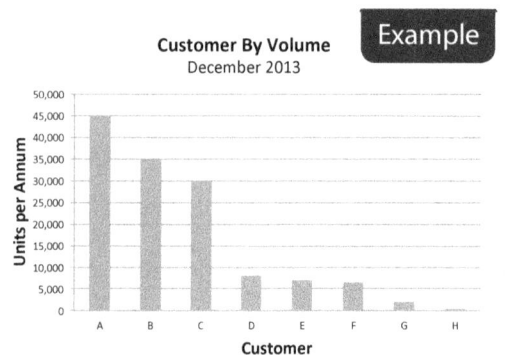

Customer By Volume — Example
December 2013

Figure 1.1

| VOICE OF THE CUSTOMER | | | | | | | Example |
PROFILE	CUSTOMER GROUP	WHO is the customer?	WHAT do they want?	WHY do they want it?	WHEN do they want it?	WHERE do they want it?	HOW do they want it?
Volume	High Volume (>80%)	Customer A					
		Customer B					
		Customer C					

Table 1.2

Step 2: Collect the Voice of the Customer

There are a few options to gather more information about the customer, and choosing a simple way to better understand their needs is best. Consider the results of the customer-grouping exercise and decide which approach will be the most applicable.

Useful sources to gather WHO, WHAT, WHY, WHEN, WHERE and HOW may include (Evans and Lindsay 1996):

USE EXISTING INFORMATION

- Sales data
- Returns or refunds data
- Sales preferences
- Contract cancellations
- Customer referrals
- Closure rates of sales calls

CREATE CUSTOMER LISTENING POSTS

- Complaint and compliment mechanisms
- Customer-facing staff
- Social networks

MAKE CUSTOMER CONTACT

- Interview
- Surveys
- Focus groups
- 'Go see for yourself'

Face-to-Face Interviews

There is a significant advantage to sitting face-to-face with someone and getting their input on matters close to the heart – product, service and performance. It is important to be well organised in terms of what you are trying to achieve and to listen intently to what the customer has to say. You will gain a unique perspective that could lead to real innovation in how problems are solved later.

Plan the Interview:

- ○ Decide on what you want to get from the interview and prepare your questions.
- ○ Decide how you will document and summarise the Voice of the Customer.
- ○ Make an appointment planning the time well (last thing on Friday is not ideal!).
- ○ Go get the Voice of the Customer.

Example of Typical Questions to Customise:

Category	Questions & Dialogue	Customer Response Example
Service Vision	How would you describe the perfect service from us?	If we received exactly what we wanted, in the quantity and place we wanted, and at the quality we wanted, we would be very happy.
Challenges	What are your greatest challenges in how we provide you with our service? On which of these challenges do you place the highest priority?	We have tremendous demand variation from our clients and find your inflexibility to adjust to this a challenge. Our clients expect a 5% cost reduction annually, and our challenge is to get our suppliers to support this goal and work together with us to find the opportunities. Our competition is hot on our heels – this is critical.
Support Needs	What can we do to improve the relationship between our companies?	More collaboration in problem solving and improved communication that support this would be helpful. Improving visibility of service levels would also support the triggering of collaborative problem solving.
Performance Needs	What performance measures do you use to rate our service to you? How well have we performed to target over the past six months?	Typically we use 'on time in full' and 'availability'. We would like to review these with you and perhaps you could also track it and give us feedback on what measures you are taking to address shortcomings? Here is your latest performance.
Way Forward	We appreciate your time and will be reviewing our performance and your comments. We will come back in a month to share how we plan to improve.	Excellent. Let's see what you manage to do.

Example

'Go See for Yourself'

'Go to gemba' means 'go where the action is' if you want to learn more about the customer's problems. This is a good approach when gathering intelligence on the Voice of the Customer. Go to where it is all happening, where the product or service is in use, and learn from what really happens. Take out the guesswork and perceptions and see for yourself.

Plan Your Observation:

o Decide what you want to get from the observations.

o Choose the right person to conduct the activity, someone who understands the purpose of the exercise.

o Brainstorm how and when you will observe.

o Decide how you will document your observations.

o Prepare how you will summarise the results in the Voice of the Customer.

o Do a trial run at one customer and refine your approach for later use.

o Make sure the people you observe understand why you are there.

o Remember to thank the customer afterwards.

Having gathered the Voice of the Customer through various means, you can update the table:

PROFILE	CUSTOMER GROUP	WHO is the customer?	WHAT do they want?	WHY do they want it?	WHEN do they want it?	WHERE do they want it?	HOW do they want it?
Volume	High Volume (>80%)	Customer A	OTIF 95% availability 95% 5% cost reduction	Flexibility Pressure from competition	12 months	Product AS34 and GU76	Improved performance tracking and collaborative problem solving
		Customer B	OTIF 90%	Delivery penalties from their customers	6 months	Product AS34; YP25; PL67	Review complaints and address
		Customer C	Improved packaging	Improve image of product	3 months	All supplies	Investigate with design team

VOICE OF THE CUSTOMER — Example

Step 3: Filter the Results

By filtering the results, you will understand how much value the customer places on certain attributes of the product or service.

Dr Noriaki Kano developed what is known as the Kano Model. Kano determined that there are three factors worth considering for the product or service:

o Dissatisfiers
   This is a basic need, without which you would not even be considered for the order. Often the customer will not feel the need to mention this, as it is implied.

o Satisfiers
   This is about a need for performance and the customer satisfaction will vary according to this. Speed, cost and ease of use would be examples.

o Delighters
   This is the excitement factor. They earn you 'brownie points' with the customer and present the opportunity to provide world-class service or products.

Visually plot the needs of the customers into the Kano Model in figure 1.2 to indicate how much they value this feature, how well you perform and the priorities for focus. This will filter some of the requirements into a prioritised order:

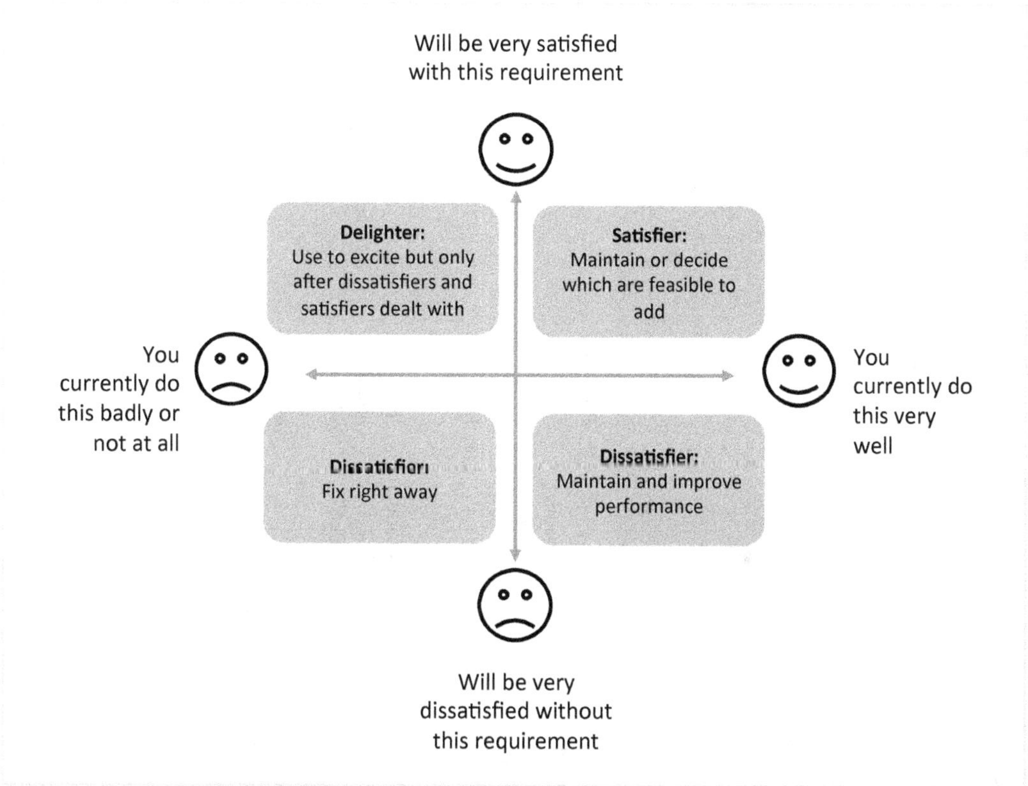

Figure 1.2

Step 4: Summarise the Priorities

Now you are able to complete the Voice of the Customer table with what is important to each of your vital customers and the priority areas for focus going forward. Keep this and the Voice of the Business in mind every time you prioritise actions and projects in the change effort. Use this to guide and define where you place your improvement energy.

VOICE OF THE CUSTOMER

Example

PROFILE	CUSTOMER GROUP	WHO is the customer?	WHAT do they want?	WHY do they want it?	WHEN do they want it?	WHERE do they want it?	HOW do they want it?	VALUE how important it is	PRIORITY level for improvement focus
		Customer A	OTIF 95% availability 95% 5% cost reduction	Flexibility Pressure from competition	12 months	Product AS34 and GU76	Improved performance tracking and collaborative problem solving	Dissatisfier	Very high
Volume	High Volume (>80%)	Customer B	OTIF 90%	Delivery penalties from their customers	6 months	Product AS34; YP25; PL67	Review complaints and address	Satisfier	High
		Customer C	Improved packaging	Improve image of product	3 months	All supplies	Investigate with design team	Delighter	Medium

✔ FOR YOU TO TRY

○ Agree on how customers will be grouped.

○ Gather necessary data and develop customer groupings.

○ Agree on how the Voice of the Customer should be determined.

○ Design the relevant approach and do the necessary planning.

○ Gather the information and summarise the results.

○ Filter the customer needs to determine a priority list.

○ Complete the Voice of the Customer table and refer back to this summary when assessing change initiatives.

THE VOICE OF THE EMPLOYEE

? WHAT IS THIS?

The Voice of the Employee is about understanding what employees are saying, what their perceptions are and their suggestions for improvement. Trying to implement a change initiative when employees experience a lack of direction, could make them feel they are in the dark or that there is no collaboration between the leadership and their employees.

Understand where the employees stand and what their areas of concern are so that when the Change Management (PART II) and Execution Strategy (PART III) is developed, it specifically addresses these shortfalls.

Figure 1.3

Figure 1.3 indicates the elements that should be assessed when evaluating readiness for change. It is recommended that a variety of positions, levels and demographics be surveyed to provide a good representation of the current state of affairs within the business.

TIPS

This is a complex and in-depth evaluation to understand the climate within the organisation. We highly recommend that a certified professional assists you in conducting such a comprehensive study.

The benefit of this is not only getting good source data from which to base decisions but also to have an impartial facilitator interpret and present the results. This ensures the information is being used in the correct way. A climate survey can also create expectations from those participating and if not handled correctly and followed through on, can lead to the destruction of the trust this element aims to create.

WHY IS THIS HELPFUL?

- Employee perceptions are better understood taking guesswork out of the equation.
- The readiness for change is established.
- Strengths and weaknesses are exposed, indicating what to play to and what to improve.
- The result provides substance to the Change Plan (PART II) and assists the leadership team in preparing an approach that breeds trust and transparency.
- A baseline is set from which to conduct periodic reviews and track progress.

HOW TO DO IT

Step 1: Communicate the Survey

The method of communication will vary from company to company but as a generic approach, the managing director (MD) or chief executive officer (CEO) addresses the staff. Background to the survey is to be explained and how the information will be used to better understand the perceptions, needs and recommendations coming from the employees.

The anonymity of the survey should also be emphasised and every employee encouraged to participate. In a large organisation, it can be fairly labour intensive to collate the results, so in this case an alternative strategy may be sought.

Step 2: Prepare the Survey Questionnaire

Table 1.3 may be used for the survey. The employee is expected to complete each question. In an organisation with literacy or language complications, it is highly recommended that a skilled facilitator handle focus groups to assist in the objective understanding of each question.

VOICE OF THE EMPLOYEE   Example

CLIMATE SURVEY

DATE

POSITION IN COMPANY
- ☐ Frontline operations
- ☐ General management
- ☐ Middle management
- ☐ Team leader
- ☐ Support staff
- ☐ Executive

INSTRUCTIONS:

○ For each question, choose the answer that best describes the question for you, and mark with an X.

○ Submit your completed survey to the lock box at the reception area or catering area.

○ The results of this survey will be presented at the next Road Show on 15 April 2014

CLEAR DIRECTION		Strongly Agree	Agree	Disagree	Strongly Disagree
1	I know our company vision by heart and can see how the strategy aims to achieve our vision.				
2	I am clear on my goals and how these link to the strategy of the company.				
3	I am in agreement with the targets set and understand how this will assist us in achieving the strategy.				
4	Our goals drive the right behaviour in my team and everyone works together towards customer satisfaction.				
5	I can see how the activities I do everyday link directly to my goals and achieving the strategy.				

COMMENTS:

Table 1.3

STRUCTURES		Strongly Agree	Agree	Disagree	Strongly Disagree
6	I believe we have the right people, in the right places, doing the right things within my team.				
7	Our team is well structured to achieve the goals set for us.				
8	I can see how our area or department adds value to the customer and the business.				
9	We have good structures and systems in place to facilitate continuous improvement activities.				
10	I am empowered to make decisions relative to my position.				

COMMENTS:

LEADERSHIP STYLE		Strongly Agree	Agree	Disagree	Strongly Disagree
11	My superior lives by our company values and personally sets an example.				
12	I feel I can raise problems without negative consequences and that my superior listens and acts.				
13	My superior works with me to solve problems and values my input and experience.				
14	My superior provides clarity and focus in the work I do and assists me to spend time on the right activities.				
15	I feel involved in decisions made and empowered to act on our vision.				

COMMENTS:

COMPANY CULTURE	Strongly Agree	Agree	Disagree	Strongly Disagree
16 There is mutual respect for people in our team, evident in how people treat each other and value others' input.				
17 There is a feeling of trust and transparency amongst co-workers, between employees and superiors.				
18 Ethical behaviour is evident and I believe employees live the values of the company, everyday.				
19 Our daily habits align to the behaviours needed to create a culture of improvement and customer satisfaction.				
20 Our company cares for its employees and people feel stable in their employment.				

COMMENTS:

CLARITY OF ROLE	Strongly Agree	Agree	Disagree	Strongly Disagree
21 I am clear on my role description and that of my superior.				
22 Role descriptions are well documented and provide me with guidance on areas for improvement.				
23 There is a formal development plan to raise my competency in my role, with regular reviews.				
24 I am clear on what I must develop to progress in the company and take on new responsibilities.				
25 There is consistency in performance between employees in the same roles.				

COMMENTS:

CHANGE MANAGEMENT	Strongly Agree	Agree	Disagree	Strongly Disagree
26 I believe change in the company is good, well planned and well executed, with involvement from the right people.				
27 I believe change in the company is good, well planned and well executed, with involvement from the right people.				
28 When obstacles to change are met, they are removed and I receive the support I need.				
29 I can see where the change is taking us and the benefit is evident in how we achieve goals and how people feel about it.				
30 Changes for the good last and the team and leadership work hard at maintaining the new methods of work.				

COMMENTS:

COMMUNICATION	Strongly Agree	Agree	Disagree	Strongly Disagree
31 I feel I can approach my superior and that his or her door is always open.				
32 I am able to freely approach my MD or any of the directors.				
33 Communication in the company is good, frequent and I feel I am up to speed with all the latest developments.				
34 Communication in the company flows well. If I send communication upwards, I always receive timely feedback.				
35 Communication from leadership is open, honest and fosters good teamwork and stability.				

COMMENTS:

TEAMWORK	Strongly Agree	Agree	Disagree	Strongly Disagree
36 Our team works together, towards a common goal of improvement and customer service.				
37 Strengths and weaknesses in our team are well understood, and used in a positive way.				
38 Our team supports our leader and there is good overall communication within the team.				
39 Our team solves problems together, in a constructive way that benefits the customer.				
40 There is consistency and respect in how people from different backgrounds are treated in our team.				

COMMENTS:

PERFORMANCE MANAGEMENT, REWARD AND RECOGNITION	Strongly Agree	Agree	Disagree	Strongly Disagree
41 I am clear on what constitutes good or poor performance, and receive constructive feedback.				
42 I know my contribution to making improvements will be praised, recognised and rewarded.				
43 A personal-development plan guides improvement in my performance.				
44 Reward and recognition is applied fairly across the company.				
45 Performance management is regular, consistent and breeds a culture of trust within my team.				

COMMENTS:

LEARNING AND DEVELOPMENT	Strongly Agree	Agree	Disagree	Strongly Disagree
26 My personal-development plan guides all training and development I undergo.				
27 My superior supports the training and development I participate in, and coaches me to apply it to my work.				
28 I am encouraged to further develop myself and set goals for future career aspirations. These are reviewed.				
29 The quality of the training and development provided to me prepares me to deliver on my responsibilities.				
30 I consider learning and development valuable and a means to achieve my goals.				

COMMENTS:

INNOVATION	Strongly Agree	Agree	Disagree	Strongly Disagree
31 My ideas are valued and I feel my superior has faith in my ability to bring forward new ideas.				
32 I have actively implemented improvements in my area to affect quality, cost, delivery, safety, environment or customer satisfaction in the past 30 days.				
33 I have actively implemented improvements in my area to affect quality, cost, delivery, safety, environment or customer satisfaction in the past 12 months.				
34 Improvements I implement are always sustained and receive the support from other team members.				
35 I am confident that I will be rewarded and recognised for the ideas I bring to exceed performance.				

COMMENTS:

Step 3: Distribute and Track Progress

It is good to get an even spread of participants across levels, positions and demographics. All employees are to be provided with the questionnaire, where they can submit the surveys anonymously to the administrator. A lock box could work well for this but ensure it is attended to.

As the surveys start coming through, the administrator should track the numbers and if the format allows for this, the level in the organisation. This feedback is to go back to the MD or CEO so that staff can be lobbied to participate until the numbers are sufficient to use. See Table 1.4 for an example:

Example	Executive Team	General Managers	Support Staff	Team Leaders	Frontline Staff
Total Employees	5	8	27	15	85
Surveys submitted to date	1	3	8	2	17
% Submitted to date	20%	37.5%	30%	13%	20%
% Target	100%	100%	60%	80%	50%

Table 1.4

An alterative method is to produce a random list of employees to complete the survey at the same time in a given location. This can be effective in managing a culture where answers may be influenced by peers.

Step 4: Consolidate Results and Assign Priority

Once the results have been tallied and transferred into a graph, it will be possible to evaluate the opportunities and the level of readiness for change in the business. The following steps should be completed:

- o Tally the results into a spreadsheet that can be used to sort the data (see Table 1.5).
- o Develop graphs to represent the data in a user-friendly format (see Figure 1.4).
- o Identify priority areas to be addressed (see table 1.6).

VOICE OF THE EMPLOYEE DATA — Example

CATEGORY	QUESTION	PARTICIPANT RESULTS										COUNT TOTALS				% TOTALS			
		A	B	C	D	E	F	G	H	I	J	Strongly Agree 4	Agree 3	Disagree 2	Strongly Disagree 1	Strongly Agree 1	Agree 2	Disagree 3	Strongly Disagree 4
	I know our company vision by heart and can see how the strategy aims to achieve our vision.	1	1	2	1	2	1	3	3	2	1	0	2	3	5	0	20	30	50
	I am clear on my goals and how these link to the strategy of the company.	1	1	1	2	3	1	2	1	1	2	0	1	3	6	0	10	30	60
	I am in agreement with the targets set and understand how this will assist us in achieving the strategy.	1	2	1	2	2	1	2	1	1	2	0	0	5	5	0	0	50	50
CLEAR DIRECTION	Our goals drive the right behaviour in my team and everyone works together towards customer.	1	2	2	2	2	1	2	2	2	1	0	0	7	3	0	0	70	30
	I can see how the activities I do everyday link directly to my goals and achieving the strategy.	2	2	1	1	2	1	1	3	2	1	0	1	4	5	0	10	40	50
	AVERAGE PER PARTICIPANT	1.2	1.6	1.4	1.6	2.2	1.2	1.8	2	1.6	1.4								
	AVERAGE FOR CATEGORY	1.6																	

Develop a spreadsheet to tally the result. Include ability to sort by level, to show the spread across the hierarchy. Summarise with an average score across all participants for each category.

Table 1.5

Example

VOICE OF THE EMPLOYEE

VOICE OF THE EMPLOYEE SURVEY
RESULTS BY CATEGORY
MARCH 2014

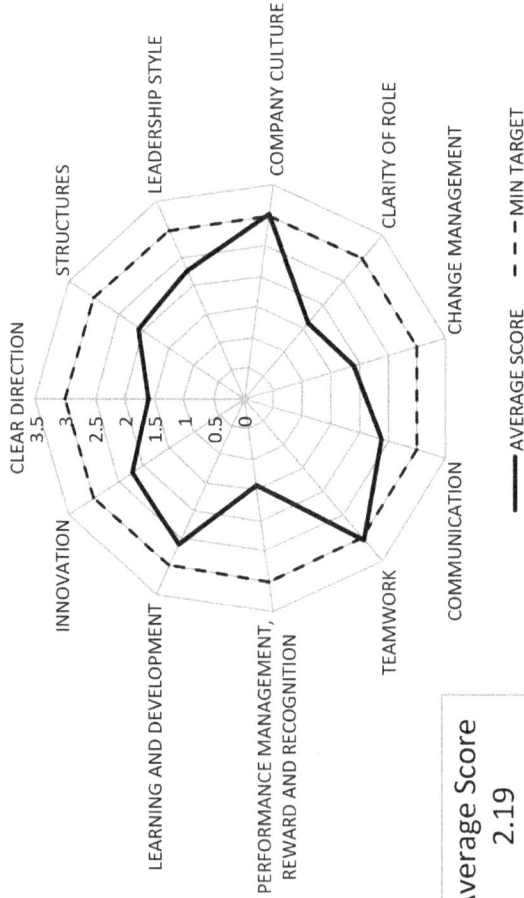

Average Score
2.19

Using the data from your spreadsheet, develop graphs to represent the results and set a baseline. The above includes a target condition (outer-ring) to achieve a score of '3' across all categories.

Figure 1.4

VOICE OF THE EMPLOYEE — Example

CATEGORY	QUESTION NUMBER	Strongly Agree 4	Agree 3	Disagree 2	Strongly Disagree 1	% SPREAD OF RESULTS	PRIORITY	YEAR 1 FOCUS	YEAR 2 FOCUS
CLEAR DIRECTION	1	0	20	30	50		HIGH	X	
	2	0	10	30	60		HIGH	X	
	3	0	0	50	50		HIGH	X	
	4	0	0	70	30		HIGH	X	
	5	0	10	40	50		HIGH	X	
STRUCTURES	6	0	10	50	40		HIGH		X
	7	0	10	70	20		HIGH		X
	8	50	40	10	0		LOW		
	9	0	10	50	40		HIGH		X
	10	0	10	50	40		HIGH		X
LEADERSHIP STYLE	11	50	50	0	0		LOW		
	12	10	20	50	20		HIGH		X
	13	0	20	30	50		HIGH		X
	14	0	50	30	20		MED		
	15	0	0	60	40		HIGH		X
COMPANY CULTURE	16	30	60	10	0		LOW		
	17	40	60	0	0		LOW		
	18	20	70	10	0		LOW		
	19	0	30	60	10		HIGH		X
	20	30	60	10	0		LOW		
CLARITY OF ROLE	21	0	0	40	60		HIGH	X	
	22	0	0	20	80		HIGH	X	
	23	0	0	40	60		HIGH	X	
	24	0	0	40	60		HIGH	X	
	25	20	40	30	10		MED	X	
CHANGE MANAGEMENT	26	0	0	30	70		HIGH	X	
	27	0	20	70	10		HIGH	X	
	28	40	40	20	0		LOW		
	29	0	0	30	70		HIGH	X	
	30	0	0	50	50		HIGH	X	
COMMUNICATION	31	50	50	0	0		LOW		
	32	0	0	60	40		HIGH		X
	33	0	40	60	0		HIGH		X
	34	0	10	60	30		HIGH		X
	35	0	60	40	0		MED		
TEAMWORK	36	40	60	0	0		LOW		
	37	0	70	30	0		LOW		
	38	70	30	0	0		LOW		
	39	50	40	10	0		LOW		
	40	0	20	60	20		HIGH		X
PERFORMANCE MANAGEMENT, REWARD AND RECOGNITION	41	0	10	30	60		HIGH		X
	42	0	0	40	60		HIGH		X
	43	0	0	40	60		HIGH		X
	44	0	0	40	60		HIGH		X
	45	0	0	40	60		HIGH		X
LEARNING AND DEVELOPMENT	46	0	0	40	60		HIGH		X
	47	10	60	30	0		LOW		
	48	50	50	0	0		LOW		
	49	0	10	60	30		HIGH		
	50	50	50	0	0		LOW		
INNOVATION	51	40	50	10	0		LOW		
	52	0	10	90	0		HIGH		
	53	0	60	40	0		MED		
	54	0	10	30	60		HIGH		
	55	0	0	60	40		HIGH		

Develop the spreadsheet to show the spread of results across the responses. Do the same exercise for each level to show how the responses vary by position. Use colour coding to distinguish priorities.

Table 1.6

Step 5: Provide Feedback

With the results and priorities in hand, it is recommended that feedback on the highlights be presented to the employees.

The intention of this session is to:

o Provide feedback to employees on the results and priority areas for the coming year/s.

o Explain how this survey will tie into the improvement strategy and the expectations placed on the leadership team.

o Encourage questions and take note of concerns.

✓ FOR YOU TO TRY

- Set up a communication session for the MD or CEO to inform all employees of

  - the upcoming survey

  - the importance of participation

  - the anonymity of the survey

  - how the results will be used

  - when feedback will be provided.

- Prepare the survey, ensuring the right categories are included and the right level of literacy is targeted. Guarantee employees that they have an anonymous method of submitting the surveys and that the collection point is manned and administered.

- Distribute to all employees and where necessary, run focus groups to assist employees to achieve a common understanding of the questions.

- Regularly track the participation results, and ensure the MD or CEO is lobbying additional support where the submissions numbers are low.

- Tally the results into a versatile spreadsheet that is capable of sorting the data by total results, by level or position and by question.

- Create graphs to visually depict the results and stimulate discussion.

- Interpret the results, assigning priority to those areas that scored low.

- Provide feedback to employees on the results, indicating the commitment from the leadership team to address the shortfalls, and how their questions or concerns will be addressed.

THE NORTH STAR SUMMARY

❓ WHAT IS THIS?

The North Star is an interesting celestial body and historically, was used in navigation to find the direction of North and determine latitude. The identity of the pole star gradually changes over time because the celestial poles exhibit a slow, continuous drift through the star field. The primary reason for this is the precession of the Earth's rotational axis, which causes its orientation to change over time.

In business, the North Star is our navigation guide towards sustained levels of improvement. This is our strategy to raise performance as well as to:

○ Make products and services that customers want to buy.

○ Satisfy shareholder needs.

○ Create stable employment.

○ Preserve the environment for future generations.

As such, we do not limit the North Star to the Voice of the Business, but include the Voice of the Customer and Employees as well.

The Voice of the Business, Customer and Employee has told us a story about where the business currently is and to where it must strive. Capturing these conclusions into a North Star Summary will provide a visual and straightforward view of the key areas of interest and provide leadership with the clear direction to cascade throughout the levels.

'Clear direction is all about maintaining one's bearing even when everything blows up all over the place. It's about following a guiding star regardless of currents and reefs and shipwrecks.'

(Ballé 2009: p300)

(?) WHY IS THIS HELPFUL?

o The business purpose in the context of the improvement drive is clear and unambiguous.

o Leaders can provide constancy of purpose through a collective understanding and application of the business direction.

o The results from the diagnostic will maintain strategic focus.

o A basis for the improvement metrics is created.

(?) HOW TO DO IT

Consolidate the Outcomes from the Evaluations

Review the results from the Voice of the Business, Customer and Employee, and capture the improvement focus onto your North Star (figure 1.5). More detail on each of the headings will be covered in the final section of Part I, and at this stage, we are interested only in clarifying the key improvement areas highlighted thus far.

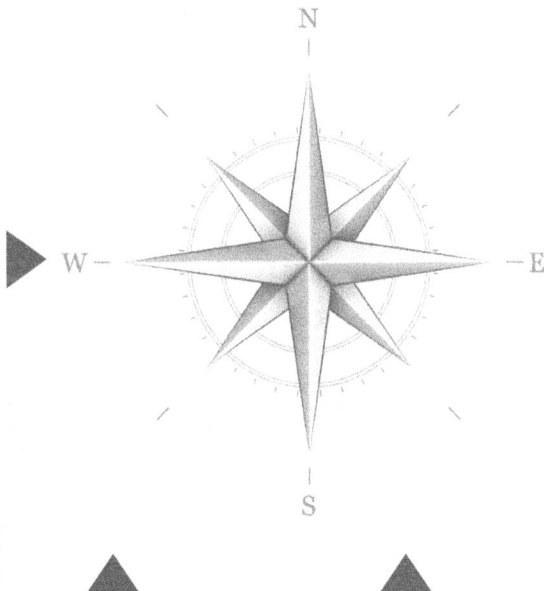

VOICE OF THE BUSINESS			Example
Business Goal (Mar 2015)	Business Objective	Existing Key Initiatives	Current Performance (Feb 2014)
Grow market share by 25%	Secure existing customer base	**Superior Service** ○ Service 80% of clients in fewer than 10 days ○ Achieve zero customer complaints	○ Lead time ranges from 10 to 60 days ○ 15 complaints received per annum
	Increase market penetration in existing markets	**Responsible Company** ○ Reduce tons of hazardous waste by 50% ○ Improve packaging recycling by 100% **Entry Incentives** ○ Service 100% of clients in fewer than 14 days ○ Implement loyalty plans with incentive ○ Offer hassle-free application process	○ Hazardous waste averages at 3 tons per month ○ 100% of packaging discarded after single use ○ Lead time ranges from 10 to 60 days ○ No loyalty plan in place ○ Complex application process
Reduce working capital by 18%	Reduce Inventory Holding by R20m		○ R120m inventory holding
	Reduce Cash-to-Cash Cycle to 45 days	*Undefined, awaiting diagnostic results*	○ 79 days financing time (cash-cash)
	Reduce capital expenditure by 25%		○ Planned capital expenditure is R50m
Reduce environmental impact on energy and water by 30%	Reduce water consumption by 30%	○ Improve cleaning process to reduce 70% water consumption ○ Reduce need for cleaning through scheduling changes	○ 150 000 m³ groundwater per
	Reduce energy consumption by 30%	○ Convert all lighting to low energy ○ Implement office auto-lighting system	○ 2500 GWh per annum
Increase net profit by 5%	Reduce operating expenses by 17%	*Undefined, awaiting diagnostic results*	○ R47m operating expenses

VOICE OF THE CUSTOMER								Example
PROFILE	CUSTOMER GROUP	WHO is the customer?	WHAT do they want?	WHY do they want it?	WHEN do they want it?	WHERE do they want it?	HOW do they want it?	VALUE how important it is	PRIORITY level for improvement for us
Volume	High Volume (>80%)	Customer A	OTIF 95% availability 95% 5% cost reduction	Flexibility Pressure from competition	12 months	Product AS34 and GU76	Improved performance tracking and collaborative problem solving	Dissatisfier	Very high
		Customer B	OTIF 90%	Delivery penalties from their customers	6 months	Product AS34; YP25; PL67	Review complaints and address	Satisfier	High
		Customer C	Improved packaging	Improve image of product	3 months	All supplies	Investigate with design team	Delighter	Medium

VOICE OF THE EMPLOYEE SURVEY
RESULTS BY CATEGORY
MARCH 2014

Average Score 2.19

— AVERAGE SCORE - - MIN TARGET

Example

NORTH STAR

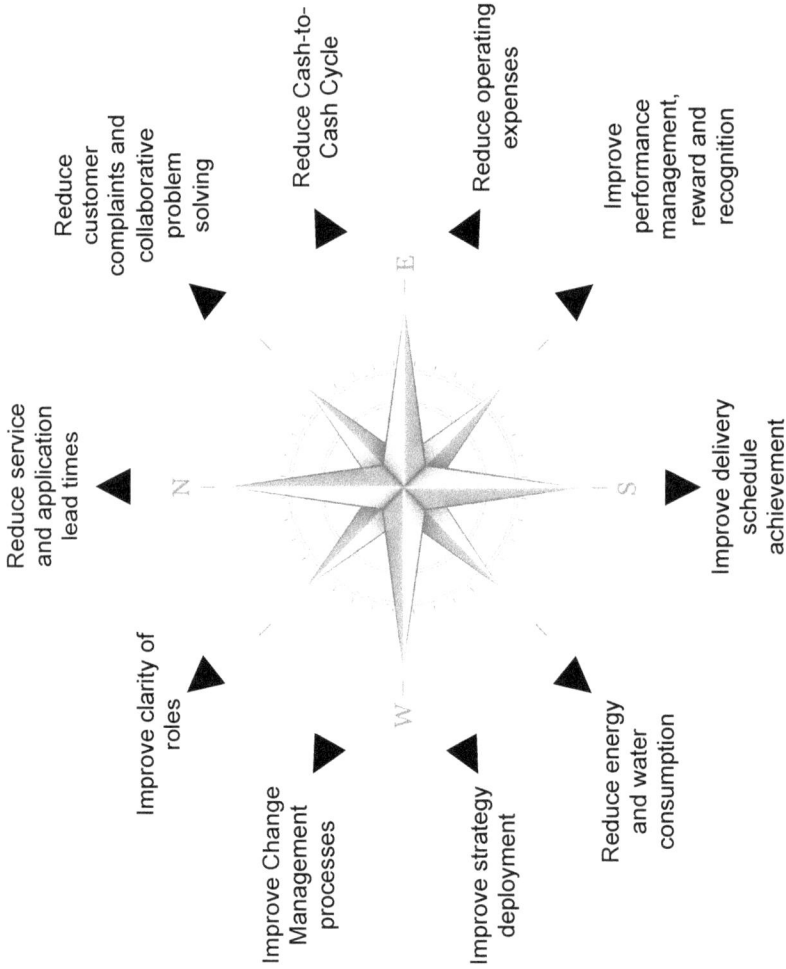

Reduce customer complaints and collaborative problem solving

Reduce Cash-to-Cash Cycle

Reduce operating expenses

Improve performance management, reward and recognition

Reduce service and application lead times

Improve delivery schedule achievement

Improve clarity of roles

Improve Change Management processes

Improve strategy deployment

Reduce energy and water consumption

Capture the Improvement Focus from the Voice of the Business, Customer and Employees. This will be improved throughout the book and the detail behind it completed in the final section of Part I.

Figure 1.5

✓ FOR YOU TO TRY

- Refer to the Voice of the Business, Customer and Employee.

- Capture the key improvement areas onto the North Star, ensuring only the top priorities for the year are included.

- Reserve including any details at this stage as this will be handled once the diagnostic is complete.

2 BEST PRACTICE EVALUATION
5P ASSESSMENT

❓ WHAT IS THIS?

The word 'culture' is often used in conversation, coupled with comments such as 'the culture in this business is preventing us from improving', 'we do not have the right culture for Operational Excellence' and 'if we could just change the culture, we could change the way we do business'.

There are many different interpretations and meanings for the word 'culture', and various models exist to describe the key aspects. For the purpose of this book, consider the definition of culture to be 'the sum of people's habits related to the work they do' (Mann, 2005). So by definition, if we wanted to 'fix' the culture, we would need to improve the 'individual habits' and the sum of these would determine the overriding culture within the organisation. These habits should drive how people perceive, think and feel in relation to problems exposed in the company.

A Best Practice is a benchmarked habit that builds the behavioural characteristics of a world-class organisation. Of course, Best Practice may vary from one industry sector to another, so the following section is designed to give you a generic approach for Operational Excellence, which you will need to compare with the Voice of your Business, Customer and Employee for relevance.

The 5P Assessment is designed to ask a series of questions related to the habits of Best Practice in the organisation that form part of the management system. It is arranged around the 5P Model (figure 2.1), namely: Purpose, Process, People, Problem Solving and Planet.

Developing strength in the practices described in the 5P Assessment will start you on a road that systematically encourages employees to think about their work from a different perspective. It will also allow them to engage in activities that directly impact the purpose of the business. Collectively, these good practices also create the management system needed to sustain the improvements.

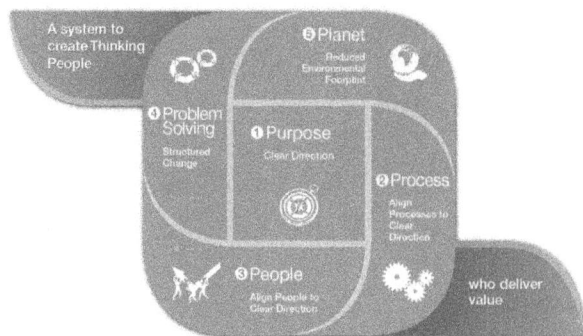

Figure 2.1

The assessment makes it possible to put a stake in the ground as to the Current State in the business and the focus areas for improvement in the short, medium and long-term.

Quick Overview of the 5P Assessment

The assessment evaluates Best Practice maturity from a level 1 to level 5 status, as follows:

Level 1	Level 2	Level 3	Level 4	Level 5
Not in place	Basic Implementation and Awareness	Intermediate Implementation	Advanced Application	Customer and Business Value

It aims to establish the current performance for each category, according to the level achieved. The following assessment areas are included for each of the 5Ps (figure 2.2):

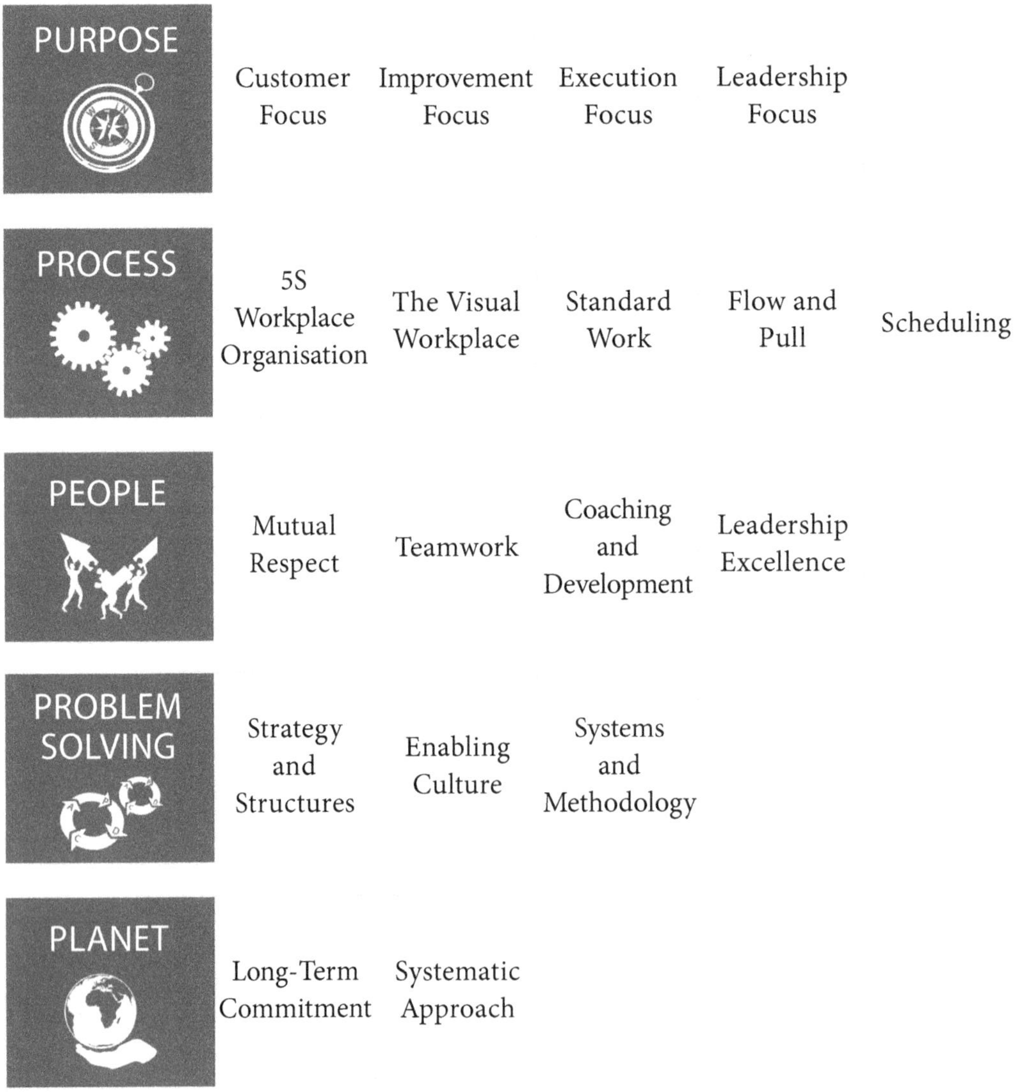

PURPOSE

Customer Focus · Improvement Focus · Execution Focus · Leadership Focus

PROCESS

5S Workplace Organisation · The Visual Workplace · Standard Work · Flow and Pull · Scheduling

PEOPLE

Mutual Respect · Teamwork · Coaching and Development · Leadership Excellence

PROBLEM SOLVING

Strategy and Structures · Enabling Culture · Systems and Methodology

PLANET

Long-Term Commitment · Systematic Approach

Figure 2.2

The Operational Excellence Matrix

This matrix is extremely useful in plotting the balance between implementation of Best Practice and performance to the North Star objectives. Improvement in both progresses an organisation towards Operational Excellence, and by positioning the score on the matrix, it is possible to see where more focus is required.

The y-axis refers to objectives set to achieve the North Star (covered in Chapter 5). The x-axis refers to the implementation of the 5Ps as described in the 5P Assessment, and therefore the management system that drives and sustains performance.

Having determined the current performance in each of the Best Practices, the results are plotted in the matrix (figure 2.3), together with the target condition:

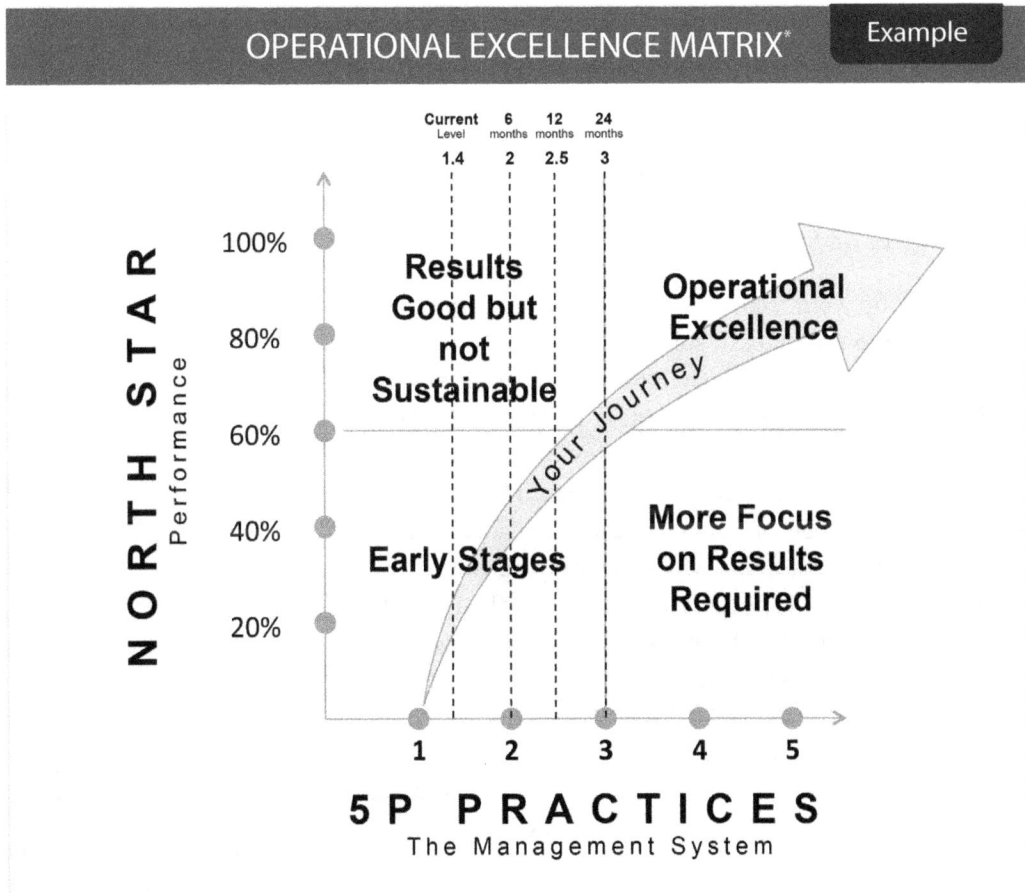

Figure 2.3

* The exact origin of the original design of this matrix is unclear, but it has been used in various forms in educational institutes, industry and by international consulting firms. We have further adapted it to apply to Operational Excellence in this context.

? WHY IS THIS HELPFUL?

o Elements of the management system needed to support the improvement culture are defined and a system's approach to implementing change is engaged.

o Habits of Best Practice are evaluated and scored, highlighting the gaps for short, medium and long-term change.

o A baseline, 'stake in the ground' is set from which to improve. This is periodically measured to visualise progress.

o Only focus areas relevant to the business are identified.

? HOW TO DO IT

The assessment is most successful when you take into account the North Star covered in the previous chapter. It is important not to follow a copy-and-paste approach to assessments. Instead, consider the real value behind the principle and how it would better help the organisations serve its stakeholders, customers and employees. If you have your North Star in hand, this becomes easier to do.

Step 1: Agree on Scope

Depending on your scope of influence, agree on how large an area to evaluate. In some cases, for example, in a small organisation of fewer than 50 employees, it may be feasible to assess the entire business in one evaluation. In the case of larger or more complex organisations, it may be prudent to evaluate by department or functional area. The advantage of breaking up the evaluation by area is that different areas will be at varying maturities of implementation (especially in PROCESS, PROBLEM SOLVING and PEOPLE), and it will be easier to pin-point specific areas for improvement by separating them.

Scope
Area 1
Area 2
Area 3
Consolidate results when done

Should you wish to have a consolidated view for the company after having developed the assessment by area, select the lowest score from each section as the company result. The theory is that the enterprise is only as strong as its weakest link, so although six out of seven areas are mature in the Best Practice, if one area is not, this determines the level for all.

Step 2: Agree on Participants

Having agreed the scope, decide on how many participants and which levels will be involved. It is always best to facilitate an evaluation rather than just hand out questionnaires for people to complete, so consider critical participants and time

constraints. Table 2.1 is a recommendation for who to involve and what ratio to aim for in this assessment type. Think about the scope when making the final decision. You may also find this varies from company to company so involvement from the front-line may not be feasible in some cases. It is also worth noting that the answers to some of the questions, particularly in PURPOSE, may not be known to all participants.

Level	Examples	Ratio
Leadership	CEO, MD, Directors, Senior Management	50% – 70% of leaders
Middle Management	Managers, Supervisory Change Agents	20% – 40% of managers
Front-line	Team Leaders, Team Members	10% of front line staff

Table 2.1

Note that a skilled facilitator is recommended to lead the assessment.

Step 3: Conduct Assessment

The agenda in table 2.2 is a guideline on how long to spend on the evaluation and can be customised to your needs. Remember to include comfort breaks. Use the generic assessment provided in table 2.3 to conduct the evaluation and look for opportunities to adjust the statements to suit your North Star.

Number	Activity	Duration
1	Provide overview and objective of the assessment.	5 min
2	Commence with PURPOSE, giving guidance on meaning and evidence.	<60 min
3	Commence with PROCESS, giving guidance on meaning and evidence.	<60 min
4	Commence with PEOPLE, giving guidance on meaning and evidence.	<60 min
5	Commence with PROBLEM SOLVING, giving guidance on meaning and evidence.	<60 min
6	Commence with PLANET, giving guidance on meaning and evidence.	<60 min
7	Develop a summary table and target condition.	<90 min
8	Confirm way forward.	5 min

Table 2.2

5P ASSESSMENT

ORGANISATION

ASSESSOR

DATE

AREA

TOTAL SCORE

PREVIOUS SCORE

INSTRUCTIONS:

○ Select the level that best describes the Current State.

○ If the assessment shows that a level 5 is in place but a level 3 is not yet achieved for the same line, choose the lowest score to highlight the gap.

○ Calculate the average score achieved. Document the top focus areas from the relevant gaps identified.

Table 2.3

NO	ASSESSMENT AREA	ASSESSMENT CRITERIA	LEVEL 1	LEVEL 2	LEVEL 3	LEVEL 4	LEVEL 5
				PLACE SCORE HERE		PLACE SCORE HERE	
1	Customer Focus	1.1 Customer satisfaction is the primary goal of employees and guides improvement behaviour.	The Voice of the Customer (VOC) is not defined or available. Individuals believe the company has unique competencies and can be prescriptive on what and how value is delivered.	The VOC is defined but does not represent true customer meaning. The VOC is based on perception rather than fact.	The VOC is gathered, defined and aligned with true customer meaning. Value from the perspective of the customer is verified and understood.	Employees understand the meaning of the VOC and can explain how their daily activities impact on customer satisfaction.	The VOC guides improvement activities and is continuously reviewed. After an improvement, the impact on the customer is evaluated.
2	Improvement Focus	2.1 A clear strategy and plan aligns the focus and activities throughout the organisation.	The business strategy and plan are not formally documented, updated or reviewed. Crisis management is a tolerated norm.	The business strategy is documented and available but the rationale behind the strategic plan is not well understood. The plan has been largely formulated through intuition rather than hard facts.	A strategic plan for the 3 to 5 years has been developed based on rigorous analysis – for example, SWOT, competitor analysis, market trends, environmental pressures and so on. Leaders are held accountable to goals and buy-in to the rationale.	The strategic plan is cascaded to departmental and team-level goals and alignment is clear, traceable and accountable. Annual improvement plans are formal and provide clarity for the annual goals and objectives.	Employees understand their respective goals and the key role they play in its success. Employees can explain how their daily activities contribute to the goals of the team and the company.

PURPOSE

NO	ASSESSMENT AREA	ASSESSMENT CRITERIA	LEVEL 1	LEVEL 2	LEVEL 3	LEVEL 4	LEVEL 5
2	Improvement Focus Continued.../	2.2 There is clarity in the current state of performance, desired target condition and how the improvement will be focused and achieved.	No diagnostic has been performed and key improvement areas to achieve the strategic plan are neither defined nor understood.	A formal diagnostic has been conducted to evaluate current performance to business, customer, environmental and employee needs. The current state is documented and key improvement areas defined. Techniques such as Value Stream mapping (Process and Green Mapping), Cash Loss Analyses and Best Practice Evaluation are used to establish the current condition.	Future State Vision has been developed. A target condition for the future has been defined and aligned to business, customer, environmental and employee needs. – for example, Future State Value Stream Map, Future State Green Value Stream Map, Target Cash Loss Analysis, Target Best Practice Score and Target Employee Survey.	An implementation philosophy has been designed to ensure the correct sequence and priority of change is documented. An implementation plan is developed with clear accountability, expectations and review phases.	Metrics have been designed to track the implementation according to the expectations in the strategic plan. There is clear alignment between the improvement areas, tools, target condition and the strategic plan.
		2.3 Periodic review of the current performance and improvement focus is structured and initiates further progress.	No review diagnostics are planned. Initial improvements may yield results but stagnate thereafter.	Some review diagnostics exist but this is not consistent across all departments and not to the same standard as the initial diagnostic performed.	Periodic review of the current performance to establish new target conditions is scheduled according to a set standard – for example, formal annual review and accountability is in place.	Review diagnostics are performed and timed to align with the updates in the strategic plan and remain focused in supporting the strategic intents.	The review diagnostics and updated plans stimulate ongoing improvement in the metrics and strategic goals. The vision is becoming a reality.

PURPOSE

NO	ASSESSMENT AREA	ASSESSMENT CRITERIA	LEVEL 1	LEVEL 2	LEVEL 3	LEVEL 4	LEVEL 5
3	Execution Focus	3.1 A formal strategy deployment system aligns strategy and execution.	Action according to the strategic plan is not achieved, not to standard or is inconsistent. Employees are frequently engaged in crisis activities that remove focus from the overall goals and objectives.	A scientific method of execution – Plan, Do, Check and Adjust (PDCA) is introduced and standardised to structure activities, align them to the strategic plan and evaluate implementation.	Leadership sets an example with the PDCA method of execution in their own actions. Leadership removes obstacles to assist employees in executing their activities.	Short term and long term review cycles and conversations around the focus areas are in place and drive good-quality action. There is no ambiguity as to what employees must spend time on to achieve their team and company goals.	Accountable employees use a standardised A3 Thinking process to structure their strategy execution plans and report on progress. The strategy is successfully implemented to plan.
		3.2 The business purpose is clear, measureable, communicated and guides behaviour.	Goals, key performance indicators (KPIs) and targets are not defined for all levels. Measurement is financially-biased.	Goals, KPIs (practical and non-financial) and targets are defined for all levels.	All goals, KPIs and targets are aligned to the Voice of the Business, Customer, Environment and Employee and balanced to Quality, Cost, Delivery, Safety, Morale and Environment (QCDSME). The right number of KPIs maintain focus.	Employees can explain the goals, KPIs and targets for their area and how they personally contribute to the achievement thereof.	Employees buy into the goals, KPIs and targets. It drives behaviour and influences incentives for bonus, recognition and promotion.

PURPOSE

NO	ASSESSMENT AREA	ASSESSMENT CRITERIA	LEVEL 1	LEVEL 2	LEVEL 3	LEVEL 4	LEVEL 5
4	Leadership Focus	4.1 Mission, vision, values drive customer focus, respect for people, environmental commitment and continuous improvement.	No mission, vision or values are available or documented.	The mission, vision and values are clearly defined and documented.	The mission, vision and values align with customer focus, respect for people, environmental commitment and continuous improvement.	Aligned mission, vision and values are communicated and employees are aware of them and can explain them.	Employees have an emotional connection to the mission, vision and values and this drives ethical behaviour.
		4.2 There is a consistent, burning platform for change.	Complacency exists in the leadership team. No defined need for change is stimulating action and employees are comfortable with the current state.	A general dissatisfaction with the current state is developing – people tell each other that something must be done about the problems and opportunities.	The leadership team has collectively designed a creative need for change to stimulate action and provide purpose to the improvement drive. The leadership team executes actions in a focused and urgent way and sets the example.	Compelling, and dramatic situations are created to help others visualise the problems, opportunities and urgency for change. The perception that the current state is acceptable is being dissolved across the organisation.	Execution of actions is focused and handled with urgency across the organisation. The need and urgency for change is reviewed periodically for relevance and the message is refreshed.

PURPOSE

NO	ASSESSMENT AREA	ASSESSMENT CRITERIA	LEVEL 1	LEVEL 2	LEVEL 3	LEVEL 4	LEVEL 5
					PLACE SCORE HERE		PLACE SCORE HERE
4	Leadership Focus Continued.../	**4.3 Senior management provide constancy of purpose.**	No formal guiding coalition is in place to direct and steer the improvement strategy. Responsibility for the improvement strategy is unclear or ambiguous.	A steering committee has been formed to guide the change but participants are not representative or lack the authority to make and execute the decisions. Attendance and participation wavers and meetings lack focus and alignment to goals.	Steering committee representation achieves the right mix and authority. Participation and responsibility is clear.	Steering committee meetings are consistent, attended and structured to an agenda. There is alignment between the strategy, execution and discussions. Members see the relationship between the steercom activities and achieving strategic goals.	Employees trust that leaders are working together to lead the organisation through the change and see their commitment in daily actions and support.
		4.4 A clear communication strategy is executed.	No formal communication strategy and execution in place. Employees feel uninformed or that leaders are not focused and aligned. Communication channels are clogged and confusion results.	Leadership understands the need and role of communication. A plan to achieve effective communication has been developed by the steering committee. The message, medium, audience, frequency and objectives are clear.	There is follow-through on the communication plan and clear, credible, heart-felt messages are cascaded to the employees. There is a growing awareness from employees regarding the improvement strategy and expectations.	Employees are clear on the improvement strategy, their role in it and how well the organisation is progressing to these goals. There are clear communication channels to and from the employees and obstacles, fears and anxiety are actively dealt with.	Employees believe the leadership team to be consistent and focused in their communications. Trust is growing between the employees and leaders, and new communications are met with openness and interest.

PURPOSE

NO	ASSESSMENT AREA	ASSESSMENT CRITERIA	LEVEL 1	LEVEL 2	LEVEL 3	LEVEL 4	LEVEL 5
4	Leadership Focus Continued.../	4.5 Obstacles are systematically removed.	Employees are in a state of apathy. They tend to give up on an improvement idea when obstacles are met.	The leadership team understands its role in removing obstacles and the importance of conveying this message to the employees.	A formal escalation and feedback process is implemented to encourage employees to raise obstacles to improvement and for leaders to provide timeous responses and relevant action.	The confidence in employees to improve is growing. More improvement activities are implemented than abandoned.	Employees, who genuinely embrace the vision and strategies, are motivated and empowered to act on them.
		4.6 Quick wins raise motivation.	Employees and leaders do not believe the improvement focus has yielded any results. There is no evidence that improvement activities are bringing the organisation closer to success – cynicism persists.	Improvement activities that will leverage the most benefit to the customer, business, environment and employees have been highlighted in the diagnostic and prioritised for implementation.	Improvements have yielded positive results in the short term (fewer than 6 months), which directly contribute to the goals of the business.	Successes from the improvement activities have been documented, visually displayed and advertised to all staff. Specific recognition is given by the leadership team to the team members who helped achieve the results.	Employees are motivated to continue with the improvement activities and can see the direct link between the effort, the results, the contribution to the customer, business environment or themselves.

PURPOSE

NO	ASSESSMENT AREA	ASSESSMENT CRITERIA	LEVEL 1	LEVEL 2	LEVEL 3	LEVEL 4	LEVEL 5
4	**Leadership Focus Continued…/**	4.7 **Change is made to stick.**	Initial improvements occur but these soon gravitate back to old ways. Tradition supersedes progress.	The leadership team recognises the importance of sustaining change through formal systems.	As part of the PDCA cycle, a formal process for sustaining change is developed by the leadership team e.g. within the 'Adjust' phase of PDCA, minimum sustainment actions are required, including induction, promotion and incentive philosophies, standard leader work and succession planning.	The PDCA process for sustainment is rigidly followed through and every project is signed off only when all phases are complete.	Critical improvements are formally tracked for a period of up to one year and sustainment is deemed successful.

AVERAGE SCORE

PURPOSE

PURPOSE SUMMARY GRAPH

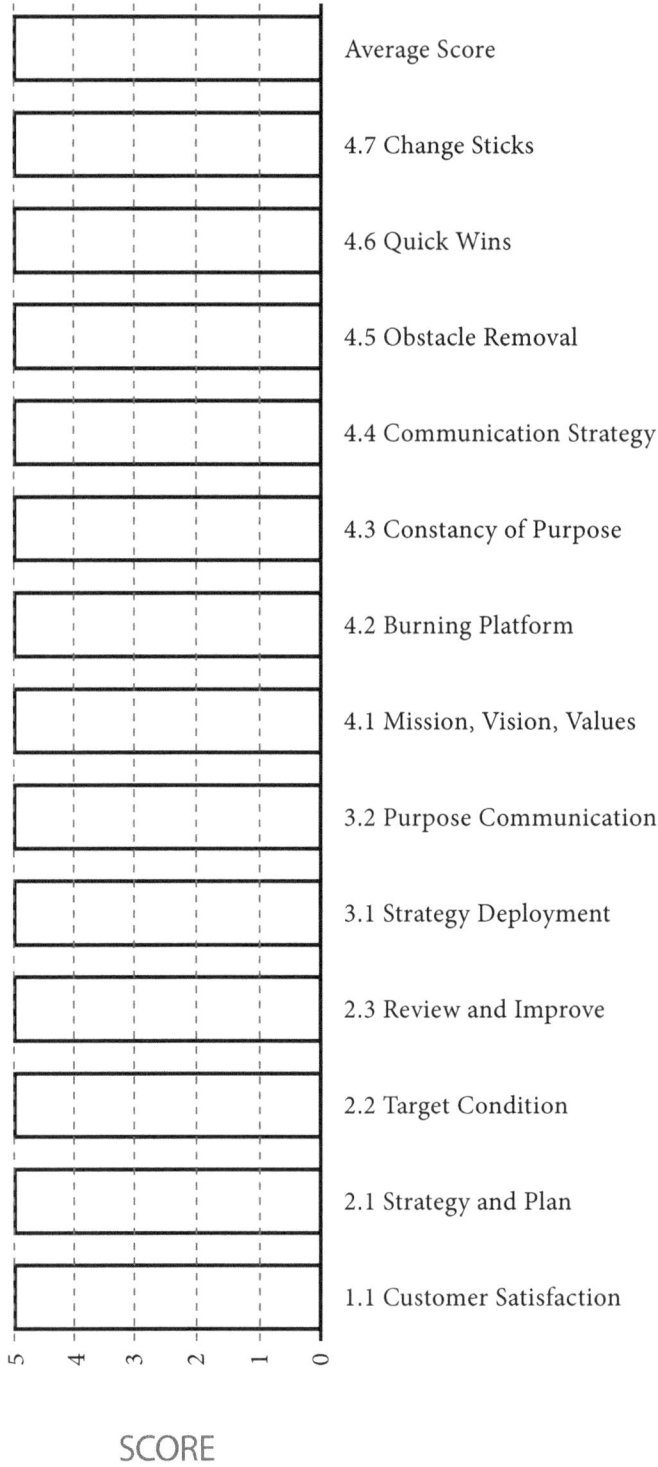

Score	Assessment Criteria
	Average Score
	4.7 Change Sticks
	4.6 Quick Wins
	4.5 Obstacle Removal
	4.4 Communication Strategy
	4.3 Constancy of Purpose
	4.2 Burning Platform
	4.1 Mission, Vision, Values
	3.2 Purpose Communication
	3.1 Strategy Deployment
	2.3 Review and Improve
	2.2 Target Condition
	2.1 Strategy and Plan
	1.1 Customer Satisfaction

5 4 3 2 1 0

SCORE

ASSESSMENT CRITERIA

Colour in the final scoring for each criterion and the average score.

PURPOSE FOCUS SUMMARY

ASSESSMENT AREA	IMPROVEMENT OPPORTUNITIES	SHORT, MEDIUM OR LONG-TERM FOCUS
CUSTOMER FOCUS		
IMPROVEMENT FOCUS		
EXECUTION FOCUS		
LEADERSHIP FOCUS		

Capture the top improvement opportunities for each assessment area and include a comment to show if it is a short, medium or long-term focus for the business:

Short: <6 months
Medium: 6 to 12 months
Long: >12 months

NO	ASSESSMENT AREA	ASSESSMENT CRITERIA	LEVEL 1	LEVEL 2	LEVEL 3	LEVEL 4	LEVEL 5
1	5S Workplace Organisation	1.1 The work area is well organised and conducive to safety, productivity, discipline and comfort. Problems are easy to identify.	The work area is dirty, cluttered and disorganised. The area is maintained by a contractor or cleaner. Employees and leaders do not hold themselves responsible for their own areas.	Only necessary items are found in the work area but the facility is unclean and disorganised. There is a standard in place to remove unnecessary items and a procedure for discarding.	Only necessary items are found in the work area and the facility is clean. However, the necessary items are not well stored and difficult to locate. Standards are in place to remove unnecessary items and maintain the cleanliness in the area. A schedule governs cleaning activities.	The work area is clean and all necessary items are properly located for easy access and retrieval. No unnecessary items are found in the area. Standards are in place to remove unnecessary items, maintain cleanliness and store items correctly. Missing items and problems are obvious.	The team actively supports and maintains the workplace organisation and sustaining the standards has become a culture. 5S scores are measured and visually displayed on boards. Outstanding actions are addressed every week.
2	The Visual Workplace	2.1 At a glance, it is possible to understand the flow and activities of the area. Performance is visual, improvement focus is clear and it drives behaviour. Visitors and newcomers understand the operations quickly.	The workplace has developed organically. Flow and the mechanics of the operation is difficult to understand at a glance. Visuals do not guide employees and visitors, performance is unclear, and activities to improve this are not visible. Reports are IT based and reactive in nature.	A meeting area is established. Some visuals have been introduced and focus on measurement as opposed to driving improvement. There is misalignment to the improvement strategy. The team does not own the visuals and these become outdated easily.	Visuals have been carefully designed to visualise the process and support the improvement focus. Relevant metrics and the current performance to target are displayed. Employees are able to explain the visuals and how they influence their daily activities.	Visuals drive daily behaviour and accountability. Employees actively review their performance to target. Actions linked to the reviews are displayed and current. Team members own the visuals and update them personally, on a daily basis.	The work area is visually appealing and provides accurate guidance as to flow, procedures, performance and improvement activities. The visuals result in focus, problem solving and improved performance.

PROCESS

NO	ASSESSMENT AREA	ASSESSMENT CRITERIA	LEVEL 1	LEVEL 2	LEVEL 3	LEVEL 4	LEVEL 5
3	Standard Work	**3.1 Variation is stabilised. The best method to perform work is documented and highly specified as to content, timing, sequence and outcome.**	Key knowledge sits with individuals and is not documented. When improvements are made, they are not compared with existing best methods. Process variation is excessive.	Critical operations are identified and standards are developed. Some variation in interpretation exists, resulting in non-conformance.	Relevant employees are trained and assessed on the updated procedures for critical operations. Adherence to standards and compliance is reviewed.	Standard work is deployed to all operations. Training and assessment is conducted. Ongoing review of adherence to standard takes place.	Variation is reduced. Standard work is used as a baseline for improvement. Improvements are initiated when the existing best method has stabilised and can be used as a reliable baseline.
4	Flow and Pull	**4.1 Speed, flexibility and flow are achieved. The Value Stream (sequence of activities to deliver product or service to the customer) provides value to the customer in the time, place and manner required.**	Operations are largely unstable and characterised by process wastes (muda), over-burden of people and equipment (muri) and variation (mura).	Critical Value Streams are identified and causes of muda, mura, and muri are highlighted. Basic stabilisation in the processes is achieved.	Further improvement to move from stabilised processes to improved flow occurs. More muda, mura and muri are eliminated. Improved performance to TAKT time (synchronising processing time with customer demand rate) and flow within the Value Stream is achieved.	With shorter, more responsive lead times and flow, the Value Stream responds more systematically to market pull. Processing is triggered by customer requirement and the ability to respond quickly.	A mixed sequence of good quality work, flowing one piece at a time, according to market pull is achieved. Flow is managed by the system, not the management.

PROCESS

NO	ASSESSMENT AREA	ASSESSMENT CRITERIA	LEVEL 1	LEVEL 2	LEVEL 3	LEVEL 4	LEVEL 5
5	Scheduling	5.1 Economies of repetition and improved flow of product or service is accomplished through scheduling principles, which give priority to streams contributing most to throughput and volume.	Product or service streams are not identified. Prioritisation and scheduling of work is inconsistent. 'Mixed factories' occur where low-volume/low-return work is allowed to delay or interrupt high-volume/high-return work. Batch sizes are large and create long lead times.	The product or service streams have been identified and prioritised into green, yellow, blue and red streams. Batch sizes to available time are evaluated.	The various streams have been interpreted and opportunities for improvement to the scheduling determined. Scheduling priorities and sequencing have been established and implemented.	Batch sizes have been reduced to facilitate flow and customer service. The schedules have been made visible and information on priorities is easily accessible.	The operation is responsive to market requirement and economies of repetition have been achieved. Physical, information and money flow in the business have improved as a result of better scheduling principles.

AVERAGE SCORE

PROCESS

PROCESS SUMMARY GRAPH

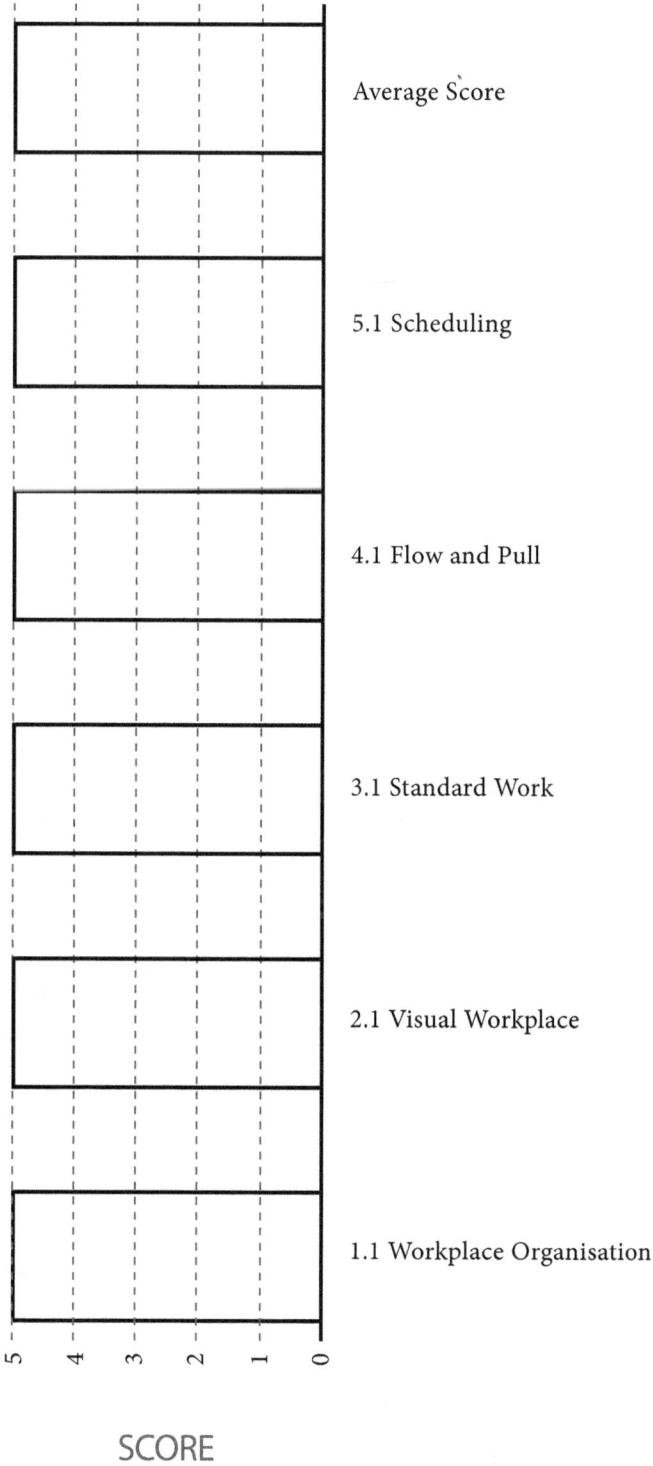

ASSESSMENT CRITERIA

Colour in the final scoring for each criterion and the average score.

Average Score

5.1 Scheduling

4.1 Flow and Pull

3.1 Standard Work

2.1 Visual Workplace

1.1 Workplace Organisation

5 4 3 2 1 0

SCORE

PROCESS FOCUS SUMMARY

ASSESSMENT AREA	IMPROVEMENT OPPORTUNITIES	SHORT, MEDIUM OR LONG-TERM FOCUS
5S WORKPLACE ORGANISATION		
THE VISUAL WORKPLACE		
STANDARD WORK		
FLOW AND PULL		
SCHEDULING		

Capture the top improvement opportunities for each assessment area and include a comment to show if it is a short, medium or long-term focus for the business:

Short: <6 months
Medium: 6 to 12 months
Long: >12 months

NO	ASSESSMENT AREA	ASSESSMENT CRITERIA	LEVEL 1	LEVEL 2	LEVEL 3	LEVEL 4	LEVEL 5
1	Mutual Respect for People	**1.1 A Collaborative approach to problem solving between the leader and employee breeds a mutual respect for knowledge and contribution.**	Leaders tell employees what to do and deprive them of the ability to think. The leader takes on a responsibility the employee should own.	The leader understands problems cannot be solved alone and they are not close enough to the process and facts. The leader is trained in problem solving, A3 Thinking and how to facilitate improvement through people. Leaders listen and take problems brought to their attention seriously.	The employee is trained and coached in the PDCA principles and appropriate problem solving tools, and is equipped to resolve root causes effectively.	The leader respects the employee's knowledge. The leader provides context and structure to assist the employee in removing him or herself from the detail and focussing on the key aspects of the problem. The leader uses A3 Thinking to coach.	Mutual respect is shown for each other's role and contribution to solving critical problems. As result, performance and sustainability improves. Employees feel that leaders take problems seriously and trust in their support.
		1.2 Operational Excellence and caring goes hand in hand and leaders actively support the needs of the employees.	Employees are expected to contribute to continuous improvement without any policy or communication regarding the release of capacity. Employees suspect improvement will result in job loss.	The leaders understand the impact of continuous improvement on capacity and have a strategy to deal with excess, including new revenue streams, reduced overtime or temporary labour, improvement activities and promotion from within.	The leadership team has formally communicated the improvement strategy and impact on the staff. The message dealing with job security is clarified and employees are able to ask questions to dispel fears.	The leaders continue to listen to the needs of the employees. Trust develops between the employees and the leaders.	Employees are confident that their contribution will be mutually beneficial. Trust has formed between the leadership team and the employees. A collaborative approach to improvement is made possible.

PEOPLE

NO	ASSESSMENT AREA	ASSESSMENT CRITERIA	LEVEL 1	LEVEL 2	LEVEL 3	LEVEL 4	LEVEL 5
1	Mutual Respect for People Continued…/	1.3 Employees are empowered to perform and know they are enabled to act on the vision.	Employees are expected to engage in improvement activities. The employee is not willing, able, authorised or accountable for the improvement. The employee is not fully engaged.	Leadership understands the role empowerment plays in developing mutual respect. The level of empowerment and strategy has been developed by the leadership team. There is clarity on what decision making is to be allowed and through what means.	An empowerment matrix has been developed to define the process to be followed, resources required, training required, timings, support required and outcomes expected. This is aligned to the improvement strategy.	Leadership understands its part in engaging and empowering the employee. The employees understand their part in achieving the required performance. Both groups actively pursue the actions defined in the empowerment matrix.	Obstacles preventing the employee from accomplishing the performance are systematically removed either by their own or leadership action. The employee engages fully in the improvement activities and achieves the goals set.
2	Teamwork Drives Value for the Customer, Business, Environment and Employees	2.1 Performing teams align their activities to the strategic goals and achieve basic stability in the operations.	Employees and functions work individually and in isolation, respectively. Team activities are met with avoidance. Meeting attendance and participation is poor. Passing blame is common.	Leaders and employees understand the importance of teamwork and how it contributes to the customer, business, environment and employees. Stable teams are formed. Team leadership is allocated and a common goal for improvement is developed.	Clear roles and responsibilities for team leaders are established and daily accountability activities are started. A shared understanding of problems is developing.	Multi-disciplinary teams engage in daily, focused reviews of performance and planning. Problem solving and action result in improved performance. Attendance and participation is strong. Strengths and weaknesses within the team are understood and used as leverage.	The teams perform to high standards and actively seek ways to improve value to the customer, business, environment and employees, together. Accountability is personal. Teamwork between shifts fosters communication and problem solving.

PEOPLE

NO	ASSESSMENT AREA	ASSESSMENT CRITERIA	LEVEL 1	LEVEL 2	LEVEL 3	LEVEL 4	LEVEL 5
3	Formalised Coaching and Development	3.1 Coaching and development is focused, structured and delivers results.	No formal or consistent approach to coaching exists. Development is adhoc and usually triggered to address a particular situation.	A learning strategy has been developed, which defines the training and coaching needs aligned to the improvement goals. Leaders and employees understand how coaching creates value.	Individual development plans have been created and aligned to the learning strategy. A structured coaching and development approach is defined and in use (A3 Thinking).	Cycles of coaching and development are frequent, short, conducted face-to-face and ultimately focus on creating value for the customer, business, environment or employee.	The ability to perform and achieve the improvement goals is accomplished. Employees have the confidence to improve and this is evident in results.
4	Leadership Excellence	4.1 Leaders become teachers and grow participation in employees (Ballé, 2009).	Training, learning and development is considered a functional responsibility, mostly handled in the human resources department.	Leaders understand their role in developing employees and how this creates mutual respect. They understand they are responsible for everyone's understanding of the job, personally. Leaders are prepared to observe, spend time, coach and assist employees to internalise the right routines.	Team leaders and group leaders spend more than 50 percent of their time on teaching and guiding employees to make real improvements, in real processes, consistently and aligned to the improvement goals. A3 Thinking is utilised to structure the learning.	Senior leaders spend between 30 and 50 percent of their time on teaching and guiding employees to make real improvements in real processes, consistently and aligned to improvement goals. A3 Thinking is utilised to structure the learning. There is no distinction between learning and improving.	The primary role of the leader is to increase improvement capability in employees. Employees actively apply their learning, everyday. Leader bonus and promotion are influenced by their ability to develop employees.

PEOPLE

NO	ASSESSMENT AREA	ASSESSMENT CRITERIA	LEVEL 1	LEVEL 2	LEVEL 3	LEVEL 4	LEVEL 5
4	Leadership Excellence Continued.../	4.2 The urgency for customer satisfaction starts with the leader and cascades through the levels to every individual (Ballé, 2009).	Customer complaints are not tracked and no reliable records are available. Issues that arise, are frequently passed over as 'someone else's problem' and restrictions within the job are more important than serving customers first.	Customer complaints are measured, captured and filed. When asked about a complaint leaders respond by referring only to the file or by referring the question to another employee. Leaders and employees are not on the pulse of customer feedback, root causes or outcome.	There is a shift in responsibility for customer satisfaction, and solving customer problems becomes a line management function. When customer feedback is received, it is addressed in a scientific, sustainable way.	Every customer complaint is treated with urgency, and is addressed by the leaders personally and immediately. Leaders can explain the details of all customer complaints, the analysis, countermeasures and outcome. PDCA is a way of life.	Leaders visit customer areas when feedback is received and customer confidence in the company is growing. Customer complaints remain top priority and the number is declining. Leaders have set a benchmark for achieving customer satisfaction and employees follow suit.
		4.3 Problem solvers are created in everyone, everyday, to address problems aligned with the improvement goals (Ballé, 2009).	Leaders and employees see the same problems every day, take them for granted and are used to living with them without solving them. Fire fighting is frequent and accepted as the nature of the business. Employees are expected to produce products or services and not to think.	Problems are seen as opportunities but only a few people are responsible for solving them. Senior and specialist staff solve basic, everyday problems, instead of more complex opportunities where they can apply specialist knowledge. There are more problems than the resources to address them.	There is clarity in the various levels of problems, who should address them and the typical techniques to prioritise and resolve. Systems to help expose problems are in place and trigger responses by the right people and the right methods. The systematic elimination of problems is starting to take place.	Every individual in the organisation can solve problems and is contributing to removing problems in a meaningful and sustainable way. Problems are always solved at the lowest level possible. Specialist functions are freed-up to focus on the difficult issues requiring their particular expertise.	There is a culture of 'building people before parts.' Problem solving is organised and supports basic stability in the operations. There is no distinction between those who solve problems and those who don't – it is everyone's responsibility to solve problems to achieve the improvement goals.

PEOPLE

NO	ASSESSMENT AREA	ASSESSMENT	LEVEL 1	LEVEL 2	LEVEL 3	LEVEL 4	LEVEL 5
4	Leadership Excellence Continued.../	4.4 Leaders 'go and see' to develop first-hand experience, grow participation and create a genuine understanding of the problems (Ballé, 2009).	Opinions on the true nature of an issue are discussed away from where the action is and misconceptions influence decision making – for example, boardroom problem solving. Solutions are sought before problems are understood and agreed to. Reading emails comes before visiting the operations.	Leaders understand the importance of Genchi Genbutsu (going to the real place, to see the real thing, gather the real facts and speak to the real people to make better decisions). More time is being spent at the operations, decision making based on real observation is improving but the activity is yet to be properly focused and made consistent.	All improvement activities include 'go-see' as a fundamental part of the PDCA. Evidence-gathering, analysis and testing largely takes place at the 'gemba' (where the action is). Support for goal achievement is structured and leaders check where employees are in their implementation and assist them with difficulties. The link between high-level goals and operational focus is improving.	Structured 'go-sees' form part of leaders' standard work. This habit takes place every day or at least every week, before the accountability meetings, according to agenda. There is clarity in the purpose of the walkabouts. Outcomes from the walkabouts are discussed, 'kaizened' (improved) and actioned, resulting in one problem solved per visit for the employee. The workplace is becoming visual and problems expose themselves.	The workplace is the teacher and go-see' is used to establish and challenge current conditions, create consensus and develop relationships. The leader is closely connected to the processes and people, and confident in how resources are invested to meet the improvement goals. Leadership commitment is visual and action oriented.

PEOPLE

NO	ASSESSMENT AREA	ASSESSMENT CRITERIA	LEVEL 1	LEVEL 2	LEVEL 3	LEVEL 4	LEVEL 5
4	Leadership Excellence Continued.../	4.5 Leaders ensure processes are managed for basic stability and improvement, and actively develop a 'kaizen spirit' in the organisation (Ballé, 2009).	There is no clarity in what is normal and what is out of standard at each process. As a result, there is no clear flow of problem solving being triggered by the right indicators. A level of complacency has set in. Functional experts find it difficult to spend time on developing standards and coaching employees. Leaders spend 80 percent of their time on crisis and only 20 percent on improvement.	Leaders understand the importance of creating the environment and conditions in which to produce good quality product or service. For critical processes, normal and abnormal conditions are defined. The conditions that must be managed in the process to create the best results are clear. Acceptable standards are set according to SMART principles (specific, measureable, accountable, realistic and time-based).	Systems are implemented that expose abnormalities compared to standard and trigger responses from employees. Based on predetermined, root cause analysis, standard routines are available as a first line of defence. Employees know when to respond, to what and how.	Experts coach employees on how to address issues within their control when abnormalities occur. Experts are able to assign their time to addressing critical issues requiring their particular knowledge, and front-line issues are dealt with by the employees directly involved. Basic stability is improving.	Incremental improvement in focus areas is accomplished, and a foundation for breakthrough improvement is in place. Leaders are able to spend 80 percent on improvement and 20 percent on crisis. Leaders and employees actively seek ways to improve on the standard through kaizen activities.

PEOPLE

NO	ASSESSMENT AREA	ASSESSMENT CRITERIA	LEVEL 1	LEVEL 2	LEVEL 3	LEVEL 4	LEVEL 5
4	Leadership Excellence Continued.../	4.6 Leaders understand the balance between improvement tools and the leadership principles to create a management system for Operational Excellence.	There is no or very little knowledge of the available tools and leadership principles needed to influence the improvement goals.	There is a basic understanding of the improvement tools and leadership principles available. Improvement tools for the sake of tools are religiously implemented and leaders are uncertain of the benefit they bring or which tools yield the right results. Employees feel there is a 'smell of the week' approach to improvement activities with little understanding of purpose or benefits.	Leaders realise that Operational Excellence is not primarily about the tools but the rationale, leadership attitude and activities that support and guide them. Although ineffective use of tools still takes place, leaders begin to actively remove the disconnect between tools and leadership by developing routine activities to advance the management system.	Which problems need to be addressed, through which tools and in what way, are clear to the employees. The management mind-set supports the application of the right tools to enable achievement of the improvement goals.	A robust management system aligned to the improvement goals drives the activities and behaviours of leaders and employees, and clear benefits can be quanitified from specific tools, and leader habits can be enabled.

PEOPLE

NO	ASSESSMENT AREA	ASSESSMENT CRITERIA	LEVEL 1	LEVEL 2	LEVEL 3	LEVEL 4	LEVEL 5
4	**Leadership Excellence Continued.../**	**4.7 Leaders maintain focus on the North Star and provide clear direction to improvement activities (Ballé, 2009).**	Improvement activities do not yield results to the triple bottom-line indicators.	Leaders understand the importance of creating a connection between budget, current state, indicators and problem solving. It is also understood that not all problems are equally important.	Leaders are clear on the target condition and the critical activities that need to take place to achieve the goals. Clear direction is developed on a few typical problems that have a few typical solutions.	Leaders provide clear direction to employees on the type, sequence and priority of problems to be tackled. Improvement activities are framed: what is to be solved, how and why is clear.	Progress to the North Star is tracked and corrected, and it is possible to see the strategy being implemented, daily. Employees see the connection between improvement activities and the goals. Time is allocated to solving a limited number of focused problems and the impact is evident.
		4.8 Leader Standard Work (LSW) guides behaviour and stabilises the management system that drives and sustains Operational Excellence (Mann, 2005).	The management system is determined by the current leader. When leaders change, the management system governing continuous improvement and management activities also changes. Leaders believe standard work is applicable only to process-related jobs.	Leaders understand that LSW is critical to sustaining the gains from continuous improvement and fosters mutual trust.	Key aspects of the management system are captured in a standard work format. Core tasks and routines are explicitly spelled out. Leaders start to follow the standard work and the focus is on compliance. Leaders who do not support LSW are dealt with accordingly.	All leaders follow the LSW and there is a shift from compliance to true understanding of the principles and benefits. There is consistency amongst leaders in how they support continuous improvement and their practices. Leaders see LSW as a means to better their own performance.	When leaders change, the improvement philosophy and practices are preserved and transition is smooth. LSW is continually reviewed and improved upon. Employees trust the constancy of leaders. Improvement gains are sustained.

PEOPLE

NO	ASSESSMENT AREA	ASSESSMENT CRITERIA	LEVEL 1	LEVEL 2	LEVEL 3	LEVEL 4	LEVEL 5
4	Leadership Excellence Continued.../	**4.9 There is clarity in leader responsibility, application and outcomes to support Operational Excellence.**	No documented leader role descriptions exist and the leader responsibilities have grown organically over time to meet the needs of the business. Variation in leader responsibilities exists. The loss of a key leader in the business has detrimental effects.	Role descriptions for leaders are developed and documented. The role does not cater for activities that support the improvement strategy of the business, but includes generic management practices. These documents are frequently outdated and vague in application.	Role descriptions have been improved to include activities required to prompt, support and sustain continuous improvement, aligned to the current strategy. Leaders understand their role to grow the capability of the business and people. Leaders have a direct responsibility to develop employees and become teachers.	Individual development plans for leaders reflect the gaps identified in their roles and leadership development is aligned. Development includes the proper understanding of the responsibilities impact to the business and tools to achieve the objectives.	Promotion of leaders is governed by the competency in their expanded roles as well as the delivery of objectives. Leaders and employees have clarity in the role the leader plays, and the expectations and outcomes are unambiguous.
		4.10 Leaders develop reward and recognition to support and stimulate continuous improvement. This is aligned to the improvement strategy and fosters teamwork.	No reward or recognition policy exists for improvement activities. This is seen by leaders as a disruptive, time consuming process that contradicts teamwork and creates a means of control by employees. Leaders are not confident in what and how to reward employees.	Leaders realise exceptional performance must be met with incentive. Criteria for excellent performance is defined and aligned to the improvement strategy. A policy for reward and recognition is agreed to for individual, team and company performance.	Gemba walks include a search for good performance and improvement ideas. Individuals and teams are recognised within a reasonable time frame. A non-monetary reward and recognition system is in place and the administration forms part of the LSW.	A monetary-based reward and recognition system has been developed aligned to team KPIs and individual performance. Employees and leaders have faith in the system to stimulate the right behaviour to create value for the business, customer and environment.	SMART targets are in place and employees are motivated to exceed normal levels of performance. Personal income is directly influenced and employees consider the system fair. Employees understand that targets are revisited to meet competitive needs.

PEOPLE

NO	ASSESSMENT AREA	ASSESSMENT CRITERIA	LEVEL 1	LEVEL 2	LEVEL 3	LEVEL 4	LEVEL 5
4	Leadership Excellence Continued…/	4.11 Succession planning is in place for all critical positions within the organisation.	The loss of a critical person in the organisation results in a disruption and crisis management. Key positions in the company are not identified and no formal plans exist to protect the continuation of these capabilities. Leadership development is not aligned to a succession plan.	Leadership understands the importance of developing subordinates in the event that critical people are lost through promotion, natural attrition, resignation or any other unforeseen circumstance. Leaders see that succession planning will create more time for leadership activities and less time will be spent micro-managing employees. A list of key positions is identified.	Employees have been approached and asked to indicate their interest in being developed for a critical position. Preference is given to those who are both interested and have the least development needs for the position. Succession planning forms part of the leader-role description and is actively pursued as an outcome of the role.	Every Leader has developed at least two subordinates for each critical position identified, for advancement at any time. Additional, interested employees are included in the development process.	There is smooth transition when a key person leaves a critical role in the organisation. Employees are clear on their individual development plans that could lead to promotion within the organisation. Individuals realise their own potential in the system and are motivated through the personal growth achieved.

PEOPLE

NO	ASSESSMENT AREA	ASSESSMENT CRITERIA	LEVEL 1	LEVEL 2	LEVEL 3	LEVEL 4	LEVEL 5
4	Leadership Excellence Continued…/	4.12 Employee flexibility and cross-skilling across all positions supports the changing needs of the organisation (Bicheno, 2004).	Employees are employed in a particular position and are expected to specialise in that function. Absenteeism, changes in demand, resignations and so on cause disorder as employees are generally unable to step into a new role without an adjustment and training period. Leaders do not encourage cross-skilling.	The improvement strategy prescribes the reason for cross-skilling and the flexibility required to meet the business needs. Leaders understand the competitive advantage and employee motivation linked to cross-skilling and evaluate the policy and grading changes required to support the principles.	A skills matrix is developed and the development plan for each employee is structured to achieve the cross-skilling within a particular area. Cross-skilling commences in each area according to a defined method of training, competence acquisition and assessment process.	The skills matrix and development plan is updated to reflect inter-area cross-skilling. Development continues according to the defined method of training, competence acquisition and assessment to increase the flexibility between departments.	Where applicable, geographical flexibility has been developed to create the ability to move employees between sites. Labour flexibility to market and demand fluctuations is achieved and supports the ability to create value for the business, customer, environment and employee.

PEOPLE

PEOPLE SUMMARY GRAPH

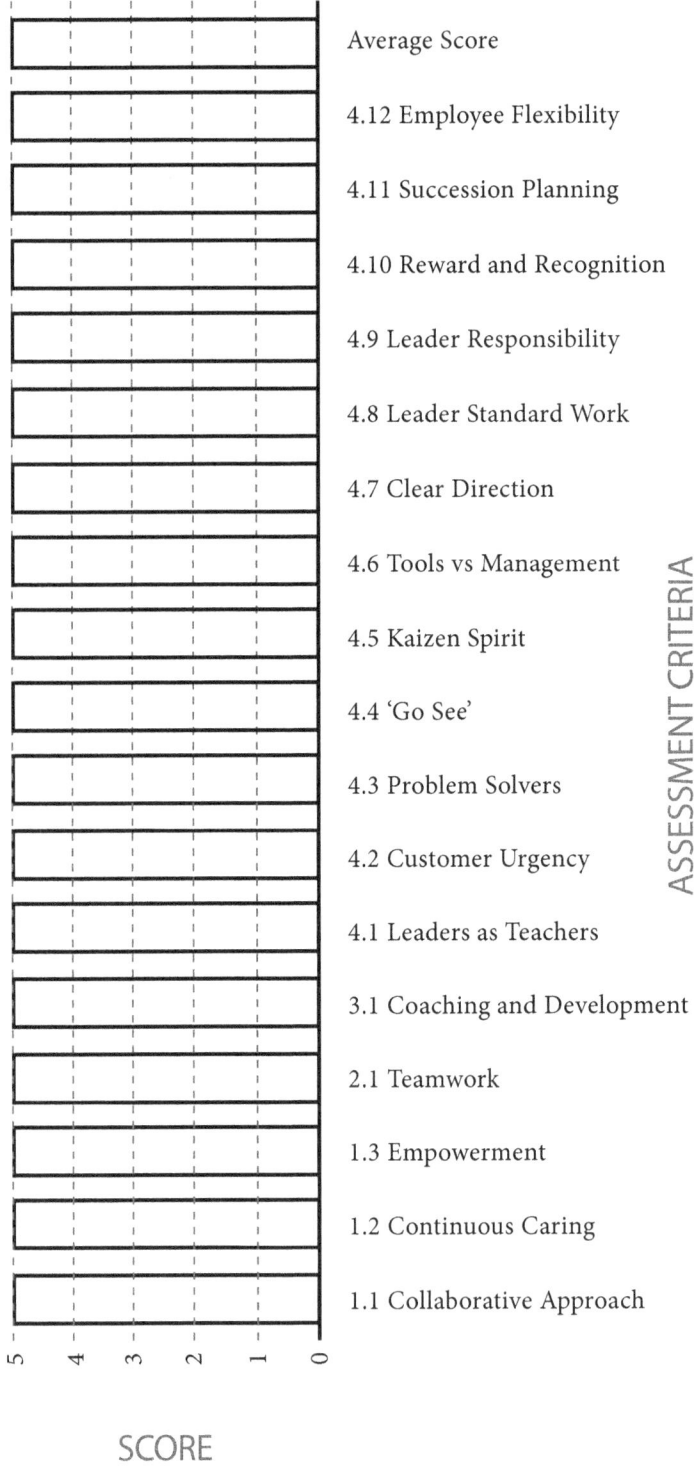

Score	Assessment Criteria
	Average Score
	4.12 Employee Flexibility
	4.11 Succession Planning
	4.10 Reward and Recognition
	4.9 Leader Responsibility
	4.8 Leader Standard Work
	4.7 Clear Direction
	4.6 Tools vs Management
	4.5 Kaizen Spirit
	4.4 'Go See'
	4.3 Problem Solvers
	4.2 Customer Urgency
	4.1 Leaders as Teachers
	3.1 Coaching and Development
	2.1 Teamwork
	1.3 Empowerment
	1.2 Continuous Caring
	1.1 Collaborative Approach

5   4   3   2   1   0

SCORE

ASSESSMENT CRITERIA

Colour in the final scoring for each criterion and the average score.

PEOPLE FOCUS SUMMARY

ASSESSMENT AREA	IMPROVEMENT OPPORTUNITIES	SHORT, MEDIUM OR LONG-TERM FOCUS
MUTUAL RESPECT FOR PEOPLE		
TEAMWORK SUPPORTS CUSTOMER VALUE		
FORMALISED COACHING AND DEVELOPMENT		
LEADERSHIP EXCELLENCE		

Capture the top improvement opportunities for each assessment area and include a comment to show if it is a short, medium or long-term focus for the business:

Short: <6 months

Medium: 6 to 12 months

Long: >12 months

NO	ASSESSMENT AREA	ASSESSMENT CRITERIA	LEVEL 1	LEVEL 2	LEVEL 3	LEVEL 4	LEVEL 5
1	**Problem Solving Strategy and Structures.**	**1.1 A strategy to address both incremental and breakthrough improvement is deployed (Bicheno, 2004).**	Problems are addressed as they surface and are reactive in nature. A formal strategy that defines how improvements are categorised and tackled does not exist. Leaders and employees are constantly engaged in solving problems, but real progress in the indicators is not achieved.	Leaders are aware that both incremental improvement and breakthrough improvement are required to move the company forward in achieving the improvement goals. A distinction is made between passive and reactive opportunities and a formal strategy to create this balance is defined.	Incremental and breakthrough kaizen activities have started. These are initiated by operators, managers and industrial engineers and are passive in nature – they are reactive to a particular situation or crisis. There is inconsistency in how often they occur. Passive examples include quality circles and team suggestions.	Incremental and breakthrough kaizen activities are pro-active in nature, and situations to stimulate improvements are engineered to keep the pressure on. Pro-active examples include kaizen events. These are structured and on a fixed, non-negotiable schedule. Dedicated resources are applied.	Continuous improvement and leaps in performance characterise the performance culture in the organisation. There is a good balance between proactive and re-active improvement. There is significant impact to the key indicators.
		1.2 Improvement leverage focuses all change activities and achieves triple bottom line impact.	Improvements are launched based on intuition, personal preferences, or the individual needs of a department. A system's approach to identifying the most pressing areas is not utilised, and selections are not backed by data and analysis.	Leaders understand the importance of creating a culture where activities are focused on areas that will have the greatest impact to the goals. The principle of allocating 80 percent of the energy to 20 percent of the problems is understood.	Most improvement projects and activities can be traced back to a need defined in the improvement strategy. Business levers drive decisions to allocate resources. Employees understand how their activities support the improvement drive.	Employees are trained to use a scientific approach to improvement and all details within each improvement activity conform to the 80/20 principle. The right problems are tackled according to the right method.	Improvement activities yield significant impact in the operations through an efficient use of resources, and improvement in the indicators is evident.

PROBLEM SOLVING

NO	ASSESSMENT AREA	ASSESSMENT CRITERIA	LEVEL 1	LEVEL 2	LEVEL 3	LEVEL 4	LEVEL 5
1	**Problem Solving Strategy and Structures** Continued…/	**1.3 Problem Solving triggers are well defined and support a culture of rapid response to problems (Mann, 2005).**	When problems occur, response is reactive in nature and often employees find creative, sometimes unconventional ways to work around the problem. There is a strong focus on 'doing what it takes' to meet schedule.	The importance of setting triggers to activate rapid response to problems is understood. For each critical area, triggers for problem solving, responsibility, method and timing are defined. A standard for rapid response to the right problems is developed.	A trigger system for out-of-standard conditions in the process prompts problem solving activities. Relevant employees are properly trained to respond rapidly according to a structured approach.	A trigger system for out-of-standard conditions in the performance indicators prompts problem solving activities. The system applies to team level, middle management and top management and drives a behaviour of continuous improvement to the right problems.	Problems are addressed pro-actively, timeously, in a structured way and by the right level. Triggers are continually reviewed for relevance to critical process areas and performance indicators. Processes are stabilising, and improvement in the indicators is evident.
		1.4 A tiered problem solving model drives multi-level improvement, escalation and feedback.	There is inconsistency in how problems are addressed and by whom. A culture of 'passing the buck' exists and a lack of accountability prevents problems being addressed effectively. Employees feel they are not supported. Concerns are raised and a lack of feedback results in de-motivation and a reluctance to participate.	Leadership understands the importance of clarity in how problems are addressed. A model describes the levels in the organisation, problem levels, typical approaches and triggers. How problems are to be escalated and under what conditions, is clear. How feedback is to be handled and accountability is clear.	A visual guide to the tiers of problem solving is implemented in all areas and employees are trained on what problems to address and when to escalate them. Leaders are trained to respond to escalations and a standard procedure is followed. Escalations are visually managed and accountability is clear and personal.	Relevant employees and leaders are trained and able to apply the methods required at each tier of problem solving. A scientific approach is used at all levels, with varying degrees of difficulty in the tools and techniques to suit the level of problem.	Problems are identified and solved at all levels (situational, systemic and strategic) by the right people, in the right way, regularly. Employees are confident they have the support and empowerment to act. Leaders are confident that problems are tackled effectively and at the correct level.

PROBLEM SOLVING

NO	ASSESSMENT AREA	ASSESSMENT CRITERIA	LEVEL 1	LEVEL 2	LEVEL 3	LEVEL 4	LEVEL 5
2	Enabling a Problem Solving Culture and Learning	2.1 Every problem is seen as an opportunity and stimulates continuous improvement, participation and growth.	Problems are hidden and employees reveal problems with negative consequences. A culture of punishment prevails. The same problems recur and although these are tackled periodically, fresh insight is lacking into possible causes and countermeasures.	Leaders understand the importance of creating an environment that enables the exposure and learning from problems. Employees are thanked when they bring a problem to the leader.	The leader provides the necessary support and guidance to resolve problems exposed by the employees. The principles of A3 Thinking actively guide this relationship and helps build the learning culture.	There is no hesitation to expose problems and address them timeously. All employees are constantly improving their knowledge of the process, product or service, and finding innovative ways to address root causes and sustain results. The recurrence of problems is declining.	Mutual respect has developed between leader and employee. New problems are being surfaced continuously. Superior process and product or service knowledge has led to innovation in creating improved value to the business, customer, environment or employee.
		2.2 Time is made available to solve problems.	Problems occur and are addressed on an adhoc basis and vary in terms of the time taken to resolve. 'Quick-fixes' become the standard and employees feel there is no time to resolve problems properly.	Leaders are committed to making time available for improvement activities. Dedicated time to problem solving is evaluated and designed into the working schedule for all employees.	Triggers prompt employees to respond to out-of-standard conditions and if the problem cannot be resolved immediately, the leader is alerted through the escalation procedure and takes the necessary action to support the employee.	Employees are empowered to 'stop the line' according to a standard procedure and response time. Morning meeting agendas allow time to problem solve performance indicator triggers. When longer time is required, problems are escalated to dedicated problem solving sessions.	Problems are resolved reactively and pro-actively, both situationally and at breakthrough level within a specified time frame. Crisis management is not tolerated and once 'quick-fixes' have stabilised impact to the customer or environment, root causes are eliminated. The impact on indicators is evident.

PROBLEM SOLVING

NO	ASSESSMENT AREA	ASSESSMENT CRITERIA	LEVEL 1	LEVEL 2	LEVEL 3	LEVEL 4	LEVEL 5
					PLACE SCORE HERE		PLACE SCORE HERE
2	Enabling a Problem Solving Culture and Learning Continued.../	2.3 The ability to continuously improve at all levels, in all areas, every day is possible (Ballé, 2004).	Specific methods for problem solving are not used. Employees rely on their own experience for each approach.	The need for specific methods of problem solving is established and defined for each tier of problem solving.	Employees are trained and effectively use situational problem solving methods – for example, 5Why (a method to uncover root causes) and Ishikawa diagrams (fishbone diagram illustrating possible causes).	Employees are trained in and are effectively using systemic and strategic problem solving methods – for example, tools and techniques commonly used in 6 Sigma training (advanced problem solving.)	A combined effort of problem solving skills at all levels, in all areas yields improved results in the indicators. Those closest to the process solve the problems using the right techniques.
		2.4 Development, evaluation, coaching and reflection in problem solving is frequent, structured and effective (Ballé, 2004).	Employees are left un-supported to deal with their problems and countermeasures. This leads to problems that are poorly defined and resolved. Employees are not confident to make bold leaps in performance and leaders are not confident in the employees' ability to achieve this.	Leaders and employees understand there is a dual responsibility in solving problems and that a structured approach is required to coach and steer individuals through the learning process. A3 Thinking is adopted to check and coach the employee through each stage of PDCA.	Leaders and change agents are trained to provide the necessary support in problem solving and A3 Thinking. Improvement projects are launched and the coaching process is initiated. There is a dual responsibility to develop A3 reports for problems.	A problem solving and coaching relationship between leaders and employees is established. The employee is self-directed, autonomous and empowered to search for the right answers to the right questions but are never abandoned. The leader steers the process, maintains motivation and drives rigour in the process.	Sustainability and effectiveness of problem solving is achieved. Confidence in applying problem solving is expanded beyond operations to new areas – for example, new equipment purchasing and strategy development. A dual responsibility to tackle problems prevails and leaps in performance are evident.

PROBLEM SOLVING

NO	ASSESSMENT AREA	ASSESSMENT CRITERIA	LEVEL 1	LEVEL 2	LEVEL 3	LEVEL 4	LEVEL 5
3	Systems and Methodology	3.1 Systems surface problems and trigger problem solving.	There is no clarity in what is normal and what is out of standard at each process. Triggers do not prompt response and problem solving.	The importance of exposing opportunity is understood and systems to expose abnormal conditions for each tier of problem is defined.	Systems are implemented to expose abnormality and trigger responses. Employees know when to respond, to what and how.	At a glance, one can see which operations are stable, issues identified and steps taken to address the situation in a structured way.	Improvement in the indicators and stability in the process is evident.
		3.2 Scientific, data-based thinking is embraced and drives every cycle of improvement.	Decisions, new products and projects, and reactive improvements are based on the instincts and gut feel of a few individuals.	The importance of experimental and, data- and, based scientific thinking is understood and a controlled approach to PDCA is established for each tier of problem solving.	Everyone is trained in the principles and application of scientific–based problem solving, relevant to their level. Under guidance and coaching (A3 Thinking), projects are initiated and the structured methods emerge in pockets of the organisation.	All employees use a scientific approach to improvement and techniques vary to suit the level of difficulty. Every improvement initiative can be evaluated for quantitative results and in most cases, the financial gains are established.	Improvement in the capability to solve problems effectively, and the resulting change in indicators has increased customer, business and employee confidence in the organisation to effectively address concerns and provide improved service.

PROBLEM SOLVING

NO	ASSESSMENT AREA	ASSESSMENT CRITERIA	LEVEL 1	LEVEL 2	LEVEL 3	LEVEL 4	LEVEL 5
					PLACE SCORE HERE		PLACE SCORE HERE
3	Systems and Methodology Continued.../	3.3 Management-level kaizen sets the example and encourages system-wide impact.	Individual department heads solve problems relevant to their own area of control and do not get involved in activities that cross borders into other functions. Employees feel leaders do not support them in removing obstacles outside of their control.	Leaders understand the need to hold regular management kaizens that tackle problems outside of the control of subordinates and create a system's approach to change.	Leaders are trained in kaizen techniques and respond to triggers and escalations timeously and in a structured way. Management kaizens take place regularly and rigorously follow the PDCA cycle of improvement.	Employee confidence in leaders to address obstacles preventing them from achieving their goals, is growing. Leader understanding of the problems is improving and stimulating new levels of performance.	A culture of improvement is achieved. Direct improvement in systemic and strategic indicators is evident and cascades down to improvements at the situational level.
		3.4 Knowledge management preserves prior learning and creates cross-learning.	No method of capturing the knowledge and learning points from improvement activities exists. Learning is lost over time and often sits with a few individuals within the company. A culture of 'reinventing the wheel' is prevalent.	The need to preserve learning from improvement activities is recognised and a policy to capture and share knowledge is developed.	A3 reports used in the coaching process are also used to capture the problem solving story and detail how the knowledge is to be shared. An effective method of storing the reports is assured for easy access and retrieval of the records.	Knowledge from improvement activities is actively shared and forms part of the leader performance appraisal. The quality of the records is improving and there is a clear flow from one step to the next within the report. Employees follow the report and deploy the learnings in their own areas.	The rate of improvement within the organisation is accelerated through knowledge sharing. Learning from the improvement activities is preserved and survives beyond employee turnover.

PROBLEM SOLVING

NO	ASSESSMENT AREA	ASSESSMENT CRITERIA	LEVEL 1	LEVEL 2	LEVEL 3	LEVEL 4	LEVEL 5
3	**Systems and Methodology Continued…/**	**3.5 Strong focus in problem definition, consensus building and the speed of implementation.**	Employees and leaders rush into solutions and implementation before consensus on problems is fully achieved.	As part of the scientific approach, employees understand the importance of problem definition in the planning stage.	Leaders and employees are trained to achieve consensus on the problem they are trying to solve, prior to proceeding.	The quality of the problem solving process is improving. This is evident in the success rate of countermeasures to address the problem.	All problems are understood slowly, by consensus and implemented quickly.

PROBLEM SOLVING

PROBLEM SOLVING SUMMARY GRAPH

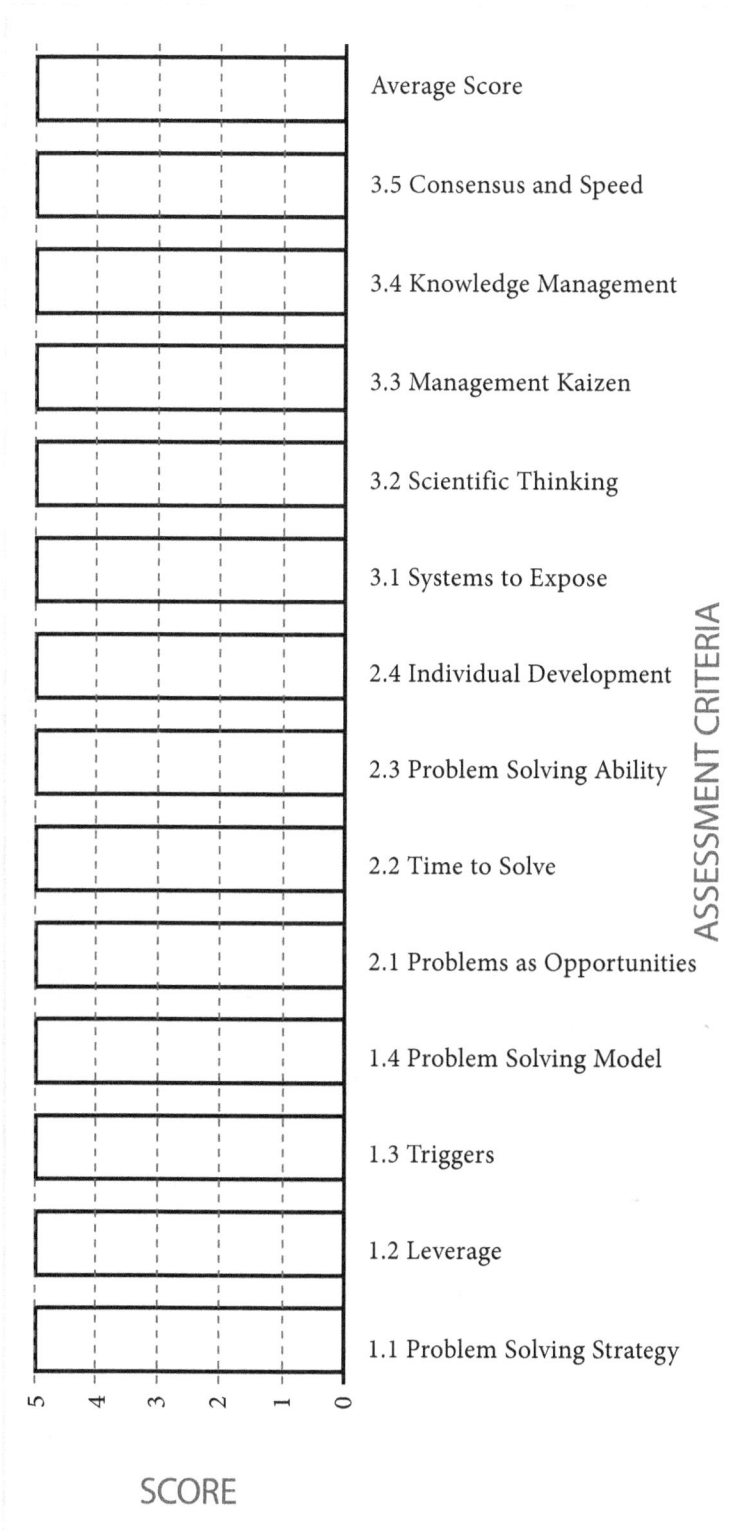

	Average Score
	3.5 Consensus and Speed
	3.4 Knowledge Management
	3.3 Management Kaizen
	3.2 Scientific Thinking
	3.1 Systems to Expose
	2.4 Individual Development
	2.3 Problem Solving Ability
	2.2 Time to Solve
	2.1 Problems as Opportunities
	1.4 Problem Solving Model
	1.3 Triggers
	1.2 Leverage
	1.1 Problem Solving Strategy

ASSESSMENT CRITERIA

Colour in the final scoring for each criterion and the average score.

5 4 3 2 1 0

SCORE

PROBLEM SOLVING FOCUS SUMMARY

ASSESSMENT AREA	IMPROVEMENT OPPORTUNITIES	SHORT, MEDIUM OR LONG-TERM FOCUS
PROBLEM SOLVING STRATEGY AND STRUCTURES		
ENABLING A PROBLEM SOLVING CULTURE AND LEARNING		
SYSTEMS AND METHODOLOGY		

Capture the top improvement opportunities for each assessment area and include a comment to show if it is a short, medium or long-term focus for the business:

Short: <6 months

Medium: 6 to 12 months

Long: >12 months

NO	ASSESSMENT AREA	ASSESSMENT CRITERIA	LEVEL 1	LEVEL 2	LEVEL 3	LEVEL 4	LEVEL 5
1	**Long-Term Committment to Sustainability**	**1.1 A holistic approach drives improvement activities to reduce environmental impact.**	Complacency around the consumption of materials and resources is evident, and levels of usage and disposal are unknown or considered acceptable.	There is a growing awareness around environmental opportunities to reduce impact and benefit the company. Improvement goals for recycling materials or resources are included in the Change Plan. Employees action formal recycling activities on purchases already made, to convert unused materials or resources to alternative uses. A quantifiable reduction in the environmental footprint is confirmed.	Improvement goals for reusing materials and resources are included in the Change Plan. Employees and leaders action formal refurbishment activities on purchases already made, to re-enter into the market. As a result, a quantifiable reduction in the environmental footprint is confirmed.	Improvement goals for reducing materials or resources required are included in the Change Plan. Employees and leaders action formal reduction activities that not only reduce the amount of purchases needed but also the impact of the resources after use. As a result, a quantifiable reduction in the environmental footprint is confirmed.	Improvement goals for eliminating materials or resources required are included in the Change Plan. Employees and leaders action formal product and process redesign activities that not only reduce the amount of purchases needed but also the impact of the resources after use. As a result, a quantifiable reduction in the environmental footprint is confirmed.

PLANET

NO	ASSESSMENT AREA	ASSESSMENT CRITERIA	LEVEL 1	LEVEL 2	LEVEL 3	LEVEL 4	LEVEL 5
2	A Systematic Approach to improve Environmental Performance	2.1 The environmental impact is visible and tactical changes to achieve the target condition are executed.	The current environmental footprint and target condition for improvement is unknown. Detailed analysis of the key contributing factors to the footprint have not been established.	Leaders understand the value of visualising environmental performance. A Current State evaluation of the organisation's environmental footprint is complete and the target condition is agreed to in line with customer requirement, business purpose, or legislative criteria. The evaluation clearly defines the key improvement areas for further mapping and exposes immediate actions for execution.	Current State Green Value Stream Maps have been created to visualise the next level of detail for critical Value Streams. Opportunities have been quantified and prioritised, Future State Maps developed, and a phased implementation plan is ready for execution.	The Future State actions have been implemented, checked, revised where needed and standardised to promote sustainability of the changes. Procedures for reducing and controlling risks, responding to emergencies and taking corrective actions are formally documented and integrated into the management system.	The cycle is repeated periodically and a new Current State environmental footprint and target condition is created to align with tighter targets in the improvement goals.

PLANET

NO	ASSESSMENT AREA	ASSESSMENT CRITERIA	LEVEL 1	LEVEL 2	LEVEL 3	LEVEL 4	LEVEL 5
2	A Systematic Approach to improve Environmental Performance Continued.../	2.2 Environmental improvement projects use scientific problem solving techniques to deliver sustainable changes.	No standard problem solving approach is used for environmental projects. Individuals select their own methods based on personal experience, resulting in different methods deployed and varied results being achieved.	The value in using problem solving best practice in projects is understood and accepted by environmental, health and safety representatives (EHS). There is alignment between the methodology defined and the continuous improvement principles inherent in an environmental management system.	EHS representatives are trained in the principles and application of scientific-based problem solving methodology, relevant to their level. Under guidance and coaching (such as A3 Thinking), projects are initiated and the structured methods are in play.	EHS representatives actively use a scientific approach to improvement and techniques vary to suit the level of difficulty. Every improvement initiative can be evaluated for quantitative results in environmental impact and in most cases, the financial gains are established.	Improvement in the capability to solve problems effectively and the resulting change in indicators has increased customer, business and employee confidence to address environmental concerns.

PLANET

PLANET SUMMARY GRAPH

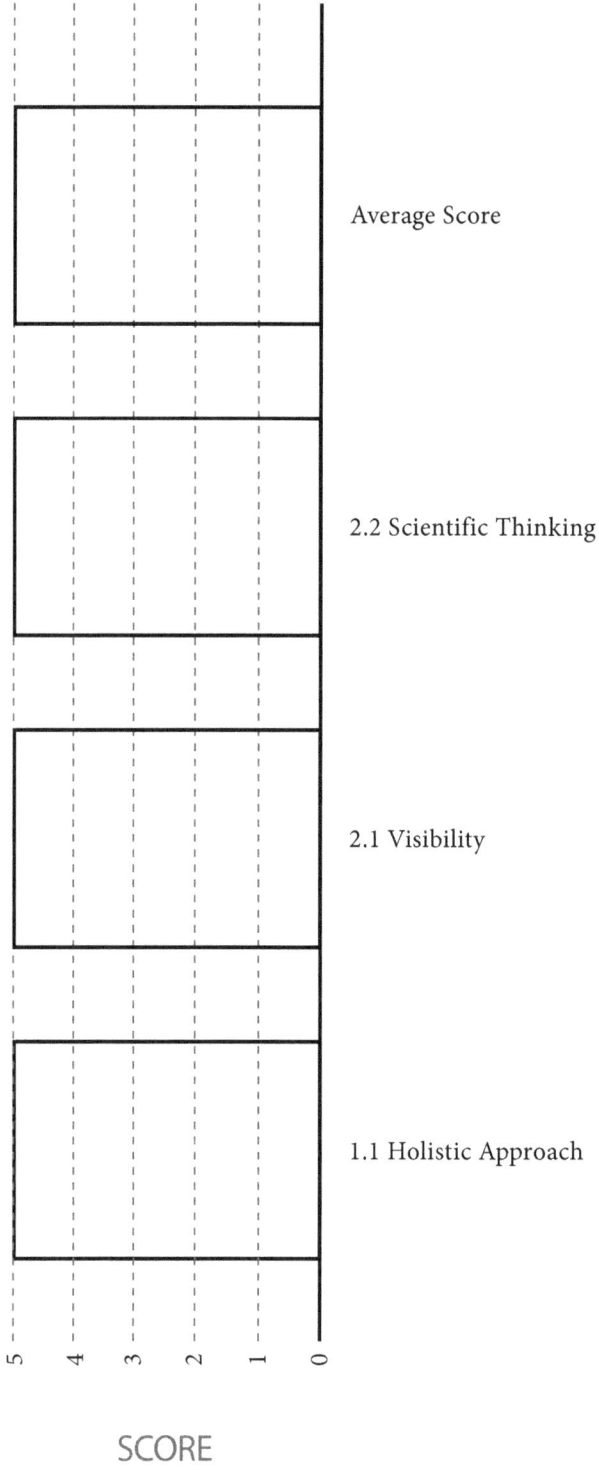

ASSESSMENT CRITERIA

Colour in the final scoring for each criterion and the average score.

Average Score

2.2 Scientific Thinking

2.1 Visibility

1.1 Holistic Approach

SCORE

5   4   3   2   1   0

PLANET FOCUS SUMMARY

ASSESSMENT AREA	IMPROVEMENT OPPORTUNITIES	SHORT, MEDIUM OR LONG-TERM FOCUS
LONG TERM COMMITMENT TO SUSTAINABILITY		
A SYSTEMATIC APPROACH TO IMPROVE ENVIRONMENTAL PERFORMANCE		

Capture the top improvement opportunities for each assessment area and include a comment to show if it is a short, medium or long-term focus for the business:

Short: <6 months

Medium: 6 to 12 months

Long: >12 months

Step 4: Summarise Results and Focus Area

It was recommended earlier in the chapter that an assessment not be treated like a 'copy and paste' exercise. The 5P Assessment shows a comprehensive way to evaluate the organisation for the best practices in place and areas for focus. However, it should be compared to the real needs of the business. For example, if the organisation has not yet completed a diagnostic (Purpose 2.2) to evaluate the Current State and true potential aligned to the business strategy, this would be a higher priority than pursuing a level 5 pull-based system (Process 4.1). The logic here is that one cannot determine the improvements required until the needs are fully understood or implement sophisticated systems until the fundamentals are in place. It is important that a skilled facilitator assists in guiding the assessment team through the critical questions to be asked to ensure the focus areas highlighted will, in fact, benefit the business and be implemented in a reasonable sequence and time frame.

Begin by summarising the scores for the 5P Assessment (figure 2.4) and then prioritise the improvement opportunities into a matrix (figure 2.5). Thereafter, capture the focus and time frames into an improvement table (table 2.4) and summarise the Current State and target condition (as shown in figure 2.3) on the Operational Excellence Matrix provided:

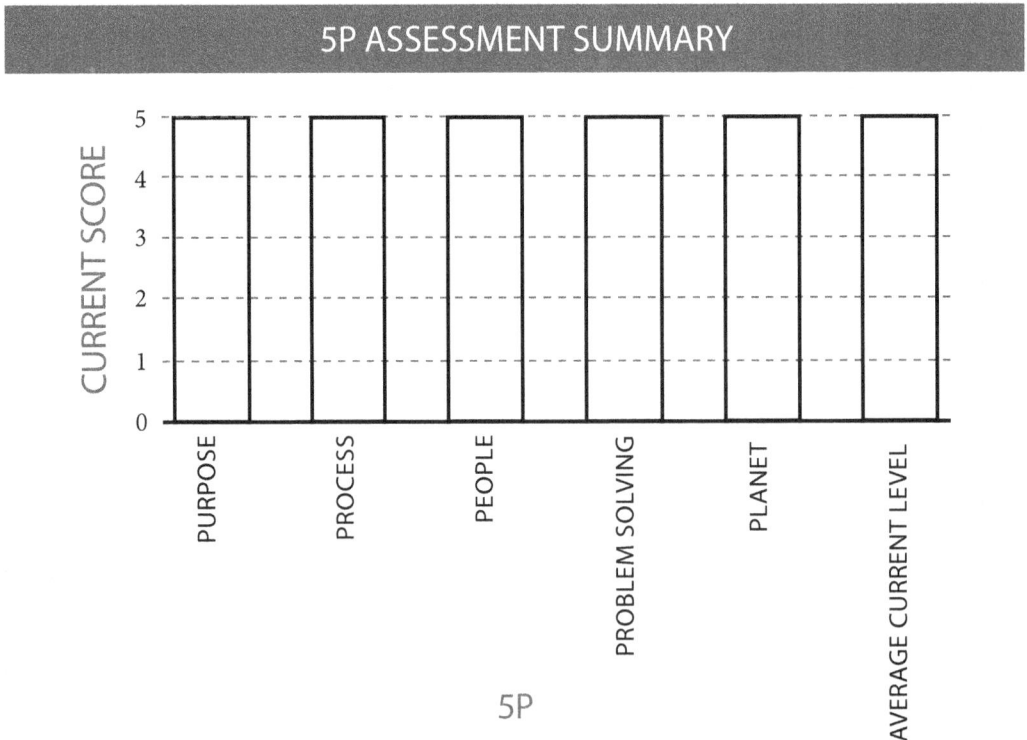

Colour in the average scoring for each of the 5Ps from the assessment results. The last bar represents the average score for all five.

Figure 2.4

PRIORITISATION MATRIX

The purpose of this exercise is to create discussion and consensus around the focus areas and their respective priorities. It is possible to skip this step and go straight to the improvement table (table 2.4) but often the debates and discussions can be of value, eventhough they require additional effort.

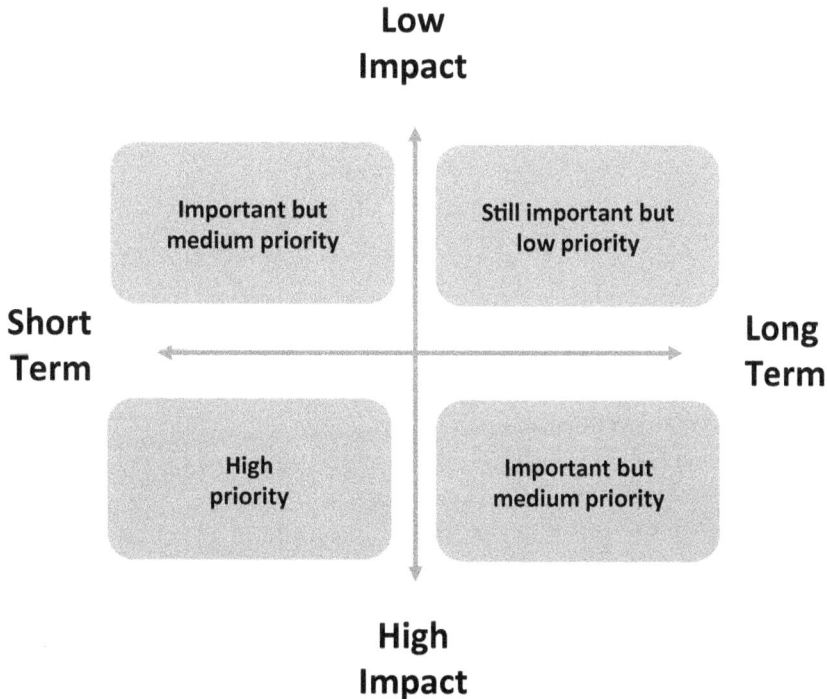

Using a flipchart and Post-it Notes, rank the improvement opportunities identified for each of the 5Ps and position on the matrix (figure 2.5) to establish a basic priority. Include the time frame on each Post-it. Consider using different colours for each of the 5Ps.

Figure 2.5

Use the following guideline, or develop your own:

- o Short term:<6 months to address

- o Medium term: 6 to 12 months to address

- o Long term: >12 months to address

- o Impact: will have a high or low impact on

    - The triple bottom line (Voice of the Business)

    - Customer satisfaction (Voice of the Customer)

    - Environmental footprint (Voice of the Business)

    - Morale (Voice of the Employee)

5P / Time Frame	Purpose	Process	People	Problem Solving	Planet
IMPROVEMENT TABLE					
Short Term					
Medium Term					
Long Term					

Using the priorities agreed to in the previous exercise, summarise the focus areas into their time frames and position them in order of priority under each of the 5P headings above.

Table 2.4

OPERATIONAL EXCELLENCE MATRIX

Take the average of the total 5P scores and mark the result on the model by drawing a vertical line through the level achieved (see figure 2.3).

Step 5: Agree on Target Condition

Refer to the summaries created for each of the 5Ps together with the improvement table and agree on a target condition (indicated by a target 5P Assessment Score) for a two-year view at a minimum.

Update the graphs on the following pages to summarise the target condition for each criteria and for each of the 5Ps.

TIPS

- Consider the business objectives when deciding on the timing of your target scores and the focus.

- Consider the resource availability (money and time) when setting the target condition.

- Be specific about what assessment criteria will be improved upon, and to what level (level 1 to 5).

- Use the expertise of a skilled facilitator to guide the discussions and debates.

- Ensure there is consensus from the senior team on the target condition, and that it is not just the hobby-horse of an individual.

- Above all, ensure the senior team understands the connection between the focus areas and achieving the business objectives – this must not be seen as an add-on to current initiatives but a means of achieving the goals sustainably.

PURPOSE TARGET CONDITION

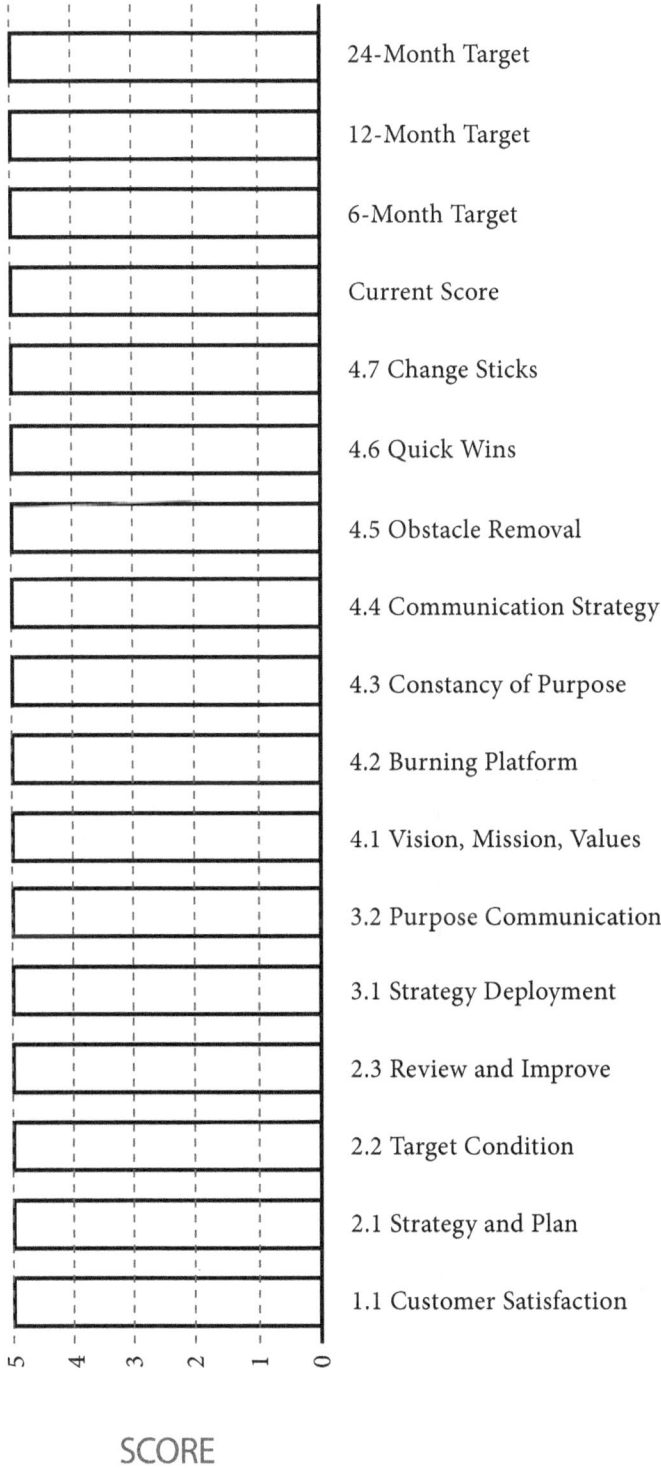

24-Month Target

12-Month Target

6-Month Target

Current Score

4.7 Change Sticks

4.6 Quick Wins

4.5 Obstacle Removal

4.4 Communication Strategy

4.3 Constancy of Purpose

4.2 Burning Platform

4.1 Vision, Mission, Values

3.2 Purpose Communication

3.1 Strategy Deployment

2.3 Review and Improve

2.2 Target Condition

2.1 Strategy and Plan

1.1 Customer Satisfaction

5 4 3 2 1 0

SCORE

ASSESSMENT CRITERIA

Colour the current score for each criterion and then use three different colours to show the progression to 6, 12 and 24 month target conditions for each bar. Calculate the average target condition for 6, 12 and 24 months respectively.

PROCESS TARGET CONDITION

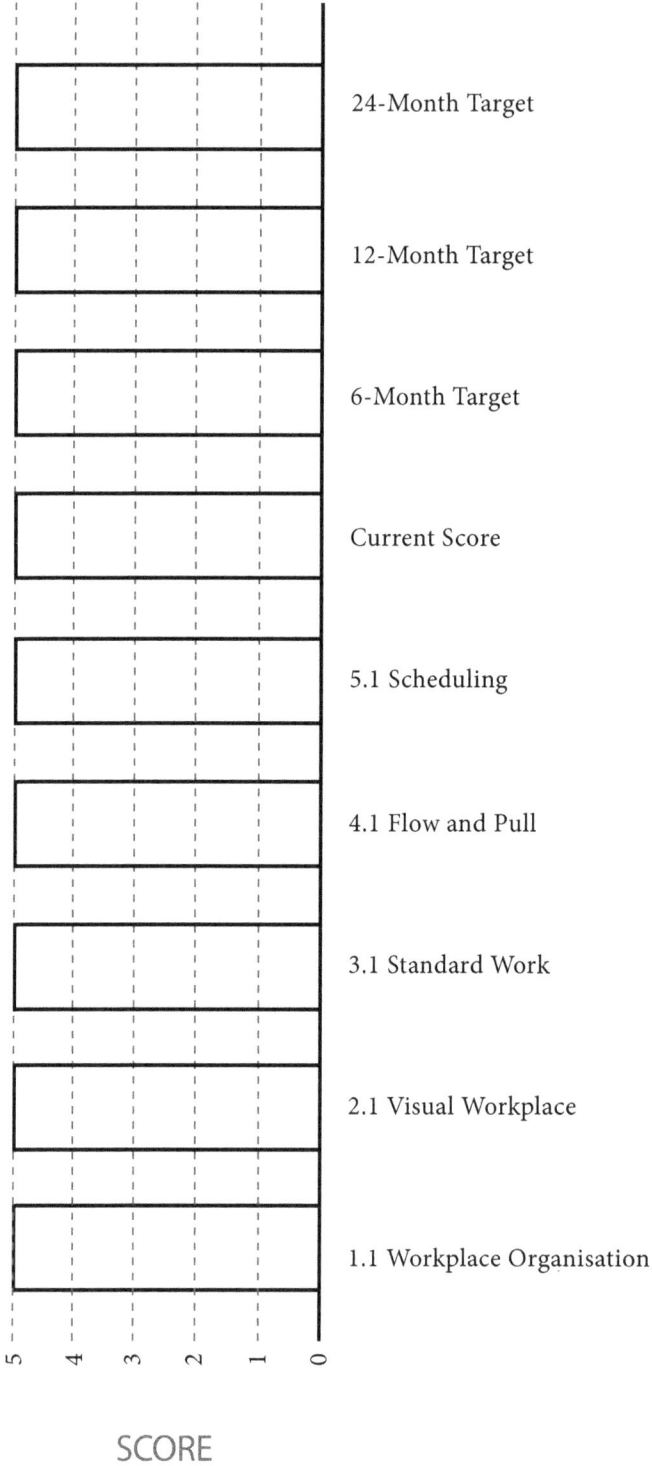

24-Month Target

12-Month Target

6-Month Target

Current Score

5.1 Scheduling

4.1 Flow and Pull

3.1 Standard Work

2.1 Visual Workplace

1.1 Workplace Organisation

5   4   3   2   1   0

SCORE

ASSESSMENT CRITERIA

Colour the current score for each criterion and then use three different colours to show the progression to 6, 12 and 24 month target conditions for each bar.
Calculate the average target condition for 6, 12 and 24 months respectively.

PEOPLE TARGET CONDITION

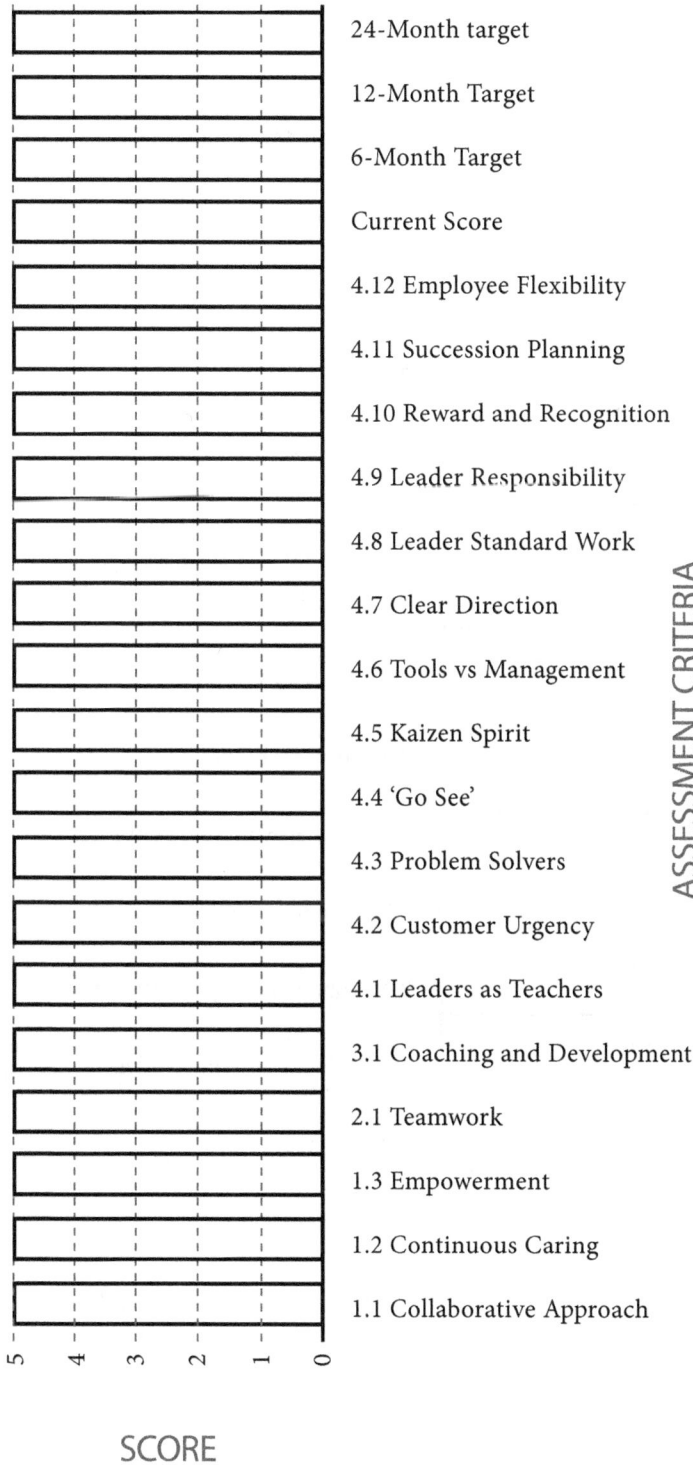

ASSESSMENT CRITERIA

Colour the current score for each criterion and then use three different colours to show the progression to 6, 12 and 24 month target conditions for each bar.
Calculate the average target condition for 6, 12 and 24 months respectively.

	24-Month target
	12-Month Target
	6-Month Target
	Current Score
	4.12 Employee Flexibility
	4.11 Succession Planning
	4.10 Reward and Recognition
	4.9 Leader Responsibility
	4.8 Leader Standard Work
	4.7 Clear Direction
	4.6 Tools vs Management
	4.5 Kaizen Spirit
	4.4 'Go See'
	4.3 Problem Solvers
	4.2 Customer Urgency
	4.1 Leaders as Teachers
	3.1 Coaching and Development
	2.1 Teamwork
	1.3 Empowerment
	1.2 Continuous Caring
	1.1 Collaborative Approach

5   4   3   2   1   0

SCORE

PROBLEM SOLVING TARGET CONDITION

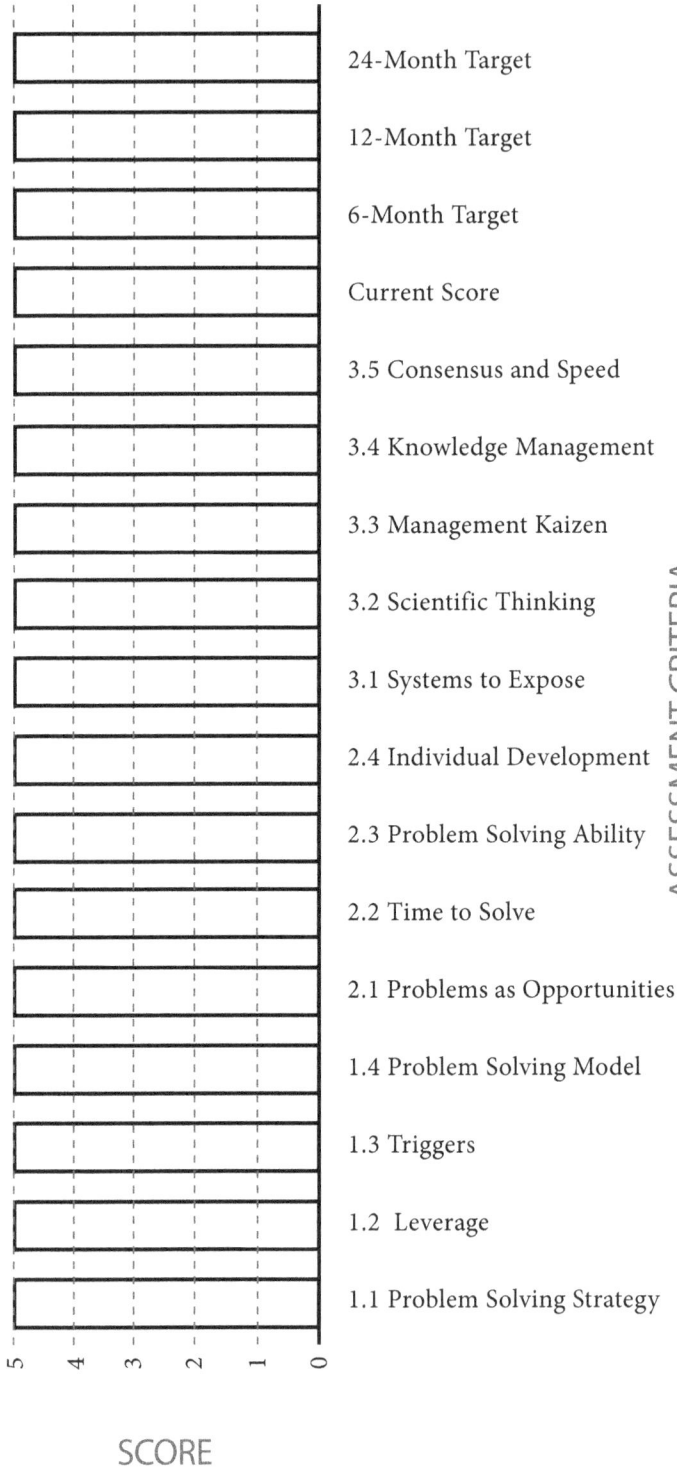

ASSESSMENT CRITERIA

Score	Criterion
	24-Month Target
	12-Month Target
	6-Month Target
	Current Score
	3.5 Consensus and Speed
	3.4 Knowledge Management
	3.3 Management Kaizen
	3.2 Scientific Thinking
	3.1 Systems to Expose
	2.4 Individual Development
	2.3 Problem Solving Ability
	2.2 Time to Solve
	2.1 Problems as Opportunities
	1.4 Problem Solving Model
	1.3 Triggers
	1.2 Leverage
	1.1 Problem Solving Strategy

Score axis: 5 4 3 2 1 0

SCORE

Colour the current score for each criterion and then use three different colours to show the progression to 6, 12 and 24 month target conditions for each bar. Calculate the average target condition for 6, 12 and 24 months respectively.

PLANET TARGET CONDITION

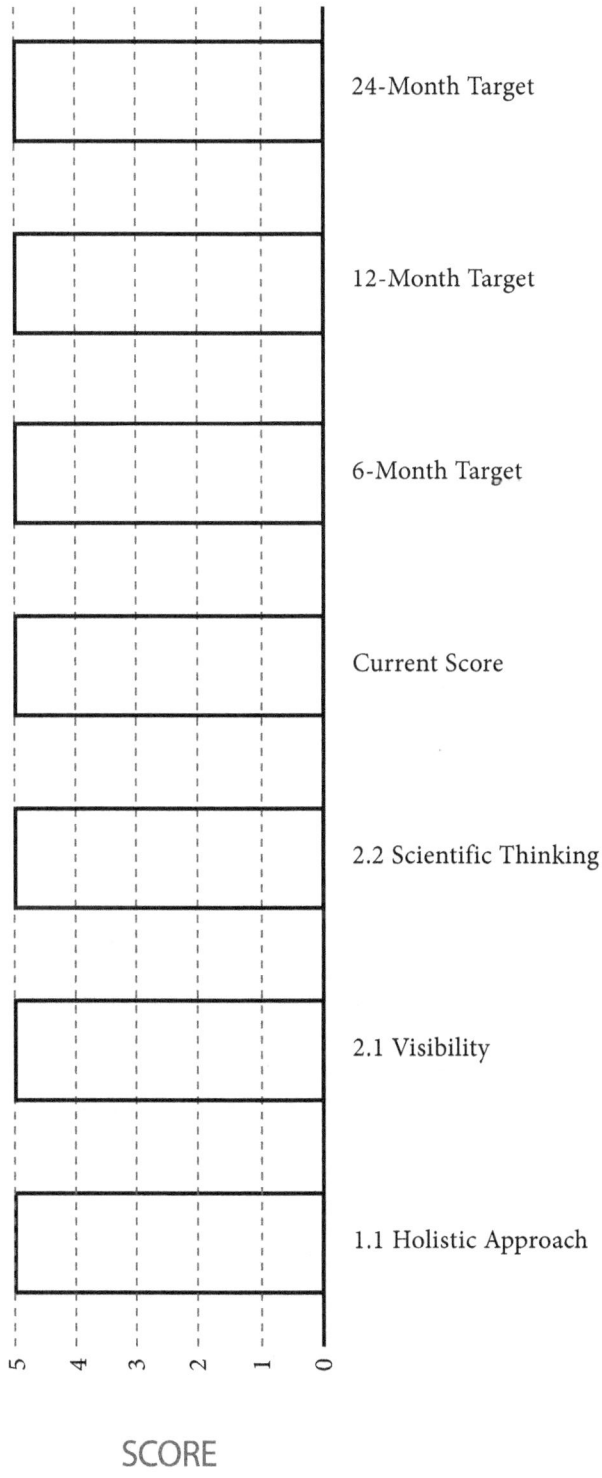

24-Month Target

12-Month Target

6-Month Target

Current Score

2.2 Scientific Thinking

2.1 Visibility

1.1 Holistic Approach

5 4 3 2 1 0

SCORE

ASSESSMENT CRITERIA

Colour the current score for each criterion and then use three different colours to show the progression to 6, 12 and 24 month target conditions for each bar.
Calculate the average target condition for 6, 12 and 24 months respectively.

5P TARGET CONDITION

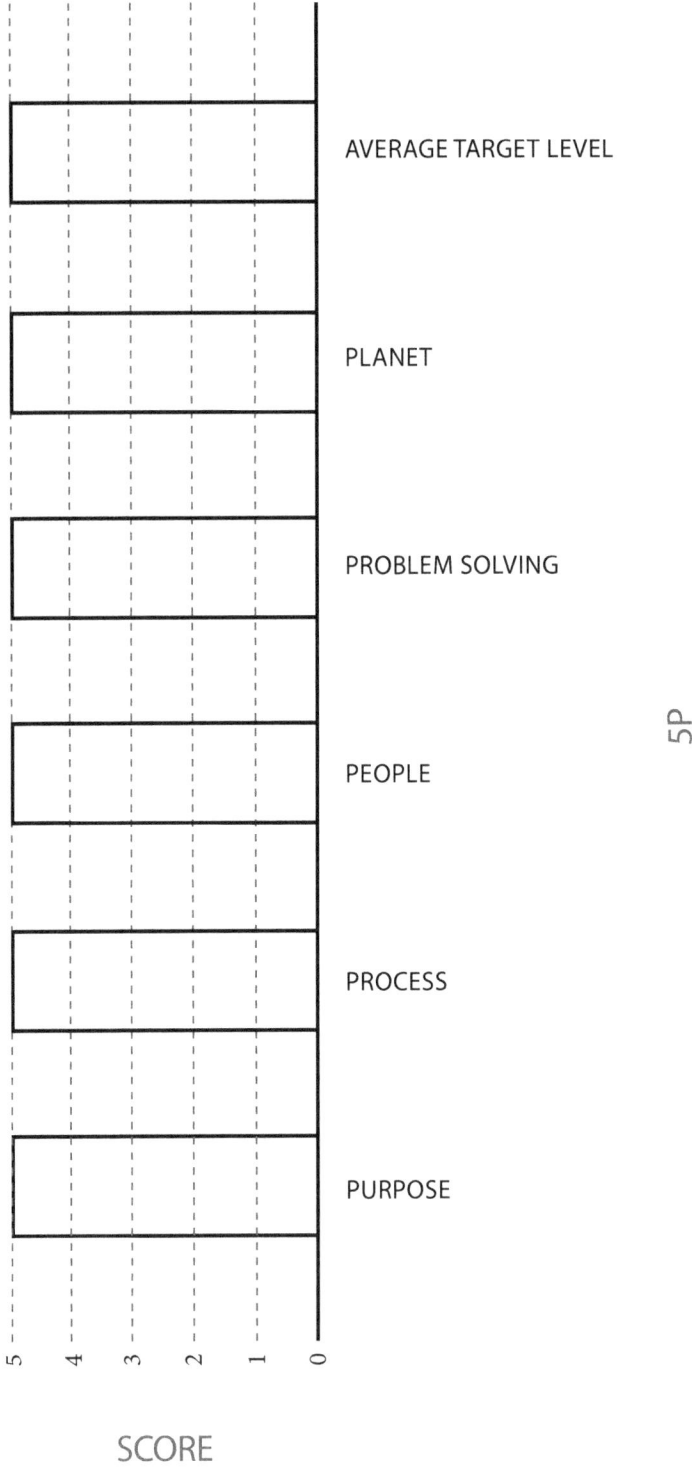

	AVERAGE TARGET LEVEL
	PLANET
	PROBLEM SOLVING
	PEOPLE
	PROCESS
	PURPOSE

SCORE

5   4   3   2   1   0

5P

Colour the current score for each of the 5Ps and then use three different colours to show the progression to 6, 12 and 24 month target conditions for each bar.

OPERATIONAL EXCELLENCE MATRIX TARGET CONDITION

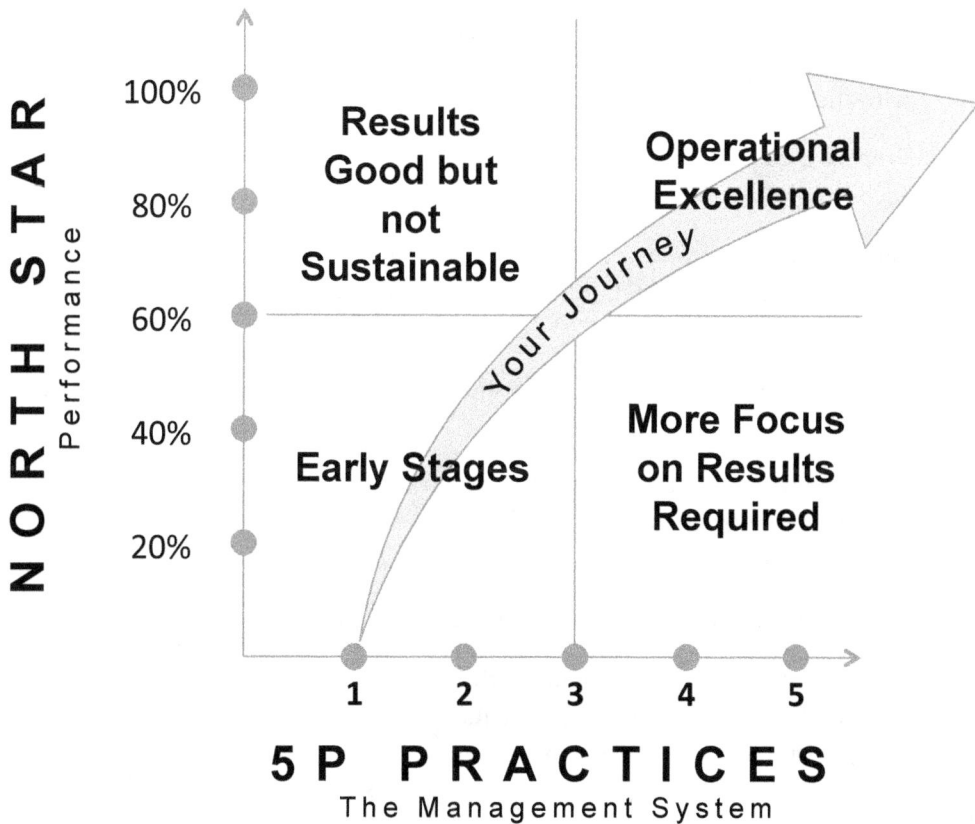

NORTH STAR
Performance

100%	
80%	**Results Good but not Sustainable**
60%	
40%	**Early Stages**
20%	

Operational Excellence

Your Journey

More Focus on Results Required

1   2   3   4   5

5P PRACTICES
The Management System

Refer to figure 2.3 for an example showing how to update the target score. Draw a vertical line through the average level targeted for all 5Ps. Consolidate the Current State and target condition onto one model for ease of reference.

✓ FOR YOU TO TRY

○ Refer to the results of the North Star in Chapter 1.

○ Agree on the scope of the assessment:

  - Which areas will be assessed?

  - Will one assessment be done for the organisation, or one per site or division?

○ Decide who will be involved, ensuring there is sufficient senior representation and a good mix of designations. Assign a strong facilitator with the required experienced to guide the activity.

○ Prepare a customised agenda with timings and schedule the participants accordingly.

○ Conduct the 5P Assessment. The facilitator is to provide guidance to ensure the group understand the statements and collectively agree on the Current State.

○ Complete the results summary to show the focus areas, priority and time frame.

○ Discuss and attain consensus on the target condition required to support the business strategy for each assessment criteria.

○ Summarise the target condition for the 5Ps.

○ Remember, this assessment will be used in conjunction with other assessments to create the final picture for the Future State.

3 VALUE STREAM EVALUATION
THE GLENDAY SIEVE ANALYSIS

❓ WHAT IS THIS?

The Glenday Sieve Analysis was developed by Ian Glenday, author of Breaking Through to Flow (Glenday, I, 2007, Breaking Through to Flow). Glenday's theory has been adapted to support this material.

The Glenday Sieve at first seems similar to the Runner-Repeater-Stranger Analysis (Pareto Analysis indicating the relative impact of volumes in production or tasks) but the interpretation of the results follows a different thought process and provokes interesting debates. We have found that even performing the basic analysis can initiate new learning and ideas around creating flow in the processes, which may contradict traditional logic and trigger breakthrough changes in performance.

Depending on how you choose to do the analysis, it will highlight which products or tasks contribute most to the bottom line, revenue, constraints or volume (green streams) and where you can pinpoint your activities for flow improvement to accelerate economies of repetition. The analysis helps discover the correct areas for the right capability improvement (yellow streams) and exposes the complexity caused by unnecessary variety that does not add value (blue streams). Finally low-volume products (red streams) are interrogated, and the potential to remove them altogether, or at least separate them from the main stream is highlighted.

It is a powerful means for understanding the flow of work through the operations and what affects it.

❓ WHY IS THIS HELPFUL?

During the phase of understanding the Current State, the Glenday Sieve Analysis provides a critical perspective on what impacts flow, what needs fixing, why, where and how. The advantages of conducting this exercise include:

- Identification of which Value Stream to concentrate efforts on for maximum impact.
- Sorted data pinpoints the products and services that pay bills, those that contribute to the 'cream' and those that steal cash.
- Areas that require capability improvement to support flow are highlighted.
- Waste caused by complexity is exposed.

○ Most people inherently prefer routine and consistency, and the analysis aims to find opportunities in which this can thrive.

○ Greater confidence in the Future State planning through a system's view that lets you think through the impact of your changes properly.

❓ HOW TO DO IT

Step 1: Choose your Team, Approach and Time Period

A big part of doing the analysis is to present problems in a way that people cannot dispute. Change management remains a challenge in any major change effort, and helping others to see the problems and solutions themselves, goes a long way in sustaining the changes later. Select a diverse, yet focused, group that can influence the supply chain and invite them to do the analysis together.

Involve the group in which data to use. Popular choices for sorting the data include:

○ Sales turnover per product or service

○ Sales volume per product or service

○ Gross profit per product or service

○ Contribution to overheads using selling price minus direct costs (Bicheno, 2004)

○ Contribution per bottleneck using the unit contribution divided by the time spent on bottleneck or constraint process (Bicheno, 2004).

If the team is uncertain of which data to use, start with sales volume to sort and extract the powerful few that complicate the flow of work through the value stream. You will also need to agree to what level to sort. If you are in manufacturing, a product may be offered only in small quantities to the market, but 'sub-products' may be common to many. This may necessitate that the analysis be done at a lower level in the bill of materials. If you are in service or maintenance, this could relate to sub-level tasks that should be analysed.

Once you have agreed which view to take from the data, decide on the time period to use. To get a good indication, use 12 months' data but if you experience sharp seasonal changes in demand, do the analysis per season. If the product or service ranges change frequently, consider going back a shorter period – for example, three months.

Step 2: Develop the Data Spreadsheet

For the purpose of the learning material, a sales turnover example will be used (table 3.1). The same process would apply to other data selections.

- o Insert the data and sort from highest to lowest.
- o Insert a cumulative column and show cumulative values running down the list.
- o Insert a cumulative percentage column and calculate the corresponding percentage to cumulative value.
- o Run down the list, and when you get to the 50 percent cumulative value, mark these products or services in green.
- o Run down from 50 percent to 95 percent and mark in yellow.
- o Run down from 95 percent to 99 percent and mark in blue.
- o Mark the last 1 percent in red.

Ranking	Product	Annual Sales Contribution per Product (Mar 2013 to Mar 2014)	% Sales Contribution per Product (Mar 2013 to Mar 2014)	Cumulative Sales Contribution	Cumulative % Sales Contribution
1	A	R 28,000,000	17%	R 28,000,000	17%
2	B	R 17,000,000	10%	R 45,000,000	27%
3	C	R 10,000,000	6%	R 55,000,000	33%
4	D	R 9,000,000	5%	R 64,000,000	39%
5	E	R 8,500,000	5%	R 72,500,000	44%
6	F	R 7,500,000	5%	R 80,000,000	49%
7	G	R 6,000,000	4%	R 86,000,000	52%
8	H	R 5,900,000	4%	R 91,900,000	56%
9	I	R 5,000,000	3%	R 96,900,000	59%
10	J	R 4,900,000	3%	R 101,800,000	62%
11	K	R 4,400,000	3%	R 106,200,000	64%
12	L	R 4,000,000	2%	R 110,200,000	67%

Example

7 products out of a total of 120 products (<6%) make up 52% of the sales turnover. They are marked in green.

Table 3.1

The list of products is too long to include here but each of the colours would highlight the relevant stream. Table 3.2 illustrates typical results according to research by Ian Glenday (Glenday, 2007).

Cumulative % Sales	Cumulative % of Product Range	Colour Code
50%	6%	Green
95%	50%	Yellow
99%	70%	Blue
Last 1%	30%	Red

Table 3.2

Step 3: Visualise your Data

A visual format to present the results will be easier to interpret and gather input. Customise a graph (figure 3.1) to your needs and let it trigger discussion around what has been learned.

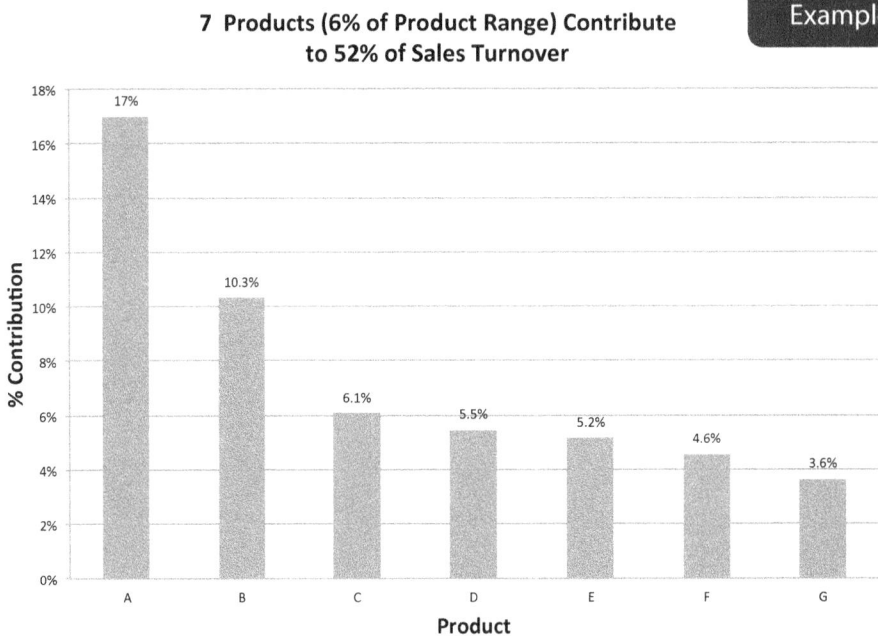

Figure 3.1

If applicable, show the results for volume, sales and profit on one graph to indicate the overlaps or differences.

Step 4: Interpret the Results

Discuss the issues identified and possible opportunities using the guidelines below as a starting point.

Green Stream

○ These are your high volume, repetitive products, services or tasks.

○ They represent the work that has the biggest impact on revenue and profit.

○ Treat these products or services like gold and protect from fire fighting.

○ Concentrate improvement efforts here first to improve on the cash-conversion cycle.

○ Investigate dedicated lines or fixed cycle scheduling to create economies of repetition.

○ Investigate real consumption, real causes of variation and possible demand smoothing.

○ Dedicate people who like repetition and routine to this type of work.

Yellow Stream

- The yellow stream makes up a good portion of the products or services analysed, making it a good leverage point for change, but there may be practical barriers to releasing the flow potential.

- It usually benefits from capability improvement – for example, reduction in changeover times, 5S (workplace organisation), maintenance management to improve available time, reduction of ramp-up losses, layout and so on.

- Investigate improvements that could help create the 'economies of repetition' enjoyed in the green stream.

- Remove barriers so that you can start treating yellows like greens and place them on a fixed cycle with the greens.

Blue Stream

- This stream adds complexity but often no value, for example, minor raw material or packaging differences.

- Investigate opportunities to rationalize these products or services.

- Reduced complexity = reduced opportunity for something to go wrong = less work = less cost.

- Resist the urge to shy away from reducing complexity due to the amount of work involved in making it happen.

- Remember that although unit cost may increase, overall cost and risk will reduce.

Red Stream

- It is not practical to include these products or services in the fixed cycle. The volumes are small, orders infrequent and the intention is to move them out of the way for high volume, repetitive offerings.

- Understand the value to the customer by asking them. Can you stop selling these products or services altogether?

- Understand the value to the business. What is the real cost of supplying these products or services? What is the benefit? Can they be removed? (see Chapter 4 for pointers on the real cost to remove a product or service).

- If you have to keep on selling these products and services, can you charge a higher price for them to compensate for the added complexity to your operations?

- Separate them from the main stream of work so that they do not hinder the flow of greens and yellows.

- Match the right people to this line of work by dedicating those who enjoy high variety.

A Motivation for Fixed Scheduling

Depending on how work is prioritised in the business, you may be experiencing frequent plan changes or a lack of regularity in the schedule. Throughout the book, it affirms how regularity breeds flow and improved quality and how by tackling this at the planning stage, you give your operations a better chance to perform at their best.

The green streams are prime candidates for fixed schedules because they are highly repetitive and contribute well to volume. By dedicating a line, or at least dedicating a planning slot to this work, you can get the bulk of the work out of the way to give you more time to focus on the 'funnies' or lower-volume work. This encourages 'economies of repetition' and supports the processing of work that generally pays the bills. The management time you spend on the green and yellow streams decrease, freeing time to solve problems often created by the blue and red streams respectively.

You may be wondering how the logic presented in this section is influenced by raging demand fluctuations. The impact of demand variation on fixed schedules will be discussed during the interpretation of the current state.

✔ FOR YOU TO TRY

○ Bring together a team to represent the critical cogs in the supply chain.

○ Agree on how you will evaluate the data, – for example, by sales, volume or gross profit contribution.

○ Decide on the time period to be reviewed.

○ Gather your data.

○ Develop your spreadsheet.

○ Sort the data from highest to lowest.

○ Highlight your top 50 percent contributors and mark in green.

○ Highlight from 50 percent to 95 percent and mark in yellow.

○ Highlight from 95 percent to 99 percent and mark in blue.

○ Highlight last 1 percent and mark in red.

○ Convert data into usable graphs for discussion.

○ Evaluate the results using the guidelines provided for each of the streams.

○ Summarise the opportunities for reducing complexity, improving flow and achieving quicker cash conversion.

DEVELOP THE CURRENT STATE MAP

❓ WHAT IS THIS?

The Value Stream Map is a valuable tool to help visualise the Current State and chart a future vision for improvement, which meets the needs of the customer and business. It focuses on the bigger picture of how to take a product or service from the start through the process into the hands of the customer.

In PURPOSE we are interested in the high-level view. This is in contrast to just looking at a single process and how to improve that in isolation, which is covered in PROCESS.

With the bigger picture represented, it is possible to evaluate the Value Stream in line with where the business needs to go (North Star), and to highlight the opportunities. It is also a system's thinking tool that encourages interrogation of all suggestions based on the impact it will have on the system.

> *'Whenever there is a product for a customer, there is a value stream. The challenge lies in seeing it.'*
>
> *(Rother and Shook 1999: Preface)*

❓ WHY IS THIS HELPFUL?

The mapping tool has several advantages that make it an attractive method for sketching problems and charting the target condition:

- You learn to focus on and fix the whole Value Stream and not just the parts.
- It shows a storyboard of the physical, information, people and money flows, and how they are linked.
- It achieves a clear and high-level, visual evaluation of the Current State and metrics.
- It achieves a clear and high-level, visual representation of the future vision and metrics.
- It is possible to see the waste, disconnects, the impact on the system and in many cases, the source of the problems.
- Prioritisation of what to fix, why, by how much and in what order is clearer.
- The processes are better documented and understood encouraging debate, consensus building and learning using a common language, especially at leadership level.

TIPS

- You need leaders to do it! This is a high-level map that will influence the improvement strategy. Too low a level constructing the map may exclude critical elements of the supply chain, which could result in sub-optimisation. It may also necessitate a significant 'selling' job to get buy-in from leaders who were not there from the start and who are not emotionally connected to the problems exposed.

- Communicate to everyone about the mapping exercise beforehand. This can boost the quality of the results. If employees know that leaders will be walking the process and asking questions, they will be more inclined to offer helpful insight to problems, causes and possible countermeasures.

- Structure the workshop well. Follow an agenda, time the breaks well, achieve attendance, respectfully enforce punctuality and maintain a strict code of conduct that will foster involvement, teamwork and progress.

- Seek the wisdom of the majority rather than the input from just one individual.

- Keep the workshop size to fewer than ten participants but have enough representation around the table to tackle the end-to-end Value Stream.

- Pursue creativity before capital investment. IT systems can be the exception in knowledge-worker environments but generally speaking, it is critical to use innovation around existing resources before bringing in additional ones.

- Think 'customer' before what is good for the individual or department. This will help steer the group away from silo thinking towards system's thinking.

- Put the process into perspective. Remind the group that the road to successful implementation is the outcome and Current State mapping is just the beginning.

- This is not about making the perfect map. Rather, it is about finding a way to make problems, which affect the flow of your product or service, obvious. Keep that in mind when you are tempted to overcomplicate the map or when heading down the dark hole of analysis-paralysis.

❓ HOW TO DO IT

Step 1: Select a Value Stream

Listed below are suggestions on where to start the mapping and how to focus the activity. It is recommended this first be discussed amongst the participants to ensure the right reasons behind the exercise have been agreed to and that consensus has been achieved before proceeding:

- As a starting point, review the North Star and where the improvement must target.

- Refer to the Glenday Sieve Analysis and identify a Value Stream that can have a significant impact on the business if improved.

- Consider any short to medium-term plans in the business that require improvement in the capability of a particular Value Stream – for example, to accommodate new markets or revenue streams. The Glenday Sieve Analysis may also have highlighted product lines requiring capability improvement to unlock a path to flow logic (Glenday, 2007).

- Develop a family matrix to highlight typical groupings in the products or services that logically occur and should be treated together when making Value Stream changes. One family may become a possible candidate for mapping and an improvement to this stream may spread a critical mass of change. The family matrix (table 3.3) entails breaking down the full product or service range into groups that can be managed together or that share a significant part of a Value Stream (Bicheno, 2004):

Example Products or Services	Process Steps					
	1	2	3	4	5	
A	X	X		X	X	Product Family A
B	X	X	X	X	X	Product Family A
C	X	X	X		X	Product Family A
D		X		X		Product Family B
E		X		X		Product Family B
F		X	X	X		Product Family B

Table 3.3

Step 2: Agree on Start-Stop Points

To ensure there is no confusion on what is included and what is not, define where the map will start and stop before proceeding – for example:

o Manufacturing – from raw material to the warehouse

o Supply chain – from marketing to money received

o Service – from the customer trigger until service delivered

o From customer request to product or service developed.

You should also consider the objectives of what must be learned and who is participating in the activity. At the risk of repeating the obvious, to have the right people around the table and to maintain focus on the Value Stream identified, remains critical. The group must not become distracted by areas outside of the scope.

Step 3: Understand Value, Muda, Mura, Muri

A vital step to fixing problems is to admit that a problem exists! To begin, it is helpful to define what 'value' means to the customer and business, and subsequently to evaluate how all activities in the chosen Value Stream are influenced by waste, over-burden and variation. This will start you on a journey of recognising and categorising problems in a structured way. We provide an introduction to muda, mura and muri here which will be expanded on in the interpretation of the Current State.

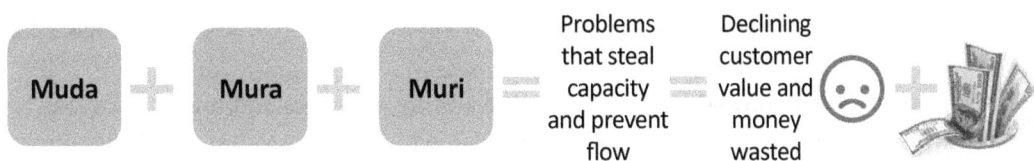

Muda = Waste

A word of caution: some believe a principle of Lean Thinking – a strong element in Operational Excellence – is mostly about finding and eliminating waste. In reality, if we do not understand the context in which this waste is taking place, we may fix many problems but with little influence to the business and zero change to the experience of the customer.

Figure 3.2 points out how the work we do is made up of three key elements as defined by the customer, namely value-adding, non-value adding and waste activities:

Value-Adding
What the customer is willing to pay for

Non-Value Adding
Does not actually create value but is necessary to do the value-adding activity

Muda
Any unnecessary activity or waste of resource

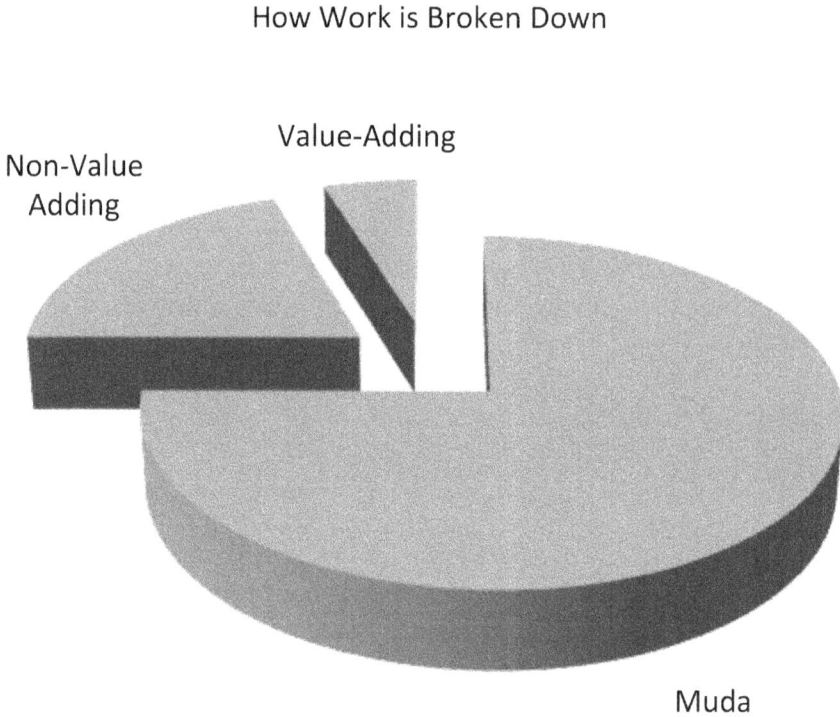

How Work is Broken Down

Value-Adding

Non-Value
Adding

Muda

Figure 3.2

You want to eliminate muda, reduce non-value adding activities and maximise value to design work that consists more of the activities for which the customer is willing to pay. See table 3.4 for examples.

Manufacturing Example of Muda	Service Example of Muda
○ A value-adding activity would be what changes the product into something the customer wants – for example, painting a car in line with the customer specification.	○ A value-adding activity would be the service for which the customer is willing to pay – for example, an insurance claim is correctly paid into the customer's account.
○ Non-value adding would be an activity that does not actually change the product but which is necessary to achieve the value adding work – for example, setting the machine to achieve the paint colour.	○ Non-value adding would be an activity that does not actually result in the service for the customer but is necessary to achieve the value-added activity – for example, the legislative requirements the insurance company must meet in order to service the customer.
○ Muda would, therefore, be everything else – for example more cars are painted than needed, reworking and touching-up required, walking to fetch the paint colours, excessive set-up time of the paint process to change products and transporting the car vast distances between processes.	○ Muda adds costs but no value to the business – for example, a queue (inventory) of claims is waiting to be processed, the claim is delayed awaiting approval from the right level, incorrect information captured for the claim requires rework, many handoffs between departments to process the claim, which results in excessive lead time.

Table 3.4

'All we are doing is looking at the timeline from the moment the customer gives us an order to the point when we collect the cash. And we are reducing that timeline by removing the non-value adding wastes.'

(Ohno 1988 :pg ix)

Taiichi Ohno provided us with a guideline on the common wastes found in processes and over time, these have been modified with new thoughts, however, the basic principles remain. The point to remember is that seeing waste is not enough. You want to see it, understand the source of it and then eliminate the waste and its root cause permanently.

Table 3.5 lists typical examples of muda to be aware of when on a gemba walk and constructing the Value Stream Map.

MUDA REFERENCE GUIDE*

Muda Category	Overview	Manufacturing Example	Service Example
Overproduction	Producing too soon, too much or just in case. This waste is the evil of all evils and in its worst form, results in all the other wastes. It hides problems and employees are not forced to think.	The customer orders 400 units, you make 800 to save on changeover time and just in case he takes them later.	Printing a duplication of statements just in case the first one was not received. The real problem is not addressed and wastes are left to fester.
Waiting	Idle time of an operator or machine. Idle time is considered less of an evil than overproducing to keep people or machines busy.	Waiting for material, work, maintenance, instructions, or standing idle watching a machine while it is cycling.	Waiting for information, IT support, approvals or the bottleneck process to finish with its work.
Transportation	Moving work from place to place between processes or departments. Excessive handling of material or information.	The layout of processes resulting in excessive movement of material.	Transferring between departments to move information or to communicate.
Over processing	Taking unneeded steps to process a product or service. Providing higher quality than is required and paid for by the customer.	Poor tool design causing unnecessary defects. Hi-tech machines providing a higher specification than the customer requires.	Unnecessary reporting. More quality checks than required to achieve good quality. Unnecessary complexity in the process to bring the service to the customer.
Excess Inventory	Excessive stock or queue sizes.	Too much raw material, work-in-progress, finished goods or consumables.	Large queues of work, e-mails or phone calls. Excessive printing or stationery inventory.
Unnecessary Movement	Any motion the employee has to perform instead of adding value – including walking, stretching, turning and bending.	Walking to fetch a drawing. Walking to find the correct tools for the job.	Walking between two departments to collect information. Walking to get an approval.
Defects	Rework or scrap. Not right the first time.	Touching up paintwork. Discarding non-conforming product.	Correcting invoicing errors and order entry information.
Unused Employee Creativity	Losing learning opportunities by not engaging with or listening to employees.	Not allowing those directly involved in the work to help solve the problems.	Not allowing those directly involved in the work to help solve the problems.
Environmental Waste	The Seven Green Wastes: energy, water, materials, transport, garbage, emissions, biodiversity (see PLANET).	Leaving machines running overnight when not in use. Poor lagging on steam pipes. In-efficient routing.	Leaving lights, computers and heaters on when not in use. Water leaks.

*Modified from Taiichi Ohno's 7 Wastes   Table 3.5

Mura = Uneveness, fluctuation, variation

Mura results in inconsistency in the operations, which makes it difficult to plan, keep costs under control and provide a reliable service to the customer. Ultimately, mura will cause muda. Examples of mura include:

o Quality variation

o Poor availability of equipment or systems

o Last-minute production plan changes

o Variation in forecast accuracy and demand patterns

o Poor achievement of the production plan versus actual performance

o Variation between employees and how they perform the work.

Some variation may already have been identified when conducting the Glenday Sieve Analysis and it is recommended that this be raised in the Current State evaluation, together with additional findings. To remain focused, consider the North Star and identify all mura that can negatively influence this. More about mura is covered throughout the book, but for now, look out for it and indicate all findings on the Current State Map for interpretation.

Muri = Overburden

Muri occurs when people, systems or equipment are over-loaded with regard to available capacity. Evidence of this can be found where:

o Machines are planned to run at maximum capacity, stealing critical preventive maintenance time and putting additional strain on the equipment.

o People are continuously scheduled to work overtime resulting in their ability to perform being affected. Morale drops, absenteeism increases and additional strain on the system results.

o Excessive amounts of work are released into the system – more than the employees or equipment can handle. The result is confusion, an inability to prioritise and ultimately the creation of a crisis situation where employees lose focus on value.

More about muri is covered throughout the book, but for now, look out for it and indicate all findings on the Current State Map for interpretation.

Step 4: Walk the Process (Go to Gemba)

Now that everyone is clear about where the focus will be, you walk the whole Value Stream. Some people prefer to start with the customer and experience the Value Stream upstream. Others select the starting point and work their way through to the end point.

The purpose of the exercise is to ensure everyone understands the Value Stream in the same way and to get out there and see what the real problems are and talk to the people along the way. This will help create a Value Stream Map that is not based on opinions but rather on real evidence and actual observation. There is no substitute for this and this step must not be skipped, even if the team is uncertain about the value:

- Provide everyone with a stack of Post-its.

- Request that each participant draw a rough sketch of the steps in the Value Stream.

- Explain that along the way they are to write down all the muda, muri and mura they observe or learn from the selected Value Stream. Set a minimum expectation – for example, no fewer than 20 Post-its per person.

- Remind them to stay focused on the Value Stream selected.

- For each step in the process, ask them to look around and talk to the responsible person about typical problems experienced.

- Remind the group to be polite and respect the people throughout the exercise.

Step 5: Draw the Current State Value Stream Map

As with most things, there is a comfortable balance to mapping. Do not overcomplicate and concentrate purely on achieving a perfect map. At the same time, do not oversimplify so that you cannot make any decisions. You want to target just the right amount of detail to expose the problems.

A common argument during mapping is, 'This is not how things normally are!' Experience shows that it is best to map as you see it and not fall into the trap of documenting how you think it usually looks. It must be a realistic picture and again, the purpose is to visualise problems and opportunities to satisfy the customer and achieve the North Star.

It is recommended that standardised icons (figure 3.3) be used to construct the map to simplify interpretation and create a common approach. Feel free to customise your own icons and standardise for your company, but those provided will help get you started.

TIPS

○ Always walk the floor first and again when you need to verify.

○ Do not rely on standard times unless there is reliable online data. Rather check for yourself.

○ Resist the urge to start talking about solutions. First understand the Current State.

○ Try not break the Value Stream up. You should see it from end to end to learn and apply system's thinking. If it becomes overcomplicated with far too much detail, consider subdividing it with caution or grouping the activities better.

○ Keep it simple, use a pencil, eraser and an A3 sheet of paper.

○ Map as you see it on the day, without any adjustment.

○ Only gather data that will help better understand and make decisions.

○ Again, never stop at the Current State! You must turn this into a Future State Vision and Action Plan.

VALUE STREAM MAPPING ICONS*

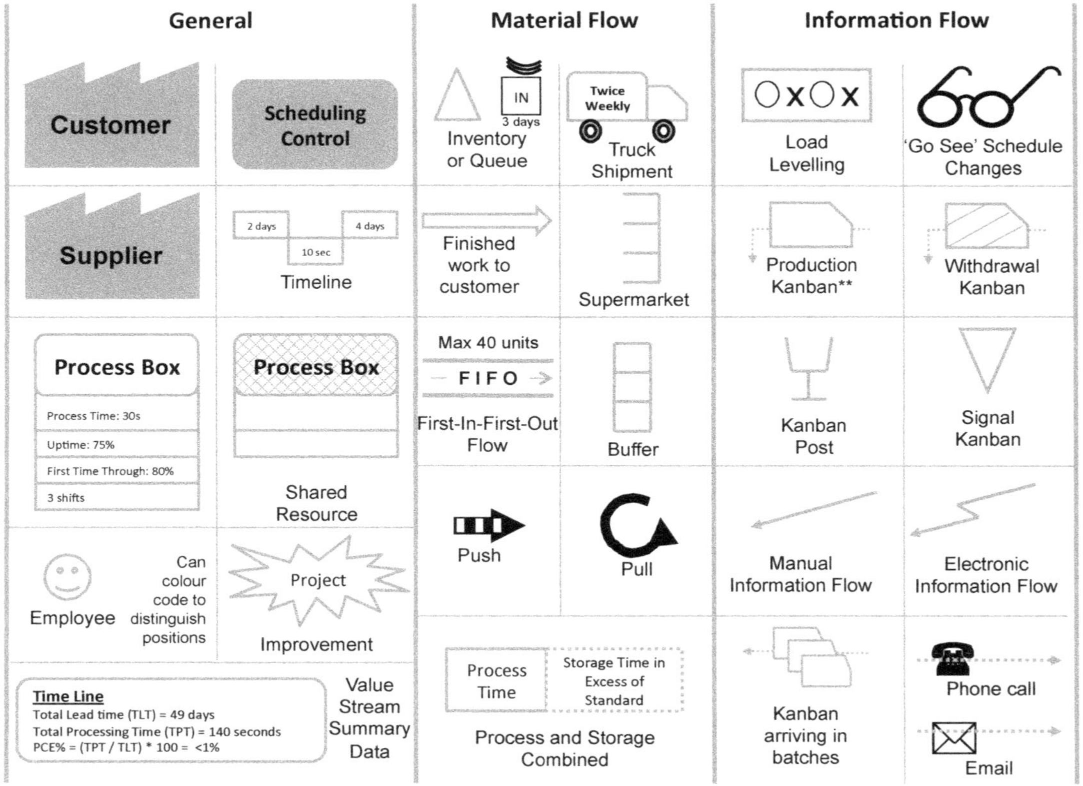

General

| Scheduling Control |
| Customer |
| Supplier |

Timeline — 2 days, 10 sec, 4 days

Process Box

Process Box
Process Time: 30s
Uptime: 75%
First Time Through: 80%
3 shifts

Shared Resource

Project

Employee — Can colour code to distinguish positions

Improvement

Value Stream Summary Data

Time Line
Total Lead time (TLT) = 49 days
Total Processing Time (TPT) = 140 seconds
PCE% = (TPT / TLT) * 100 = <1%

Material Flow

Inventory or Queue — IN 3 days

Finished work to customer

Max 40 units — FIFO — First-In-First-Out Flow

Push

Twice Weekly — Truck Shipment

Supermarket

Buffer

Pull

Process Time — Storage Time in Excess of Standard — Process and Storage Combined

Information Flow

'Go See' Schedule Changes

Load Levelling

Withdrawal Kanban

Production Kanban**

Signal Kanban

Kanban Post

Electronic Information Flow

Manual Information Flow

Phone call

Kanban arriving in batches

Email

*The Value Stream Mapping process and list of icons have been adapted to suit this book (Rother and Shook, 1999)
**Kanban is a Japanese word and translated means signboard, signal or card. It refers to a system utilising standard containers, each of which has a card designating what and when to produce (Japan Management Association, 1985)

Figure 3.3

Draw the Customer

Refer to the Voice of the Customer to have the customer in mind when building the map.

Add the customer and requirements.

In some cases the customer and supplier may be the same entity (figure 3.4).

Example

Customer

Demand: 800 per day

Figure 3.4

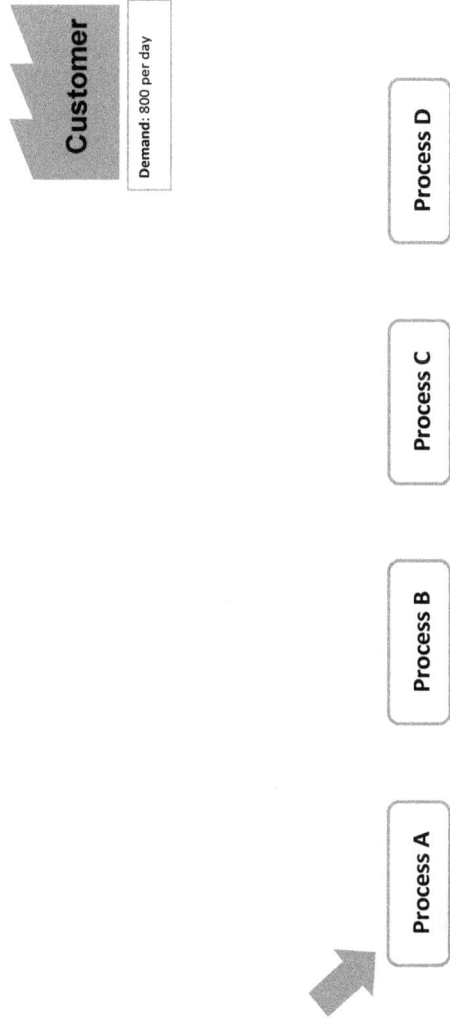

Draw the High-Level Process Steps

Show one area of material flow rather than all the individual processing steps or activities (detailed maps are covered in PROCESS).

The process box stops where material flow stops and batches are transferred. Each block could be identified by a significant break in the timeline illustrated by a build-up in WIP or a handoff.

If sub-processes join the mainstream, select the key components to include and draw in parallel (figure 3.5).

Example

Customer

Demand: 800 per day

Process A   Process B   Process C   Process D

Figure 3.5

Add Data to the Process Boxes

Data illustrates how well the Value Stream performs to customer needs. Consider the North Star when selecting metrics.

The intention is to capture a high-level view so some indicators listed below may better serve a process-level map:

- ○ Processing or cycle times to do the work
- ○ Changeover time
- ○ First Pass Yield (FPY) – what made it through the process the first time
- ○ Complete and Accurate % (C&A%) – incoming work that is 'usable as is' and does not require corrections, additions or clarification
- ○ Uptime or availability
- ○ Batch size
- ○ Number of shifts
- ○ Number of people
- ○ Shared resources (figure 3.6)

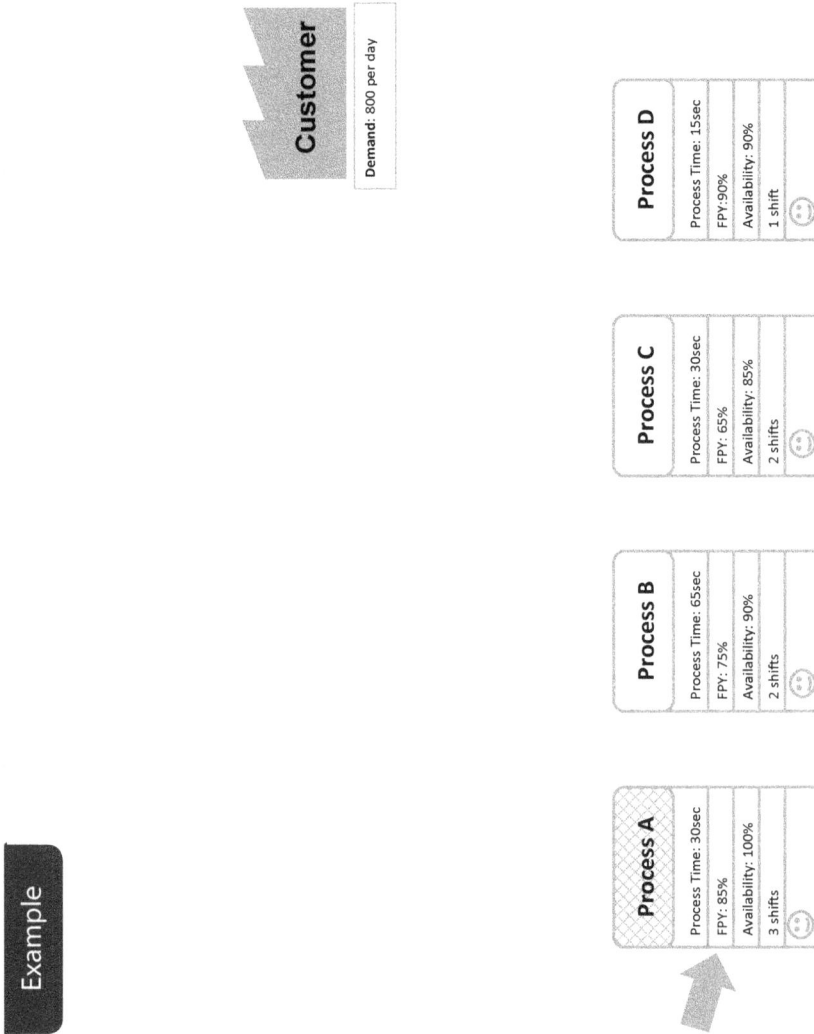

Example

Customer

Demand: 800 per day

Process A

Process Time: 30sec
FPY: 85%
Availability: 100%
3 shifts

Process B

Process Time: 65sec
FPY: 75%
Availability: 90%
2 shifts

Process C

Process Time: 30sec
FPY: 65%
Availability: 85%
2 shifts

Process D

Process Time: 15sec
FPY: 90%
Availability: 90%
1 shift

Figure 3.6

TIPS

o Conduct a simple time study (table 3.6) to understand the actual cycle or processing times (Rother and Harris, 2001). This is a high-level view, so you are not interested in the individual work element or activities (this is discussed in PROCESS).

SIMPLE STUDY TIME		
Process	Observed Times	Lowest Repeatable Time
A		
B		
C		
D		

Table 3.6

o If quality is highlighted in the North Star, FPY and Roll Through Yield (RTY) are powerful measures to show how much work made it through the process the first-time-right. C&A% may be used if the terminology is more suitable.

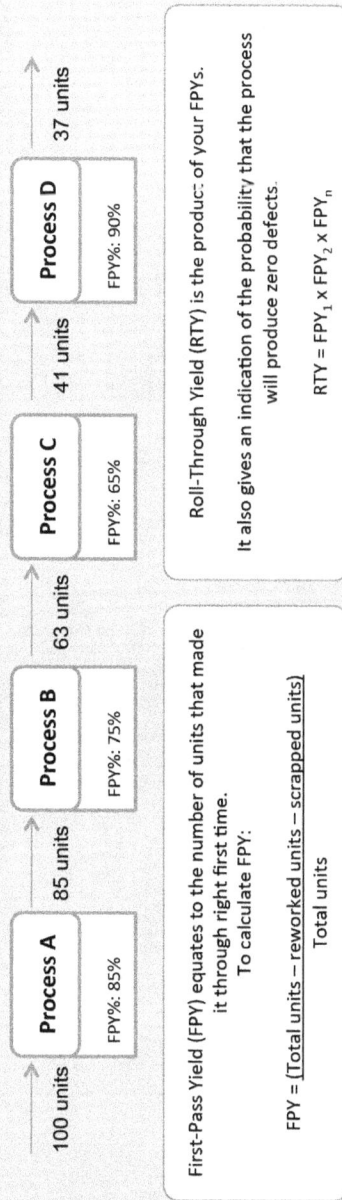

100 units → **Process A** FPY%: 85% → 85 units → **Process B** FPY%: 75% → 63 units → **Process C** FPY%: 65% → 41 units → **Process D** FPY%: 90% → 37 units

First-Pass Yield (FPY) equates to the number of units that made it through right first time.
To calculate FPY:

$$FPY = \frac{(Total\ units - reworked\ units - scrapped\ units)}{Total\ units}$$

Roll-Through Yield (RTY) is the product of your FPYs.

It also gives an indication of the probability that the process will produce zero defects.

$$RTY = FPY_1 \times FPY_2 \times FPY_n$$

Figure 3.7

Although 100 units were put into the system, only 37 made it out right the first time – imagine the cost and time implications (figure 3.7).

Add Inventory or Queues

Show the queues or work-in-progress (WIP) where flow stops and work waits. This could be product, people or information depending on what you are processing. Choose the symbol that makes sense for you:

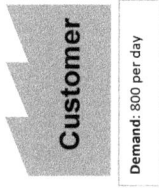

IN

3 days
Inventory
or Queue

If queues accumulate in more than one location for the same Value Stream, draw a symbol for each one.

In manufacturing, if the raw material for this Value Stream is used in many products, take the stock for that Value Stream only and divide it by the demand for the same Value Stream. If this is not feasible, brainstorm how you can best represent the queue time at the raw material triangle.

You may need to pull some data from the system but be sure to visit the Value Stream to see for yourself (figure 3.8).

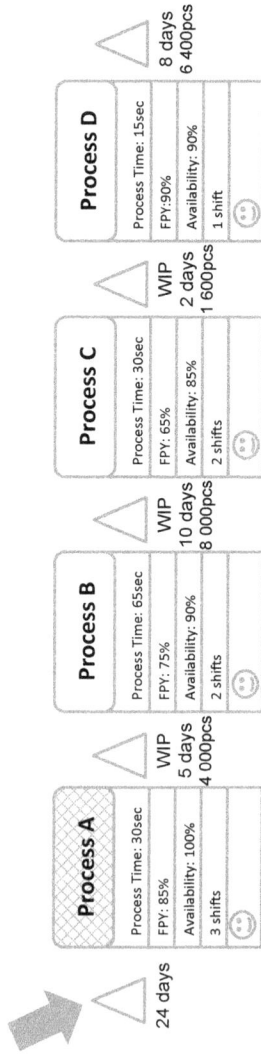

Customer

Demand: 800 per day

To calculate the number of days for each triangle:

$$\triangle = \frac{\text{Total in Queue}}{\text{Daily Demand}} = \frac{4\ 000\ \text{pieces}}{800\ \text{per day}} = 5\ \text{days}$$

WIP
5 days
4 000pcs

Process A

Process Time: 30sec
FPY: 85%
Availability: 100%
3 shifts

24 days

WIP
5 days
4 000pcs

Process B

Process Time: 65sec
FPY: 75%
Availability: 90%
2 shifts

WIP
10 days
8 000pcs

Process C

Process Time: 30sec
FPY: 65%
Availability: 85%
2 shifts

WIP
2 days
1 600pcs

Process D

Process Time: 15sec
FPY:90%
Availability: 90%
1 shift

8 days
6 400pcs

Figure 3.8

Add Customer Delivery Information

Show how often delivery or supply to the external customer takes place and how.

Take note of any special customer requirements that are relevant to understanding the Current State. Information from the Voice of the Customer exercise (Chapter 1) may be helpful.

This contributes to the big picture of flow and how well a product or service moves through the Value Stream and into the hands of the customer – only when the customer receives what they want and when they want it, is the delivery of value complete (figure 3.9).

Example

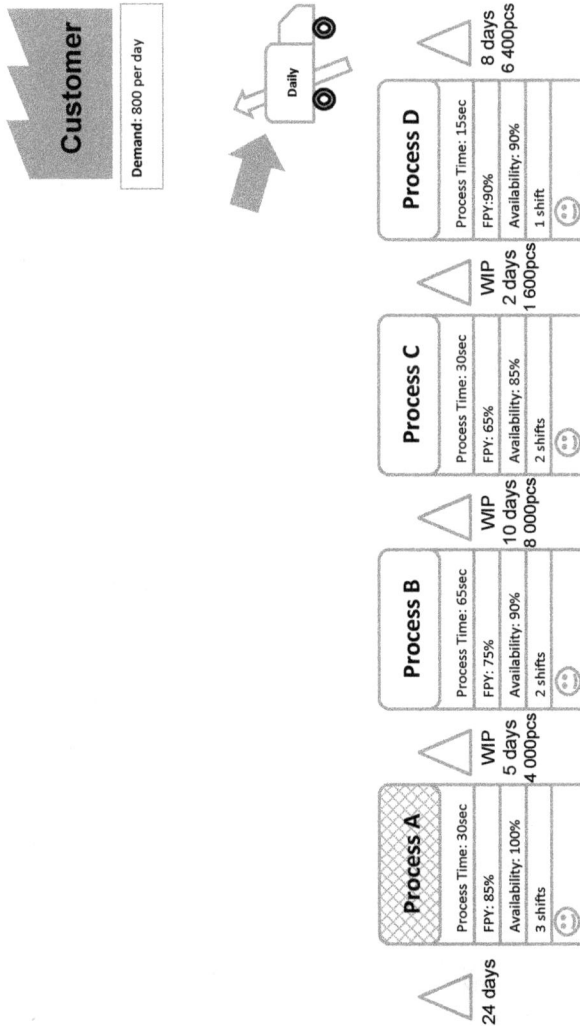

Customer

Demand: 800 per day

Daily

Process A
Process Time: 30sec
FPY: 85%
Availability: 100%
3 shifts

24 days

WIP
5 days
4 000pcs

Process B
Process Time: 65sec
FPY: 75%
Availability: 90%
2 shifts

WIP
10 days
8 000pcs

Process C
Process Time: 30sec
FPY: 65%
Availability: 85%
2 shifts

WIP
2 days
1 600pcs

Process D
Process Time: 15sec
FPY:90%
Availability: 90%
1 shift

8 days
6 400pcs

Figure 3.9

Add Supplier Delivery Information

A Value Stream is only as strong as its weakest link so the map includes relevant information to understand how well material or inputs flows from the supply-side.

Consider including:

o Frequency of supply

o The method of supply

o Critical raw materials or inputs

o Pack size or batch size

o Other relevant details that affect the flow in.

If there are many materials or inputs supplied, choose only the critical ones to include in the map that will have the greatest impact (figure 3.10).

Example

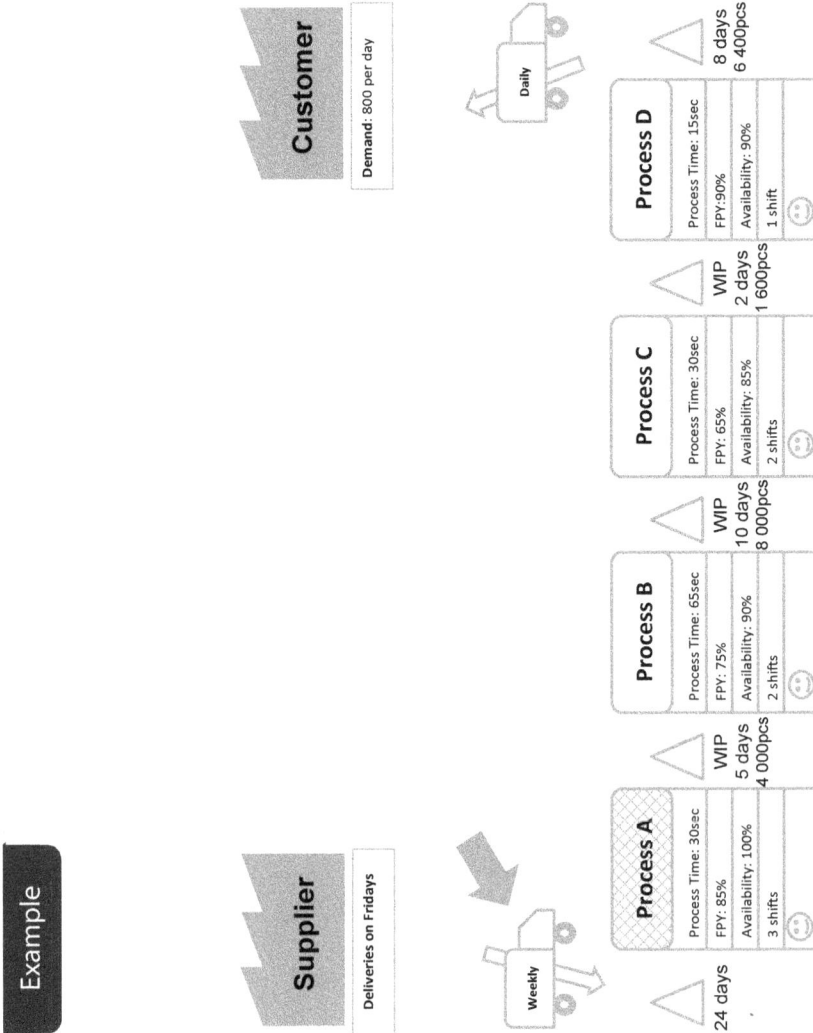

Figure 3.10

Add Information/Communication Flow

This is where the map can become quite busy. Think carefully about what to include. Too much and you lose yourself in detail. Too little, and the muda, mura and muri created by how the information flow is executed, may be overlooked.

Consider the following:

- Quality of information coming from the customers
- Quality of information going from you to the suppliers or contractors
- Quality of information sent to the front-line operations
- Manual adjustments to how work is prioritised using the 'go see' glasses
- Different systems that house this information.

If flow is disrupted in the Value Stream, what part did the information flow play in this (figure 3.11)?

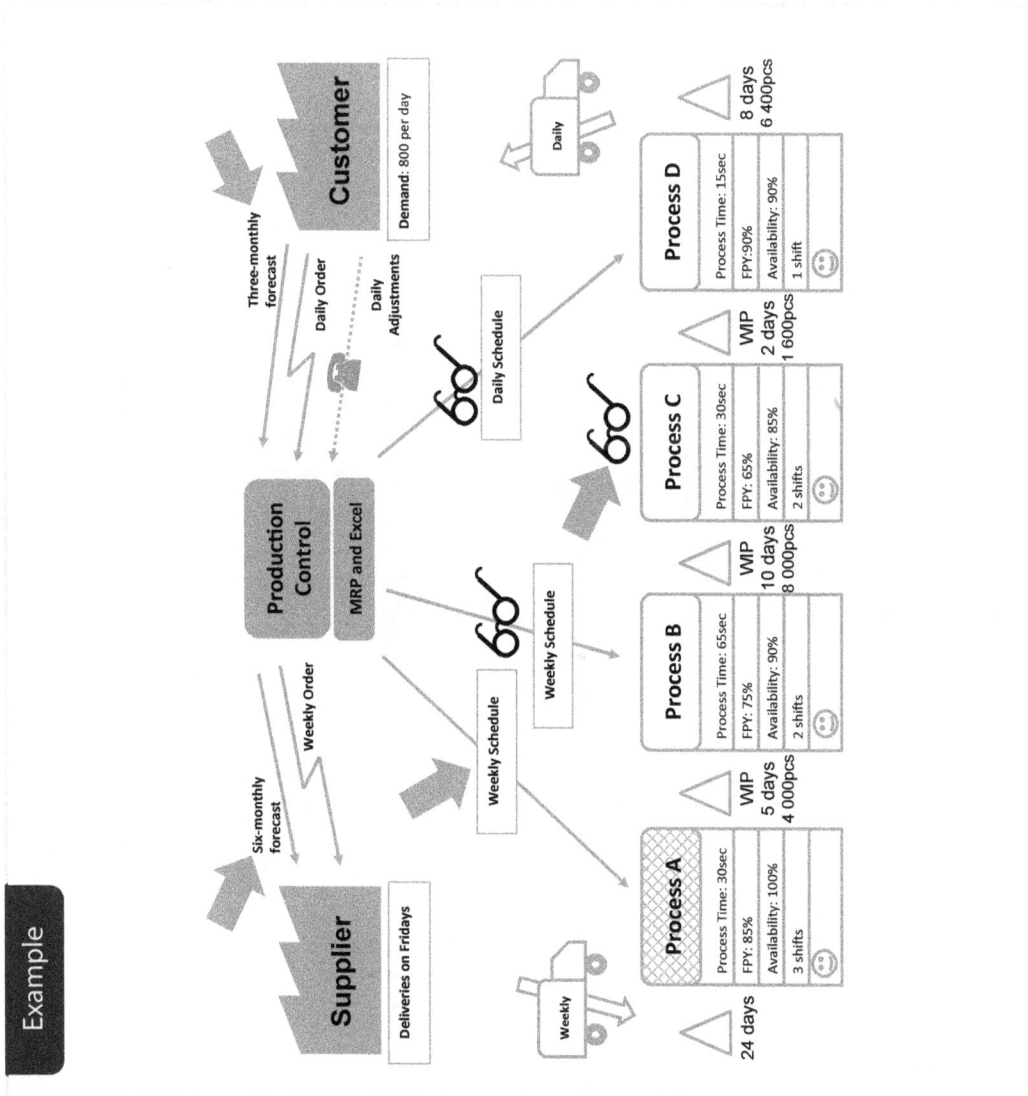

Example

Figure 3.11

TIPS

o Do not not fall into the trap of 'so much information, you can't see anything!'

o Always walk the flow of the process, speak to the people involved and find out how information is received and used. Often it helps to see where the main points of material or service transfer are, and speak to the person receiving the information there.

o Consider how performance measures are influencing the flow of information. How an area is managed can cause adjustments and this should be looked into – 'Show me how you measure me, and I'll show you how I behave.'

o If you have a 'push' system (see explanation on the following page), consider how this affects the daily work, and how the system copes with changes in customer demand.

o Ask about the customer information:
- Does the customer supply a forecast. How often?
- How often does the customer place orders in the system – weekly or monthly? Does the customer have daily call-offs?
- Are 'manual' adjustments to requirements made by phone or email, that cause disruption to flow? How often? What is the impact?

o Ask about the planning and scheduling of workload:
- How is work prioritised?
- Where are computerised systems used?
- Be careful not to get too wrapped up in this detail, just indicate where and what – for example, material requirements planning systems and stand-alone spreadsheets.

o Ask about the supplier information or information going to outside sources:
- Is a forecast provided to the supplier?
- How often does the supplier receive the order or information?
- What 'manual' adjustments are made by phone or email? Speak to the person at the supplier who receives the information. How often does this happen? What is the impact?

Add Physical Flow Triggers

Pull is when demand is triggered by the customer process and there is a defined limit on the amount of work-in-progress allowed in the system. You would use this symbol :

Push is usually triggered by a schedule or as work comes in. In theory, in a push system, work can move into the system beyond the capacity of the system. If you observe evidence of 'pushing' work to the next process, before it is ready for it, you use this symbol:

Push

For transference through pipe work, for e.g. from one tank to another, use this symbol:

Process A → **Process B**

On the map, indicate if this is a pull or push system and what triggers the work to move (figure 3.12).

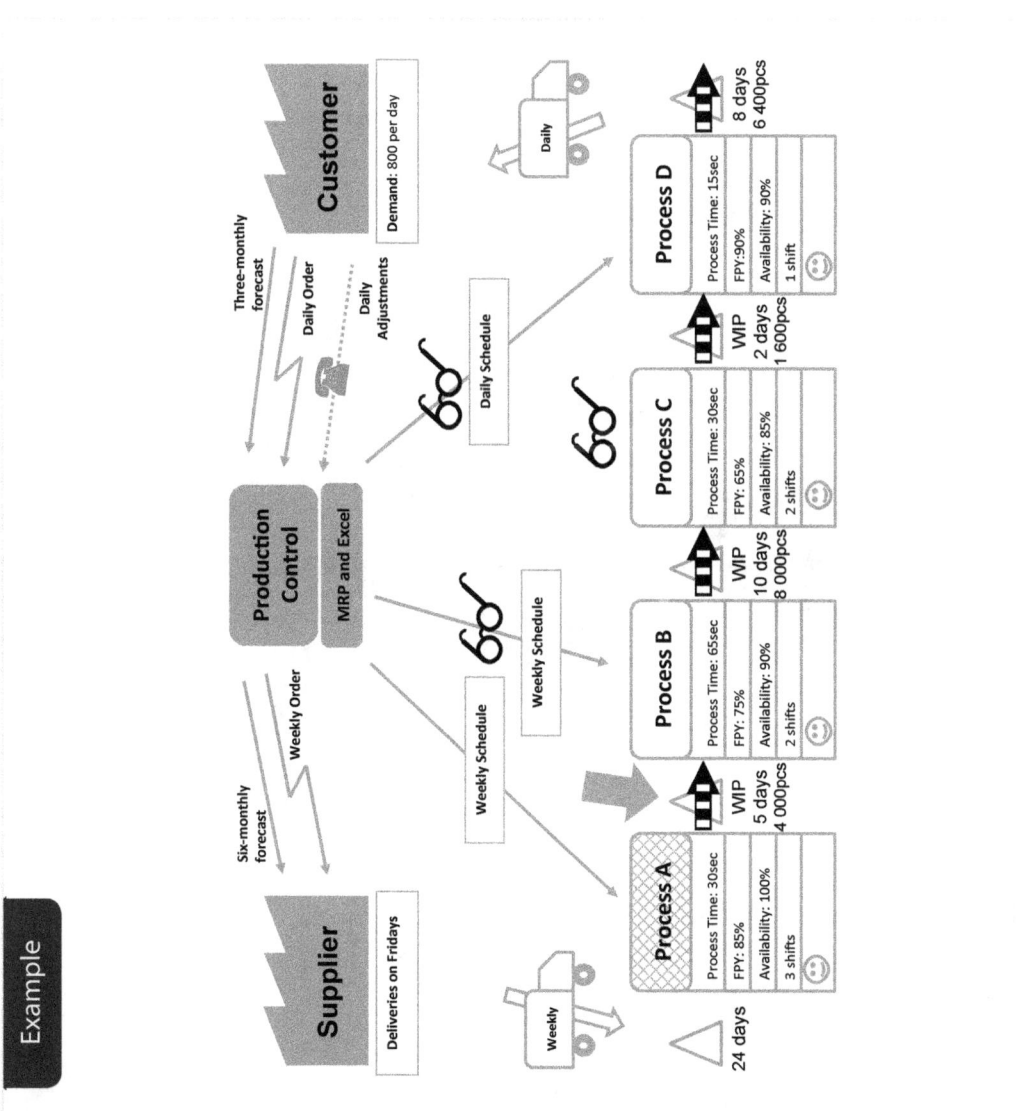

Example

Figure 3.12

Add your Timeline

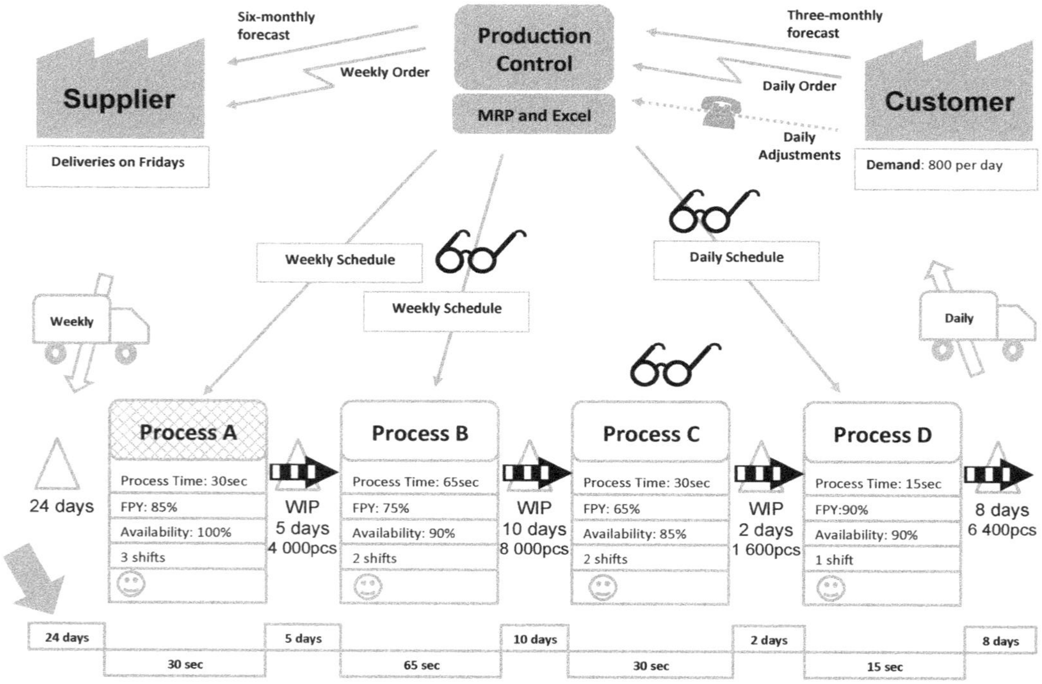

Summarise the Current State through a metric that can be used to understand current performance and track the improvement.

It shows the time taken from when the work arrives in the system until it lands in the hands of the customer, and is made up of queue and processing times.

Depending on where your focus lies, you can vary this but refer to the exercise you did to understand the 'start' and 'stop' points in your Value Stream Map.

If dealing with batch processing whereby several units are processed at the same time, do not divide the cycle time by the number of parts in the batch. If you were to mark the work to see how long it takes to move through, it would be for the full batch time (figure 3.13).

Example

Figure 3.13

Summarise Timeline and Money Line

○ Add up the top timeline (all the triangle times)

○ Add up the bottom timeline (all the processing times)

○ Calculate Process Cycle Efficiency (PCE%)

$$PCE\% = \frac{Total\ Process\ Time}{Total\ Lead\ Time} \times 100$$

○ Evaluate what percentage is actually spent on processing activities.

Next, calculate the money line to show how long money is tied up for:

○ Add up the top timeline (all the triangle times)

○ Find out the debtor and creditor days

○ Calculate the financing time (FT).

$$FT = Inventory\ Days + Debtor\ Days - Creditor\ Days$$

(figure 3.14)

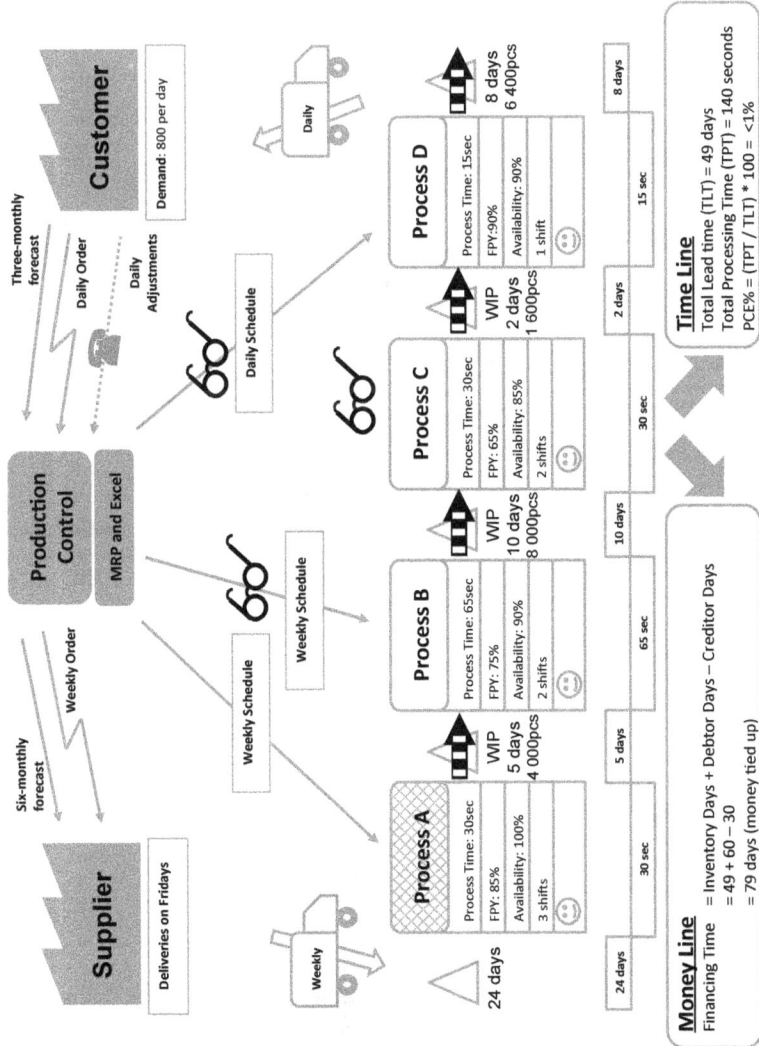

Example

Supplier
Deliveries on Fridays

Production Control
MRP and Excel

Customer
Demand: 800 per day

Six-monthly forecast
Weekly Order
Three-monthly forecast
Daily Order
Daily Adjustments
Weekly
Daily
Weekly Schedule
Daily Schedule

Process A
Process Time: 30sec
FPY: 85%
Availability: 100%
3 shifts

WIP
5 days
4 000pcs

Process B
Process Time: 65sec
FPY: 75%
Availability: 90%
2 shifts

WIP
10 days
8 000pcs

Process C
Process Time: 30sec
FPY: 65%
Availability: 85%
2 shifts

WIP
2 days
1 600pcs

Process D
Process Time: 15sec
FPY: 90%
Availability: 90%
1 shift

8 days
6 400pcs

24 days

24 days | 30 sec | 5 days | 65 sec | 10 days | 30 sec | 2 days | 15 sec | 8 days

Money Line
Financing Time = Inventory Days + Debtor Days – Creditor Days
= 49 + 60 – 30
= 79 days (money tied up)

Time Line
Total Lead time (TLT) = 49 days
Total Processing Time (TPT) = 140 seconds
PCE% = (TPT / TLT) * 100 = <1%

Figure 3.14

Additional Visuals

Figure 3.15 illustrates the lead time critical path (Bicheno, 2004). This is a good, system's tool to establish which elements have the greatest affect on lead time and money tied up, prompting improvement focus.

Start at the order trigger until the service is complete and the money is received.

Consider subdividing each contributor up into value-adding versus non-value adding elements to visualise the extent of the opportunities.

Figure 3.16 illustrates a lead time bar graph and the major contributors.

Figure 3.17 illustrates a variation graph and the variation in lead time around the average.

These visuals may help in summarising the current state picture to enable further debate and ideas.

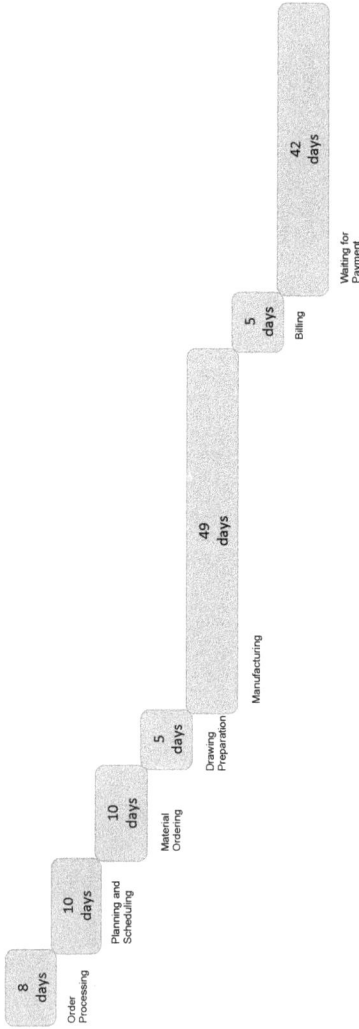

Figure 3.15

Figure 3.16

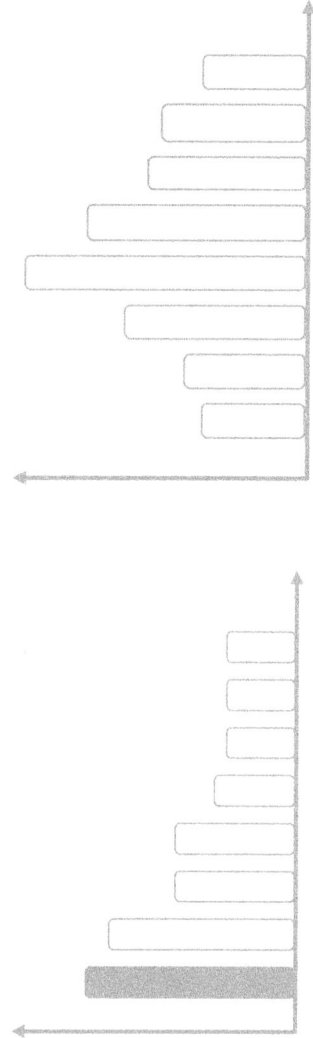

Figure 3.17

FOR YOU TO TRY

- Prepare a room for the activity with sufficient wall space.

- Select the right mix of participants for the mapping team, with sufficient decision-making power and influence on the supply chain.

- Agree on how the Value Stream will be selected:

  - Green stream

  - Product or service family

  - Target Value Stream for capability improvement

  - Other.

- Agree on where the map will start and stop and ensure the team understands the scope.

- Create an understanding of what value is in the eyes of the customer, and how to recognise muda, mura and muri on the gemba walk.

- Prepare the team with materials and instructions for the gemba walk.

- Conduct the gemba walk and return with rough sketches of the process flow together with completed Post-it Notes of initial findings.

- Draw the Current State Value Stream Map ensuring the team completes all the steps in the guideline.

- Summarise the Current State performance through effective summary visuals.

INTERPRET THE CURRENT STATE MAP
EVALUATE TAKT TIME

❓ WHAT IS THIS?

TAKT time is a pacing mechanism to align operations with customer demand. If your customer is buying one product every 60 seconds, then your processes must make one product within 60 seconds. Therefore the TAKT time is 60 seconds.

TAKT time is not the same as cycle time. Cycle time is measured by observation and a stop watch whereas TAKT time is calculated using a formula.

There are many theories published on where TAKT time originated, and some indicate that TAKT is derived from the German word taktzeit, which loosely translates to 'rhythmic time' or 'keeping a beat', similar to the ticking of a metronome or the movement of a conductor's baton.

The 'drumbeat' is dictated by the customer's requirements. When TAKT time is calculated, it becomes apparent as to how often the customer requires production or servicing, and this provides the target for pacing operations to meet this. Be aware, it may prove difficult to drive TAKT awareness if there is instability in the process or team preventing the very consistency needed to support cadence. Consider this success factor when designing TAKT awareness in the Future State.

As such you will find a close connection between understanding TAKT time and the next section, which covers the interpretation of flow opportunities.

❓ WHY IS THIS HELPFUL?

TAKT time is a great place to start when interpreting the Current State. You will better understand the customer demand, and what it means with respect to the available time operations have at their disposal. Then you will be in a position to evaluate how well operations are geared up to cope with this demand. Calculating TAKT time can also lead to the following benefits:

- Creates TAKT awareness and helps measure performance to requirement.
- Encourages standardised work in operations.
- Aligns the pace of operations to the customer buying-rate.

○ Pacing to demand = less overproduction and waiting = less waste = more value.

○ Assists when balancing the workload amongst resources.

○ Highlights the constraint and exposes opportunities for improvement.

○ Optimising the number of people required becomes possible.

○ It provides a baseline to do 'what-if' scenario planning when demand fluctuates.

❓ HOW TO DO IT

Step 1: Calculate the TAKT Time

There are two sets of data needed to start:

Available Working Time

This is the total time available in a day, minus the planned downtime. Examples of downtime include lunch breaks, tea breaks, daily meeting times and housekeeping times. Be very careful of subtracting preventive maintenance times from the total time available. If there is a set, non-negotiable, planned time for preventive maintenance, then subtract this. If operations experience unplanned or reactive maintenance, then do not subtract this, as it is only building waste into the calculation.

Customer Demand

This is the daily customer demand. Agree amongst the mapping team what makes the most sense here. Typically companies use the average demand per day. If the company experiences fluctuations in demand over the year – for example, seasonality – then two TAKT time calculations may be required to cater for two very different demand patterns. Be careful not to fall into the trap of trying to calculate a TAKT time for every occasion, as it is also intended to bring stability to your processes.

Once you have gathered the necessary data, the following formula is used to calculate the TAKT time:

$$\text{TAKT Time} = \frac{\text{Available Working Time}}{\text{Demand}}$$

- The operation runs 9.5 hours per day
- There is one lunch break of 30 minutes, and two tea breaks of 15 minutes each
- There are daily meetings for 20 minutes and a planned shutdown for 20 minutes
- The customer's average demand is 800 products per day

$$\text{TAKT Time} = \frac{\text{Available Working Time}}{\text{Demand}}$$

$$= \frac{(9.5\text{hrs} \times 60\text{min}) - (30\text{min} + 30\text{min} + 20\text{min} + 20\text{min})}{800}$$

$$= 0.59 \text{ minutes}$$

(multiply by 60 to convert from minutes to seconds)

$$= 35 \text{ seconds}$$

This means the customer is buying one product every 35 seconds, and therefore requires one product every 35 seconds, so the operations must be capable of producing one product at least every 35 seconds.

Update your Current State Map with the result of the TAKT time calculation (figure 3.18):

Customer

Demand: 800 per day
Takt time: 35 seconds

Figure 3.18

Step 2: Compare the Current Performance to TAKT Time

You performed a simple study (table 3.6) to establish times for each process. Represent this information in a graph and show how each process performs to TAKT Time (figure 3.19). Identify areas for reduction to meet requirement and include your findings on the Current State Map.

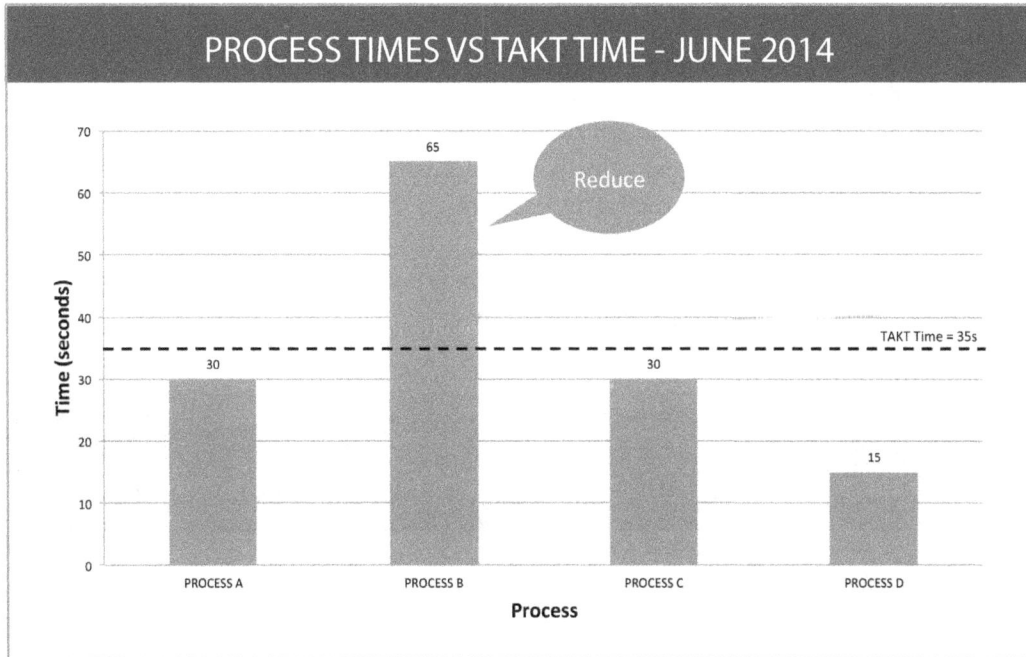

PROCESS TIMES VS TAKT TIME - JUNE 2014

Figure 3.19

It is sufficient to make high-level decisions from this. It will however be necessary to improve the quality of data at a later stage especially when more detailed action plans are required.

Exposing muda, mura and muri in the Value Stream Map already tells a tale of where capacity is lost and some of the reasons behind not meeting customer requirement. It may however not be clear as to what the process is capable of doing or how much capacity is in fact being lost. This is where capacity studies (covered in PROCESS) and the measurement of Overall Effectiveness can be invaluable to understanding this difference.

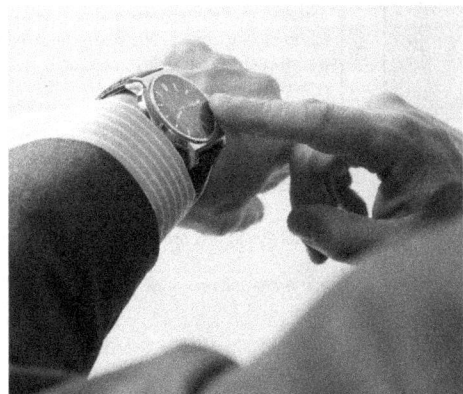

An Introduction to Overall Effectiveness

Measuring OE may seem excessive but the upfront investment in data will create a much smoother path to solving the issues uncovered. The formula used is:

$$OE\% = (Availability\ Rate\ x\ Performance\ Rate\ x\ Quality\ Rate)\ x\ 100$$

You may already be measuring quality performance or lost time but often these metrics are looked at in isolation by different departments. OE is a complex metric influenced by several variables, and the real value is to demonstrate the net effect of all the losses influencing the ability of the process to perform.

Table 3.7 illustrates how the variables within the OE metric take the available capacity and erode it to the actual performance of the system.

		OVERALL EFFECTIVENESS The True Impact of Loss in Manufacturing and Service	Example
AVAILABILITY	A	Available working time less planned downtime e.g. 470 minutes	
	B	Available working time less unplanned downtime e.g. 470 – 110 = 360 minutes	Lost 110 minutes due to: • Breakdowns and failure • Waiting time • Set-ups and adjustments
PERFORMANCE	C	Output as the process is designed to achieve e.g. the process is designed to do one unit every 10 minutes 360 minutes x 10 minutes per unit = 3 600 units per day	
	D	Actual output the process makes (good quality, rework and scrap combined) e.g. the actual output is tracked daily and shows 2 900 units per day	Lost 700 units due to: • Reduced speed • Minor stops • Interruptions
QUALITY	E	Actual output the process makes e.g. 2 900 units per day	
	F	Actual good units produced e.g. 2 400 units per day	Lost 500 units due to: • Scrap • Additions • Rework • Clarifications • Backtracking • Corrections

Table 3.7

Element 'A' represents the available time and potential for optimum performance. Element 'F' represents the net effect of all the losses and the actual performance achieved. The results of OE would therefore be calculated by:

OE% = (Availability Rate x Performance Rate x Quality Rate) x 100

Availability Rate	= B/A = 360 / 470 =	0.766
Performance Rate	= D/C = 2 900 / 3 600 =	0.806
Quality Rate	= F/E = 2 400 / 2 900 =	0.828

OE% = (0.766 x 0.806 x 0.828) x 100

= 51.2%

OE can also be used to compare performance to TAKT time but detailed capacity studies would be needed to verify the cycle times (covered in PROCESS). If you have this data available, use table 3.8 (or your own version of it) to establish what can be accomplished on a normal day, the OE rating and the resulting cyle time with losses built in:

CURRENT STATE OVERALL EFFECTIVENESS (OE) JUNE 2013 TO JUNE 2014								
Process	Observed Times (Seconds)	Effective Cycle Time (Seconds)	Quality (Q)	Availability (AV)	Performance (Pf)	OE (QxAVxPf)	TAKT Time	Actual Cycle Time (Seconds)
Process A	30	32	0.85	1	0.95	0.81	35	38
Process B	65	64	0.75	0.9	1	0.68	35	85
Process C	30	34	0.65	0.85	0.75	0.41	35	54
Process D	15	18	0.9	0.9	0.95	0.77	35	22

Informal time study (table 3.6)

Based on formal capacity studies

Performance after OE losses that can be compared to TAKT time

Table 3.8

If the operational environment is too complex to warrant measuring OE throughout the process, it can be focused to the constraint or process consistently holding up the rest of the operation. Transfer the data into a graph to expose processes that are not performing well enough to TAKT time (figure 3.20).

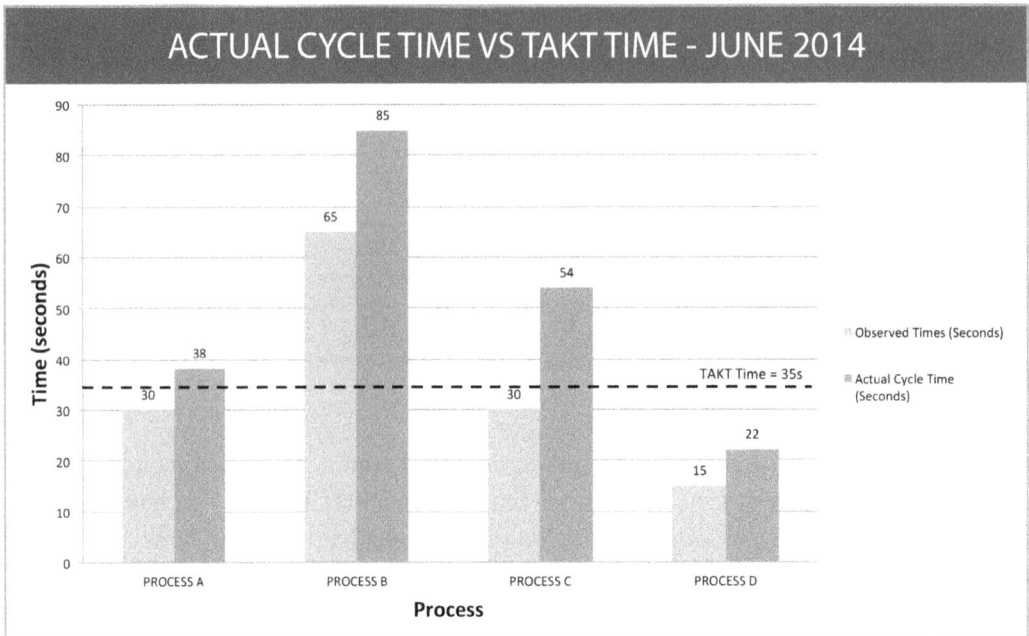

ACTUAL CYCLE TIME VS TAKT TIME - JUNE 2014

Figure 3.20

The results of the study show that process 'A' and 'C' require improvement and not just process 'B' as originally thought.

Step 3: Interpret the Results

With the TAKT time and current performance clear, evaluate the Current State as follows:

Overproduction Potential

At first glance, do any of the processes run the risk of overproducing? Now review your Current State Map. Is there evidence of a build-up of inventory at this process? Is there a system in place to limit the production and prevent excess supply?

Identify the Weakest Link

The terms 'constraint' and 'bottleneck' are often used interchangeably, but it is useful to differentiate between processes that by their current design will not be capable of producing to requirement, and processes that should be capable but are behaving like bottlenecks due to losses.

- o Identify the constraint: Review the effective cycle times. Are there any processes incapable by design of keeping up with the customer requirement?

- o Identify the bottleneck: Review the actual cycle times. Are there any processes struggling to keep up with requirement as a result of losses? Which loss is having the greatest impact?

Visual Performance Measurement

How does the employee know how he or she is doing in relation to the requirement? Is there a visual board that shows in regular intervals how the performance to target is progressing? Is this target aligned with the TAKT time? Is the reason for not meeting target clearly written next to interval?

Standard Work

Review the works instructions, job aids and standard operating procedures at the workstation. Compare these documents to how the work is actually being performed. Is the standard work designed and followed to meet the TAKT time?

Flexibility to Changing Demands

Review what happens when demand fluctuates. Are there contingency plans developed for when the demand increases or when the demand drops so that manning is adjusted according to a standard (figure 3.21)? If not, how does the process cope with these fluctuations?

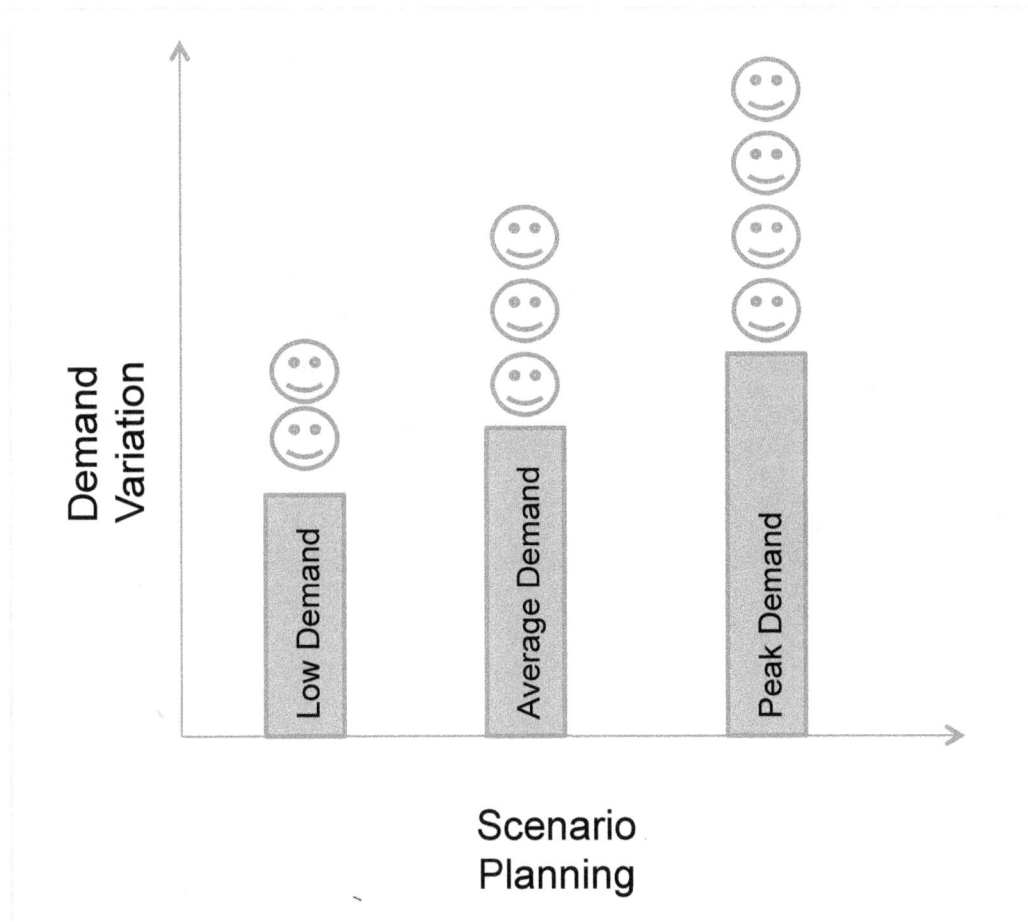

Figure 3.21

Based on your investigation conclude if the system is paced to TAKT Time or not and where the opportunities lie to improve on this. Add your findings to the map (figure 3.22).

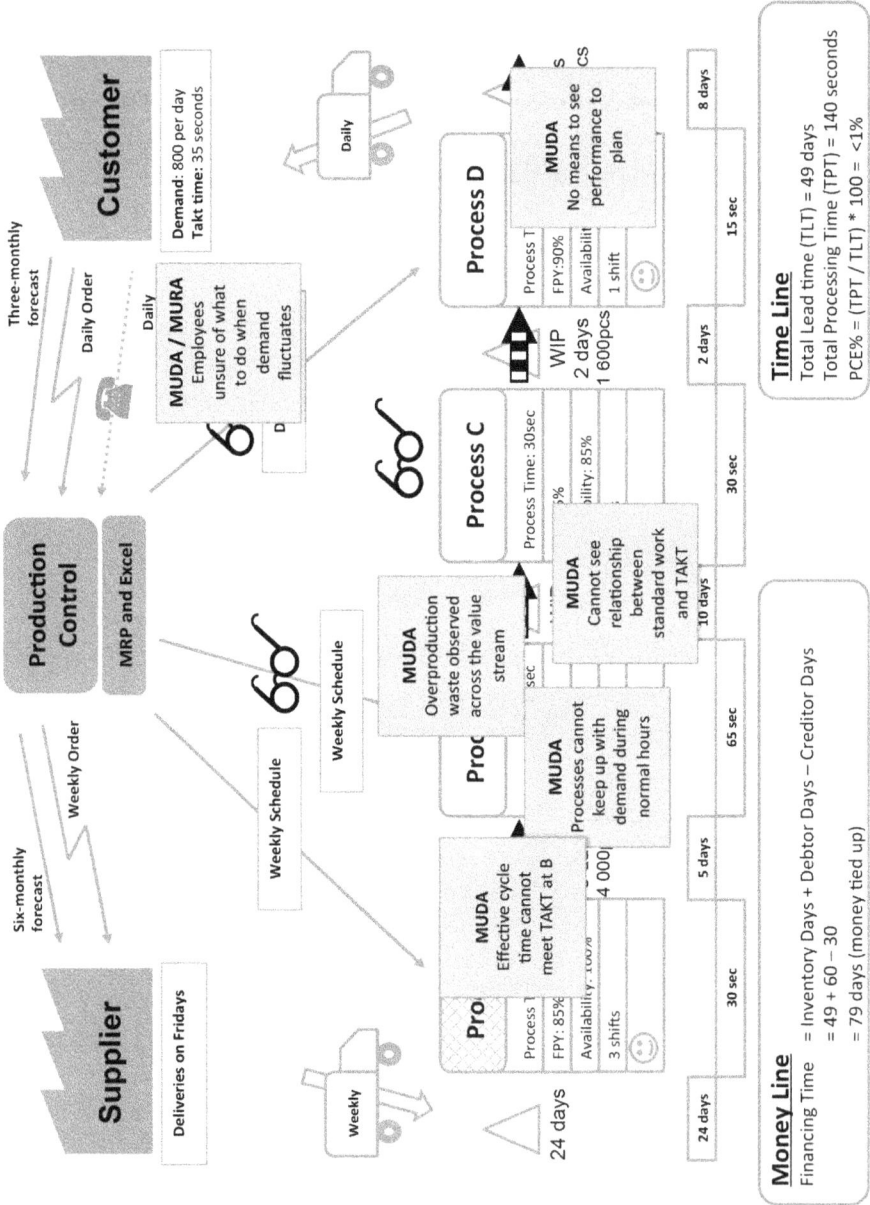

Supplier

Deliveries on Fridays

Six-monthly forecast

Weekly Order

Production Control

MRP and Excel

Three-monthly forecast

Daily Order

Customer

Demand: 800 per day
Takt time: 35 seconds

Daily

MUDA / MURA
Employees unsure of what to do when demand fluctuates

Weekly Schedule

Weekly Schedule

Weekly Schedule

Process D

Process T
FPY:90%
Availabilit
1 shift

MUDA
No means to see performance to plan

MUDA
Overproduction waste observed across the value stream

MUDA
Cannot see relationship between standard work and TAKT

MUDA
Processes cannot keep up with demand during normal hours

MUDA
Effective cycle time cannot meet TAKT at B

Process C

Process Time: 30sec

WIP
2 days
1 600pcs

Weekly

24 days

Money Line
Financing Time = Inventory Days + Debtor Days – Creditor Days
= 49 + 60 – 30
= 79 days (money tied up)

Time Line
Total Lead time (TLT) = 49 days
Total Processing Time (TPT) = 140 seconds
PCE% = (TPT / TLT) * 100 = <1%

| 24 days | 30 sec | 5 days | 65 sec | 10 days | 30 sec | 2 days | 15 sec | 8 days |

Figure 3.22

✔ FOR YOU TO TRY

- Gather the demand and available time data.

- Calculate TAKT time using the formula provided.

- Establish the current performance of the Value Stream:

  - Use the results from a simple time study

  - If the data is available, use the results from a detailed
    capacity study and calculate OE.

- Develop summary graphs to show the current performance to TAKT time.

- Interpret the results and include your findings on the Current State Map.

INTERPRET THE CURRENT STATE MAP
FIND FLOW OPPORTUNITIES: MUDA, MURA, MURI

❓ WHAT IS THIS?

The best way to understand 'flow' is to think of a river. If the river is flowing, with no obstructions (rocks and meanders) to slow it down, the water will reach its destination in the shortest possible time and distance, with the least amount of loss. It is this standard of flow we look to achieve in our processes, and in order to create flow you first need to understand what prevents flow.

Rother and Harris describe flow as a mixed sequence of good quality work, flowing one piece at a time according to market pull through TAKT Time (Rother and Harris, 2001). This means flexible processes are needed that can cope with the variety demanded by the market at the pace they need it, in the order they need it, at the quality they require it. It also implies that the product or service must flow into the hands of the customer without delay – if one piece is moving through the process without delay, there is minimal build-up and queuing to slow it down.

You stand a better chance of removing flow inhibitors by following a logical sequence to seek them out and deal with them. You first learned to spot muda, mura and muri in the Current State mapping excercise and the sections that follow expand on this method to give you a better grasp of symptomatic effects and root causes of barriers to flow.

MUDA, MURA, MURI IN OPERATIONS

Muda

Mura

Muri

Value

Removing muda is not enough to deliver value. The source of waste may be generated through mura and muri, resulting in a frustrating recurrence of the problem if not addressed.

The method presented has been adapted from a fundamental principle of just-in-time thinking with its origins in the Toyota Production System (figure 3.23).

Figure 3.23

? WHY IS THIS HELPFUL?

Understanding what obstructs flow and therefore value makes problems more visible and opportunities more accessible. Assuming you take advantage of these findings, the following benefits will also flow:

- Improved stability in the operations
- Shorter lead time and improved responsiveness to customer requirement
- Improved quality and the ability to see normal from abnormal
- Increased productivity and reduced cost by doing more with less effort
- Increased throughput for the system, assuming the extra output results in increased sales and revenue
- Better use of available resources and facilities
- A better working environment
- Improved sustainability of problems eliminated.

There are many advantages to improving flow but it is vital to select projects that will benefit the customer or the business, and align perfectly with the North Star. Be aware of this when embarking on a flow-improvement hunt. What you detect and solve, must drive a true benefit.

? HOW TO DO IT

An introduction to muda, mura and muri was covered in Current State mapping. Table 3.9 expands on these concepts and provides additional guidelines that may not have been obvious from the initial walkabouts. Some examples provided in the table can actually be found under more than one of the three headings. Do not be not too concerned about this – it is more important to recognise problems that hinder flow, the source and to accept there may be some overlaps.

FINDING FLOW OPPORTUNITIES

Flow Obstruction	Description	Evidence to Look For	Guidelines
Muda	**Muda** is waste. This is any unecessary use of resources in a way that does not add value to the needs of the customer.	○ Overproduction ○ Waiting ○ Transportation ○ Over processing ○ Excess inventory ○ Unecessary movement ○ Defects ○ Unused employee creativity ○ Environmental waste (see PLANET)	Step 1: Evaluate the muda Post-it Notes. Step 2: Compare customer requirement to actual production. Step 3: Evaluate the constraint. Step 4: Draw a spaghetti diagram.
Mura	**Mura** is uneveness, fluctuation or variation in the processes, product or service.	○ Quality, availability and performance variation ○ Scheduling complexity ○ Last-minute production plan changes ○ Variation in forecast accuracy ○ Spikes and troughs in demand patterns ○ Lack of standardisation and standard times ○ Variation in shift patterns	Step 5: Evaluate the mura Post-it Notes. Step 6: Break OE into key losses. Step 7: Evaluate scheduling principles. Step 8: Review forecast accuracy. Step 9: Evaluate plan verses actual performance. Step 10: Review shift patterns.
Muri	**Muri** is over-burden. People, systems or equipment are overloaded with respect to their available capacity.	○ Overloading of capacity ○ Reactive maintenance ○ Equipment or system unavailability ○ Excessive overtime ○ High absenteeism ○ High safety incidents ○ No time for problem solving ○ Excessive work released into the system	Step 11: Evaluate the muri Post-it Notes. Step 12: Compare available capacity to actual loading. Step 13: Evaluate maintenance principles. Step 14: Review overtime and absenteeism. Step 15: Review safety incidents. Step 16: Evaluate problem-solving enablers.

Table 3.9

Step 1: Evaluate the Muda Post-It Notes

During the gemba walk, muda, mura and muri were identified and captured on Post-Its. Evaluate each of the muda found and place it on the map where it occurs. Remove those that are not relevant to the North Star.

Step 2: Compare Customer Requirement to Actual Production

The thinking here is straight forward. What did the customer require and what was actually produced? Was more or less than required processed?

Agree amongst the team on how far back to go, but typically a minimum of three months' data is useful to detect any evidence of overproduction (or underproduction). Sales will be able to verify what the customer actually ordered and the production or operational records will confirm what was actually processed. Consider calculating the average variance and also show the deviation from the average each month (table 3.10).

Example	CUSTOMER REQUIREMENT VS ACTUAL PRODUCTION MARCH TO JUNE 2014		
	Actual Customer Requirement	Actual Production	% Variation
March	200	220	110%
April	350	500	143%
May	100	0	0%
June	650	720	111%
Total	1300	1440	111%

Table 3.10

The Value Stream Map will expose excess build up and queues. Look for these and highlight them on the map. If evidence of overproduction is found, investigate why this has happened and update the Current State Map with the findings.

Step 3: Evaluate the Constraint

From the Current State Map you can see at a glance the entire system and the interdependencies. Having identified the constraint earlier in the chapter it is now possible to evaluate factors that prevent the system from performing to optimum levels by concentrating on the weakest link and its problems:

A Loss at the Constraint, is a Loss to the System

Similarly, the improvement of a non-constraint, unless for the benefit of a constraint, is a phantom improvement. Evaluate OE at the constraint as explained in the section comparing current performance to TAKT time. If the constraint data indicates losses incurred through supporting processes, evaluate the OE at these processes too. Highlight your findings on the Current State Map.

Wasted Effort and Balancing Principles

Are efforts being made to try and balance the capacities perfectly instead of balancing flow (Bicheno, 2004)? There will always be faster and slower processes in your operations and this energy can be better used to exploit the opportunities at the constraint. Are there unnecessary queues of work at non-constraint processes? From a system's perspective, queues at a non-constraint will not achieve more throughput. These may as well be controlled and the energy placed elsewhere. Does the constraint govern the flow of product, or are non-constraints allowed to govern the rate of throughput? Update your findings on the Current State Map.

Where to Batch

This will differ from industry to industry but a typical approach is to reduce the batch sizes at the non-constraint processes, and increase the batch sizes at the constraint to optimise utilisation. The batch should, of course, not exceed customer requirement and the changeover at the constraint must first be optimised (covered in PROCESS). This means the non-constraints will be kept busier with the additional changeovers but it also means they will be able to respond to the needs of the constraint better. The constraint will be less plagued by losses due to changeovers and shortages. Evaluate the logic in your operation's batching and include your findings on the Current State Map.

Starvation and Protection of the Constraint

Evaluate the lost time information gathered to calculate the availability (Av) element of OE. Was the constraint waiting for material or input in this data? Was the constraint starved of material or input resulting in delays and loss to the system? Are set, non-negotiable buffers in place before the constraint to protect it? Are the best skills made available to the constraint? Are all required employees in place at the constraint? Is there a contingency plan when a constraint employee is absent or on annual leave? Update your findings on the Current State Map.

Work Released into the System

Is the amount of work released into the operations greater than what the constraint can handle? This results in muda (excess inventory and congestions points) but also affects muri by burdening the system with more work than can be handled. If this is the case, update your findings on the Current State Map.

Transferring of Batches from the Constraint

The work coming from a constraint is too valuable to have to wait. Where feasible, this work must be passed on to the next process timeously to make its way through the rest of the operation. If transference influences waiting time at the constraint the impact should be reflected in the OE data. Evaluate the size of 'transfer batches' from the constraint and update your findings on the Current State Map. Understand the reasons behind the current transfer batch size.

Non-Process Related Constraints

Sometimes the constraint affecting the system has nothing to do with the processing capability but is coming from another source. Is the constraint coming from the market (demand less than supply), from employee behaviour or management policy making? Update your findings on the Current State Map.

TIPS

If the constraint is not internal in the system, then the processes are adequate to supply to demand and the constraint lies out there in the market.

Improving the market constraint is beyond the scope of this book, but important to remember at this stage is that you do not want to overproduce just because you have available capacity. True throughput is defined by the rate at which the system generates money through sales. If there are no sales and you are producing, then this is a waste. In this case, you would skip this analysis and review the purpose of your Value Stream mapping before proceeding.

Step 4: Draw a High-Level Spaghetti Diagram

From the gemba walk, draw a spaghetti diagram on a layout or flipchart to show the flow of work, motion and transportation – as the name suggests, it will most likely look like spaghetti. Indicate how the work actually moves, and measure the number of steps. Include this distance on the diagram as you will use this as a baseline measurement later (figure 3.24).

The same diagram can be done for a material handler or other employee if this makes sense, but the work example below usually gives a good indication of the transportation waste and the potential for layout improvement. Again, capture the findings on the Current State Map but discuss only those improvements that will have an impact on the North Star.

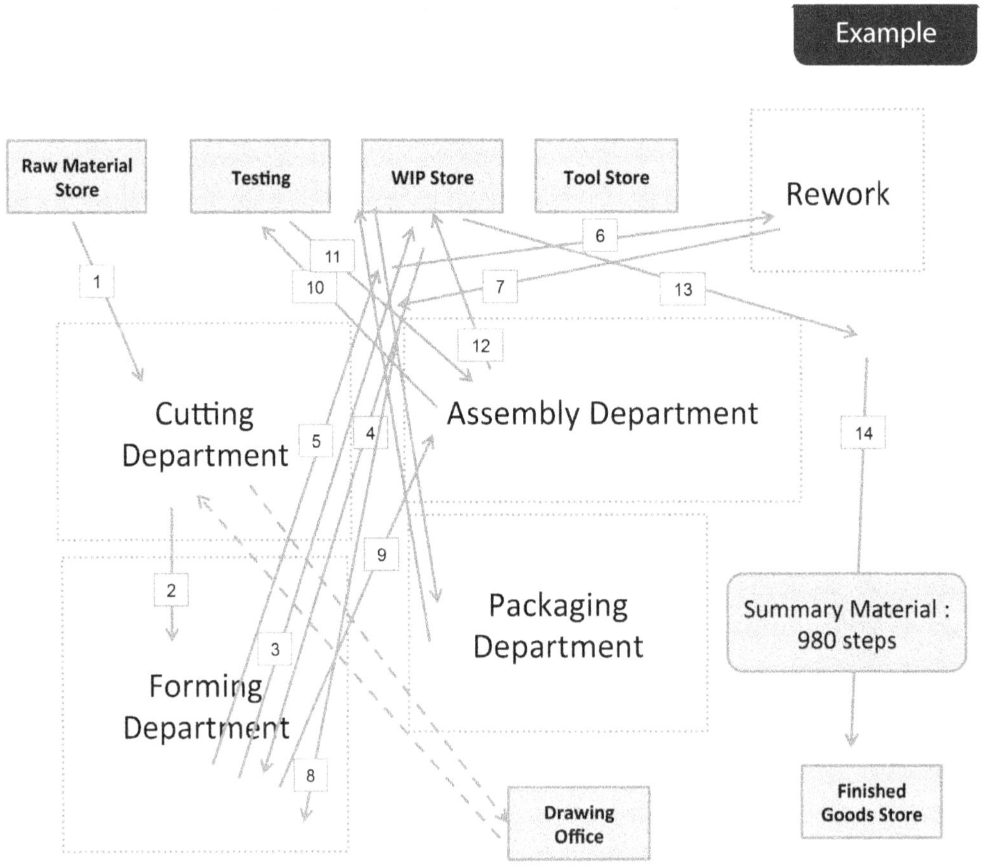

Example

Figure 3.24

Having included all muda findings on the Current State Map (figure 3.25), it may start to get quite busy. The sections that follow will guide you on how to clean it up and retain focus.

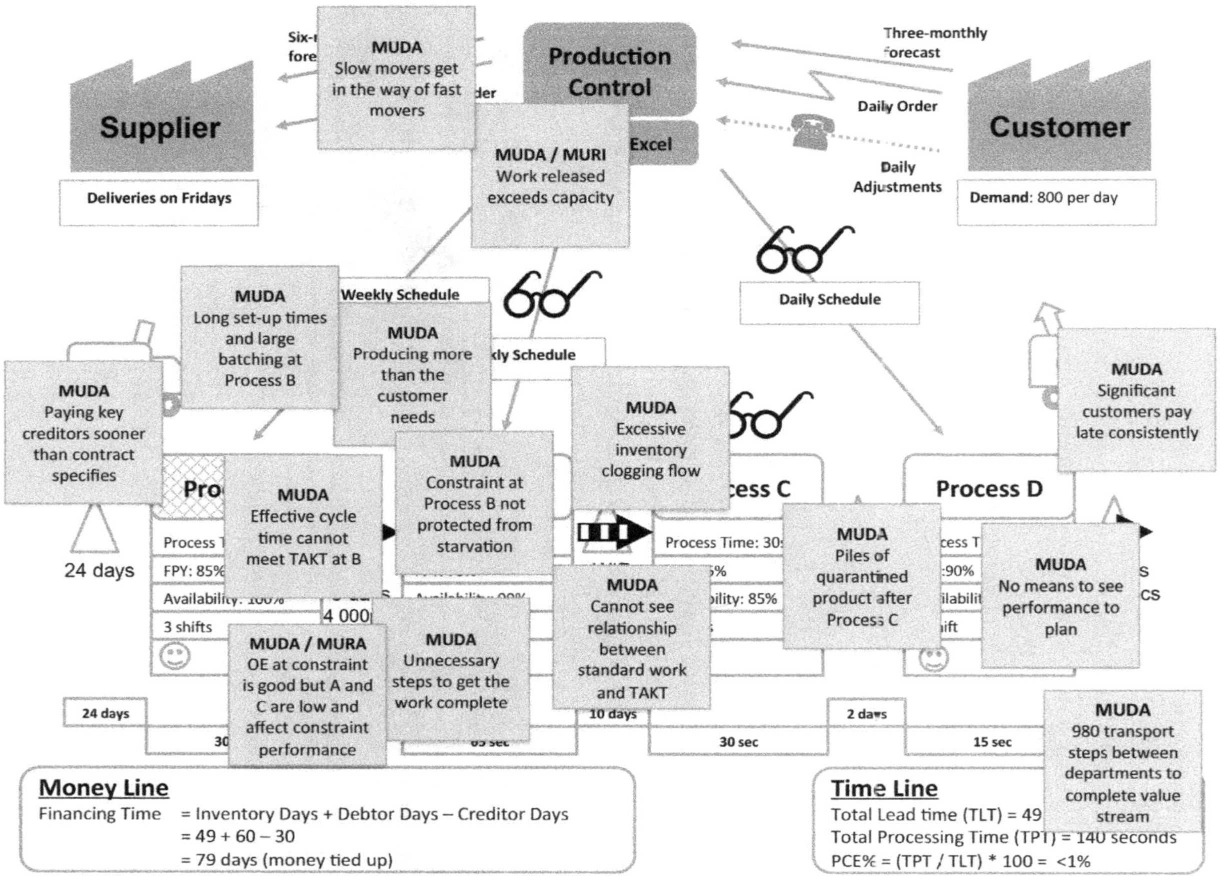

Supplier

Deliveries on Fridays

Production Control

Excel

Customer

Demand: 800 per day

Three-monthly Forecast

Daily Order

Daily Adjustments

Daily Schedule

Weekly Schedule

Process D

Process C

MUDA
Slow movers get in the way of fast movers

MUDA / MURI
Work released exceeds capacity

MUDA
Paying key creditors sooner than contract specifies

MUDA
Long set-up times and large batching at Process B

MUDA
Effective cycle time cannot meet TAKT at B

MUDA / MURA
OE at constraint is good but A and C are low and affect constraint performance

MUDA
Producing more than the customer needs

MUDA
Constraint at Process B not protected from starvation

MUDA
Unnecessary steps to get the work complete

MUDA
Excessive inventory clogging flow

MUDA
Cannot see relationship between standard work and TAKT

MUDA
Piles of quarantined product after Process C

MUDA
No means to see performance to plan

MUDA
Significant customers pay late consistently

MUDA
980 transport steps between departments to complete value stream

Process Time: 30

FPY: 85%

Availability: 2004

4 000

3 shifts

24 days

24 days

10 days

2 days

30 sec

15 sec

Money Line
Financing Time   = Inventory Days + Debtor Days − Creditor Days
                     = 49 + 60 − 30
                     = 79 days (money tied up)

Time Line
Total Lead time (TLT) = 49
Total Processing Time (TPT) = 140 seconds
PCE% = (TPT / TLT) * 100 = <1%

Figure 3.25

Step 5: Evaluate the Mura Post-it Notes

During the gemba walk, muda, mura and muri were identified and captured on Post-Its. Evaluate each of the mura (variation and unevenness) found and place it on the map where it occurs. Agree in terms of the North Star, which mura will be pursued. Consolidate your findings and remove those that are not relevant.

Step 6: Break OE into Key Losses

OE has already been discussed and this step aims to take what has been learned and break it down one level more to pinpoint mura-related issues. This can become quite complex as there are many variables that influence OE performance – we remind you not to go as far as the root causes (covered in PROBLEM SOLVING), only down to the key losses that will be further investigated at a later stage.

Review Longer-Term Trends

Figure 3.20 illustrated that Process B was a constraint (by design it could not meet demand) but Process A and B were behaving like bottlenecks due to losses. This exposed areas that must improve to comfortably meet TAKT time. Taking a closer look at the detailed performance may present further problems to the stability of the processes, and table 3.11 is an example of the data collection used to visualise the variation in performance using longer-term trends. Complete this exercise for all processes not currently capable to meet TAKT time) although only A is shown here:

Example	OE PERFORMANCE AT PROCESS A JUNE 2013 TO MAY 2014			
	Quality	Performance	Availability	OE
June	95%	85%	100%	81%
July	92%	86%	100%	79%
August	91%	84%	100%	76%
September	85%	85%	100%	72%
October	84%	83%	100%	70%
November	78%	83%	100%	65%
December	77%	85%	100%	65%
January	74%	86%	100%	64%
February	72%	87%	100%	63%
March	69%	87%	100%	60%
April	68%	86%	100%	58%
May	80%	85%	100%	68%
Average	**80%**	**85%**	**100%**	**69%**

Table 3.11

Visualise Data One-Level Down

Looking at it in isolation you may not be too concerned with your first impressions of the OE monthly trend. Performance in figure 3.26 is declining somewhat but the variation at a glance does not set off any significant warning bells. However, this is a complex measure, with many variables influencing it so take a closer look at the next level of data as this may tell a different story:

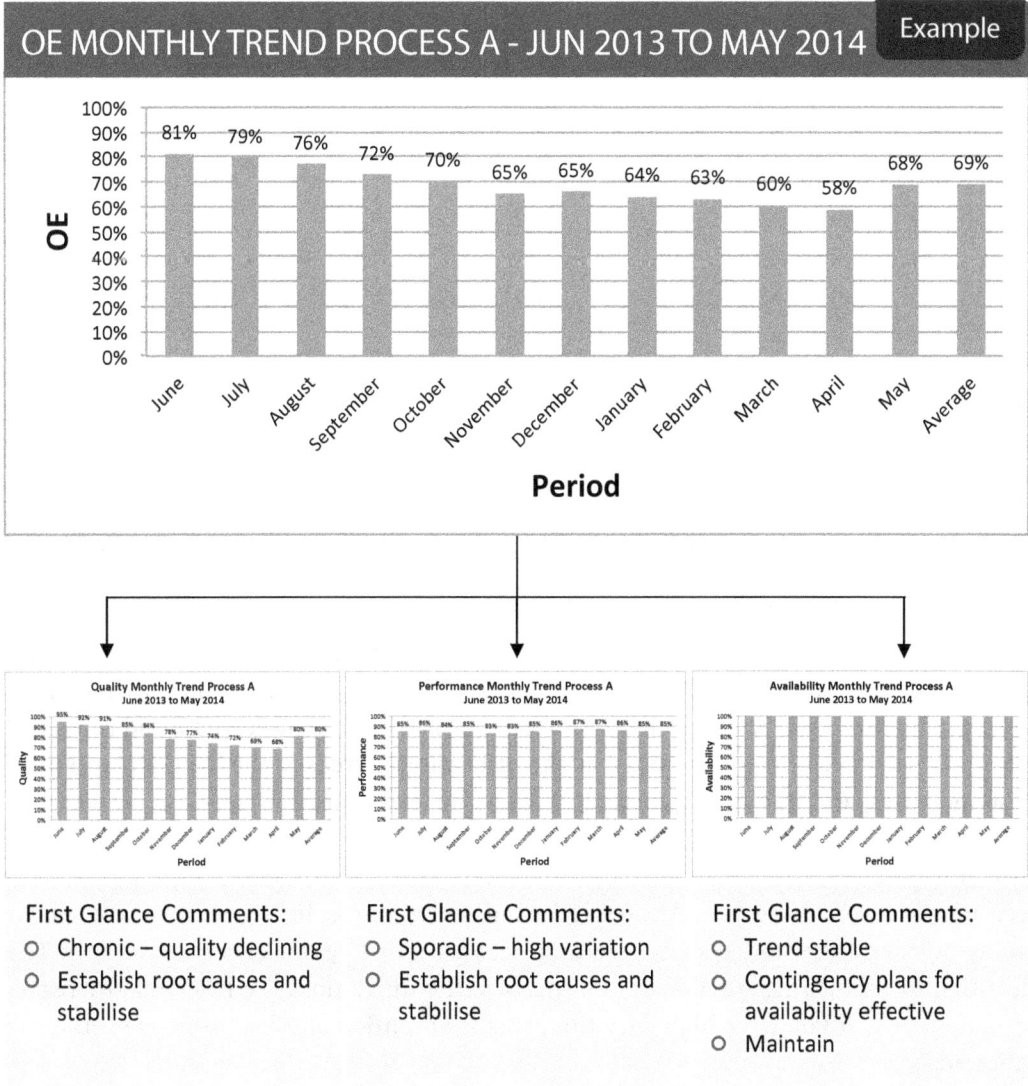

First Glance Comments:
- Chronic – quality declining
- Establish root causes and stabilise

First Glance Comments:
- Sporadic – high variation
- Establish root causes and stabilise

First Glance Comments:
- Trend stable
- Contingency plans for availability effective
- Maintain

Figure 3.26

Include comments on the Current State Map to highlight which aspects need further investigation to reduce mura.

Remember the Law of Factory Physics

Hopp and Spearman have proven a series of fundamental relationships in manufacturing that are particularly useful to mention at this point (Hopp and Spearman, 2000). They explain principles that relate well to the section on mura and scheduling principles. Refer to figure 3.27 in the example below describing one such relationship:

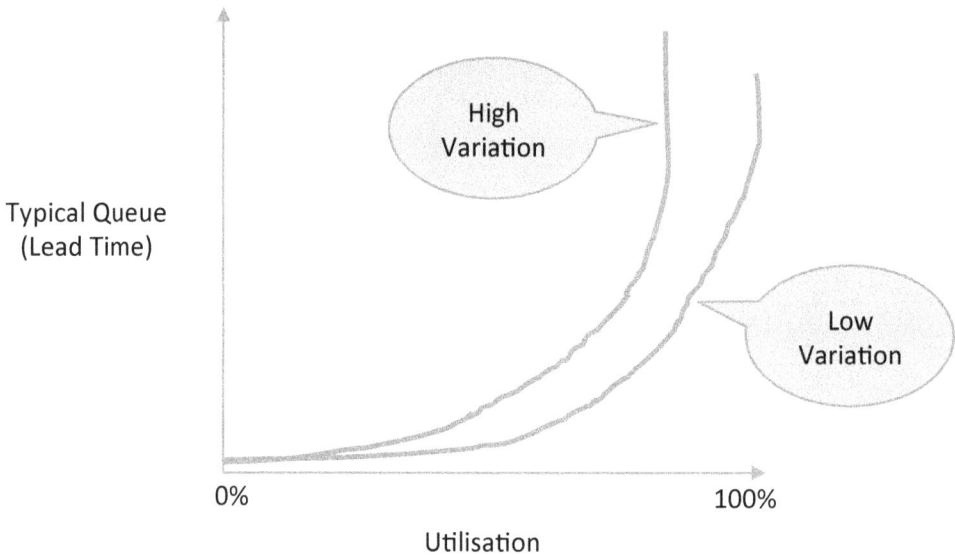

Figure 3.27

Imagine you are driving on a highway and the traffic is moving consistently. As you get closer to peak hour, a few more cars come onto the road but the traffic is not too severe and the cars are still flowing. However, as you get closer to peak time and the cars on the road gradually increase, so the congestion on the roads starts to get worse and the speed of travel is reduced. In other words, as the utilisation increases, the 'work-in-progress' also increases, and this subsequently increases the lead time.

Now imagine you have impatient drivers on the road consistently changing lanes and causing variation in the flow. Although the individual thinks he is getting to where he is going quicker, the whole system is actually slowed down by this erratic behaviour. The learning in this? In figure 3.27 as you increase the utilisation, the lead time increases exponentially. If you have high variation, this is amplified and lead time is even more affected.

From a planning perspective, you might think you will achieve more throughput by stealing some of the meeting or maintenance time to run for longer but in fact, the system could become less capable as the utilisation increases. If you are increasing sales and loading more into the production plan, again, as the utilisation increases the lead time could also increase. If you have high variation in the process – as the OE calculations show in the previous section – then the lead time increases further, and the system becomes even less capable.

Step 7: Evaluate Scheduling Principles

Mura will also be influenced by how the operation is scheduled and the contributing factors inherent in the system design (figure 3.28).

Demand variation, unplanned changeovers, red streams interfering with greens, outdated information in the system and so on all play a part in how work is scheduled and interrupted. To reduce mura, you want to better understand how the scheduling is affecting your ability to achieve smooth flow. We recommend the following questions to help get you started:

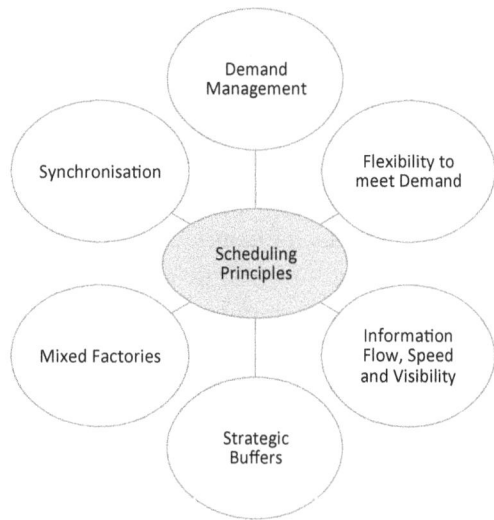

Figure 3.28

Demand Management

Different batching and decision-making policies along the supply chain can play havoc with the demand to which you are responding. This is sometimes referred to as the 'hockey stick' effect that causes the entire system to respond knee-jerk-style to amplifications in demand, rather than the real needs of the end-customer. The trick is to understand the true demand and filter out the noise created along the way. Figure 3.29 illustrates the phenomenon quite well (Womack and Jones, 2005).

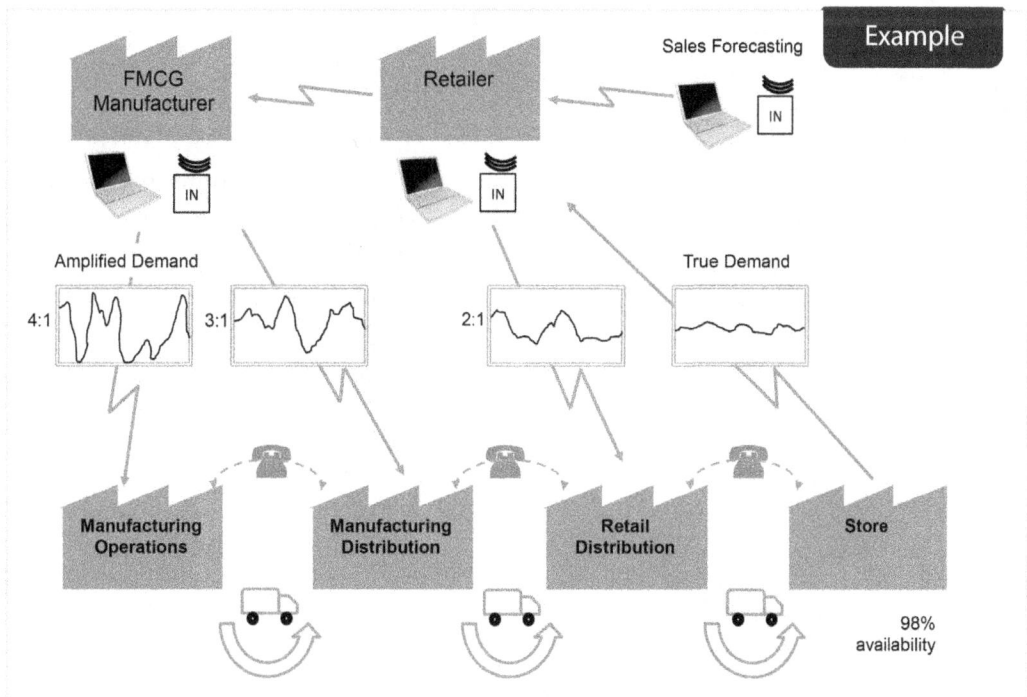

Figure 3.29

The farther up we move the system away from the customer, the more distorted the link between the actual demand and what is being relayed to operations becomes. In figure 3.29 the manufacturing operations have to respond to the amplified demand which is radically different to the true needs. This results in more changeovers, higher inventory levels to compensate for the variation, more infrequent delivery cycles and a far less-efficient supply chain. True customer demand may well get lost in all the chaos.

Taking this thinking to your Value Stream, you may find a similar disconnect with the customer needs. In manufacturing for example, as a result of long changeovers and large batches, operations may be altering the true needs of the customer to accommodate the complexities in the processes.

Evaluate the demand-pattern variation, its impact on the schedule and the avoidable causes driving the disturbances. The following list should trigger questions around your own demand amplification (Bicheno, 2004):

External Reasons for Demand Amplification

- Incentives and discounts creating spikes in demand.
- High variety early-on in the process due to product or service design adding complexity to the scheduling process.
- Poor accountability for excessive demand variation whereby it is not discussed and resolved regularly at systemic-level accountability meetings.
- Performance measures driving behaviour that runs inventory high and then suddenly depletes it in an attempt to meet the targets set.

Internal Reasons for Demand Amplification

- A high number of items share common subassemblies that are not grouped together in the schedule (see Glenday Sieve).
- Scheduling is planned to meet the capacity of the operation without a buffer to compensate for problems, catch-up or demand fluctuation.
- Employees overreact to create situations of extreme behaviour rather than using systems to stabilise and adjust in times of demand changes.
- Priority is not given to regular orders and 'funnies' are allowed to disrupt flow.
- Overproduction or problems in OE steal precious scheduling time from real demand.

You should have a handle on the varieties affecting flow, the current batch-logic in play and some initial findings to make improvements from. This stimulates a move toward flow-logic.

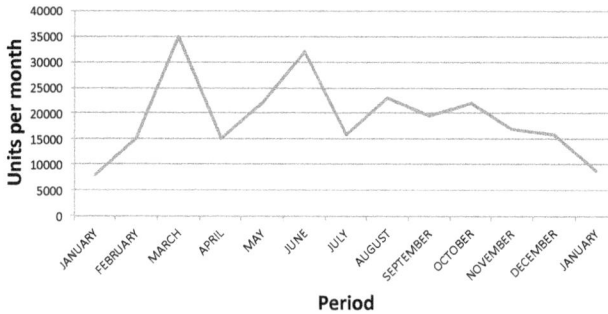

DEMAND VARIATION JAN 2013 TO JAN 2014   Example

Figure 3.30

Expect scepticism with respect to the viability of moving the greens onto a fixed-scheduling system to reduce complexity and protect 'money spinners' from fire fighting. One of the most common arguments against flow-logic, is the impact of demand variation: 'How can we put these items on a fixed schedule when our demand pattern looks like this?'. Figure 3.30 illustrates an erratic demand pattern common to many industries, both in products and services. It is true that such a pattern will make even the bravest of change agents hesitate in moving to fixed cycles. It is therefore worth mentioning that most organisations have two types of demand affecting what gets processed in the available time:

○ Value demand
   This what the end customer actually consumes.

○ Failure demand
   This is the demand that comes into the system as a result of unreliability, system design and error. It does not accurately reflect what the customer actually consumes. There are several causes of failure demand and figure 3.31 indicates a selection typically found:

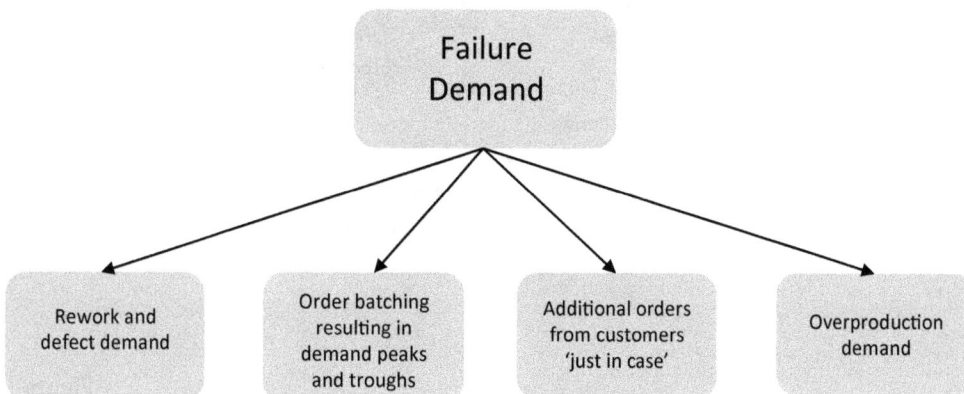

Figure 3.31

It is recommended data be gathered to differentiate between value and failure demand, exposing opportunity to reduce mura and maximise the chance of smooth demand patterns. Assuming alignment to your North Star focus, this may be fundamental to achieving optimum flow. Figure 3.32 and 3.33 illustrates the level of visibility to aim for and data that can motivate a need for demand smoothing.

DEMAND VARIATION AND CONTRIBUTING FACTORS JANUARY 2013 TO JANUARY 2014

Example

Figure 3.32

BREAKDOWN OF FAILURE DEMAND JANUARY 2013 TO JANUARY 2014

Example

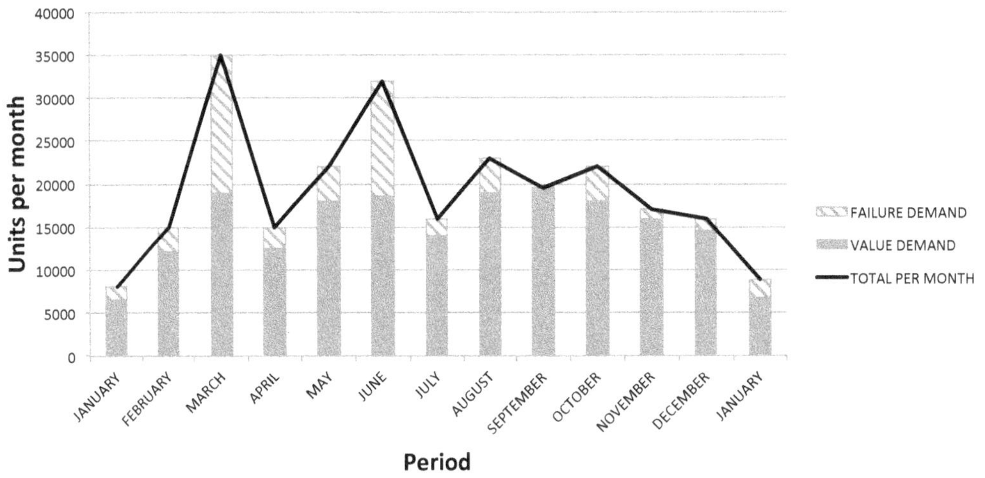

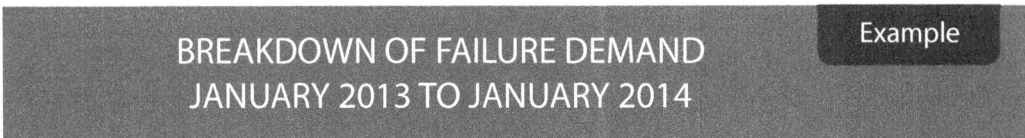

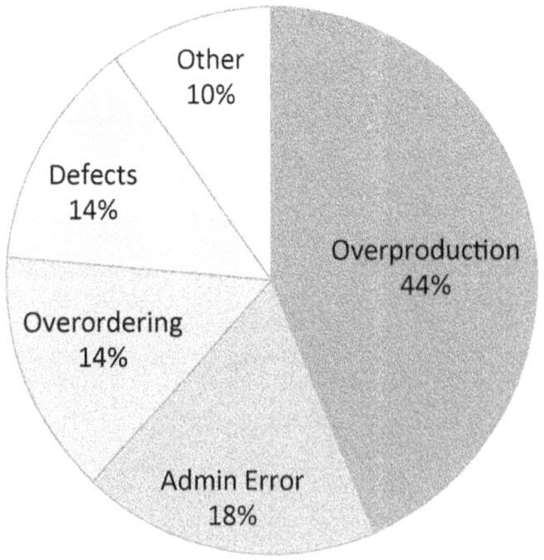

Figure 3.33

Flexibility to meet Demand

Can operations handle a variety of products or services in line with customer needs, in smaller lots or are large batches of product or service put through the schedule, resulting in longer lead times, greater congestion and less flexibility?

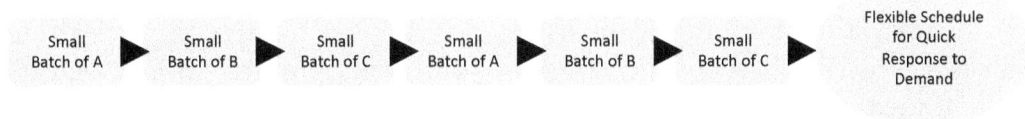

Figure 3.34

Figure 3.34 describes what happens when a more frequent EPEI or 'Every Product Every Interval' is accomplished. This is a good measure for the current level of flexibility which you can compare to requirement. The objective of a good EPEI is to make a batch as small as possible within the available time and with as many planned changeovers as possible. Depending on what EPEI meets your market requirements, this could also trigger the need for changeover reduction techniques (see PROCESS). Bear in mind this section brings focus to mura so excessive, unplanned changeovers is the opposite end of the spectrum you want to steer clear of.

A good schedule is a boring, predictable one (Bicheno, 2004) and the advantages of optimised EPEI are many, including:

○ The ability to schedule products or services at regular intervals to provide context for economies of repetition, regularity and standardisation.

○ A fundamental building block to achieve customer pull.

○ Improved predictability in planned changeovers and resulting available working time.

Calculate EPEI:

To understand your Current State of flexibility, work out the EPEI and evaluate how well this currently satisfies the needs of the market. Take the past three month's production or operations records (actuals) and capture the schedule. The example in table 3.12 shows the current schedule for six products (A to F) for the line:

				Example	
Day Week	Monday	Tuesday	Wednesday	Thursday	Friday
1	A	A	A	A	B
2	A	A	A	B	B
3	C	C	C	D	D
4	E	F	F	A	A

Table 3.12

The system currently schedules every product over an 18-day cycle before it repeats, therefore EPEI is Every Product Every 18 working days or put another way, Every Product Every 3.6 work-weeks.

Compare Current EPEI to the North Star:

Refer to the Voice of the Customer or discuss flexibility with the department closest to the customer needs – sales, marketing or customer service. How does current flexibility meet the needs of the critical customers both at present and for future requirements? Is the current EPEI sufficient to meet the goals of the North Star?

Calculate the Potential EPEI:

To complete this exercise, first calculate the run time which represents the amount of time required each day to produce the mix of products demanded (table 3.13 and figure 3.35). Then test various EPEI scenarios to establish a reasonable target EPEI to aim for (table 3.14).

Example	Cycle Time (sec)	Demand Per Day	Run Time (min)	Changeover Time (min)
A	46	235	180	30
B	50	144	120	30
C	48	38	30	30
D	52	35	30	30
E	49	37	30	30
F	45	40	30	30
Totals			420	180

Table 3.13

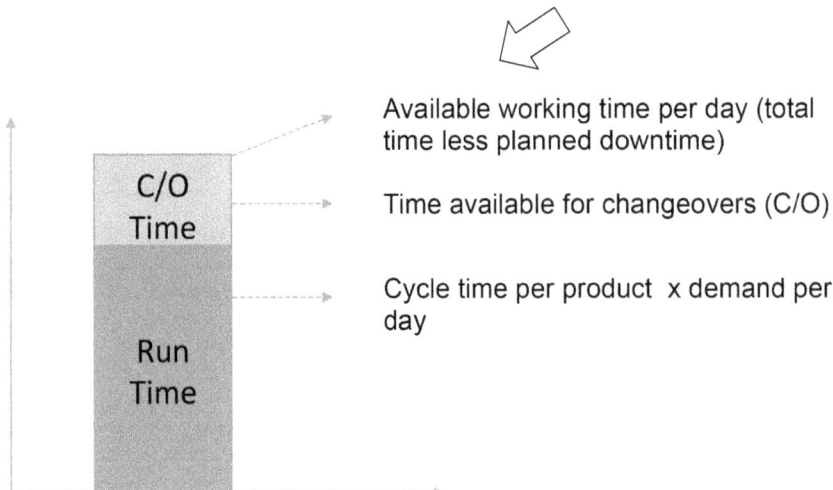

Available working time per day (total time less planned downtime)

Time available for changeovers (C/O)

Cycle time per product x demand per day

C/O Time

Run Time

Figure 3.35

Time needed to run each product in the day

Time needed for all changeovers throughout the day

Run time + changeover time

Working time less planned downtime

Is there enough time in a day for the total run time or not?

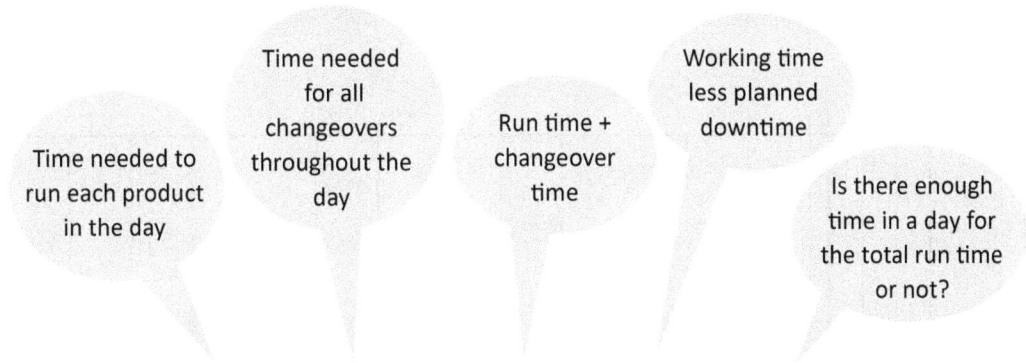

	Run Time (min)	Changeover Time (min)	Total Run Time (min)	Available Time (min)	Balance (Avail-Tot Run)	Is This EPEI Possible?
Every Day	420	180	600	476	-125	No
Every 2 Days	840	180	1020	950	-70	No
Every 3 Days	1260	180	1440	1425	-15	No
Every 4 Days	1680	180	1860	1900	40	Yes
Every 5 Days	2100	180	2280	2375	95	Yes

Table 3.14

Information Flow, Speed and Visibility

Take a closer look at the information flow in the Current State Map. Is this a bigger spaghetti than the flow of the product or service? Is there complexity in how the information is brought from the control tower down to the individual operations creating instability in how the front-line responds?

Have a look at how long the information takes to get from the customer to the people doing the work? Are there delays in passing the information down the ranks and are operations reacting to old information at the front-line?

How visible is the schedule to those concerned? Is it in a top-secret place for the elite few or has it been well displayed, properly updated. Is performance to schedule obvious?

Use the checklist provided in table 3.15 as a starting point, customise the content and evaluate where information flow hinders the physical flow resulting in unnecessary mura. Allocate a score of 1, 2 or 3 depending on the current state of the information flow, and sum up the total to show the possible areas for change. Make a list of improvements required and include comments on the Current State Map. Remember to go to the operations and speak to the real people influenced by the information.

INFORMATION FLOW EVALUATION
ACCURATE • TIMELY • RELEVANT

DEPARTMENT		ASSESSOR	
AREA		DATE	
INFORMATION TYPE			

CATEGORY	DESCRIPTION	1 POOR	2 AVERAGE	3 GOOD	IMPROVEMENT REQUIRED
VISIBILITY	CRITICAL INFORMATION TO GET WORK DONE IS VISIBLY DISPLAYED IN THE RIGHT PLACE				
	MEASUREMENT OF PERFORMANCE TO REQUIREMENT IS VISUALLY DISPLAYED				
EASE OF INTERPRETATION	INFORMATION IS EASY TO READ AND EASY TO INTERPRET				
TIMELY PROVISION	INFORMATION NEEDED BY OPERATIONS TO DO THE WORK IS PROVIDED IN GOOD TIME WITH NO DELAYS				
TIMELY RESPONSE	EMPLOYEES HAVE THEIR FINGERS ON THE PULSE AND INFORMATION HELPS THEM RESPOND TIMEOUSLY TO PROBLEMS OR REQUESTS				
RELEVANCE	INFORMATION PROVIDED TO GET THE WORK DONE IS CURRENT AND CRITICAL TO THE WORK AT HAND				
ACCURACY	INFORMATION IS FREE OF ERRORS AND CONSISTENT TO STANDARD				
AVAILABILITY	INFORMATION IS READILY AVAILABLE TO THOSE WHO REQUIRE IT, WHERE THEY REQUIRE IT				
COMPLEXITY	INFORMATION IS AVAILABLE FROM A SINGLE SOURCE WITH RELIABLE REVISION CONTROL				
STANDARDISATION	INFORMATION IS PROVIDED IN A STANDARD FORMAT ACROSS THE DEPARTMENTS				
OWNERSHIP	ACCOUNTABILITY FOR THE ACCURACY AND PROVISION OF INFORMATION IS CLEAR				
TOTAL SCORE OUT OF 30					

Table 3.15

Strategic Buffers

Buffers are used to guard against fluctuations and promote the flow of work. Too much, and you run the risk of congestion and queues; too little and the constraint may be starved of work bringing the system to a stand-still. A strategic buffer is about having the right stock, in the right place, in the right quantities for the right reasons. In service, this refers to having the right work available and ready so that critical processes do not have to wait. If this is well executed it will bring more stability and flow to the operation, resulting in less mura.

Consider your own operations and the following questions:

○ Do queues, work-in-progress and inventory fluctuate depending on the dynamics of the process, or have strategic, well-planned buffers been installed to regulate flow?

○ How has the position of the buffer been determined?

○ Is the buffer designed to protect the constraint and is it carefully calculated according to common disruptions established from data or is there fat built in to handle unusual, just-in-case events?

○ When buffers are depleted, does this trigger production to replenish according to consumption or do parts just arrive 'unannounced'?

Include comments on the Current State Map to bring attention to how buffers are currently handled, and possible impact on mura.

Mixed Factories

Although we use the term 'factory' loosely this is equally relevant to service and knowledge worker environments. Refer to the results of the Glenday Sieve Analysis and previous observations:

○ In the schedule, are there two distinctly different 'factories' grouped together?

○ Are the high volume, repetitive green stream items disrupted by low volume, irregular red stream items?

○ Is there a conscious effort made to keep them separate either physically – for example, dedicated line or department – or at least give each stream a dedicated time slot in the schedule?

Quality guru, Philip Crosby, provides us with an excellent analogy describing how some businesses operate like a ballet performance, whereas others behave like ice hockey games constantly entertaining mura.

In a ballet performance every routine is carefully planned, coordinated and performed the same way, each time, with absolute precision.

The dance flows, the audience knows what to expect, and when there is a mistake, the dancers quickly adjust to bring it all back on track again. The movement is smooth, predictable, repeatable, accurate and beautiful.

With hockey every game is an adventure! You never know what to expect. It is survival of the fittest and if a player loses concentration for one second, he may be injured. From the time the game starts until the end of the game, players have to be alert, responding to every crisis. As much as players have practised, there is no guarantee that they will win. At the end of the game, players are exhausted but pleased to have survived another one!

Think about how your organisation operates, and in particular the scheduling. Is it more like ballet or ice hockey? Why do you think this is and what are the opportunities that must be detailed on the map to drive regularity?

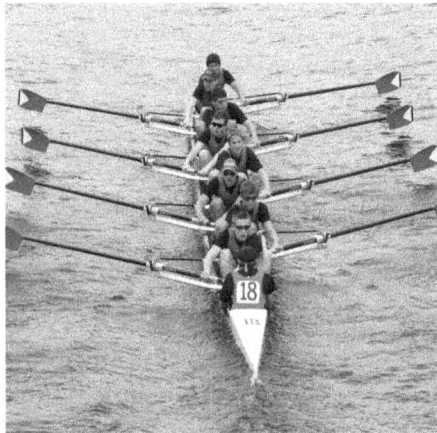

Synchronisation

The coxswain is a person who steers, paces and navigates a boat and his crew during a race. He provides a steady cadence that drives each rowers' individual performance towards a common goal – to win!

In operations, it is just as important to set a pace and govern this methodically, so that when targets are missed or exceeded, the system speeds up or slows down respectively.

We discussed TAKT time and what to pace the operations to. Now it is necessary to evaluate the 'coxswain' of the process – the system that drives the synchronisation of operations to the customer demand rate. Consider the following questions:

○ How do people and departments know what to do, and when? Is everyone synchronised to the same beat, whereby they operate independently, but are driven by the same objectives?

○ Does one operation set the pace for the rest, or are there several 'chiefs' influencing the flow?

○ Does the system respond automatically to variations in performance or are adjustments adhoc and reactive resulting in more mura?

Often, operations will pace and synchronise to the constraint process to achieve the most throughput. In other cases, the pace is set by a process closer to the customer, to align better to actual customer needs. Good synchronisation relies heavily on smooth demand, so if you do have a pacemaker or coxswain, evaluate how well this is working.

Step 8: Review Forecast Accuracy

Demand and sales and operations planning is beyond the scope of this book, but forecast accuracy can play a major role in planning and control, the proper utilisation of resources and the satisfaction of customers. At this point, we recommend that the forecast accuracy be reviewed for any irregularities to raise awareness of its generation of mura.

To understand the Current State of forecasting, gather data on the accuracy as well as the variation to understand the possible impact to the planning function. Figure 3.36, shows that although the forecast accuracy average is 93 percent, which is reasonable, the monthly variation is cause for concern.

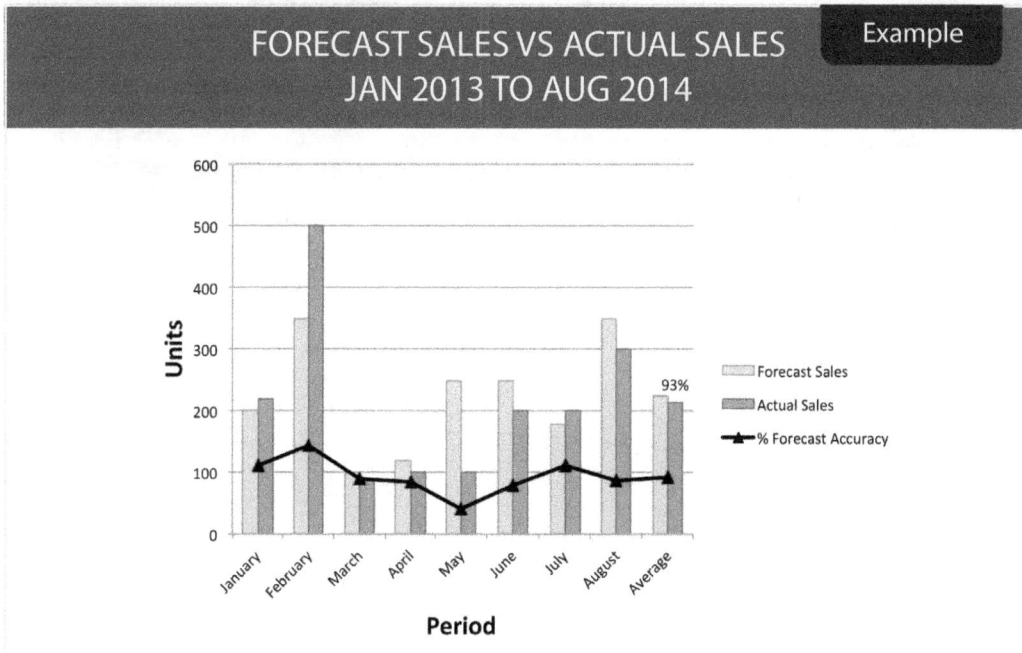

Figure 3.36

When demand is predicted accurately, it can be met in a timely and accurate manner. The opposite is also true and variation in accuracy is key. Planning of people, material and cash flow are just a few of the headaches to expect and the bottom line impact from holding excessive inventories, lost sales, stock outs and losing customers to competition feature as well. Discuss the following among the team:

- o Is the forecast accuracy affecting good planning practices?

- o Is forecast accuracy measured and who is held accountable for the accuracy?

- o Is it frequently reviewed in communication meetings. How are the variations dealt with?

- o Is the forecast trusted, and if not, do tweaked forecasts make their way into the system?

The goal is not to solve all the forecasting issues at this stage but to evaluate the Current State and its impact on the ability to serve the customer.

Step 9: Evaluate Plan Versus Actual Performance

Now that the customer requirement to actual production, as well as forecast accuracy, has been revealed, run a quick check on the plan versus what was actually processed. Using actual production or operations records and the schedule, compare and highlight any variation in what was planned relative to what actually happened (figure 3.37). If variation is evident, find out the reasons for the deviation.

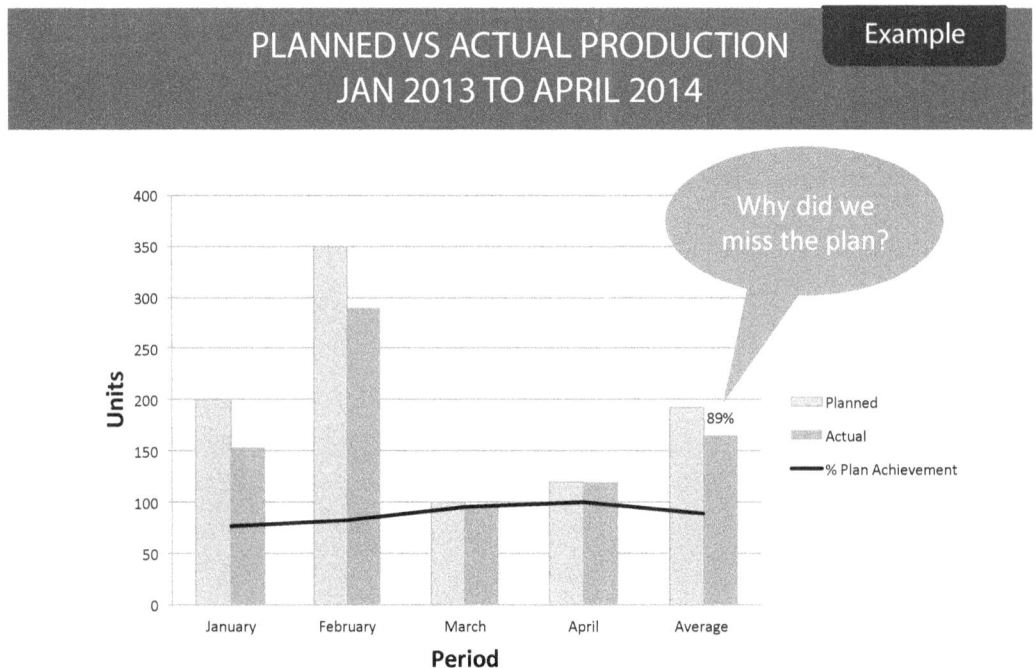

Figure 3.37

Step 10: Evaluate Shift Patterns

The right people need to be in the right places to facilitate flow and ensure processes are not standing due to poor people planning.

Variation in forecast accuracy can play havoc in labour-intensive environments that need to gear up in advance for increases in demand and plan their shifts in good time. It is a critical balance to strike between advanced capacity planning and investing at the right time.

Short-term planning also needs to be acccurate enough to ensure shift patterns are properly managed for each area. An excess in one area could generate overproduction, and a shortage in another could cause a system stand-still. As such the variations we create in the people flow to meet the work flow can make the difference between delivering value and producing mura. Refer to the Current State Map data boxes:

- Look for differences in shift patterns that can cause disruption to the smooth continuation of work across teams.

- Identify unbalanced manpower allocation between departments or process areas that create ebbs and flows in the movement of work.

- Evaluate the variations in shift patterns that impact the constraint and their respective queues.

Update your findings onto the Current State Map (figure 3.38) and continue to verify alignment with the North Star objectives:

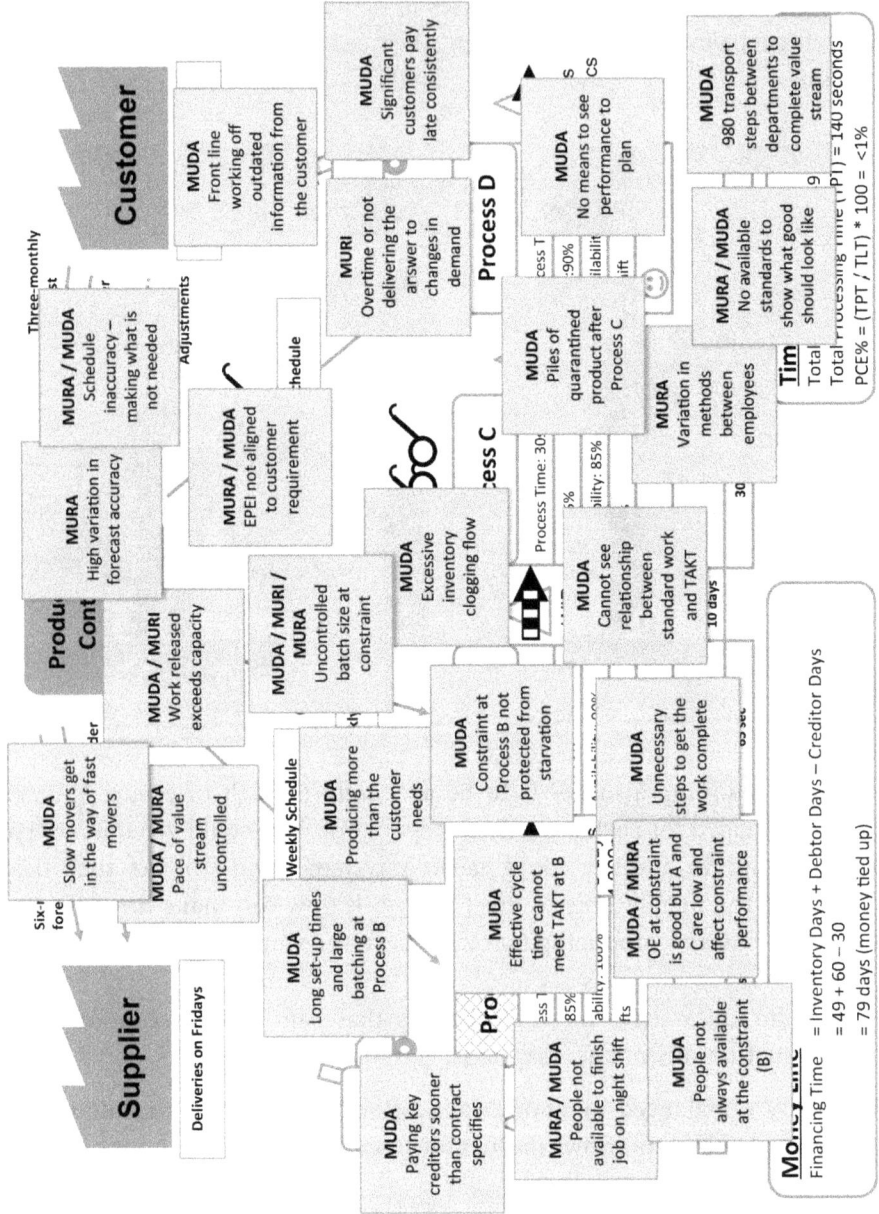

Customer

MUDA Front line working off outdated information from the customer

MUDA Significant customers pay late consistently

MURI Overtime or not delivering the answer to changes in demand

MUDA No means to see performance to plan

Process D

MUDA 980 transport steps between departments to complete value stream

MURA / MUDA No available standards to show what good should look like

Total Processing Time (TPT) = 140 seconds

PCE% = (TPT / TLT) * 100 = <1%

Three-monthly

MURA / MUDA Schedule inaccuracy – making what is not needed

MURA High variation in forecast accuracy

MURA / MUDA EPEI not aligned to customer requirement

Adjustments

MUDA Piles of quarantined product after Process C

MURA Variation in methods between employees

MUDA Slow movers get in the way of fast movers

MUDA / MURA Pace of value stream uncontrolled

MUDA / MURI Work released exceeds capacity

MUDA / MURI / MURA Uncontrolled batch size at constraint

MUDA Excessive inventory clogging flow

MUDA Cannot see relationship between standard work and TAKT

10 days

Weekly Schedule

MUDA Producing more than the customer needs

MUDA Constraint at Process B not protected from starvation

MUDA Unnecessary steps to get the work complete

MUDA Long set-up times and large batching at Process B

MUDA Effective cycle time cannot meet TAKT at B

MUDA / MURA OE at constraint is good but A and C are low and affect constraint performance

Supplier

Deliveries on Fridays

MURA / MUDA People not available to finish job on night shift

MUDA People not always available at the constraint (B)

MUDA Paying key creditors sooner than contract specifies

Money Line

Financing Time = Inventory Days + Debtor Days – Creditor Days

= 49 + 60 – 30

= 79 days (money tied up)

Figure 3.38

Step 11: Evaluate the Muri Post-It Notes

During the gemba walk, muda, mura and muri were identified and captured on Post-Its. Evaluate each of the muri (overburden) found and place it on the map where it occurs. Agree in terms of the North Star, which muri will be pursued. Consolidate your findings and remove those that are not relevant.

Step 12: Compare Capacity to Loading

Whether it be machines or people, you can schedule only so much work into a day and over-loading them can result in muda such as waiting time, defects and rework.

If machines are consistently over-burdened, eventually the wear will result in breakdowns and lost time.

If people are consistently over-burdened, they too will 'wear' and the result may be increased absenteesim, reduced morale and productivity. Sometimes short cuts in standards are taken because there just is not enough time to do it the right way! Over-burdening with regards to responsibility also has a part to play. Review the following questions to determine if capacity loading is a problem:

○ If data is available, evaluate the available capacity at the constraint and bottlenecks in comparison to their loading (figure 3.39). What proportion are they loaded? Is this enough to perform critical activities such as maintenance or problem solving?

○ Is there a policy in place that governs the loading of your resources? What percentage loading has been agreed to and does the data show this is properly upheld?

Capacity is defined as the maximum amount of product or service (output) a process can deliver over a continuous period of time (George, 2005).

Methods for calculating capacity are covered in detail in PROCESS.

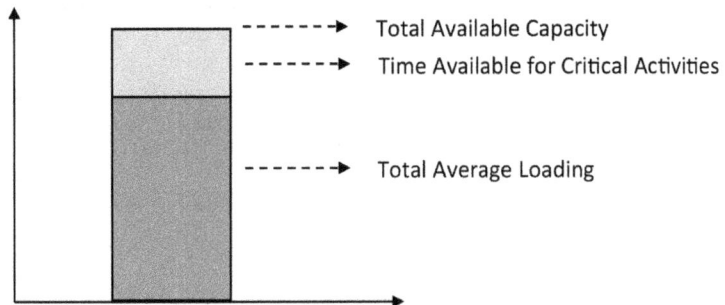

- - - - - → Total Available Capacity
- - - - - → Time Available for Critical Activities

- - - - - → Total Average Loading

Figure 3.39

Step 13: Evaluate Maintenance Principles

This is not a detailed asset care assessment (provided in PROCESS) but there are a few basic questions that can be asked at this stage to outline any concerns with the Current State. Review the results from the OE calculations (availability) and take a walk to the constraint and bottleneck processes. Talk to staff members manning the area as well as those taking care of the equipment. Evaluate what measures are in place to maintain the performance of the equipment:

- Are there any availability problems that cause concern and if so, what, in their opinion, are the major contributing factors. Verify with OE data.

- Are there standard, daily checks to find and fix problems with the equipment?

- Is there a formal handover process to the next shift? If there is a problem with equipment or system availability, how is this handled?

- Are there proper operating instructions and training for the equipment, to ensure it is operated and set correctly?

- Are critical spares kept to ensure that if there is a failure, the downtime is kept to a minimum?

- Is there scheduled maintenance, which takes place according to a standard procedure within a strict time frame?

- Who conducts the repairs, and how well are they trained to perform the procedure?

- Does the maintenance time get tracked, and does it take place according to schedule (or within 10 percent of schedule)?

- Are faults tracked and trends evaluated for problem solving and root cause analysis?

- Are the proper tools available to the technician or operator to conduct the maintenance?

- Is maintenance typically preventive or reactive?

- Is there good cooperation between maintenance personnel and the operators?

- Are operators coached by maintenance staff in the proper use and care of equipment?

If in a service environment, consider the questions applicable to the critical systems and equipment in use.

Step 14: Review Overtime and Absenteeism

How much overtime and the level of absenteeism is a good indication of morale and how severely employees are affected by over-loading. If no overtime is worked, then consider skipping this exercise. If no overtime is worked and there is high absenteeism in comparison to industry standards, there is most likely a cause outside the scope of this exercise that requires attention.

Examples

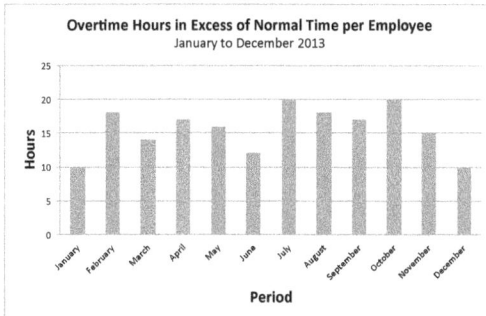

Figure 3.40

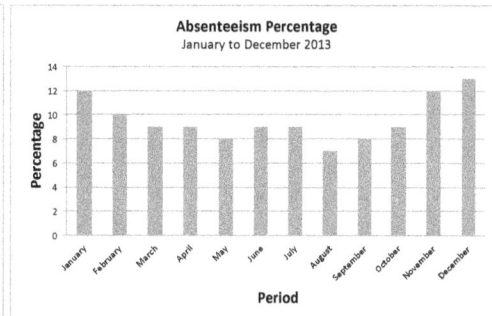

Figure 3.41

o Evaluate working hours and discuss the reasons why overtime is worked (figure 3.40) and what the impact to the employee is.

o Evaluate the absenteeism rate for the company and by area. Is absenteeism higher than the industry standard specific to your sector (figure 3.41)? Is this cause for concern? What is the impact to the constraint and bottlenecks?

Step 15: Review Safety Incidents

There may be several contributing factors to safety incidents, even unrelated to the over-burdening of resources. However, it is worth reviewing what these are and the major causes behind them:

o Review incidents and near misses as well as their documented causes (figure 3.42).

o Highlight issues related to over-burdening.

MAJOR CAUSES OF INCIDENTS AND NEAR MISSES JANUARY TO DECEMBER 2013
18 Incidents and 57 Near Misses

Example

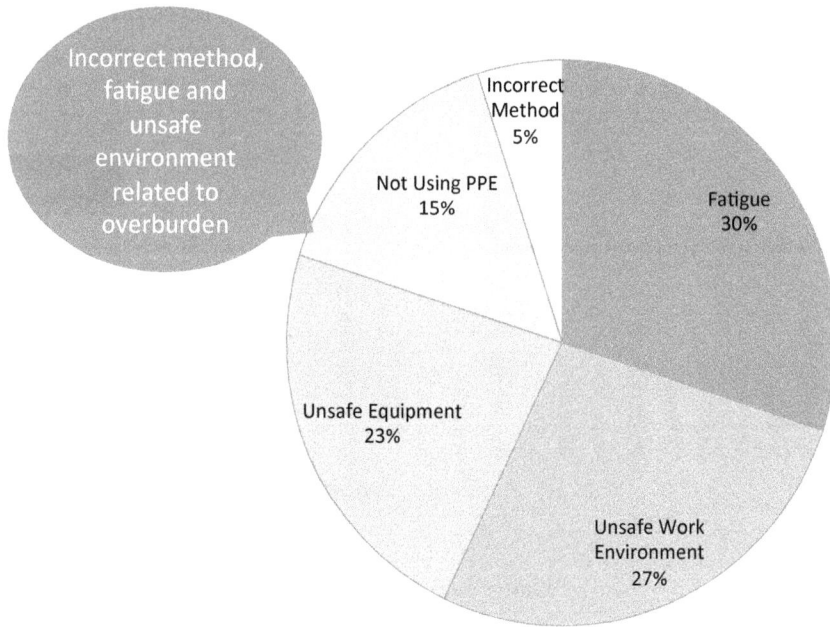

Incorrect method, fatigue and unsafe environment related to overburden

Incorrect Method 5%

Not Using PPE 15%

Fatigue 30%

Unsafe Equipment 23%

Unsafe Work Environment 27%

Figure 3.42

Step 16: Evaluate Problem-Solving Enablers

Ongoing crisis management and chasing 'the smell of the week' is already an indication that the practice of problem solving is not embedded in the culture of the company and that little time is made available to do it within. Completing the 5P Best Practice Evaluation has already exposed opportunities to improve PROBLEM SOLVING but here are a few simple questions that could reveal much about the effectiveness of exposing and fixing problems:

○ Is time formally allocated to reviewing performance and problem solving?

○ Is problem solving a habit and done soon after the event or is the cause already stale by the time someone allocates time to it?

○ Is crisis management rife or do employees stop to reflect and fix problems?

○ Are problems selected formally triggered?

○ Is a simple, yet structured, problem solving approach used to explore, find root causes, implement countermeasures and sustain the gains?

○ Are the same problems constantly being fixed?

○ If a team cannot solve a problem, is there a way to escalate the problem and get formal feedback?

Update your findings onto the Current State Map (figure 3.43) and interrogate alignment with the North Star objectives:

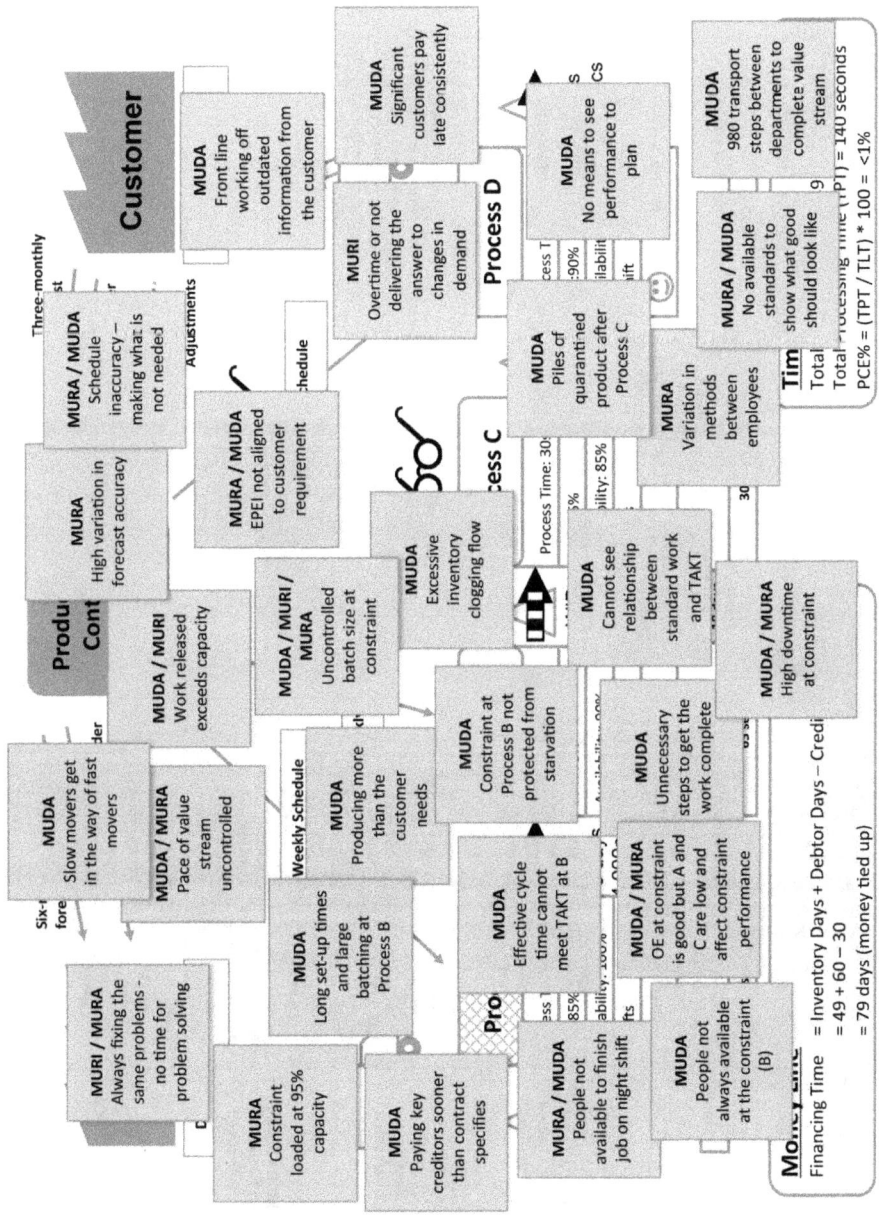

Customer

MUDA
Front line working off outdated information from the customer

MUDA
Significant customers pay late consistently

MURI
Overtime or not delivering the answer to changes in demand

MUDA
No means to see performance to plan

Process D

MUDA
980 transport steps between departments to complete value stream

MURA / MUDA
No available standards to show what good should look like

MURA / MUDA
Schedule inaccuracy – making what is not needed

MURA
High variation in forecast accuracy

MURA / MUDA
EPEI not aligned to customer requirement

Product Control

MUDA / MURI
Work released exceeds capacity

MUDA / MURI / MURA
Uncontrolled batch size at constraint

MUDA
Excessive inventory clogging flow

MUDA
Cannot see relationship between standard work and TAKT

MURA
Variation in methods between employees

MUDA
Slow movers get in the way of fast movers

MUDA / MURA
Pace of value stream uncontrolled

MUDA
Producing more than the customer needs

MUDA
Constraint at Process B not protected from starvation

MUDA
Unnecessary steps to get the work complete

MUDA / MURA
High downtime at constraint

MURI / MURA
Always fixing the same problems - no time for problem solving

MURA
Constraint loaded at 95% capacity

MUDA
Long set-up times and large batching at Process B

MUDA
Effective cycle time cannot meet TAKT at B

MUDA / MURA
OE at constraint is good but A and C are low and affect constraint performance

MUDA
Paying key creditors sooner than contract specifies

MURA / MUDA
People not available to finish job on night shift

MUDA
People not always available at the constraint (B)

Time

Total Processing Time (TPT) = 140 seconds
PCE% = (TPT / TLT) * 100 = <1%

Money tied
Financing Time = Inventory Days + Debtor Days – Credi
= 49 + 60 – 30
= 79 days (money tied up)

Figure 3.43

CLUSTERING OF MUDA, MURA AND MURI

Example

PHYSICAL FLOW			INFORMATION FLOW	PEOPLE FLOW	MONEY FLOW
MURI Overtime or not delivering the answer to changes in demand	**MURA** Constraint loaded at 95% capacity	**MUDA / MURA** Pace of value stream uncontrolled	**MURA / MUDA** Schedule inaccuracy – making what is not needed	**MURA / MUDA** People not available to finish job on night shift	**MUDA** Paying key creditors sooner than contract specifies
MUDA Slow movers get in the way of fast movers	**MUDA** Long set-up times and large batching at Process B	**MUDA** Excessive inventory clogging flow	**MUDA** Front line working off outdated information from the customer	**MUDA** People not always available at the constraint (B)	**MUDA** Significant customers pay late consistently
MUDA / MURI / MURA Work released exceeds capacity	**MUDA** Effective cycle time cannot meet; TAKT at B	**MURA / MUDA** EPEI not aligned to customer requirement	**MURA / MUDA** No available standards to show what good should look like	**MURI / MURA** Always fixing the same problems - no time for problem solving	
MURA High variation in forecast accuracy	**MUDA / MURI / MURA** Uncontrolled batch size at constraint	**MUDA / MURA** OE at constraint is good but A and C affect constraint performance	**MUDA** No means to see performance to plan		
MUDA Unnecessary steps to get the work complete	**MUDA** Constraint at Process B not protected from starvation	**MUDA** Constraint at Process B not protected from starvation	**MUDA** Cannot see relationship between standard work and TAKT		
	MUDA / MURA High downtime at constraint	**MUDA** 980 transport steps between departments to complete value stream			
	MUDA Piles of quarantined product after Process C	**MURA** Variation in methods between employees			

To help you navigate the next section cluster each of the Post-Its from 3.43 under the headings shown in table 3.16. Expect some overlap between the headings and for cause-effect relationships between the headings. Consider labeling each Post-It to refer back to the map, or photograph the map to show where the problem was first positioned.

Table 3.16

✔ FOR YOU TO TRY

- Evaluate the muda Post-Its from the gemba walk.
- Compare what the customer wants to what is actually produced or provided.
- Evaluate the constraint and discuss ways to exploit the current resources.
- Capture the transport and motion waste in a spaghetti diagram.
- Evaluate the mura Post-Its from the gemba walk.
- Understand and break down OE to expose variation.
- Evaluate the scheduling principles in play that produce mura.
- Compare the forecast to actual sales and the impact on planning.
- Compare the plan to actual performance exposing reasons for missing the target.
- Review the people flow and impact of variation in shift patterns, especially on the constraint.
- Evaluate the muri Post-Its from the gemba walk.
- Compare the capacity capability to how the resources are actually loaded.
- Review the preventive measures in place to preserve equipment or system availability.
- Understand the loading of people and the impact on absenteeism and performance.
- Review safety incidents and near misses for evidence of over-burdening.
- Evaluate how often and how well problem solving activities take place to prevent the recurrence of problems.
- Structure all the findings into a holistic view on the Current State Map.
- Cluster the findings under headings to show the split between the physical, information, people and money flow to prepare for the next section.

DEVELOP THE FUTURE STATE
CREATE THE FUTURE STATE VISION

❓ WHAT IS THIS?

A tremendous amount of work has now been done understanding the needs of the customer and the business, developing the Current State Map, evaluating the Current State and summarising the findings into areas of focus. Without taking the next steps to develop the Future State Map, implementation may be vague at best, and implementation may not be representative of the true needs of the business.

'You've got to think about big things while you're doing small things, so that all the small things go in the right direction.'

Alvin Toffler, writer and futurist

The Future State Vision is developed prior to the Future State Map and provides guidance to its design and which tools, techniques and methodologies should be included on the map, and later, the implementation plan (figure 3.44). The Future State Vision can be described as follows:

- It is a formal clarification of where the business needs to go to become successful – the ultimate, desired target condition for the Value Stream.

- It confirms what must not be altered in the process – what to preserve that is working.

- It helps to establish the pattern of activities that will collectively shape the business towards a future reality.

- It focuses people's efforts to avoid the overall direction derailing through contradicting ideas and opinions.

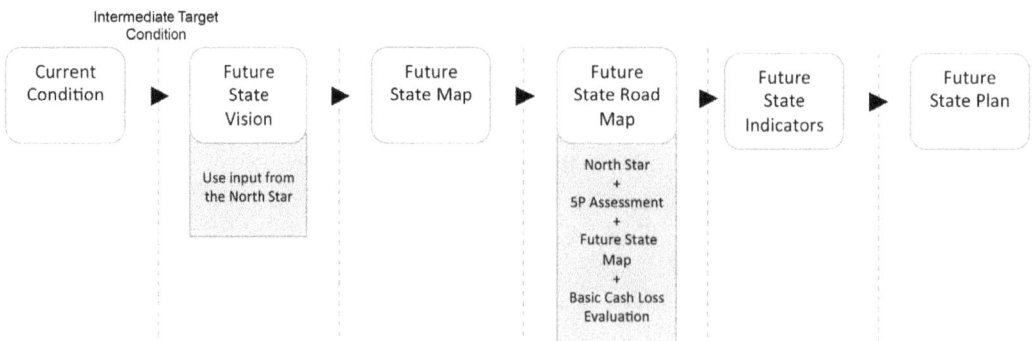

Figure 3.44

Not all employees will be able to relate to the long-term vision for the Value Stream. Current perceptions will include all the 'sacred cows' so it may seem like an impossible feat, to which they are unable to connect. It is up to leadership to have a plan for the long-term vision and to create intermediary visions or bite-size chunks that will lead towards the North Star. This may be easier for employees to digest.

You know the vision is successful when employees are able to relate their daily activities to it. You may have heard the example of the cleaner who worked at NASA. When asked what we was doing (and he was performing his cleaning duties at the time), he answered, with sincerity, that he was helping put people on the Moon. He could clearly see how his activities would achieve the vision.

Once a target condition or vision is defined, it should be preserved until the needs of the North Star change. However, the means for achieving it may vary over time.

❓ WHY IS THIS HELPFUL?

Defining the Future State Vision for the Value Stream is critical to the success of the improvement strategy – for example:

- ○ It defines the situation the business must reach at specific milestones in the future.
- ○ It creates clear direction to ensure all activities are given the correct priorities, and that employees are able to establish whether what they are working on contributes to or hinders progress.
- ○ When obstacles are encountered along the way, it is possible to overcome them and keep moving towards the goal, rather than choosing a different, easier path.
- ○ It protects the business and employees from poorly-focused 'fads' forced from above.
- ○ It motivates employees to contribute and take action.
- ○ Proposals are not evaluated independently but as part of the steps to strive towards the vision.

❓ HOW TO DO IT

Step 1: Align the Future State Vision to the North Star

Refer to the results of the North Star before proceeding. This will help to re-engage the team and clarify the direction this exercise must take. Remind everyone involved of the key areas for change to address strategic intents that will help the business to prosper and which of these are influenced by the Value Stream construct.

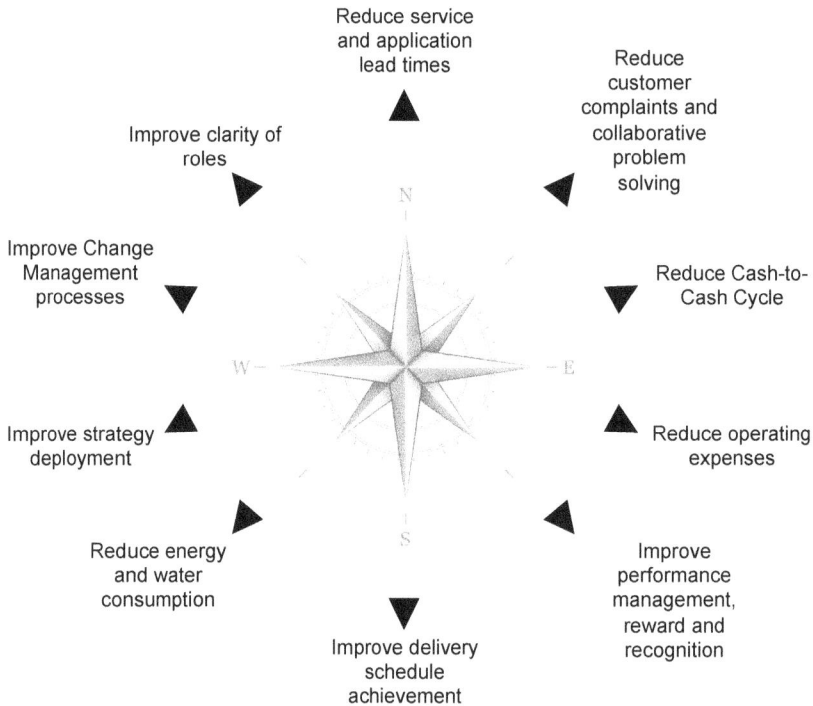

Step 2: Evaluate Process-Volume Type

There are many paths to developing an improvement strategy. Be cautious of adopting and replicating what other companies have implemented without customising it first. To copy and paste what others are doing can result in a lot of energy being wasted by introducing 'improvements' that actually have little or no impact. Having said this, there is certainly value in learning from others and saving time in developing an approach from scratch, just be sure the approach taken is what the customer requires and where the business needs to go.

Using the Product-Process Matrix in figure 3.45 puts the current condition of the Value Stream into perspective and calls attention to the influence volume and product life cycle will have on the process design going forward. This will provide additional insight into what elements of Operational Excellence are more suitable to incorporate into the Future State Map, and which companies to use as a benchmark.

PRODUCT-PROCESS MATRIX*

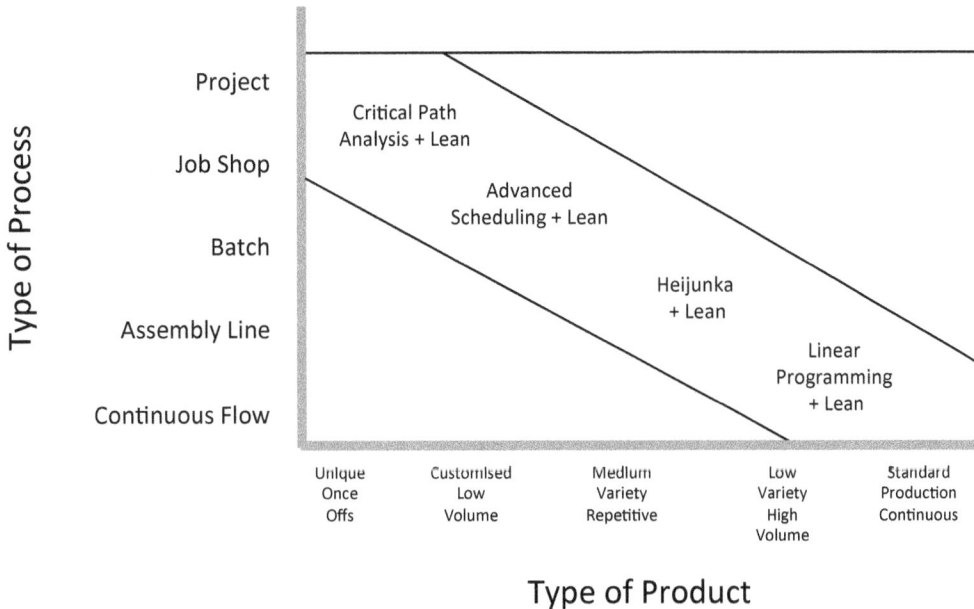

Type of Process (vertical axis)

- Project
- Job Shop
- Batch
- Assembly Line
- Continuous Flow

Critical Path Analysis + Lean

Advanced Scheduling + Lean

Heijunka + Lean

Linear Programming + Lean

Type of Product (horizontal axis)

| Unique Once Offs | Customised Low Volume | Medium Variety Repetitive | Low Variety High Volume | Standard Production Continuous |

Figure 3.45

*Hayes and Wheelright (1984) originally proposed the product-process matrix to match the type of product with the appropriate production process and the matrix has been published in various formats in the context of manufacturing strategy (Hill, 2000), operations strategy (Grütter, 2010) and lean thinking (Bicheno, 2004).

The matrix suggests that the process design and layout evolve as the volume of products or services moves through its life cycle. Failure to adjust process design and systems could lead to a Value Stream that is out of alignment and not fit for purpose.

Several principles of Operational Excellence will apply across the matrix but how the workload is scheduled and managed, will vary depending on volumes and process type. This is important because it will influence where you place your emphasis when designing the Future State Map. Although the Heijunka System (workload levelling) and pull systems may work extremely well in automotive manufacturing, this could be a very expensive exercise in a construction business with one-off projects that require more focus on project management best practices.

The Glenday Sieve Analysis conducted earlier in the book provided data on the process and volumes. It is quite common that an organisation will have two or more areas marked on the matrix, and as such, the Future State design may need to accommodate this. If one of these streams was selected to concentrate on in the mapping exercise, continue this train of thought through to Future State. Keep in mind that different streams have different volumes, different process designs and may need to be handled individually, each with their own Future State Map.

Step 3: Create a Common Understanding of Value Stream Velocity

If your North Star describes specific goals for quick lead times, customer responsiveness, flexibility, fast cash-conversion and so on, the need to improve Value Stream performance would be non-negotiable. But what is an adequate vision for a world-class Value Stream? Speed comes to mind, but then the nagging sensation follows that speed is not enough. If the Value Stream delivers speed but the wrong quality or the wrong product, you may end up with a lot of cost and very little customer satisfaction. Speed in the right direction, however, is a powerful marriage and the vision for an optimised Value Stream can build on this point of departure – a vision for velocity that encompasses speed, flexibility and the delivery of value.

There are a multitude of principles, tools and techniques available, and the sum of these will not amount to an improvement vision. First, define a target condition and then match the right principles, tools and techniques to collaborate towards it. This is more compelling and will drive the correct behaviours. For example, the vision is not to implement Hoshin Kanri (Policy Deployment), 5S and standard work. The vision is to create velocity in the Value Stream and the means will include a variety of carefully selected activities implemented collectively, to result in the right behaviours and outcomes that deliver on the North Star. Value Stream velocity comprises the following characteristics:

Speed

Delivering the product or service in the shortest possible time, from the time the need is triggered until the customer has been satisfied.

Flexibility

Adapting to the changing needs of the customer and market. Low-cost flexibility is a competitive advantage for organisations and is achieved through various means:

- Process Flexibility
  To achieve a mixed sequence of products or services, one-piece at a time according to market pull through TAKT time.

- Product Flexibility
  To standardise products and bring customisation as close to the end of the Value Stream as possible.

- Volume Flexibility
  To separate mixed factories into their own management strategies to cope with diverse volumes.

- People Flexibility
  To cross-skill, create a pipeline of skills and develop contingencies for demand fluctuation.

Value

Removing obstacles that deflect from delivering value. The systematic removal of muda, mura and muri to flow value into the hands of the customer.

Equipped with an image of what good looks like in Value Stream performance, the team can move forward to developing a vision to achieve the target condition.

Step 4: Agree the Scope and Longevity for the Future State Vision

Different enterprises may approach the Future State Vision differently depending on their individual needs. It is recommended that the scope of the vision be agreed before developing it. For example – will the Future State Vision:

- o Apply locally to a particular Value Stream, area or division only?
- o Be developed for the entire Enterprise?
- o Extend to the entire Supply Chain?

Discuss the scope and agree for what the vision is being developed for, as well as for how long.

Step 5: Develop an Improvement Vision for the Future State

The vision will depict in a few words, a bold, ongoing commitment to achieve a desired condition. It must be so clear that it can be articulated in less than one minute and written on a single page. It is also a shared vision – communicated, supported and ultimately achieved by the senior leadership team. The more participation and involvement obtained during the development, the better the acceptance and emotional connection will be. See the example provided on the following page.

Example

FUTURE STATE IMPROVEMENT VISION

In two years' time, we aim to be the African leader in protecting our customers against unforeseen circumstances. As the leader in Africa, we will:

- Outshine our competition in our ability to turnaround claims, first time right.
- Develop and challenge our employees to be the best in the industry.
- Satisfy our stakeholders through improved profitability.

We will achieve this, by:

- Achieving velocity in all critical processes.
- Developing skilled problem solvers throughout the organisation to address customer problems.
- Reducing the environmental footprint to preserve the planet for future generations.
- Focusing on the reduction of unnecessary cash losses.
- Raising the performance of our people practices.
- Improving the climate for change and growth.

We will know we have achieved our vision, when:

- Market share has grown by 25 percent.
- Working capital is down by 18 percent.
- Water and energy consumption is down by 30 percent.
- We have achieved a consistent year-on-year growth in net profit of 5 percent.
- Problems are solved daily, at the lowest level in the organisation, using a scientific method.
- Employee retention has improved by 80 percent.

FOR YOU TO TRY

- Consider who should take part in the development of the Future State Vision.

- Review the North Star to refresh the team on the critical focus areas for change.

- Refer to the Glenday Sieve Analysis, which shows the summary of the typical streams in the business.

- Evaluate the Product-Process Matrix and agree where the organisation is positioned. Discuss possible implications to the Future State Vision.

- Review the characteristics of a performing Value Stream and understand the contributing factors to achieving velocity.

- Agree on the scope of the Vision and how far across the organisation it will be applied.

- Agree on how far into the future the Vision will be designed for.

- Develop a clear, compelling message that describes to what the business is aspiring, how it aims to achieve this, and how it will know when it gets there.

DEVELOP THE FUTURE STATE
CREATE THE FUTURE STATE MAP

❓ WHAT IS THIS?

Armed with a Future State Vision and the gaps identified during the Current State mapping, you are now in a position to develop the Value Stream Map into a blueprint for improvement. The Future State Map will serve as a visual target condition for the purposes of:

- Gaining consensus for the improvement strategy.
- Designing how a vision for velocity will look in the future.
- Evaluating the improvement potential in the form of Future State metrics.
- Breaking it down into manageable, implementation phases.

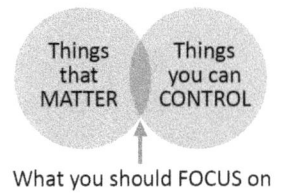

Things that MATTER

Things you can CONTROL

What you should FOCUS on

If it was agreed to develop intermediate target conditions to achieve a longer-term vision, then it is worth also developing intermediary maps to show the way in stages. A 'pie in the sky' Future State Map can often lead to disillusionment and disconnect between where the enterprise is going and the steps to get there. For example, if the vision caters for a five-year plan, consider developing a map for the five years with input from the key decision makers, but then develop a one-year Future State Map with input from those whose buy-in will be critical and that leads to the five-year plan.

There will be problems identified that cannot be resolved in the short term due to technology limitations, product design, resource availability and so on. Focus on those aspects that can be changed in the required time frame, and find a good mix of short, medium and long-term improvements to lead to the vision.

This is a dynamic process and the Future State developed today, becomes the Current State of tomorrow. Perodically evaluate the North Star to trigger new improvement needs, which in turn will trigger the need to review the Current State again.

❓ WHY IS THIS HELPFUL?

The greatest advantage of completing a Future State Map, is to have a means to realise improvements identified during the Current State mapping. As mentioned earlier, improvement aligned to the North Star is impossible by completing the Current State alone. Advantages include:

- A system's approach to improving the whole.

- A blueprint plan to guide the implementation.

- A visual way to see what must be done, the outcome expected, and how well the implementation is fairing against that expectation.

- The Future State Map will become the baseline for the next improvement.

❓ HOW TO DO IT

This section presents guidelines to reduce muda, mura and muri to evolve a well-rounded Future State that takes all perspectives of flow into account. In the introduction to Current State mapping, the Value Stream map was described as a storyboard of the physical, information, people and money flows, and how they are linked. You will use the clustering of opportunities completed in table 3.16 to create your own storyboard of what must change in the Value Stream to achieve the vision.

Develop the Physical Flow:

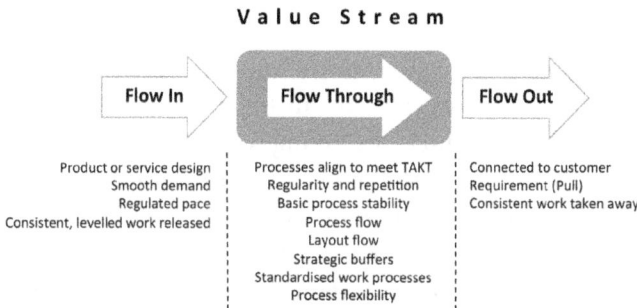

Value Stream

Flow In   Flow Through   Flow Out

Product or service design
Smooth demand
Regulated pace
Consistent, levelled work released

Processes align to meet TAKT
Regularity and repetition
Basic process stability
Process flow
Layout flow
Strategic buffers
Standardised work processes
Process flexibility

Connected to customer
Requirement (Pull)
Consistent work taken away

- Improve product or service design

- Smooth demand

- Improve performance to TAKT time

- Create regularity and repetition

- Reduce quality variation

- Create continuous flow

- Position strategic buffers

- Pace the system

- Connect to demand.

Develop the Information Flow:

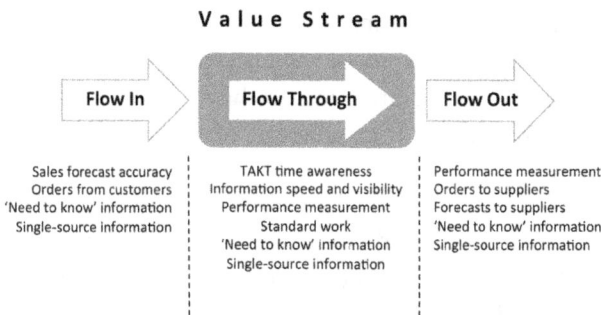

Value Stream

Flow In   Flow Through   Flow Out

Sales forecast accuracy
Orders from customers
'Need to know' information
Single-source information

TAKT time awareness
Information speed and visibility
Performance measurement
Standard work
'Need to know' information
Single-source information

Performance measurement
Orders to suppliers
Forecasts to suppliers
'Need to know' information
Single-source information

- Create a TAKT image

- Facilitate velocity through information

- Align performance measurement

- Reduce manual adjustments

- Synchronise information flow.

Develop the People Flow:

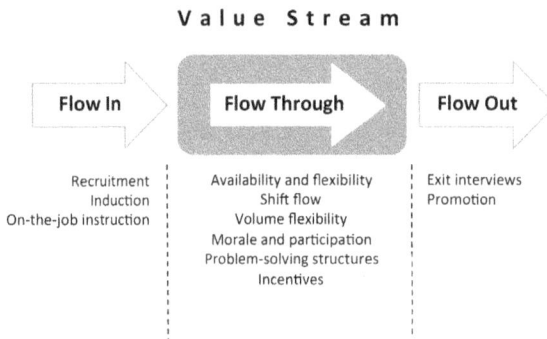

Value Stream

Flow In → Flow Through → Flow Out

Flow In	Flow Through	Flow Out
Recruitment	Availability and flexibility	Exit interviews
Induction	Shift flow	Promotion
On-the-job instruction	Volume flexibility	
	Morale and participation	
	Problem-solving structures	
	Incentives	

- Put the best skills at the constraint
- Develop a plan for people availability
- Develop a plan for people flexibility
- Develop a scenario plan for volume flexibility
- Design shifts to facilitate flow.

Develop the Money Flow:

Value Stream

Flow In → Flow Through → Flow Out

Flow In	Flow Through	Flow Out
Debtor management	Lead time	Creditor management
	Operational expense	
	Performance measurement	

- Improve throughput
- Reduce inventory
- Reduce operating expenses
- Link projects to financial gains.

Some elements may be covered in one of the other books in the series, but the Value Stream diagrams above show the context in which the changes are recommended. If it is clear that a particular section is not relevant to the Future State Vision agreed to, skip to the next part and proceed with the thought process. The intention is to use the guidelines to trigger debates on options to achieve the true potential for the Value Stream. At this stage, all root causes for the problems identified may not be clear, so bear in mind that this step is still to be taken.

Step 1: Gather the Critical Stakeholders

The critical stakeholders may be the same team that developed the Current State Map but consider how far into the future you will be mapping, and decide from there. If you are about to create a five-year Future State Map, you will require the key decision makers in the process who also have a system's view of the enterprise. If you are about to create a six-month or one-year Future State plan, consider having the right decision makers and participants who are closer to the management of the area involved. In choosing who will participate:

- Use a facilitator to guide the discussions and preserve the bigger picture. Some enterprises will use an outside facilitator or if an internal facilitator is used, ensure he or she has the support of the top leadership.

- The right decision makers need to be present because decisions will have to be made.

○ Diverse knowledge should be available to properly assess the recommendations and possibilities. If this is a supply chain example, you would expect to see representation from each of the main departments within the supply chain. If critical process design changes are in store, including representation from safety, health and environment may also be required.

Step 2: Agree on the Scope

When the Current State Map was developed, one of the steps involved agreeing on the start and stop points.

The team that will complete the Future State Map will more than likely use the same points to depict the scope of the Future State Map, however, it is worthwhile confirming this in case the team requires clarification or a different decision has been made on the scope of the Future State.

If new team members have been included in the Future State mapping, include a review of the findings from the Current State mapping activities as well as the Future State Vision before proceeding.

Step 3: Develop the Physical Flow

The goal of improving the physical flow is to establish what must look different in order to achieve velocity in how the product or service is moved through the process into the hands of the customer. It relates to the physical path taken, as well the time taken to achieve this. Figure 3.46 summarises three aspects that should be explored when designing the Future State and we will discuss a selection of them to address the muda, mura and muri identified in the Current State. Review your own findings, and select the best countermeasures to develop the Future State with, and capture each decision on a flipchart.

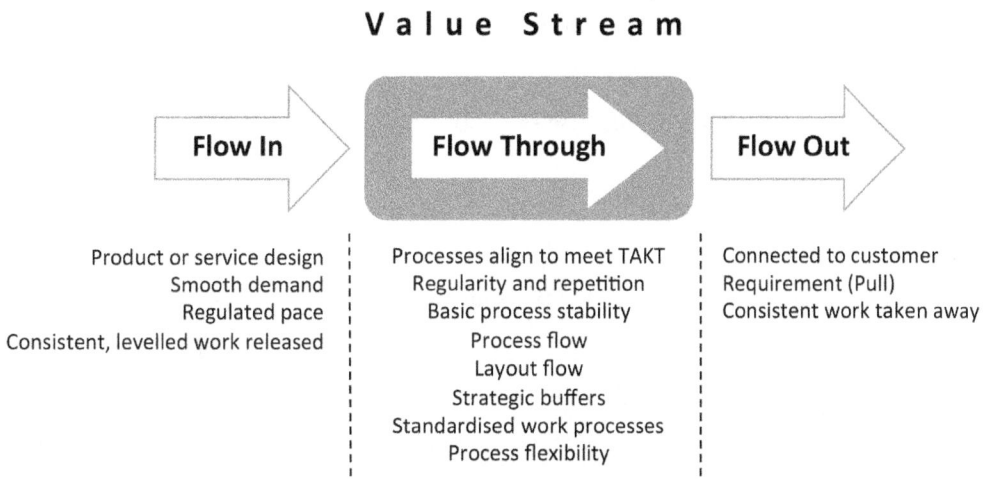

Value Stream

Flow In	Flow Through	Flow Out
Product or service design	Processes align to meet TAKT	Connected to customer
Smooth demand	Regularity and repetition	Requirement (Pull)
Regulated pace	Basic process stability	Consistent work taken away
Consistent, levelled work released	Process flow	
	Layout flow	
	Strategic buffers	
	Standardised work processes	
	Process flexibility	

Figure 3.46

Improve Product or Service Design

○ Refer to the results of the Glenday Sieve Analysis. Rationalise by improving designs of blue stream items to meet yellow or green status. The impact on parts, materials and tool rationalisation can be significant, where the benefit far exceeds the effort. This is not a small job and usually requires a dedicated team but the returns in inventory savings and reduced process complexity make it an attractive challenge.

○ Rationalisation also means improving on specifications and standards and may appear uneconomic at first but the payoff in simplicity of control, flexibility, inventory and customer responsiveness, is worth it.

○ Improve the product or service design to allow for standard processing as far downstream as possible so that customisation to suit the customer takes place as far down the process as is possible. This will positively impact demand smoothing covered in the next point.

○ The conversion of red streams into yellow streams and yellow streams into green streams should be fundamental in achieving Operational Excellence. In one organisation, 52 types of stock were reduced to just 18 to demonstrate the potential of this countermeasure.

Smooth Demand

Accommodating failure demand as opposed to value demand will prevent the successful implementation of many of the suggestions that follow. Think back to the Current State findings on actual work processed versus true demand. Make decisions to reduce failure demand, match processing capability to value demand and stay on top of the pulse of the customer's real needs:

○ Incentivise customers and distributors for regular orders and promote better buying practices.

○ Offer better deals for placing orders early to capitalise on improved forecasting, planning and regularity.

○ Reduce internal incentives that promote spikes in demand, and increase incentives that stabilise demand.

○ Introduce product or service variety as far downstream as possible.

○ Adjust systemic meeting agendas to visualise demand performance, assign accountability for demand variation and to trigger response to problems.

○ Improve performance to drive behaviours that promote regularity in inventory levels.

o Group common sub-assemblies together into the schedule. Be aware of overproducing as this should be used for regular orders or firm orders of the red and blue streams.

o Allocate formal 'catch-up' time into the schedule. Be aware not to promote overproduction but rather use any excess capacity for problem solving and improvement time.

o Give preference to regular orders and separate the erratic orders from the main stream.

o Be aware of very large orders disrupting the schedule of the rest of the orders. Negotiate with customers to break them down into buckets of regular supply to allow for a mixed-model approach.

Align Processes to Meet TAKT Time

Refer to the findings illustrating the process times in relation to TAKT time:

o Identify which process times must improve to meet TAKT time and by how much.

o Typically process times will have a 10 percent buffer built in to accommodate losses – for example, if TAKT time is 58 seconds, your processes should be geared to meet 52 seconds.

o If the processes are all currently capable of achieving TAKT time consistently, either the team will agree that no changes are required or that further improvement could yield savings in labour time, the flexibility to support other areas in peak times or just to have more time available to conduct problem solving activities.

o Set a policy to include TAKT time in standard operating procedures to ensure the documented timing of each step to TAKT time is available.

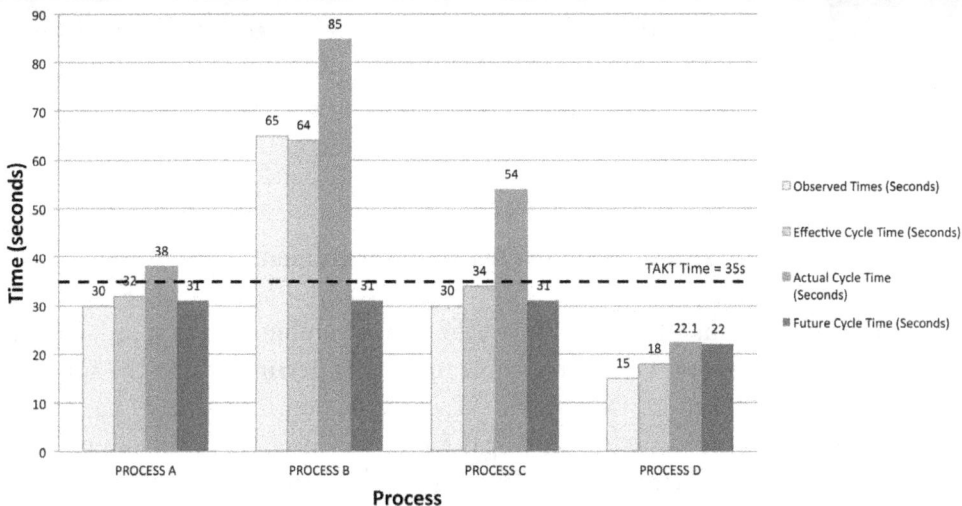

Figure 3.47

Figure 3.47 now includes the Future State cycle time that must be achieved. In the example the team would engage in kaizen activities to eliminate unncessary losses identified in OE and reduce the times to acceptable standards. This is discussed further in PROCESS and PROBLEM SOLVING.

Create Regularity and Repetition in the Schedule

The results of the Glenday Sieve Analysis highlighted issues that can be addressed by the way in which processes are scheduled:

- Protect green stream items by giving them a fixed slot in the schedule or by dedicating resources to this line only. If any green stream items fall into a declining market and are at the end of their life cycle, consider excluding them from the fixed schedule.

- Dedicate employees who enjoy repetition to the green stream.

- Identify the capability changes required to convert yellow streams to green streams. Include converted yellow stream items into the fixed schedule.

- Identify red stream items that should be removed, separated into their own 'job shop', outsourced or charged more for. Be aware of red streams of strategic importance and refer to Chapter 4 for ways to determine the true cost savings.

- Agree on the cycle of 'every product every interval' to be achieved. Develop a Future State schedule to reflect the transition to the new EPEI (table 3.17):

| Day | Every Product Every 4 Days On Line 1 | | | | | | Example | |
| | Product | | | | | | Total Changeover Time (min) | Total Run Time (min) |
	A	B	C	D	E	F		
Monday	445						30	475
Tuesday	275	170					30	475
Wednesday		310	120				30	460
Thursday				120	120	120	90	450
Friday	445						30	475
Total	1165	480	120	120	120	120	210	2335

Table 3.17

Create Basic Process Stability through Quality Improvement

It was mentioned previously that to achieve velocity is a combination of speed, flexibility and delivering value. Speed, however, of poor quality is detrimental to the survival of a cost-conscious organisation. During the OE exercise, you may already have tackled some of this section. If the losses influencing the ability to meet TAKT time were affected by quality performance – defects, rework, backtracking, clarifications and corrections – actions may already have been agreed to (figure 3.48):

- Identify processes that require improvement in quality yield.

- Set targets for improvement based on historical performance and process capability for improved throughput yield.

Figure 3.48

Improve Flow between Processes

Some of the points covered in this section may be more suitable to process-level improvement (see PROCESS) but we include it here should there be changes which may influence the development of the high-level mapping. If this is unsuitable for the level you are designing, skip to the next section.

In many Value Streams, overproduction, inventory, instability, changeover times and so on have significant effects on the batch sizes moving through the processes. Figure 3.49 illustrates a typical batch operation where work is allowed to build up impacting on lead time, quality and productivity:

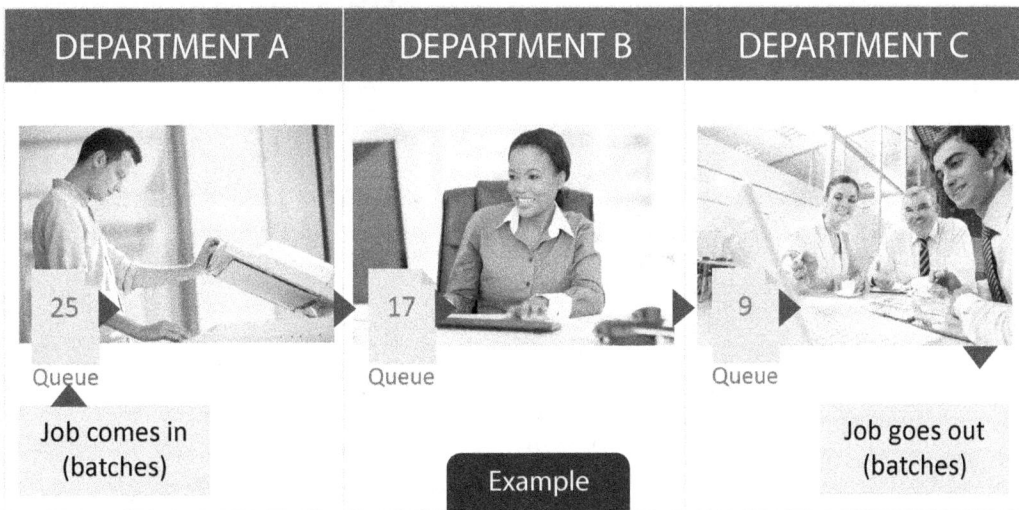

Figure 3.49

Refer to your clustering of Post-It notes and pinpoint possible effects coming from this cause. Agree on how this will be changed using the following as a guideline:

- Preserve:
  Decide on processes that are to remain in batches. If this is a shared resource or a constraint this may be best left to batch-logic.

- Reduce:
  Identify processes where batch sizes are too large resulting in unnecessary congestion. Understand possible reasons for the batch size selected and reduce the batch size accordingly (figure 3.50).

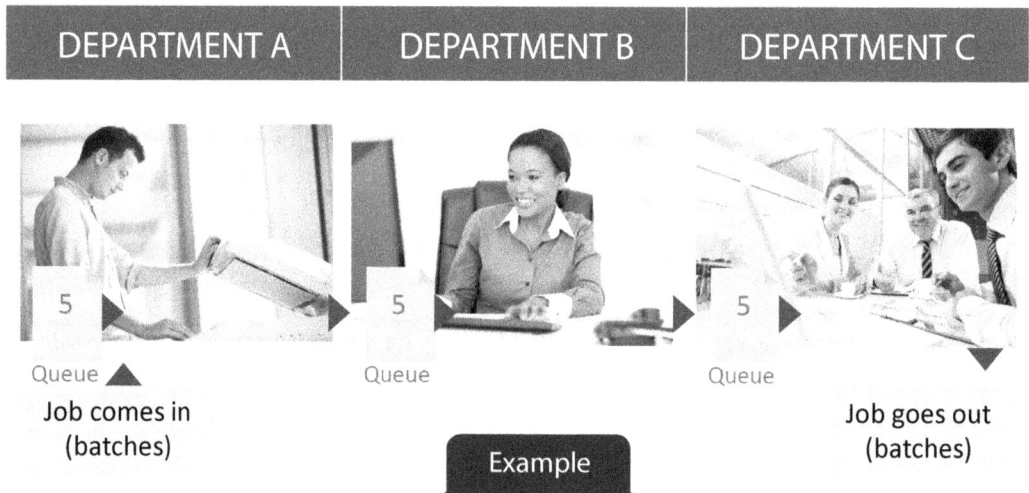

Figure 3.50

- Connect:
  Decide on processes that can transition to one-piece flow. This offers the potential to connect processes together where one unit is passed on at a time between resources with no queuing inbetween. Process times are reasonably balanced to TAKT time and quality problems are easier to spot. This cell could be fed by a batch process that is shared between departments (figure 3.51).

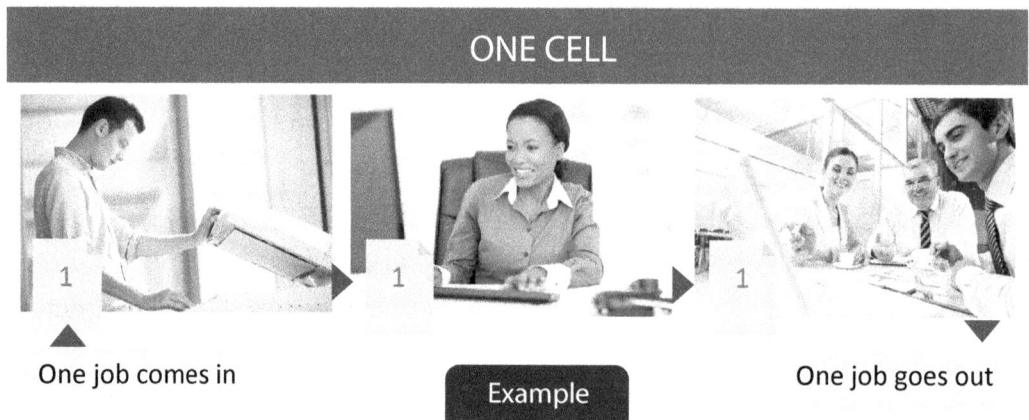

Figure 3.51

○ Combine:

Identify processes that can be combined so that one cell performs the entire process using one resource. One employee has the required skills and facilities to complete the task for all departments and meet TAKT time. Lead time and ownership improve, and this cell could be fed by a batch process supporting many cells (figure 3.52).

ONE CELL

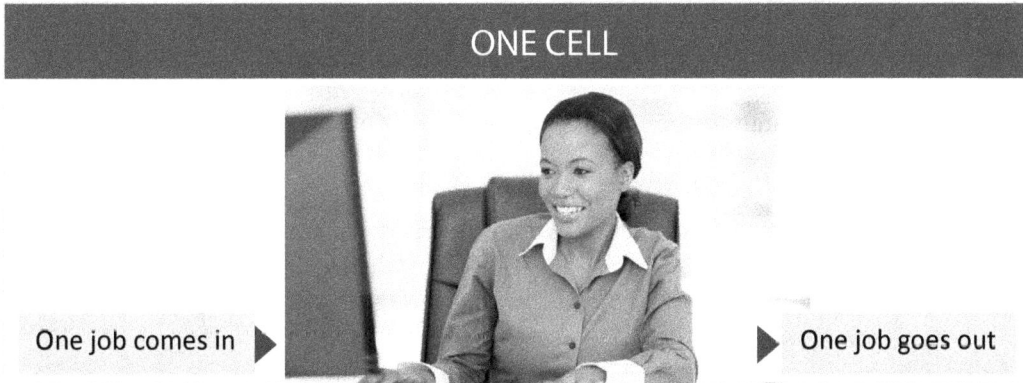

One job comes in ▶   ▶ One job goes out

Figure 3.52

Balancing tactics, paper kaizen, standard work and employee numbers will be covered in PROCESS.

TIPS

Dealing with 'freed' capacity can be tricky. It is important that Operational Excellence not be associated with retrenchment or staff cuts because the change effort relies on the support and buy-in of employees. Having a strategy to deal with changes in capacity, as a result of the improvements, is key. Consider the following options when developing this strategy:

○ Create new revenue streams and absorb extra capacity there.

○ Coach and mentor employees to take on new challenges, with career growth in mind.

○ Reduce overtime and temporary labour costs.

○ Move out-sourced work in house.

○ If there is very little or no growth in the market, make use of natural attrition strategies and review new-hire strategies.

○ Improve quality levels of the work you do.

○ Take the time to build stronger customer relationships.

○ Use the opportunity to refine and grow supplier relationships.

○ Use the available time to accelerate continuous improvement activities.

○ Improve flexibility and capacity going forward through cross-training.

Improve the Layout Flow

The motion of people, information or products was evaluated using the spaghetti diagram and with the muda of transportation and operator motion visualised, it can now be minimised. At the high-level you are interested in reducing the inter-departmental motion (figure 3.53) and at the process-level you will reduce movement through improved cell design and process layout. The future state design in PURPOSE is concerned with the high-level view:

○ Review Current State spaghetti diagram and batching decisions

○ Evaluate waste of motion and what can be avoided

○ Design proposed spaghetti diagram and indicate the savings in distance.

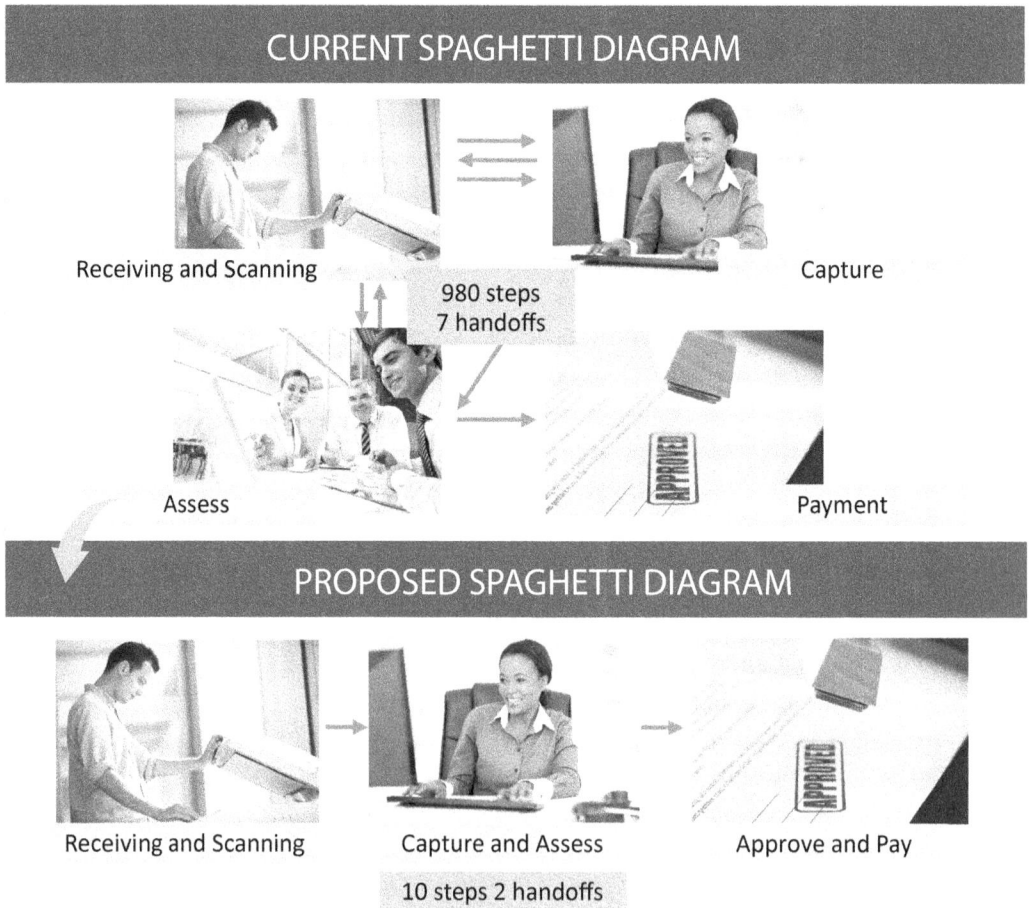

Figure 3.53

It will not always be possible to optimise layouts for all products or services, but reviewing the green stream items by volume, provides you with a priority list to design from. Flexibility and simplicity is the key to good layout design. Customer needs will change over time, so be careful not to design a layout that will be difficult to adjust to changing markets. This can be an expensive mistake!

Position Strategic Buffers

Buffers were described earlier as shields used to guard against fluctuations and promote the flow of work, and are positioned in such a way as to prevent the disruption of supply. Where to place a buffer (figure 3.54), and how big to make it can make or break the flow in the system. Position buffers when you need to deal with the following in your Future State:

○ A resource is shared and cannot be connected.

○ There are differences in processing times, making it impossible to connect the flows.

○ The constraint waits for work.

○ You need to produce to stock to buffer against varying demands.

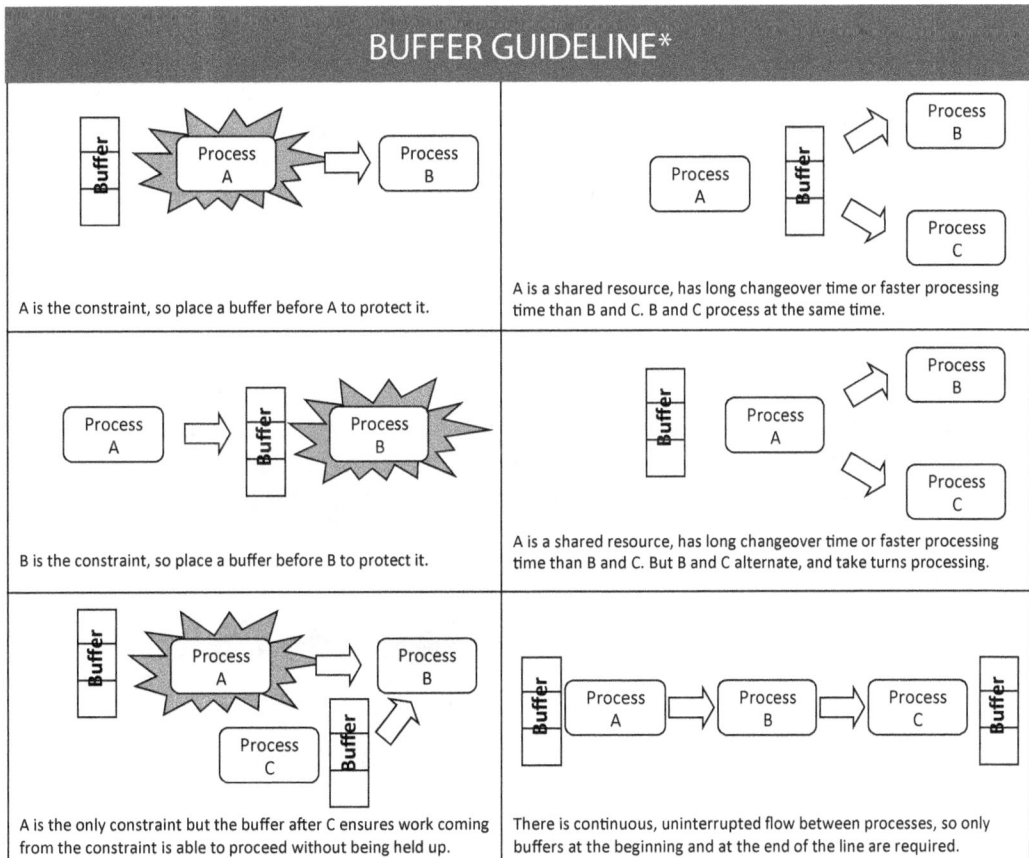

BUFFER GUIDELINE*

A is the constraint, so place a buffer before A to protect it.	A is a shared resource, has long changeover time or faster processing time than B and C. B and C process at the same time.
B is the constraint, so place a buffer before B to protect it.	A is a shared resource, has long changeover time or faster processing time than B and C. But B and C alternate, and take turns processing.
A is the only constraint but the buffer after C ensures work coming from the constraint is able to proceed without being held up.	There is continuous, uninterrupted flow between processes, so only buffers at the beginning and at the end of the line are required.

*Adapted from the Six Building Blocks (Bicheno, 2004)   Figure 3.54

The objective is to create velocity, and often it is necessary to position strategic buffers to achieve this. Although strategic buffers are necessary, they are still waste, and the reasons for needing the buffers must be addressed to continuously improve on the lead times and costs.

TIPS

The word 'supermarket' is often used in Lean Thinking. In processing terms, this works much like a supermarket in that the employee will 'shop' for the parts needed, and when it reaches a certain level, it will be replenished. Any of the buffers mentioned in figure 3.54 could operate like a supermarket buffer, and it will depend on the needs of the process flow as to what this design looks like.

Regulate the Pace of the Value Stream

Having determined at what tempo the system should be paced to meet customer demand, where flow can be created and where buffers will tie the processes together, it is necessary to develop a method to synchronise the processes to achieve this as one system. This means deciding on where to schedule work so that the processes can connect to the customer pull. Decide at what single point the Value Stream will be scheduled and synchronised from:

○ **The Constraint Process**

In many cases, it is best to set the pace at the constraint process. This way, work released into the system will not exceed the capability, and each process can work in synch with the slowest process. The benefit is a system paced to customer demand and capability, and the opportunity for overproduction is limited.

○ **The Process Closest to the Customer**

Where you position the pacemaker will also determine the lead time to supply the customer. Having created flow and removed disruption, there may be more flexibility to place the pacemaker as close to the customer as possible. With short, responsive lead times, the upstream processes will be able to respond timeously to real demand. The advantage is realised when the pacemaker is able to respond to triggers coming directly from the customer, which in turn will trigger the rest of the system to respond to the right requests.

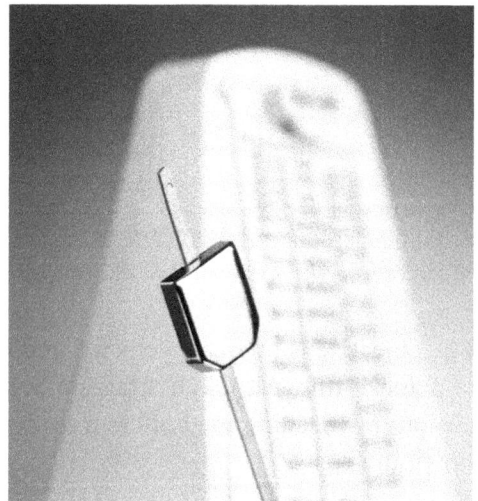

Both options have the advantage of providing one process from which to pace the workload running through the Value Stream and this reduces the risk of amplifying problems unnecessarily. In a system where no pacemaker has been set, it can set in motion a complex scheduling process. For example if waste was identified whereby each process worked to its own pace, its own schedule and in silos, there may be a great opportunity to connect these processes and simplify the scheduling by installing one pacemaker. The pacemaker relies on as smooth a demand as is possible so the sequence of change is important:

- Stabilise the process
- Create flow
- Then process to customer demand rate.

Level the Workload Volume

Velocity needs the Value Stream to operate with as little volume deviation as possible. Perhaps the demand variation has been smoothed, but some variation will always exist, and how the system responds to that variation can influence the ability to achieve the vision.

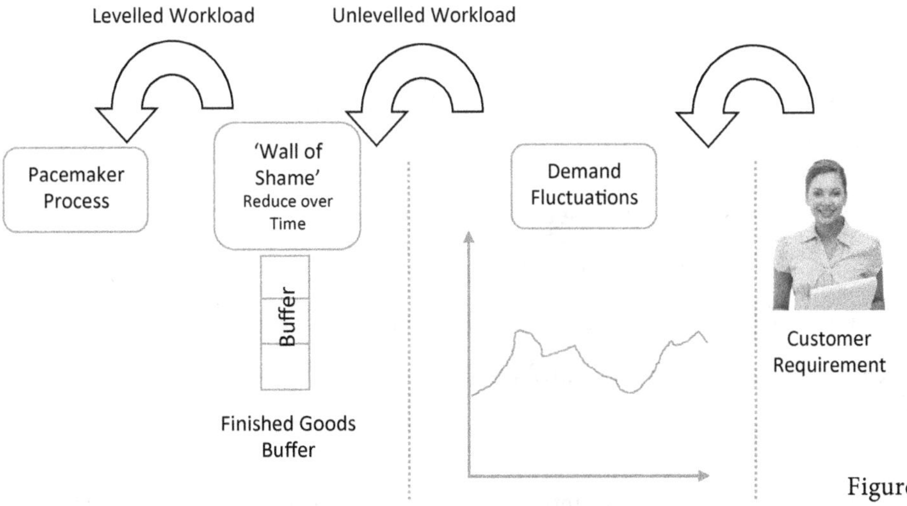

Figure 3.55

In figure 3.55, the demand fluctuations from the customer are cushioned through the finished goods buffer. As work is moved from finished goods to the customer this triggers a message to the process to replenish, however, the volume has been levelled to protect the processes from the variation that still exists. The 'Wall of Shame' acts as a shield against the sea of changes and should be seen as a necessary evil that requires reduction over time.

So although variation exists the long-term averages for demand will be stable and can be planned for, and this is often more cost effective than building in capacity to cope with the peaks. The Glenday Sieve Analysis provides source data to review the long-term averages from and to decide on a level volume to send to the front-line.

Release Level and Consistent Volumes

In order to achieve a regular pace in the process, the discipline of TAKT time must be adhered to from the word go. If work is released into the system in large, inconsistent batches it will be difficult to compare performance to requirement and the process could become 'constipated' with excessive work in the system. This is a major cause of muri. Releasing work too often will also have its drawbacks. The goal is therefore to level the workload volume that is issued to the front-line in such a way that the quantity and frequency of work support velocity. This will present the 'speed of awareness' necessary to maintain the pace set.

How often are we releasing work into the system - hourly, daily or weekly?

One way to create this 'speed of awareness' is to set a management time frame or pitch for the work which means there is a practical increment to release work into the system, and to take away work from the pacemaker. This means you will be able to:

- Pace how often work is released into the system
- Pace how often work is taken away
- Check performance to customer requirement
- Create a quicker response to problems
- Produce a more consistent volume over time.

The formula for pitch is used to define the management time frame. Calculate the pitch for your Value Stream, and include in your Future State design.

Pitch = TAKT Time x Practical Quantity of Work

The 'practical quantity of work' seems non-descript but it is important to decide what a feasible amount of work at a time should be transported and processed. In manufacturing, this is often based on a pack-out quantity in a container or a multiple thereof. For example – if your TAKT time is 35 seconds and your practical quantity of work is 100 at a time:

Pitch = 35 sec x 100 units of work

    = 3500 sec

    = 58 min

Approximately every hour, 100 units of work should arrive and be taken away.

Level the Mix of Work to the Value Stream

Batching work together can make it difficult to supply the customer in the order and quantity required. In manufacturing, you want to supply a variety of products matching the demand, and in service, you also need to be flexible to varying requirements. Where you have exclusive lines devoted to particular products or services (figure 3.56), you run the risk of keeping excess capacity to deal with the demands. Where you have one line that deals with a variety, but in large batches, you run the risk of not processing to requirement or holding large inventories.

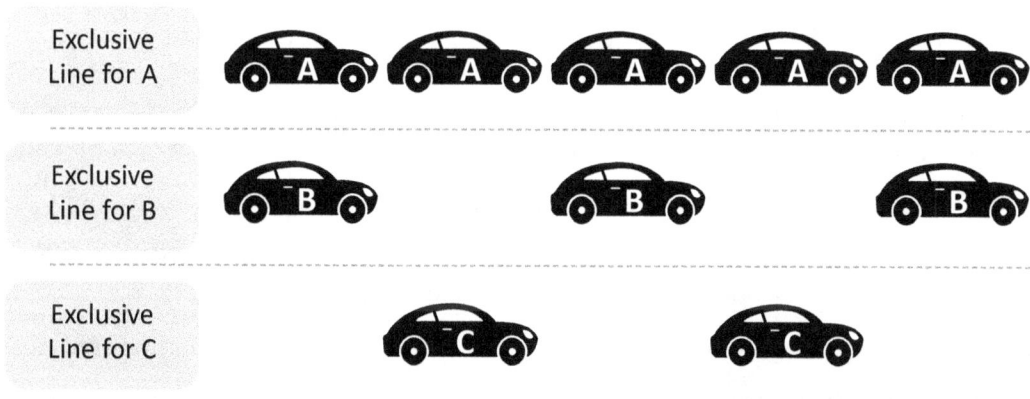

Figure 3.56

In a mixed-model process, you find a way to merge these lines into one flow, and even out the mix of product or service worked on to meet the varied needs in the market. The ultimate is one piece at a time but in some workplaces, this is not feasible and some batching is needed. The example in figure 3.57 shows how the mix is merged and the load is smoothed to meet the requirement:

Figure 3.57

In an earlier section it was mentioned how regularity in the schedule can support improved flow and how calculating the EPEI could help in deciding how much flexibility to incorporate. This must be developed in line with the North Star and your Future State Vision, otherwise it could be a very expensive exercise without any real benefit.

Connect the Value Stream to Demand

With stable processes, that flow and can process to demand, you can begin to think about systems that will connect the Value Stream to the customer demand. This means developing systems that automatically trigger the processes to produce what is required, or replenish what has been consumed. A practical example can be found in a sushi bar:

○ A customer sits down.

○ The customer removes a plate of sushi from the conveyor belt.

○ The customer consumes the sushi.

○ The chef sees the plate has been removed and this triggers production. In many cases production is triggered in batches, so he will wait until a batch has been consumed before starting.

○ The chef assembles the sushi that has been consumed and places it back on the conveyor belt.

○ The system is back in balance.

Now consider all the enablers that need to be in place for the sushi system to work:

○ The demand pattern is understood and this is reflected in the product mix placed on the conveyor. The customer has a good chance of finding what he or she wants.

○ The number of chefs and plates varies to match peaks and troughs in demand.

○ The chef is able to respond quickly to consumption (short lead time, good flow, good work area layout, good training and good tools).

○ There is controlled work-in-progress – for example, sliced salmon and prepared rice.

○ Work processes are standardised – quality and time to process is consistent.

Figure 3.58 illustrates the tranformation from a traditional batch and queue Value Stream to the ultimate one-piece-flow design for velocity. It also puts into perspective the need to connect to demand as you move away from a push system that in theory could push work into the system beyond its capacity.

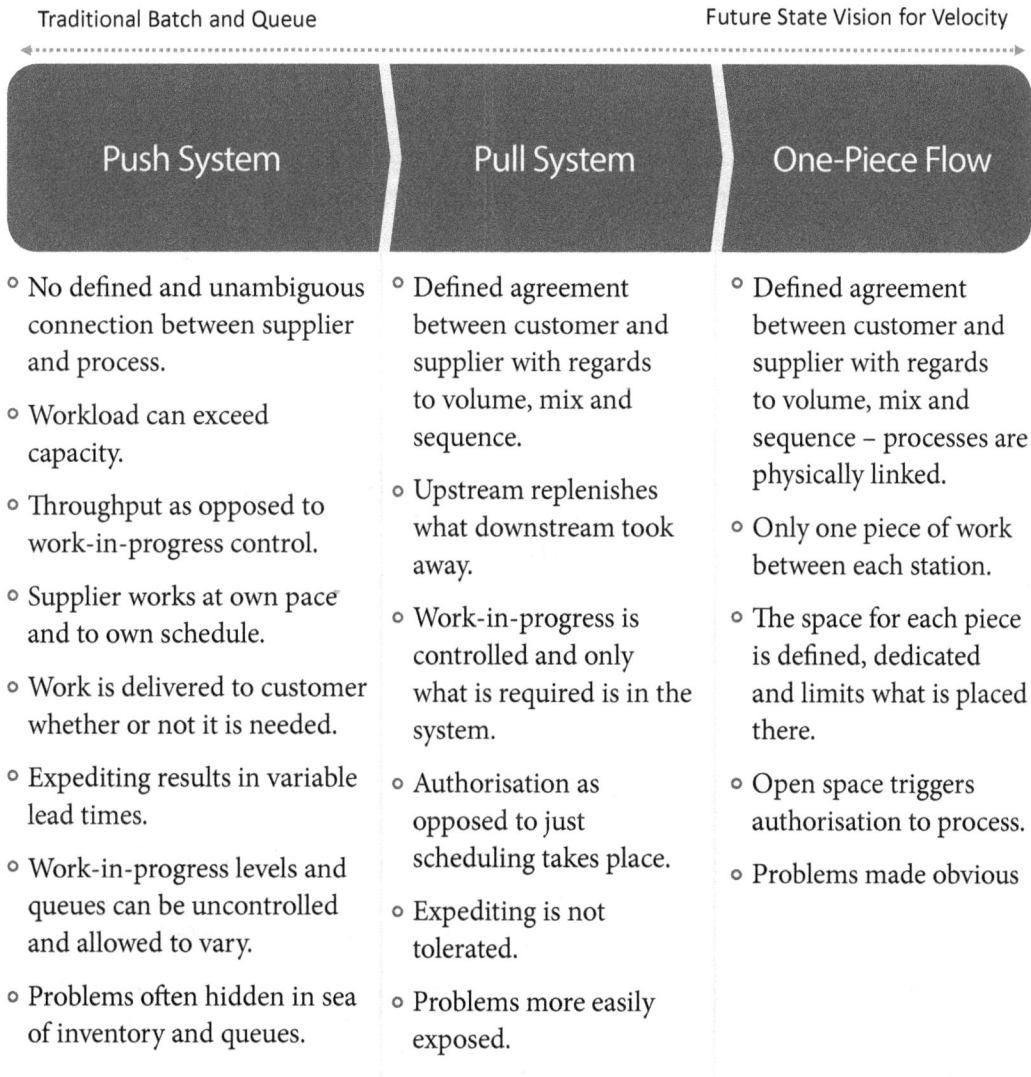

Traditional Batch and Queue   Future State Vision for Velocity

Push System	Pull System	One-Piece Flow
° No defined and unambiguous connection between supplier and process.	° Defined agreement between customer and supplier with regards to volume, mix and sequence.	° Defined agreement between customer and supplier with regards to volume, mix and sequence – processes are physically linked.
° Workload can exceed capacity.		
° Throughput as opposed to work-in-progress control.	° Upstream replenishes what downstream took away.	° Only one piece of work between each station.
° Supplier works at own pace and to own schedule.	° Work-in-progress is controlled and only what is required is in the system.	° The space for each piece is defined, dedicated and limits what is placed there.
° Work is delivered to customer whether or not it is needed.		
° Expediting results in variable lead times.	° Authorisation as opposed to just scheduling takes place.	° Open space triggers authorisation to process.
° Work-in-progress levels and queues can be uncontrolled and allowed to vary.	° Expediting is not tolerated.	° Problems made obvious
° Problems often hidden in sea of inventory and queues.	° Problems more easily exposed.	

Figure 3.58

Your Future State Vision will dictate the level of change required and how far towards one piece flow the Value Stream is expected to shift, but provided the requirement to trigger work based on customer pull is identified, you will need to investigate the right system to match your needs. The following sections will explain the common types of pull systems at your disposal. Compare each system to your requirements and select the one or design your own that will assist in achieving the vision.

Kanban Pull System:

As defined earlier, kanban is a Japanese word meaning signboard, signal or card. In the context of operations it refers to a system utilising standard containers (figure 3.59), each of which has a card designating what and when to produce (Japan Management Association, 1985).

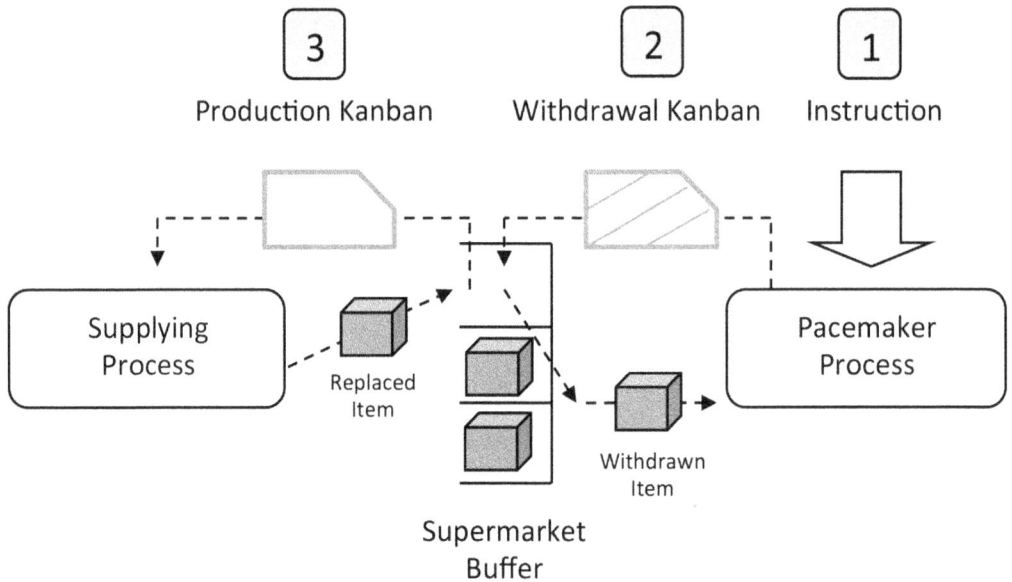

Figure 3.59

- o The pacemaker or customer process receives an instruction – for example levelled instruction.

- o The material handler – sometimes called the spiderman – withdraws the parts needed from the supermarket buffer using the withdrawal kanban as the authorisation. This is done within the pitch time and is then moved to the pacemaker for processing.

- o This triggers a production request (production kanban) that goes to the supplying process, to replace the item consumed.

- o In most cases the pacemaker gets the schedule (instruction) and the other processes just respond to the triggers.

- o This pull system is more suited to repetitive processes and the purpose of kanban is to reduce kanban over time.

- o The number of kanbans (cards) in the system governs the amount of work-in-progress.

There are six rules for kanban that are good to have in hand when setting up and sustaining the system (Japan Management Association, 1985):

- Rule 1: Do not send defective product to the next process.
- Rule 2: The next process comes only to withdraw what is needed.
- Rule 3: Process only the exact quantity withdrawn by the next process.
- Rule 4: Equalise production and ensure load levelling.
- Rule 5: Use kanban as a means to fine tuning, not for massive change.
- Rule 6: Stabilise and rationalise the process by eliminating muda, mura, muri.

FIFO Lanes:

The FIFO lane is a simple connection mechanism to couple processes, buffer variation in work times and create flow. It is a first-in-first-out sequenced queue between processes and is particularly useful when expiry of items is a risk (figure 3.60).

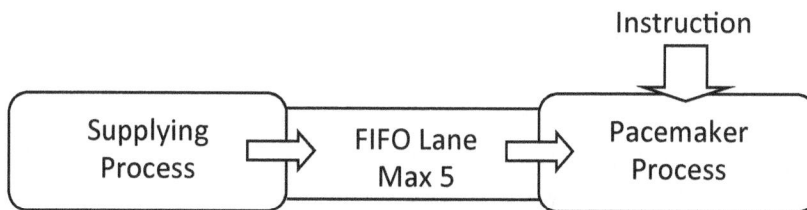

Figure 3.60

- The pacemaker or customer process receives an instruction.
- The work is removed from the FIFO lane and processed (or consumed).
- The open space in the lane triggers the supplying process to replenish.
- Process is controlled and linked to consumption:
    - FIFO lane is full, processing stops
    - FIFO lane is open, processing triggered.
- The queue has a defined number of spaces to limit the work-in-progress.
- No kanban cards, just a visual system triggering a response.

Constant Work In Progress System (CONWIP):

The CONWIP system, sometimes called the hybrid, is applicable to a wider spectrum of environments (figure 3.61). It links the last process to the first process through a multi-stage signalling system, and results in an automatic buffer before the constraint. In a Value Stream where the constraint moves around, this can be a simple way to connect the flows and trigger processing, without knowing where the constraint is or how big the buffer should be.

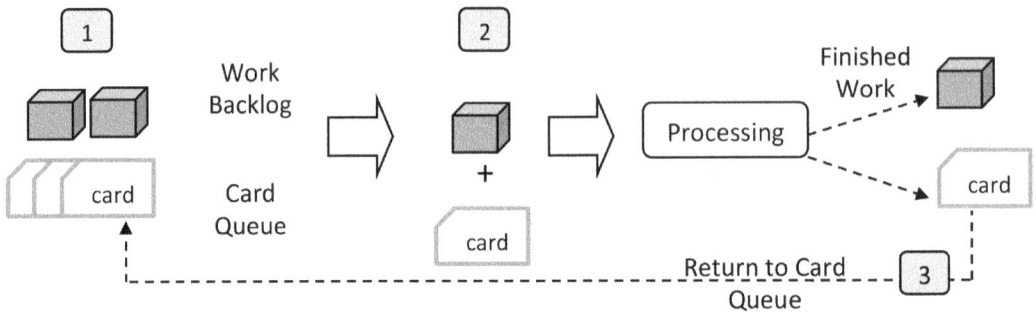

Figure 3.61

○ A card is attached to the container or work at the beginning of the line.

○ The container or work makes its way through line and at the end of the process, the card is removed from the container and is taken back to the beginning of the process.

○ The card then joins a queue of cards and awaits to be attached to the next container or work.

○ The card is line specific, not product or service specific and is allocated an identification number at the start of the process. This identification relates to a prioritised backlog list of work.

○ Work is prioritised from the backlog but authorisation to process is only possible if a card is available and work is allowed to be released into the system.

○ It relies on standard containers or standard batches of work being passed on between processes.

CONWIP is similar to a technique used in air traffic control (Spearman, Woodruff and Hopp, 1990). On days with heavy air traffic, a departing aeroplane will sometimes be held on the ground at the originating airport rather than being allowed to take off. The plane remains in a holding pattern at the congested destination airport. The object is to avoid delays at the destination airport (in the air) so planes are held even if take-off runways are free at the originating airport. The result is greater safety and lower fuel consumption with no added delay.

The CONWIP pull system is unique in that it allows for prioritisation and scheduling but work is 'pulled' into the system only when the system is able to process it. Even if the beginning process is idle, work is not permitted to be 'pushed' into the system. This has the advantage of controlling work-in-progress and ensuring that a job is not started until there is a vacant space for it in the system. Excessive work in the system increases the queue size and of course, the lead time. The number of cards will help to govern this.

It is also critical that sufficient work be pulled into the system so that the constraint is never idle bearing in mind that a loss at the constraint is a loss to the system.

This system works well in an environment operating close to capacity and achieving this balance, creates the highest throughput with the lowest work-in-progress. See table 3.18 for a quick comparison of CONWIP and Kanban.

COMPARING KANBAN AND CONWIP	
Kanban System	CONWIP System
o Uses cards to control work content of line.	o Uses cards to control speed of line.
o Sequence can be determined through load levelling.	o Backlog and prioritisation is used to dictate sequence.
o Card is linked to part number.	o Card is linked to line.
o Work is pulled.	o Work is pushed once a card has authorised it to start.
o Not tolerant to set-ups or too many part numbers.	o A feedback loop creates a unique push-pull combination and performs as a 'natural capacity check' where the system responds automatically to available capacity.
o Planning and sequencing done at the front-line operation, by front-line staff.	
o WIP usually sits upstream from the bottleneck and is controlled.	o Set-ups can be incorporated into the planning process.
	o Planning and sequencing is done by planning and scheduling personnel – for example, production control.
	o WIP tends to collect at the constraint, which keeps the constraint active and increases throughput. Usually lower WIP than kanban.

Table 3.18

TIPS

Can different systems be found under one roof? It is not uncommon to see a combination of approaches being used – for example, kanban and material requirements planning. Having evaluated the Glenday Sieve Analysis, you may have found a 'mixed factory' depicted by the various streams. As such, you should design systems to suit the various streams, evaluating the feasible outcome to the customer each time.

Drum, Buffer, Rope System:

Both the CONWIP and Drum, Buffer, Rope (DBR) approach control the release of work into the system so there are strong similarities between the two, even though developed along different reasoning. Whereas CONWIP can be applied to more environments than kanban, it is not well suited to a job shop environment. This is where the DBR can be successfully brought in (figure 3.62). Where CONWIP and DBR are both applied in flow lines, the result is quite similar (Spearman, Woodruff and Hopp, 1990).

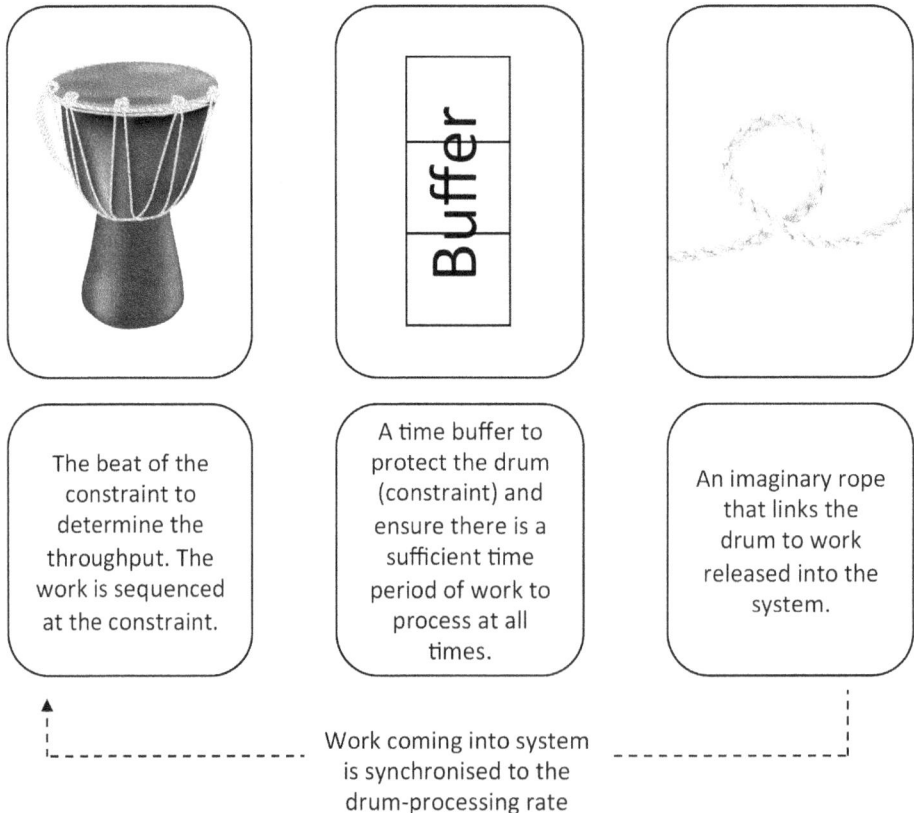

| Buffer |

The beat of the constraint to determine the throughput. The work is sequenced at the constraint.

A time buffer to protect the drum (constraint) and ensure there is a sufficient time period of work to process at all times.

An imaginary rope that links the drum to work released into the system.

Work coming into system is synchronised to the drum-processing rate

Figure 3.62

- The drum sets the pace and the constraint is protected from starvation by the time buffer.

- Non-constraint operations are scheduled to maintain the time buffer.

- The rope ensures work or parts are released into the system only as the bottleneck uses them up, controlling the work-in-progress in the system.

- The bottleneck utilisation is the highest amongst the operations so the drumbeat for the line is maintained.

TIPS

Anytime you start up a pull system it will probably fail in a short period of time. However, it is exactly this failure that will help expose the problems and where the system still needs work. It is therefore critical that a pull system be a visual regulator of flow and that it also prompts response and improvement. Consider implementing the pull system on a small scale and improving bit by bit. In this way, the problems are exposed and solved in manageable chunks.

Heijunka System (Load Smoothing):

The Heijunka Box has mostly been associated with production control for operations but the first applications were found in maintenance at car manufacturer, Toyota (figure 3.63). Managers found it useful to create boxes with hourly time intervals for scheduling preventive maintenance activities. Work content for each activity was carefully timed and the tasks to be completed were visually displayed with the time intervals clearly marked. The pace of work was set and care was taken not to load too many activities in one time interval, so as to negatively impact the customer. This was then adapted to suit production and it is interesting to see that the widest application has been with suppliers to govern the withdrawals of inventory and pace the output of supplier lines to that of the TAKT time at the customer cells (Smally, 2004).

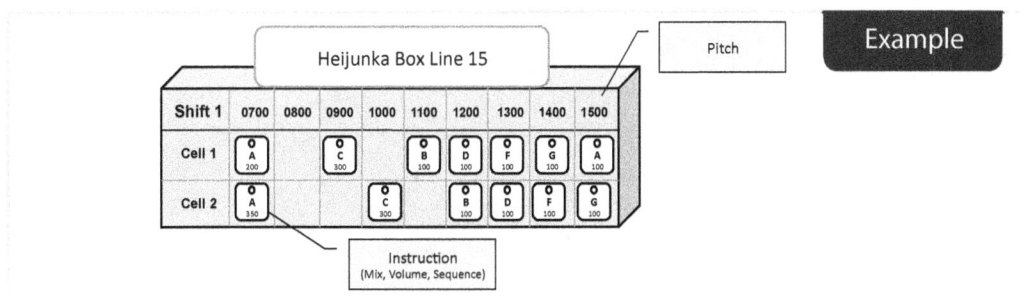

Figure 3.63

The heijunka system is a way to pull it all together, visually depict the schedule and ensure the pace, sequence, volume and mix is regulated and precise. It also authorises processing so that what is planned according to the principles above, is done. It is typically used with the kanban system, and at the pacemaker.

The system is most commonly used by the front-line operations, where the team leader or supervisor has direct control over how the operation is scheduled, however, this may vary depending on how the system has been designed and the environment in which it is being implemented. The system functions as follows:

- The requirement comes in from the customer – this could be triggered by consumption from the finished goods supermarket or directly from the customer.

- A 'sorter' takes the requirement and rearranges it into a predefined sequence by item type – this could be to minimise changeover complexity or to break up large batches of demand into smaller allocations. The 'sorter' may also group green stream items and then leave a space in the schedule at the end for red stream items.

- The 'sorter' then defines the maximum quantity to be processed in one pass.

- The mix, volume and sequence of work can now be visually displayed to the operational employees.

- The line follows the processing exactly to the visual display, ensuring the work is completed within the pitch time.

- Any issues are highlighted and solved immediately. If problems occur, and the targets are missed, this is to be investigated and resolved. This means the system may temporarily go out of sequence, but the team must strive to get back to the intended sequence as soon as possible. This should be the exception rather than the norm.

This should not be seen as a system to support only manufacturing environments. It can be adapted to any operation that requires a visual system to pace processing according to demand, in a manner that levels the volume and mix or work being tackled. As such, it is not uncommon to see the system working in financial environments, hospitals, receiver of revenue services and back-office operations.

Having measured the degree of batching and flexibility through the EPEI calculation, it was possible to develop an optimum EPEI for the Future State. This may require that some process improvements take place in order to achieve it, but if velocity is the vision for the future, this could be a critical element to the improvement strategy.

| Day | Every Product Every 4 Days On Line 1 | | | | | | Example | |
| | Product | | | | | | Total Changeover Time (min) | Total Run Time (min) |
	A	B	C	D	E	F		
Monday	445						30	475
Tuesday	275	170					30	475
Wednesday		310	120				30	460
Thursday				120	120	120	90	450
Friday	445						30	475
Total	1165	480	120	120	120	120	210	2335

Table 3.19

In addition to this, having completed the Glenday Sieve Analysis and identified the various streams in the business, it was possible to select which items (green streams) should be on a fixed, regular schedule, and which items (red streams) should be treated as strangers in the schedule. This information together with the EPEI will help you determine how the load should be smoothed, both in terms of the levelled volume as well as the levelled mix at the pacemaker (table 3.19). Remember, the outcome of this system must be to improve in areas important to the customer and the business, so continue to test your design against these criteria.

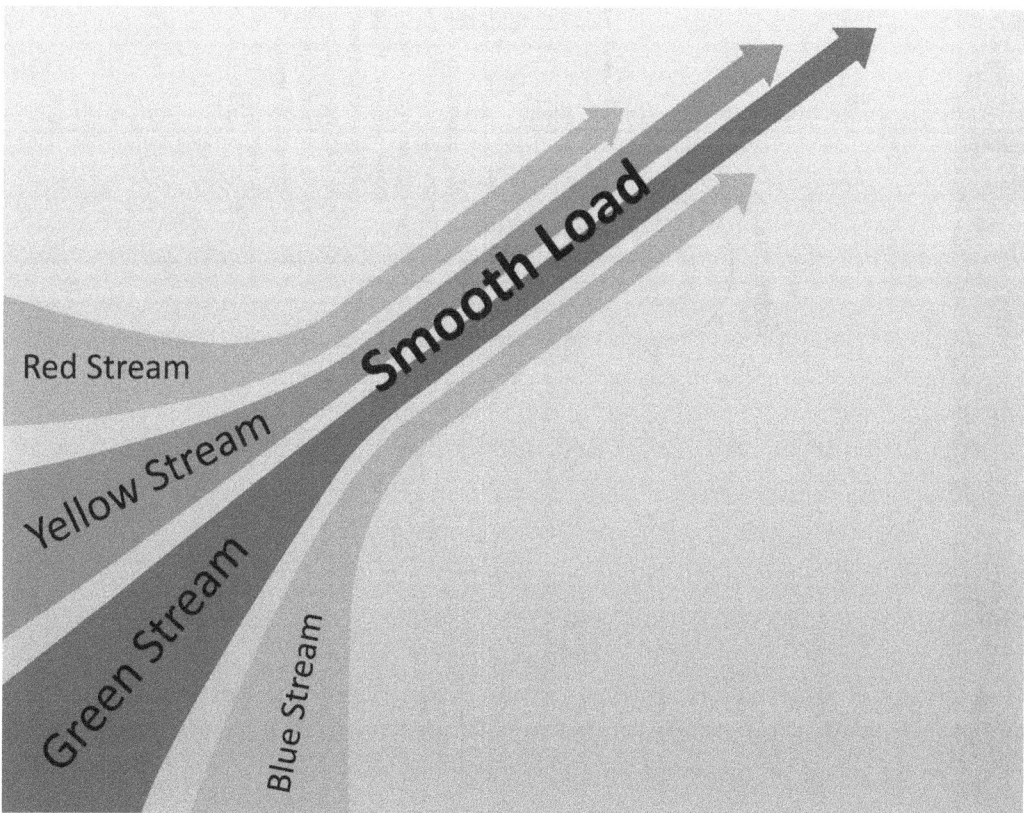

Example

AN EXAMPLE OF PULLING IT ALL TOGETHER – MANUFACTURING

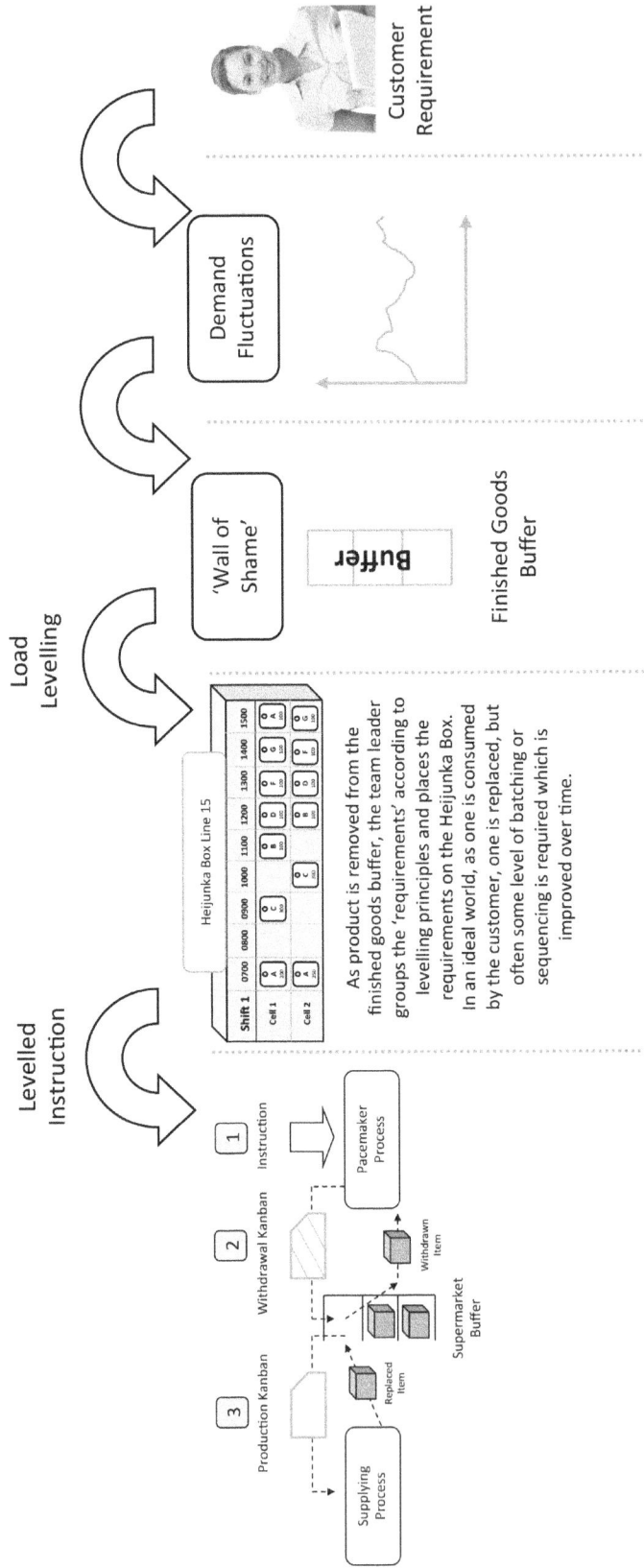

Customer Requirement

Demand Fluctuations

'Wall of Shame'

Buffer

Finished Goods Buffer

Load Levelling

Levelled Instruction

Heijunka Box Line 15

As product is removed from the finished goods buffer, the team leader groups the 'requirements' according to levelling principles and places the requirements on the Heijunka Box. In an ideal world, as one is consumed by the customer, one is replaced, but often some level of batching or sequencing is required which is improved over time.

1 Instruction

Pacemaker Process

2 Withdrawal Kanban

Withdrawn Item

Supermarket Buffer

3 Production Kanban

Replaced Item

Supplying Process

Figure 3.64

AN EXAMPLE OF PULLING IT ALL TOGETHER - SERVICE

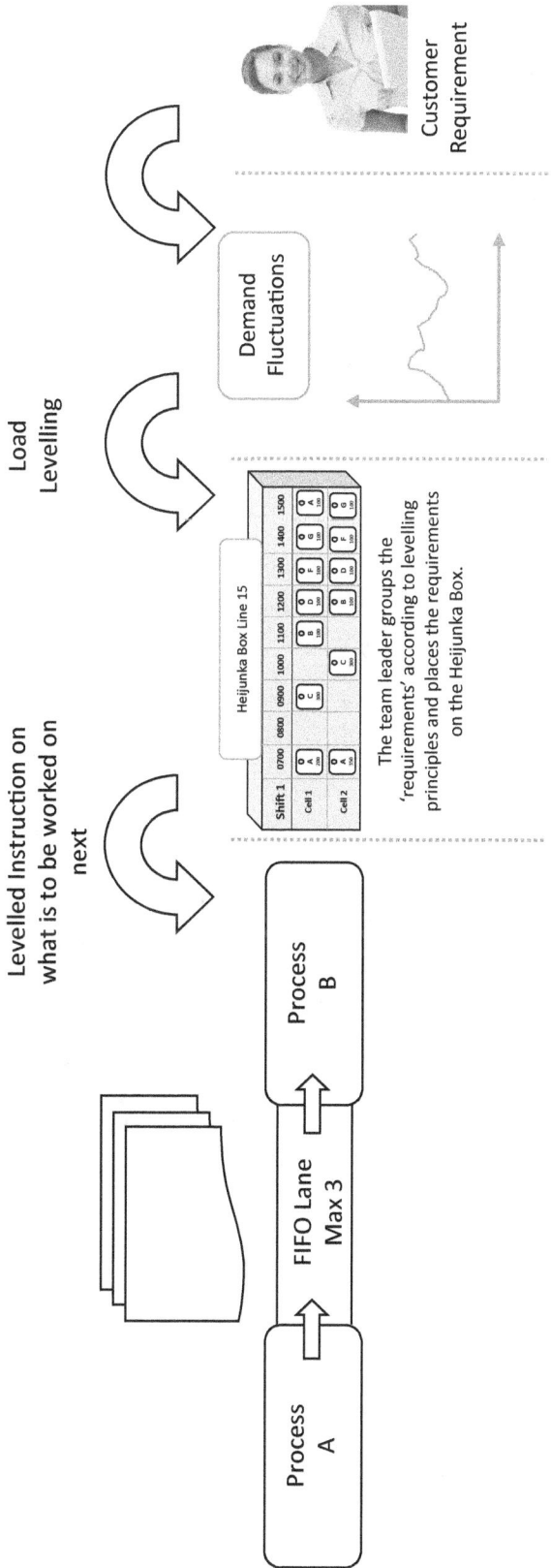

Customer Requirement

Demand Fluctuations

Load Levelling

Heijunka Box Line 15

The team leader groups the 'requirements' according to levelling principles and places the requirements on the Heijunka Box.

Levelled Instruction on what is to be worked on next

Process B

FIFO Lane Max 3

Process A

Figure 3.65

Example

Start building the Future State Map, capturing all the decisions made so far (figure 3.66):

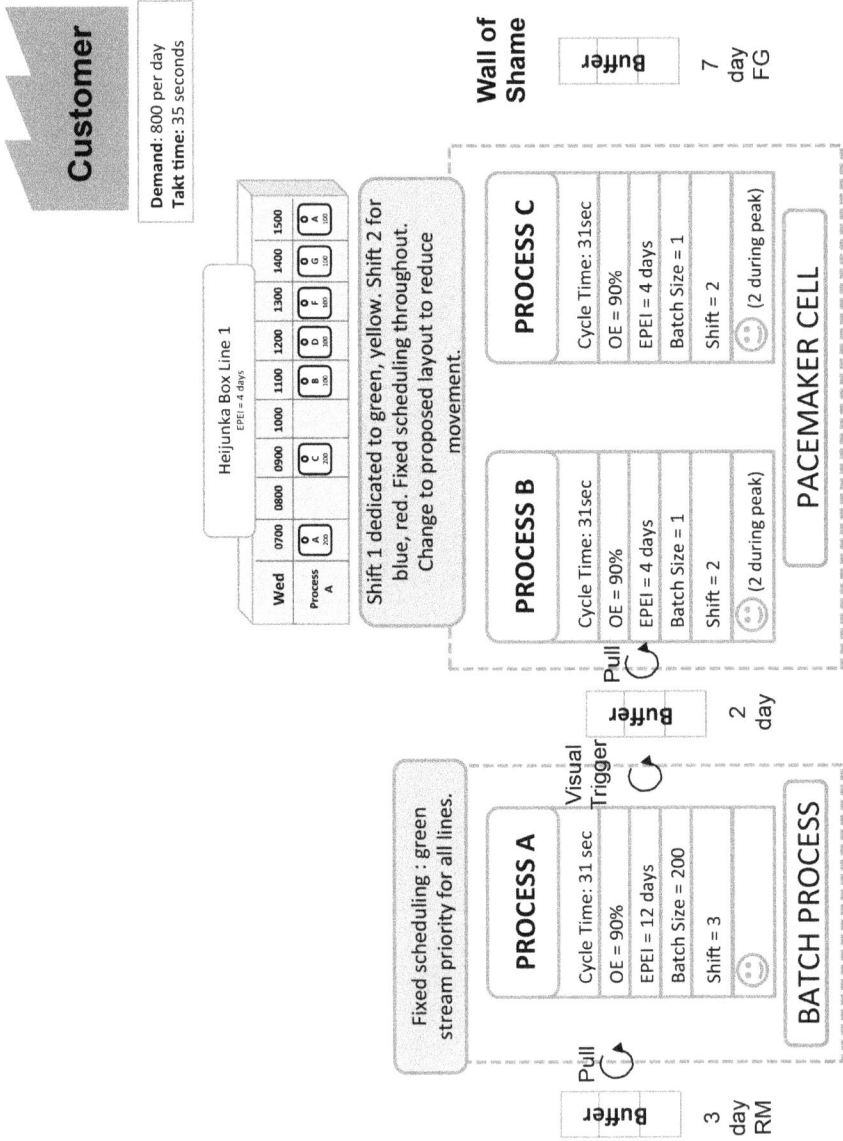

Customer

Demand: 800 per day
Takt time: 35 seconds

Heijunka Box Line 1
EPEI = 4 days

Wed	0700	0800	0900	1000	1100	1200	1300	1400	1500
Process A	A 200		C 200		B 100	D 100	F 100	G 100	A 100

Shift 1 dedicated to green, yellow. Shift 2 for blue, red. Fixed scheduling throughout. Change to proposed layout to reduce movement.

Wall of Shame

Buffer

7 day FG

PROCESS C

Cycle Time: 31sec
OE = 90%
EPEI = 4 days
Batch Size = 1
Shift = 2
(2 during peak)

PROCESS B

Cycle Time: 31sec
OE = 90%
EPEI = 4 days
Batch Size = 1
Shift = 2
(2 during peak)

PACEMAKER CELL

Pull

Buffer

2 day

Fixed scheduling : green stream priority for all lines.

Visual Trigger

PROCESS A

Cycle Time: 31 sec
OE = 90%
EPEI = 12 days
Batch Size = 200
Shift = 3

BATCH PROCESS

Pull

Buffer

3 day RM

Figure 3.66

CLUSTERING OF MUDA, MURA AND MURI

Example

PHYSICAL FLOW	INFORMATION FLOW	PEOPLE FLOW	MONEY FLOW

Physical Flow

- **MURI** ~ Overtime or not delivering the answer to changes in demand
- **MUDA** Producing more than the customer needs
- **MUDA / MURA** Pace of value stream uncontrolled

- **MUDA** Slow movers get in the way of fast movers
- **MUDA / MURI** Work released exceeds capacity
- **MURA** Constraint loaded at 95% capacity
- **MUDA** Excessive inventory clogging flow

- **MURA** High variation in forecast accuracy
- **MUDA / MURI / MURI** Uncontrolled batch size at constraint
- **MUDA** Long set-up times and large batching at Process B
- **MUDA / MUDA** EPEI not aligned to customer requirement

- **MUDA** Unnecessary steps to get the work complete
- **MUDA / MURA** High downtime at constraint
- **MUDA** Effective cycle time cannot meet TAKT at B
- **MUDA / MURA** OE at constraint is good but A and C are low and affect constraint performance

- **MUDA** Piles of quarantined product after Process C
- **MURA** Variation in methods between employees
- **MUDA** Constraint at Process B not protected from starvation
- **MUDA** 980 transport steps between departments to complete value stream

Information Flow

- **MURA / MUDA** Schedule inaccuracy – making what is not needed
- **MUDA** Front line working off outdated information from the customer
- **MURA / MUDA** No available standards to show what good should look like
- **MUDA** No means to see performance to plan
- **MUDA** Cannot see relationship between standard work and TAKT

People Flow

- **MURA / MUDA** People not available to finish job on night shift
- **MUDA** People not always available at the constraint (B)
- **MURI / MURA** Always fixing the same problems - no time for problem solving

Money Flow

- **MUDA** Paying key creditors sooner than contract specifies
- **MUDA** Significant customers pay late consistently

Mark off the muda, mura and muri that have been addressed so far.

Table 3.20

✔ FOR YOU TO TRY

- Gather the team to take part in the Future State Map.

- Gain consensus on time frame, scope and the vision for achieiving the Future State.

- Improve the physical flow of work to achieve the vision by focusing on aspects such as:

    - Product or service design

    - Demand patterns

    - Process capability to meet TAKT time

    - Scheduling

    - Basic stability

    - Process flow

    - Layout flow

    - Strategic buffering

    - Value Stream pacing mechanism

    - Workload volume and mix levelling

    - Connecting the Value Stream to demand.

- Update the Future State Map.

- Cross off the muda, mura and muri that have been addressed.

Step 4: Develop the Information Flow

The goal of improving the information flow is to establish what must look different in order to achieve velocity through clear, relevant and timeous information. Figure 3.67 summarises three aspects that should be explored when designing the Future State and we will discuss a selection of them to address the muda, mura and muri identified in the Current State. The physical flow is directly influenced by the information flow and relates to what information is made available, why, how, to whom and how quickly. Review your own findings, and select the best countermeasures to develop the Future State with, and capture each decision on a flipchart.

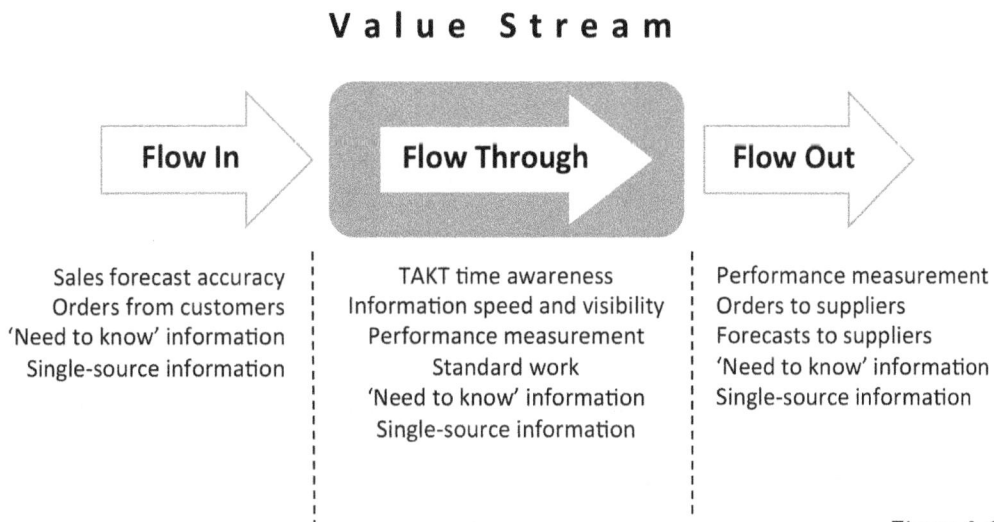

Value Stream

Flow In	Flow Through	Flow Out
Sales forecast accuracy	TAKT time awareness	Performance measurement
Orders from customers	Information speed and visibility	Orders to suppliers
'Need to know' information	Performance measurement	Forecasts to suppliers
Single-source information	Standard work	'Need to know' information
	'Need to know' information	Single-source information
	Single-source information	

Figure 3.67

Create a TAKT Image

In the previous section, the options for connecting processes to the customer and how to synchronise with TAKT time were discussed. It is also necessary to monitor performance to TAKT time in a simple, visual way so that when a problem occurs and a target is missed, the situation is exposed and the team is able to investigate and adjust accordingly. If TAKT time or pitch was not the focus for your Future State, it is still possible to use these principles to monitor performance. Creating a TAKT image involves the following:

- Develop a system to measure performance to TAKT time frequently – for example within pitch time – to ensure the team is aware of the expectations and what their response to out-of-standard conditions should be.

- Construct a visual display where the work happens to show the TAKT image and trigger response to missed targets (figure 3.68). Include the employees during the design phase – keep it simple and focused.

- Deal with causes indicated on the visual board within the shift in which they occur or at a minimum, in the daily meetings.

VISUAL BOARD

Example

MEASURE • EVALUATE • IMPROVE

AREA	CELL 2 PROCESSING	TAKT TIME:
TEAM LEADER	GERRY	**1 UNIT EVERY 60SEC**
DATE	15 AUGUST 2014	

PITCH	TARGET / CUMULATIVE	ACTUAL / CUMULATIVE	VARIATION	REASON FOR MISSING TARGET	RESOLVED & PREVENTED
07h00 to 08h00	3600 / 3600	3700 / 3700	100	200 OVERPRODUCTION FROM 14TH	✓
08h00 to 09h00	3600 / 7200	3400 / 7100	-100	MC 2 JAM	
09h00 to 10h00	3600 / 10800	3300 / 10400	-400	MC 2 JAM	PROBLEM SOLVE
10h00 to 11h00	3600 / 14400	3800 / 14200	-200	TEAM LEADER SUPPORTED	
11h00 to 12h00	3600 / 18000	3700 / 17900	-100		
12h00 to 13h00	2000 / 20000	2100 / 20000	0		
13h00 to 14h00	3600 / 23600	3400 / 23400	-200		
14h00 to 15h00	3600 / 27200	2200 / 25600	-1600	NO GLUE	✓
15h00 to 16h00	3600 / 30800	3400 / 29000	-1800		
16h00 to 17h00	2000 / 32800	1900 / 30900	-1900		

ITEMS FOR ESCALATION:	ITEMS FOR PROBLEM SOLVING:
NO STOCK OF CRITICAL SPARE	PROBLEM SOLVE REASONS FOR MC 2 JAM

Figure 3.68

Facilitate Speed and Visibility of Information

Remove the 'information noise' from what your employees receive and give them what they need, where they need it, when they need it, to facilitate velocity. Good information flow is dependent on the following:

○ How visible the information is

○ The ease of interpretation

○ Receiving the information in good time

○ Receiving information that is relevant and accurate

○ Ensuring the right people have access to the information and not an elite few

○ Reducing the hassle-factor to get or process information by consolidating the variety of systems

○ Creating a standard way to provide information, consistently, so that employees know what to expect

○ Ensuring the ownership for providing information is clear.

Refer to the Information Flow Checklist you completed in Table 3.15 and agree on the Future State changes that will help to achieve the vision. Table 3.21 illustrates an example checklist.

TIPS

- Custom design the board to suit your process and the needs of the customer.

- Get the employees who will use it involved in the design.

- Make sure the board achieves the full cycle of 'measure, evaluate, improve'. Just measuring can become a waste but measuring to evaluate the causes and improve for tomorrow, is powerful.

- Ensure the visual board improves visibility, timeliness and accuracy of performance. It must expose problems to trigger a response.

Example

INFORMATION FLOW EVALUATION
ACCURATE • TIMELY • RELEVANT

DEPARTMENT	CLAIMS PROCESSING	ASSESSOR	MARY
AREA	HOSPITAL CLAIMS	DATE	15 AUGUST 2014
INFORMATION TYPE	INFORMATION TO ENSURE CLAIMS ARE PROCESSED TIMEOUSLY		

CATEGORY	DESCRIPTION	1 POOR	2 AVERAGE	3 GOOD	IMPROVEMENT REQUIRED
VISIBILITY	CRITICAL INFORMATION TO GET WORK DONE IS VISIBLY DISPLAYED IN THE RIGHT PLACE	1			STANDARD PROCEDURES NOT VISIBLE
	MEASUREMENT OF PERFORMANCE TO REQUIREMENT IS VISUALLY DISPLAYED	1			NO PERFORMANCE TO DAILY TARGET
EASE OF INTERPRETATION	INFORMATION IS EASY TO READ AND EASY TO INTERPRET		2		DIFFICULT TO INTERPRET INPUT FORMS FROM CUSTOMER
TIMELY PROVISION	INFORMATION NEEDED BY OPERATIONS TO DO THE WORK IS PROVIDED IN GOOD TIME WITH NO DELAYS		2		LOST TIME INDICATES 5% DUE TO WAITING FOR INFORMATION – DOES NOT GET CAPTURED IMMEDIATELY ONCE RECEIVED
TIMELY RESPONSE	EMPLOYEES HAVE THEIR FINGERS ON THE PULSE AND INFORMATION HELPS THEM RESPOND TIMEOUSLY TO PROBLEMS OR REQUESTS		2		PERFORMANCE DATA SHOULD BE DAILY NOT WEEKLY TO TRIGGER QUICKER REACTIONS
RELEVANCE	INFORMATION PROVIDED TO GET THE WORK DONE IS CURRENT AND CRITICAL TO THE WORK AT HAND		2		OUTDATED PROCEDURES. SOME INFORMATION PROVIDED BY CUSTOMER NOT REQUIRED
ACCURACY	INFORMATION IS FREE OF ERRORS AND CONSISTENT TO STANDARD	1			CONSISTENT ERRORS IN CODES AND ASSESSMENT INTERPRETATION
AVAILABILITY	INFORMATION IS READILY AVAILABLE TO THOSE WHO REQUIRE IT, WHERE THEY REQUIRE IT	1			NOT ALL INFORMATION NEEDED TO ASSESS CLAIMS IS MADE AVAILABLE TO STAFF AT POINT OF USE
COMPLEXITY	INFORMATION IS AVAILABLE FROM A SINGLE SOURCE WITH RELIABLE REVISION CONTROL		2		FOUR SYSTEMS USED TO COMPLETE ASSESSMENT WITH OVERLAP AND DUPLICATION
STANDARDISATION	INFORMATION IS PROVIDED IN A STANDARD FORMAT ACROSS THE DEPARTMENTS	1			SOME VARIATION DEPENDING ON WHO IS IN SUPPORT ROLE
OWNERSHIP	ACCOUNTABILITY FOR THE ACCURACY AND PROVISION OF INFORMATION IS CLEAR		2		NO ONE TAKES OWNERSHIP FOR THE SPECIFICATIONS PROVIDED. UNCLEAR AS TO WHAT AND WHO IS CORRECT
	TOTAL SCORE OUT OF 30	5	12	0	17 / 30

Table 3.21

Align Performance Measurement to the Vision

'Show me how you measure me and I'll show you how I behave' is a phenomenon well worth remembering when evaluating if a performance measure compliments or hinders flow. Goal alignment is covered in PART III of the book but at this point, it is recommended that the team agrees on changes to prevent the disconnect between behaviour and required performance in the Future State.

○ Align your measures to velocity:

For example, the supply chain is concerned about overproduction but an individual area overproduces in one product (which meets the daily target) and under-produces in another (because it is a complex product and takes longer). The result is that targets are met but the customer requirement and cost targets are not.

○ Balance your measures:

For example, the area is measured on volume, and consistently meets this, but achieves the target through overtime and overloading of people and equipment. The performance measurement is not balanced to include morale, cost factors and quality, but instead concentrates only on the numbers processed. Typically, enterprises aim to balance measures to quality, cost, delivery, safety, morale and environment (QCDSME).

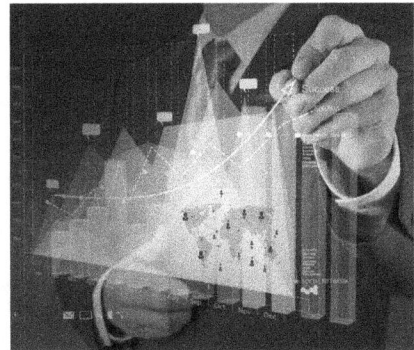

Example

CURRENT	FUTURE
MEASURES NOT ALIGNED TO SUPPLY CHAIN	ALIGN MEASURES TO SUPPLY CHAIN GOALS
MEASURED ON VOLUME AND QUALITY ONLY	BALANCE ALL MEASURES TO QCDSME
NO FOCUS ON OTIF	INVESTIGATE INCENTIVE CHANGES

Reduce Schedule Adjustments

During the interpretation of the Current State, you may have observed examples of manual adjustments taking place as a result of unplanned changes or inaccuracies. You indicated these with 'go see' glasses on your Current State Map.

- Run through the reasons for manual adjustments and identify the changes required to support regularity. These may already have been covered in your physical flow design but if not, agree what needs to be changed.

- Set a limitation on how late an adjustment can be made. For example, schedules are frozen two days before delivery, but the reasons for the adjustments are also addressed – note that just setting limits could negatively impact the customer.

- Make someone accountable for forecast accuracy and how it will be tracked and improved going forward. If a forecast accuracy target is set to support the Future State, ensure this is a phased target and properly supported by the leadership team.

The impact of these changes may seem more dramatic in a manufacturing environment but if improving a service environment, consider examples where the workflow has been disrupted to accommodate higher-priority work. This disrupts flow and can often be avoided. The cause-and-effect diagram in figure 3.69 illustrates how the discussion could be facilitated – additional techniques will be detailed in PROBLEM SOLVING.

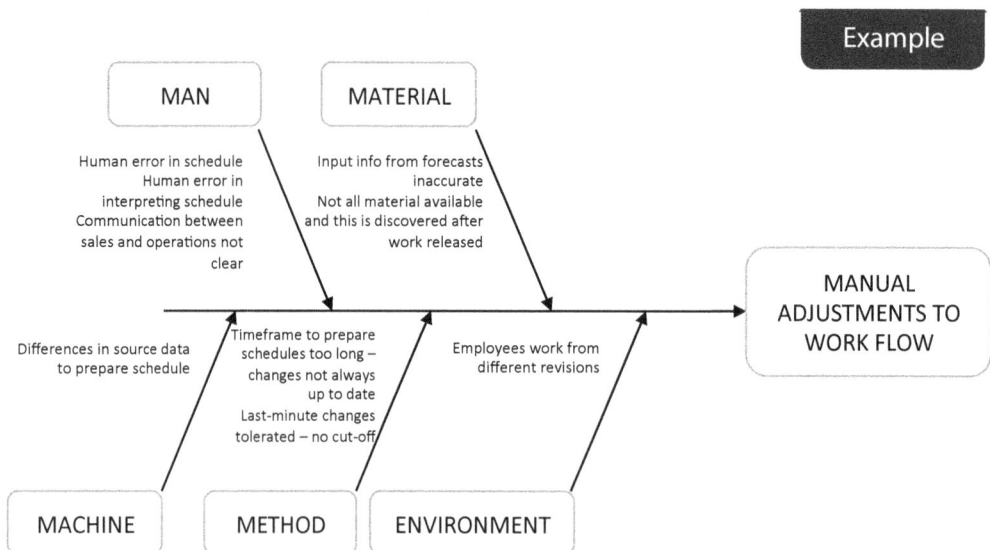

Figure 3.69

Synchronise Information

Looking at the Current State Map and the high-level information flow, there are three main elements affecting the physical flow:

- Customer needs
- Information to suppliers or contractors
- Information to the operations.

Review the information for all three elements and identify where possible disconnects occur and information becomes unbalanced:

- Ensure information received from your customers is passed to your suppliers in the same interval
- Ensure information received from your customers is passed to the operations in the same interval.

If there is a disconnect between the three flows, invariably one part of the flow will be working with outdated information or be responding too late. Consider a standard interval for the Future State.

Example

Update the Future State Map with the information flow decisions (figure 3.70):

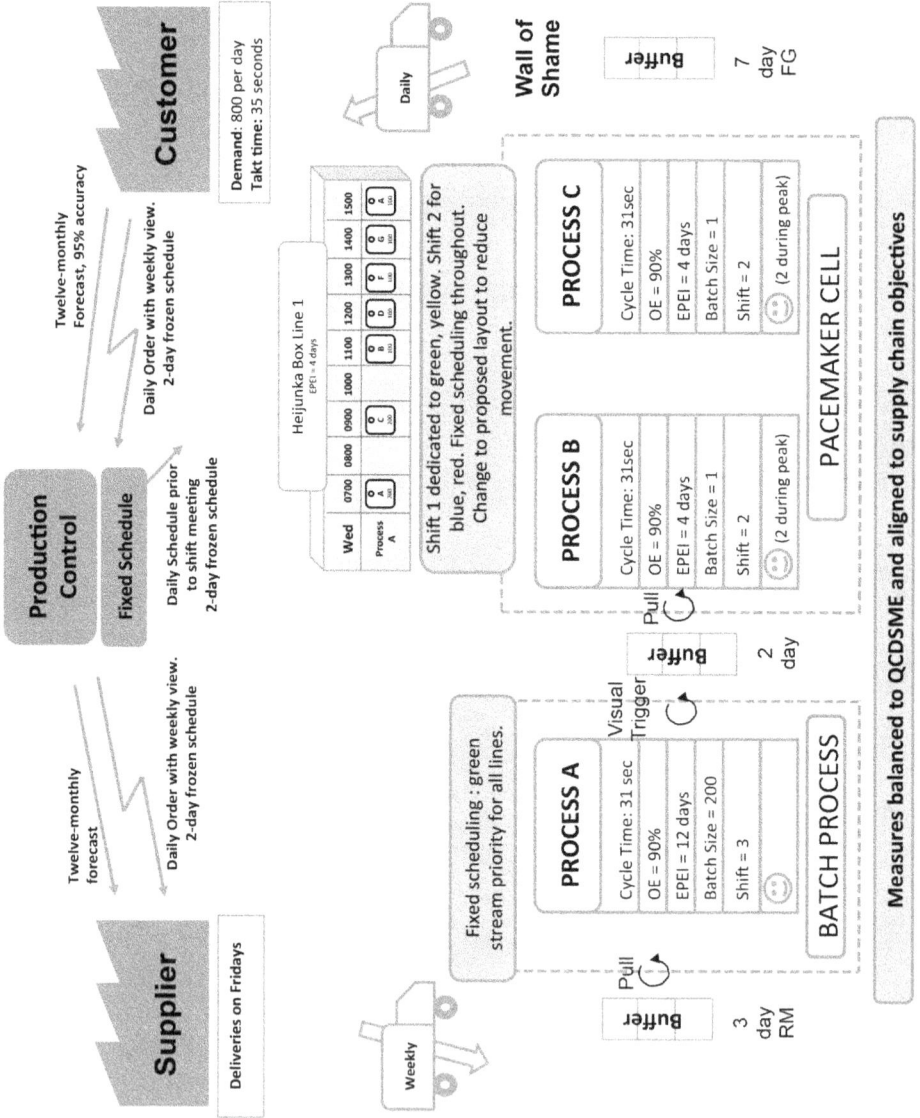

Supplier

Deliveries on Fridays

Twelve-monthly forecast

Daily Order with weekly view. 2-day frozen schedule

Production Control

Fixed Schedule

Daily Schedule prior to shift meeting 2-day frozen schedule

Twelve-monthly Forecast, 95% accuracy

Daily Order with weekly view. 2-day frozen schedule

Customer

Demand: 800 per day
Takt time: 35 seconds

Daily

Heijunka Box Line 1
EPEI = 4 days

Wed	0700	0800	0900	1000	1100	1200	1300	1400	1500
Process A	O A 100		O C 100		O B 100		O F 100	O G 100	O A 100

Shift 1 dedicated to green, yellow. Shift 2 for blue, red. Fixed scheduling throughout. Change to proposed layout to reduce movement.

Wall of Shame

Buffer

7 day FG

Fixed scheduling : green stream priority for all lines.

PROCESS A

Cycle Time: 31 sec
OE = 90%
EPEI = 12 days
Batch Size = 200
Shift = 3

Visual Trigger

Pull

Buffer

2 day

PROCESS B

Cycle Time: 31sec
OE = 90%
EPEI = 4 days
Batch Size = 1
Shift = 2
(2 during peak)

PROCESS C

Cycle Time: 31sec
OE = 90%
EPEI = 4 days
Batch Size = 1
Shift = 2
(2 during peak)

PACEMAKER CELL

Pull

Buffer

3 day RM

Weekly

BATCH PROCESS

Measures balanced to QCDSME and aligned to supply chain objectives

Figure 3.70

Example

CLUSTERING OF MUDA, MURA AND MURI

PHYSICAL FLOW				INFORMATION FLOW	PEOPLE FLOW	MONEY FLOW

MONEY FLOW

MUDA Paying key creditors sooner than contract specifies

MUDA Significant customers pay late consistently

PEOPLE FLOW

MURA / MUDA People not available to finish job on night shift

MUDA People not always available at the constraint (B)

MURI / MURA Always fixing the same problems - no time for problem solving

INFORMATION FLOW

MUDA Front line working off outdated information from the customer

MURA / MUDA Schedule inaccuracy – making what is not needed

MURA / MUDA No available standards to show what good should look like

MUDA No means to see performance to plan

MUDA Cannot see relationship between standard work and TAKT

PHYSICAL FLOW

MUDA / MURA Pace of value stream uncontrolled

MUDA Excessive inventory clogging flow

MURA / MUDA EPEI not aligned to customer requirement

MUDA / constraint OE at constraint is good but A and C are low and affect constraint performance

MUDA 980 transport steps between departments to complete value stream

MURA Constraint loaded at 95% capacity

MUDA Long set-up times and large batching at Process B

MUDA Effective cycle time cannot meet TAKT at B

MUDA Constraint at Process B not protected from starvation

MURA Variation in methods between employees

MUDA Producing more than the customer needs

MUDA / MURI Work released exceeds capacity

MUDA / MURI / MURA Uncontrolled batch size at constraint

MUDA / MURA High downtime at constraint

MUDA Piles of quarantined product after Process C

MURI Overtime or not delivering the answer to changes in demand

MUDA Slow movers get in the way of fast movers

MURA High variation in forecast accuracy

MUDA Unnecessary steps to get the work complete

Mark off the muda, mura and muri that have been addressed so far.

Table 3.22

✔ FOR YOU TO TRY

○ Improve information flow to achieve the vision by focusing on aspects such as:

- Takt awareness

- Speed and visibility of information

- Performance Measurement

- Synchronising information across the Value Stream.

○ Update the Future State Map.

○ Cross off the muda, mura and muri that
have been addressed.

Step 5: Develop the People Flow

The goal of improving the people flow is to establish what must look different in order to achieve velocity in how the human resources and their skills are made available. Figure 3.71 summarises three aspects that should be explored when designing the Future State and we will discuss a selection of them to address the muda, mura and muri identified in the Current State. The physical flow is directly influenced by the people flow. Review your own findings, and select the best countermeasures to develop the Future State with, and capture each decision on a flipchart.

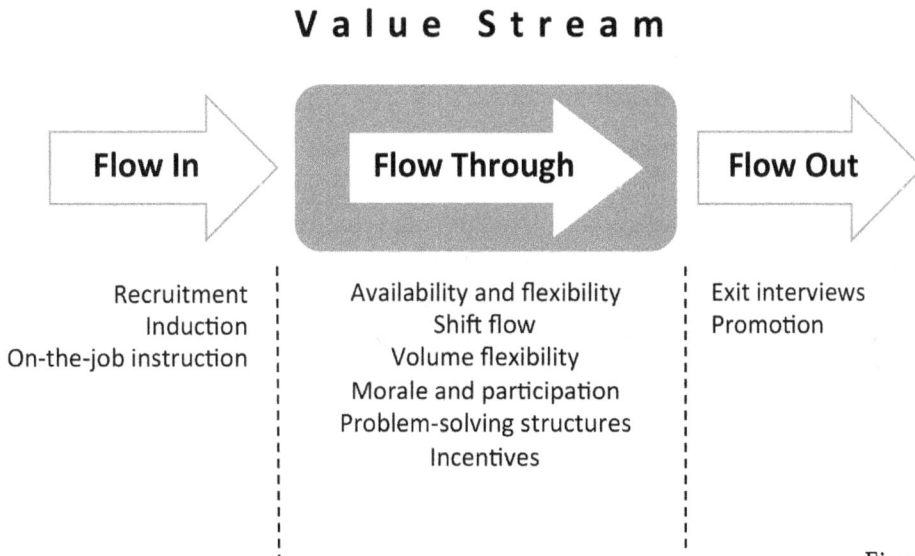

Value Stream

Flow In	Flow Through	Flow Out
Recruitment	Availability and flexibility	Exit interviews
Induction	Shift flow	Promotion
On-the-job instruction	Volume flexibility	
	Morale and participation	
	Problem-solving structures	
	Incentives	

Figure 3.71

Put the Best Skills at the Constraint

The constraint governs the throughput of the process, and as indicated in earlier sections, a loss at the constraint is a loss to the system. As such, having the best skills available at the constraint at all times is essential:

- Fill all positions at the constraint.

- Make their development a priority, and ensure the right skills mix and competency to perform the work to standard.

- Develop a contigency plan for absenteeism, leave periods or if an employee takes up a position elsewhere.

- Create a succession plan for the critical skills at the constraint.

- Assign a management team to deal with problems at the constraint. Set accountability to resolve issues in the shortest possible time.

Build a Plan for People Availability

Having the right skills available ensures each process is able to meet TAKT time as planned. Putting a system in place to do a daily check on skill availability and having a set of contingency plans ready will facilitate having the right people positioned in the right places, without disruption. Develop a plan for availability as follows:

- Implement a system to check who is available at work each day.
- Develop a plan that shows how to rotate or replace a skill when it is not available at a critical process.
- Conduct proper leave planning to ensure absent skills are staggered.
- Stagger starting times to facilitate flow.
- Stagger break times to facilitate flow.

Attendance should be considered key to achieving velocity and it is recommended that daily reviews be a priority for each leader and be visually managed. This has the added benefit that individuals prefer not to be highlighted as the employee who is absent or consistently late. Some organisations even use a forward-planning attendance matrix (Mann, 2004) – at the end of each day they ask team members to fill out their attendance for the next day:

- Yellow: I will be on leave tomorrow
- Blue: I am assisting another area tomorrow
- Grey: I will most likely be on sick leave tomorrow

The next morning prior to shift start, the actuals are updated with colour codes to represent (figure 3.72):

- Available
- Absent without leave
- Late

Example

ATTENDANCE VISUALS

AVAILABLE • FLEXIBLE • SKILLED

MONTH:	AUGUST 2014
AREA:	CELL 15 PROCESSING
LEADER:	BILLY

EMPLOYEE	1	2	3	4	5	6	7	8	9	10	11	12	13	14	15	16	17	18	19	20	21	22	23	24	25	26	27	28	29	30	31
JOHN																															
VUSI																															
ANGELO																															
JOHAN																															
THABO																															
GINA																															
ANGUS																															
BENJAMIN																															
THABASENG																															

COLOUR CODES:				
	PLANNED LEAVE	LOANED OUT	SICK LEAVE	AVAILABLE
	AWOL	LATE		

Figure 3.72

Build a Plan for People Flexibility

Although a strategy for human resource development is beyond the scope of this book, a selection of discussion points is included here to facilitate a basic plan for flexibility. Stability in the processes relies on flexibility to allow organisations to ride out the ups and downs of the market, cope with skills lost or deal with succession planning. This can be unsettling to the employees, and costly to the organisation, but the long-term vision for velocity may rely on a short-term sacrifice for a long-term benefit (Mann, 2004). Discuss the applicability of these points to your Future State:

○ Sales, operations, planning and human resources work together towards a common goal of flexibility.

  - Sales have a firm grasp on the market and communicate sales plans based on a sound development process.

  - Planning are able to take the plans and create level schedules.

  - Operations are able to plan the workforce based on flexible systems.

  - Human Resources are able to coordinate the hiring and transfering of staff.

○ There is a strategy to have as few job classifications as possible to ensure no employees 'own' particular jobs, and are considered part of a team able to move around. The transfer of employees between jobs is possible when the market requires it.

○ There is a strategy for cross-training to ensure employees have as many skills as possible to rotate:

  - If an employee is skilled in several jobs, when the need arises (temporarily or permanent) he or she is moved to facilitate teamwork and flow.

  - If an employee is skilled in only one position, and has spent years developing this seniority, he or she is less likely to be supportive of flexibility.

○ Shifts are planned to facilitate overtime flexibility. For example, two shifts are worked to allow overtime into the third shift where required. Excessive overtime can create muri but controlled overtime can be a powerful buffer against demand variation. Overtime used to continuously buffer process instability (lost time, defects, performance) must not be considered acceptable and steps to address this, are critical to facilitating flow.

○ Operations planning facilitate overtime flexibility. For example, under normal conditions, overtime is scheduled into the plan and employees are able to make the necessary personal arrangements in advance.

○ The use of temporary staff is used as a secondary strategy to react to changing customer demand, while balancing long-term employment security for permanent employees. There is a policy on the maximum ratio of temporary to permanent employees. Temporary staff are involved, trained and oriented to the same standard as permanent employees.

- Temporary or variable employees could be fully integrated into orientation, training and participation in team activities to promote morale, mutual trust and skill flexibility.

- Succession planning is done proactively.

A skills matrix can be a handy tool in keeping track of cross-skilling requirements and progress (figure 3.73). When the daily attendance is reviewed, it serves as a visual indicator for contingencies.

SKILLS MATRIX

AVAILABLE • FLEXIBLE • COMPETENT

| AREA: | CELL 15 PROCESSING | Next Training: A1 TRAINING 5 SEPT |
| LEADER: | BILLY | Participants: Johan, Thabo, Vusi |

SKILL	A1 Operation	A2 Operation	A3 Operation	5S	Team Meetings	Visual Performance	Quality at Source	Problem Solving	Autonomous Maint	ACTION BOARDS
JOHN										
VUSI										
ANGELO										
JOHAN										
THABO										
GINA										
ANGUS										
BENJAMIN										
THABASENG										

| SKILL CODES: | Not Yet Trained | | Competent |
| | Training Planned & Booked | | Able to Train Others |

Figure 3.73

Develop Scenario Plans for Demand Fluctuations

When there are changes in demand, overtime, cross-skilling or temporary staff could assist in varying the resources to match. It is recommended that scenario planning be done to encourage a consistent approach for leaders to follow and adjust their resources when demand fluctuates. See figure 3.74 for examples:

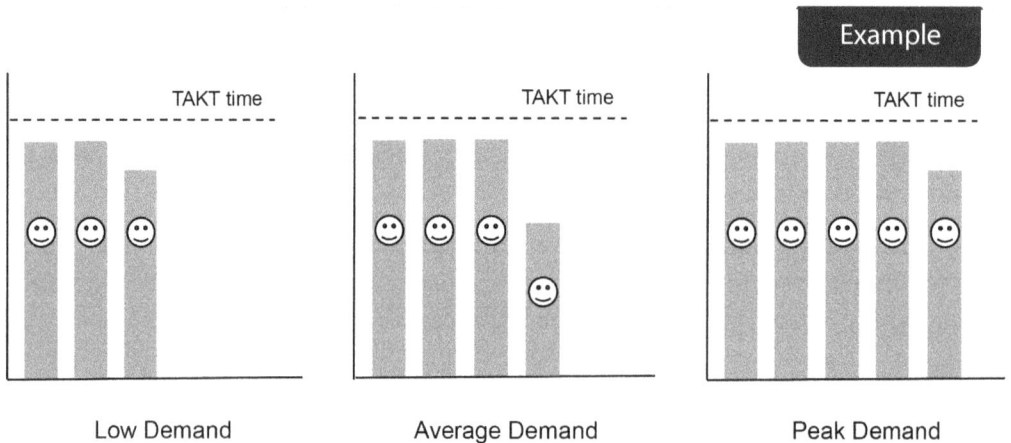

Low Demand · Average Demand · Peak Demand

Figure 3.74

o Develop the most likely scenarios to be encountered for the year based on sound knowledge of demand variation and forecasting.

o Agree when skills will be transferred (from within the department, other departments or other sites).

o Agree when overtime will be employed.

o Agree when temporary staff will be utilised.

Design Shifts for Flow

In addition to designing shifts to allow for fluctuations in demand and the ability to facilitate controlled overtime, flow of product or service through the Value Stream can also be influenced by the shift patterns. Consider what changes to the shift pattern may be required in the Future State to facilitate velocity (figure 3.75):

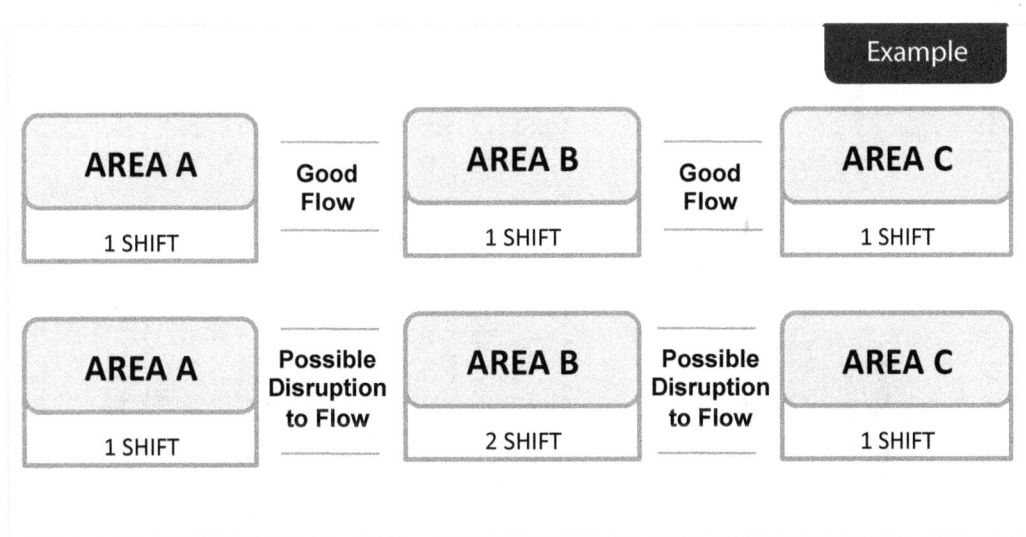

Figure 3.75

Example

Update the Future State Map with the people flow decisions (figure 3.76):

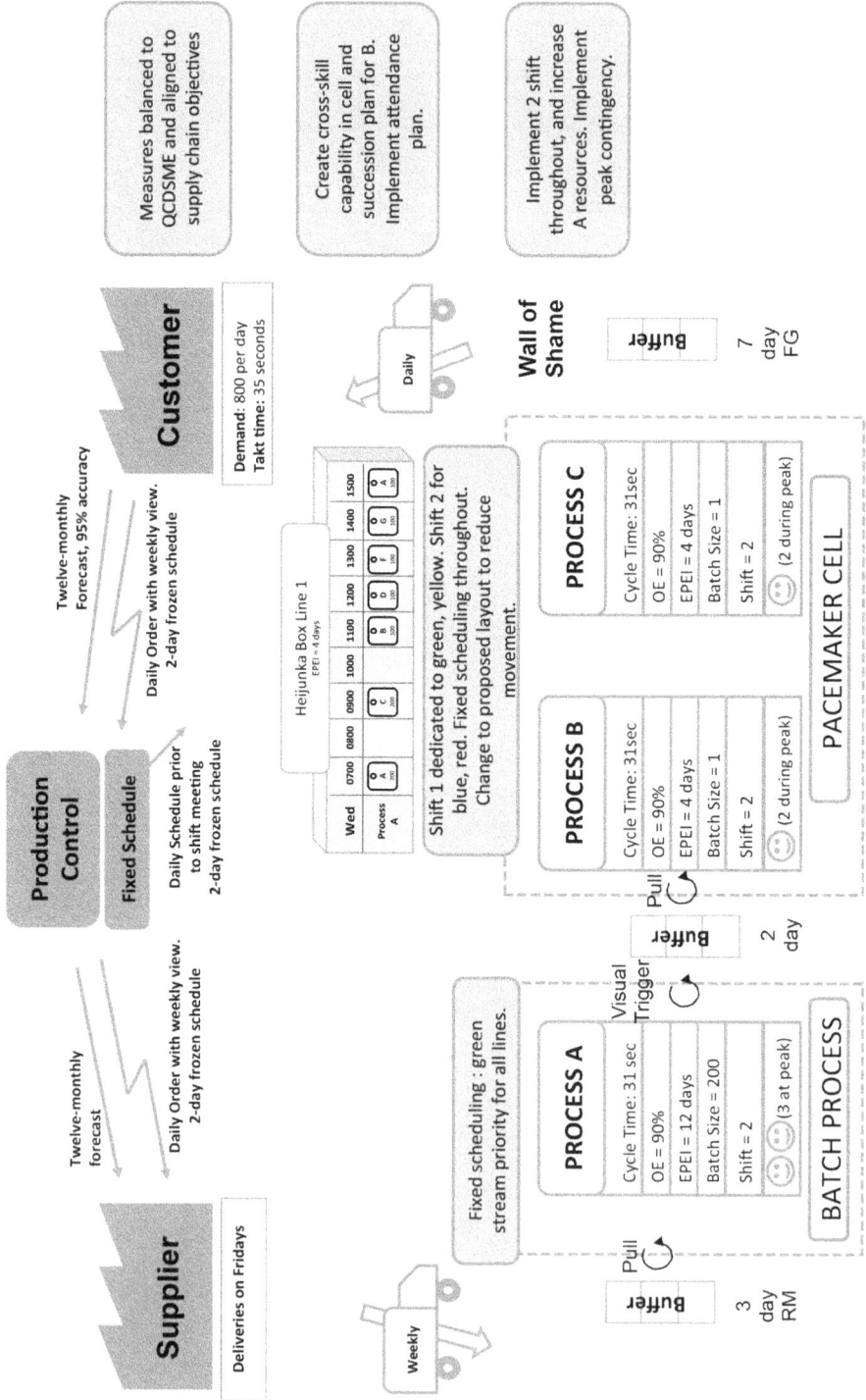

Supplier

Deliveries on Fridays

Twelve-monthly forecast

Daily Order with weekly view. 2-day frozen schedule

Weekly

Production Control

Fixed Schedule

Daily Schedule prior to shift meeting 2-day frozen schedule

Twelve-monthly Forecast, 95% accuracy

Daily Order with weekly view. 2-day frozen schedule

Customer

Demand: 800 per day
Takt time: 35 seconds

Daily

Measures balanced to QCDSME and aligned to supply chain objectives

Create cross-skill capability in cell and succession plan for B. Implement attendance plan.

Implement 2 shift throughout, and increase A resources. Implement peak contingency.

Heijunka Box Line 1
EPEI = 4 days

Wed	0700	0800	0900	1000	1100	1200	1300	1400	1500
Process A	A xxx 100		C xxx 100		B D 100 100	O D 100 100	O F 100	O G 100	O A 100

Shift 1 dedicated to green, yellow. Shift 2 for blue, red. Fixed scheduling throughout. Change to proposed layout to reduce movement.

Wall of Shame

Buffer

7 day FG

PACEMAKER CELL

PROCESS B

Cycle Time: 31sec
OE = 90%
EPEI = 4 days
Batch Size = 1
Shift = 2
(2 during peak)

PROCESS C

Cycle Time: 31sec
OE = 90%
EPEI = 4 days
Batch Size = 1
Shift = 2
(2 during peak)

Pull

Buffer

2 day

Fixed scheduling : green stream priority for all lines.

Visual Trigger

PROCESS A

Cycle Time: 31 sec
OE = 90%
EPEI = 12 days
Batch Size = 200
Shift = 2
(3 at peak)

BATCH PROCESS

Pull

Buffer

3 day RM

Figure 3.76

CLUSTERING OF MUDA, MURA AND MURI

Example

MONEY FLOW

MUDA
Paying key creditors sooner than contract specifies

MUDA
Significant customers pay late consistently

PEOPLE FLOW

MURA / MUDA
People not available to finish job on night shift

MUDA
People not always available at the constraint (B)

MURI / MURA
Always fixing the same problems - no time for problem solving

INFORMATION FLOW

MUDA
Front line working off outdated information from the customer

MURA / MUDA
Schedule inaccuracy – making what is not needed

MURA / MUDA
No available standards to show what good should look like

MUDA
No means to see performance to plan

MUDA
Cannot see relationship between standard work and TAKT

PHYSICAL FLOW

MUDA / MURA
Pace of value stream uncontrolled

MURA
Constraint loaded to 95% capacity

MUDA
Producing more than the customer needs

MURI
Overtime or not delivering the answer to changes in demand

MUDA
Excessive inventory clogging flow

MUDA
Long set-up times and large batching at process B

MUDA / MURI
Work released exceeds capacity

MUDA
Slow movers get in the way of fast movers

MURA / MUDA
EPEI not aligned to customer requirement

MUDA
Effective cycle time cannot meet TAKT at B

MUDA / MURI / MURA
Uncontrolled batch size at constraint

MURA
High variation in forecast accuracy

MUDA / MURA
OE at constraint is good. OE at A and C affect constraint performance

MUDA
Constraint at Process B not protected from starvation

MUDA / MURA
High downtime at constraint

MUDA
Unnecessary steps to get the work complete

MUDA
980 transport steps between departments to complete value stream

MURA
Variation in methods between employees

MUDA
Piles of quarantined product after Process C

Mark off the muda, mura and muri that have been addressed so far.

Table 3.23

✓ FOR YOU TO TRY

- Improve people flow to achieve the vision by focusing on aspects such as:
  - Skills at the constraint
  - People availability
  - People flexibility
  - Scenario plans for demand fluctuations.
- Update the Future State Map.
- Cross off the muda, mura and muri that have been addressed.

Step 6: Develop the Money Flow

The goal of improving the money flow is to ensure the improvements yield financial benefits. Organisations are conscious of maintaining stakeholder interest in the improvement drive, and if clear benefits are categorised and assigned a financial value, it is a powerful statement for continuation. Figure 3.77 summarises three aspects that should be explored when designing the Future State and we will discuss a selection of them to address the muda, mura and muri identified in the Current State. Review your own findings, and select the best countermeasures to develop the Future State with, and capture each decision on a flipchart.

Value Stream

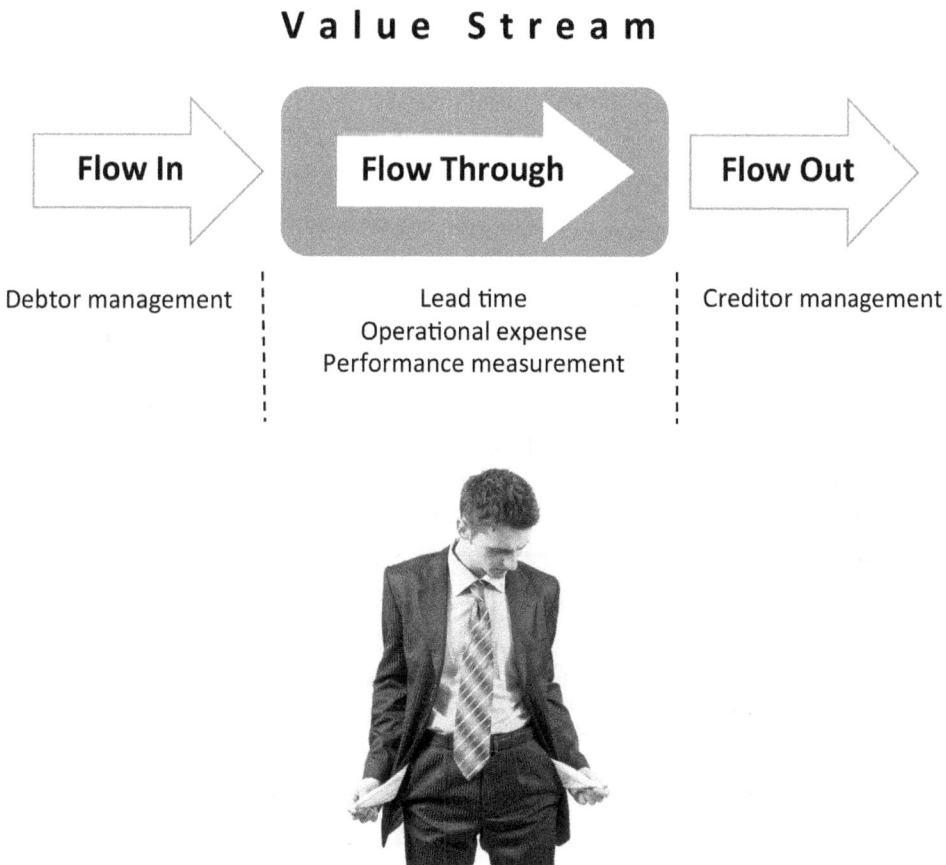

Flow In	Flow Through	Flow Out
Debtor management	Lead time Operational expense Performance measurement	Creditor management

Figure 3.77

By developing the Current State Map, it is possible to see for how long the Value Stream is 'financing' operations. The Cash-to-Cash Cycle describes how long it takes the organisation to spend money to produce a product or service, until the time the customer has paid for the product or service. By improving cash velocity, the cash-to-cash cycle is reduced. Some organisations operate with a different business model and receive the cash upfront for services but there are principles to follow that will still apply. Involvement from a qualified financial person is critical in these discussions. Review the Current State Map Money Line and discuss the following:

Improve Net Profit, Return on Investment (ROI) and Cash Flow

The good news is that it is possible to improve on these financial goals by establishing the right focus in operations. The trick is to translate these goals into tangible, operational elements that if changed would have a signficant financial impact for the business. Figure 3.78 describes how the aim of an organisation driven by financial goals, is to maximise money coming in, reduce money in the system and reduce money paid out:

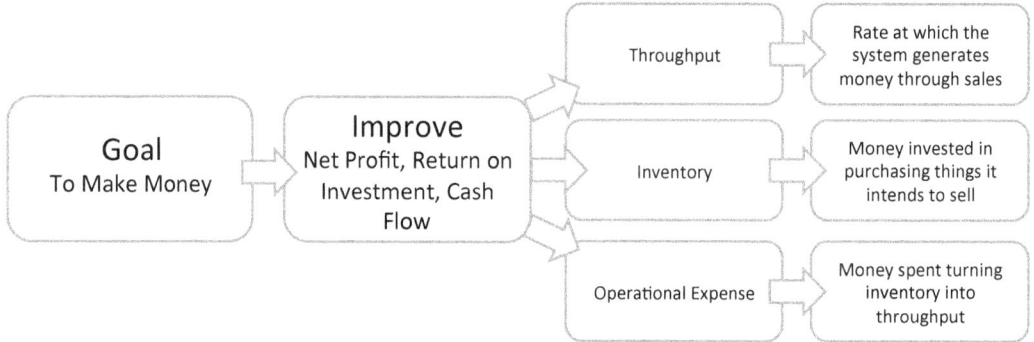

Figure 3.78

In theory, throughput should first be improved, followed by inventory and then operating expense (figure 3.79). This is because throughput has an immediate positive impact on the three financials (net profit, ROI and cash flow) and a company can afford to increase inventory and expense, provided the throughput also improves. Decreasing inventory has a once-off effect on cash and can reduce lead time. Be careful as this could also reduce throughput. Likewise, operating expense could be reduced but at the risk of losing skills. Often companies tackle this the opposite way around, which may have a short-term benefit but the long-term implications for recovery are dire (Goldratt, 2004).

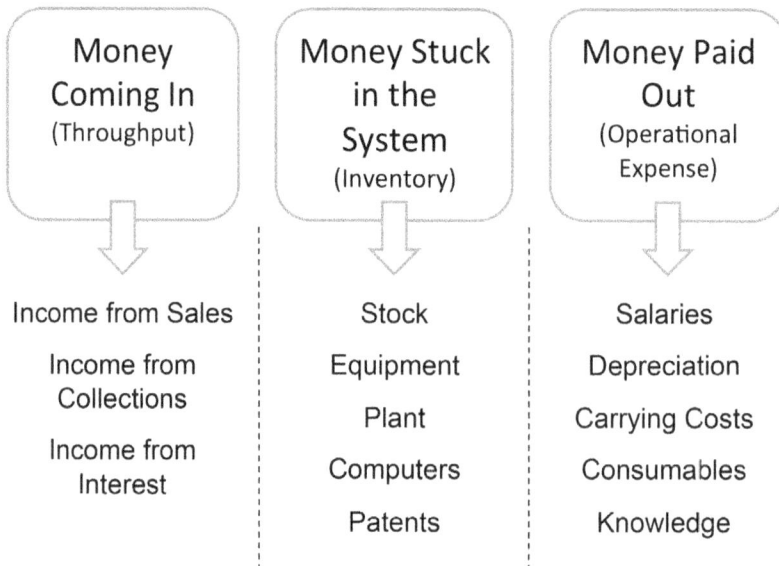

Figure 3.79

Raise the Throughput of the Value Stream

Manage Debtors (money owed to you):

o Make someone accountable for debtor days.

o Evaluate if discounts offered and penalties administered yield early or on-time payment.

o Send invoices out timeously and according to a regular schedule.

o Deal with bad payers immediately and consistently.

o Request large payments to be divided into partial payments if this will improve cash flow.

o Deposit cheques promptly.

o Revise credit limits based on customers' changing financial health.

o Obtain collateral or deposits to minimise risks.

o If feasible, offer delayed payment terms to stimulate demand.

o Conduct stringent health checks on customers (and their industries) before extending credit.

Money Coming In (Throughput)

Income from Sales

Income from Collections

Income from Interest

Reduce Losses:

o Reducing the losses will make more capacity available to process work (figure 3.80).

o The additional capacity will impact the bottom line only when additional throughput is achieved – the system is able to generate additional money through sales.

- If there is an insatiable market, benefit is realised.

- If there is no additional market to sell to, then no benefit is realised.

- If lost sales from late delivery is improved, benefit is realised.

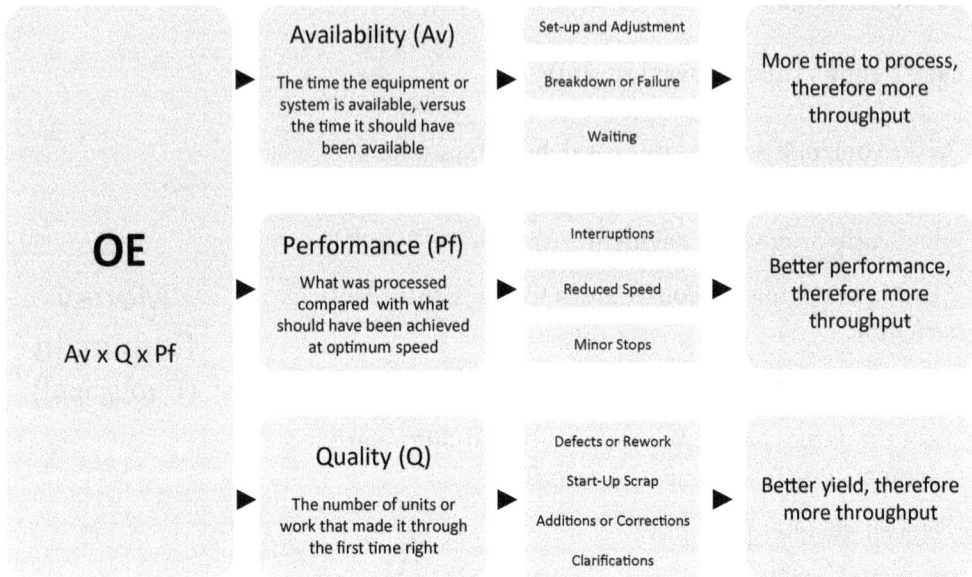

OE

$Av \times Q \times Pf$

Availability (Av)

The time the equipment or system is available, versus the time it should have been available

Set-up and Adjustment

Breakdown or Failure

Waiting

More time to process, therefore more throughput

Performance (Pf)

What was processed compared with what should have been achieved at optimum speed

Interruptions

Reduced Speed

Minor Stops

Better performance, therefore more throughput

Quality (Q)

The number of units or work that made it through the first time right

Defects or Rework

Start-Up Scrap

Additions or Corrections

Clarifications

Better yield, therefore more throughput

Figure 3.80

Reduce Inventory Levels

In the context of Value Stream mapping, this topic has been extensively covered in creating the physical, information and people flow, and will be summarised in the final Future State Map at the end of this section. In summary, the following improvements will have a direct impact on inventory as described in money flow (figure 3.81):

- o Strategic Inventory Management
  - Raw material inventory reduction
  - Work-in-progress reduction
  - Finished goods reduction
- o Queue size reduction
- o Overall lead time reduction
- o Deferred capital investment.

Money Stuck in the System (Inventory)

Stock

Equipment

Plant

Computers

Patents

```
┌─────────────────────────────────────┐
│         Current State Lead Time       │
└─────────────────────────────────────┘
                    ⇩
┌─────────────────────────────────────┐
│          Current State               │
│          Waste Identified            │
└─────────────────────────────────────┘
                    ⇩
        ┌───────────────────┐
        │    Future State    │
        │     Lead Time      │
        └───────────────────┘
                    ⇩
             Reduced
            Inventory
```

Figure 3.81

Reduce Operational Expense

Manage Creditors (money you owe):

○ Make someone accountable for creditor days.

○ Centralise payment of creditors to meet obligations at the most profitable time.

○ Divide payments into partial payments.

○ Spread payments out over the month to better align with money coming in.

○ Negotiate and improve payment terms with suppliers.

○ Align the timing of payments to payment terms rather than falling prey to paying early for convenience sake.

○ Conduct old-fashioned bartering by offering suppliers product or service in exchange for their product or service.

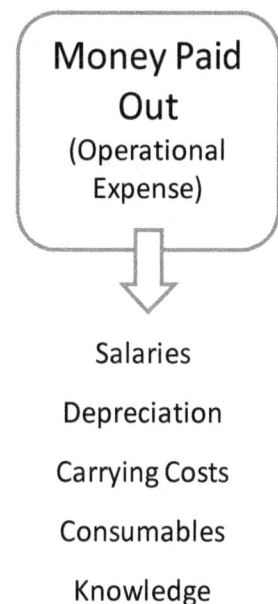

Money Paid Out
(Operational Expense)

⇩

Salaries

Depreciation

Carrying Costs

Consumables

Knowledge

Conduct a Basic Cash Loss Evaluation:

Analyse the cost drivers in the business and link projects identified in the Future State to them (figure 3.82). Refer to Chapter 4.

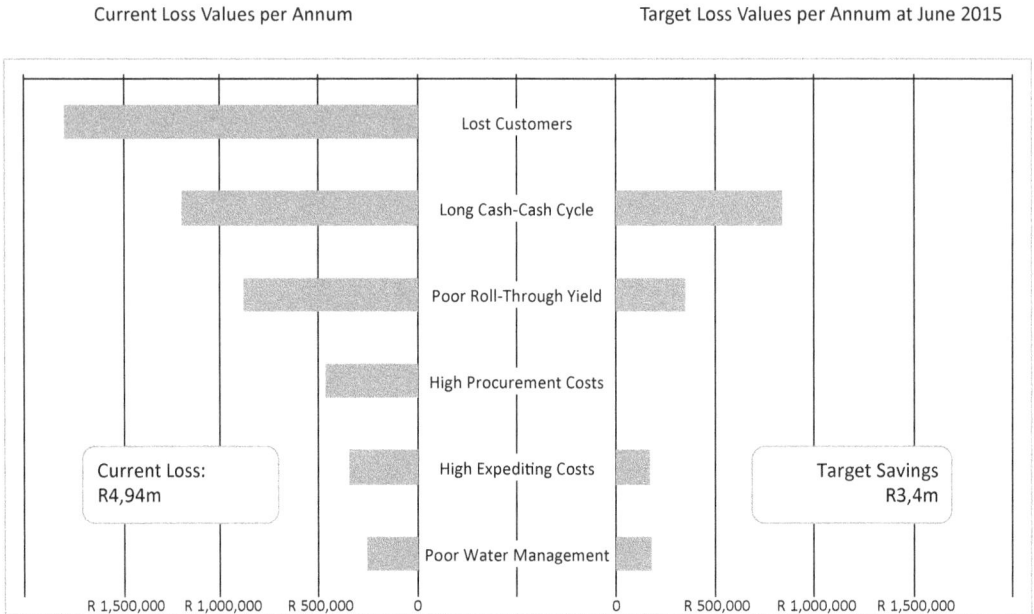

Current Loss Values per Annum   Target Loss Values per Annum at June 2015

	Lost Customers	
	Long Cash-Cash Cycle	
	Poor Roll-Through Yield	
	High Procurement Costs	
Current Loss: R4,94m	High Expediting Costs	Target Savings R3,4m
	Poor Water Management	
R 1,500,000 R 1,000,000 R 500,000 0		0 R 500,000 R 1,000,000 R 1,500,000

Figure 3.82

Use a Structured Approach to Projects

All projects identified must be structured according to plan, do, check and adjust (PDCA) and feature a return on investment focus – for example:

○ Every project is signed off by a financial representative

○ Cost to implement is clarified

○ Financial gains are clarified

○ Return on investment is calculated.

Typically organisations will utilise a project charter approach as used in the Six Sigma problem-solving methodology. It is recommended that such an approach be adopted to ensure the projects are implemented systematically, timeously and to meet the goals. This is further discussed in PROBLEM SOLVING.

Update the Future State Map with the money flow decisions (figure 3.83):

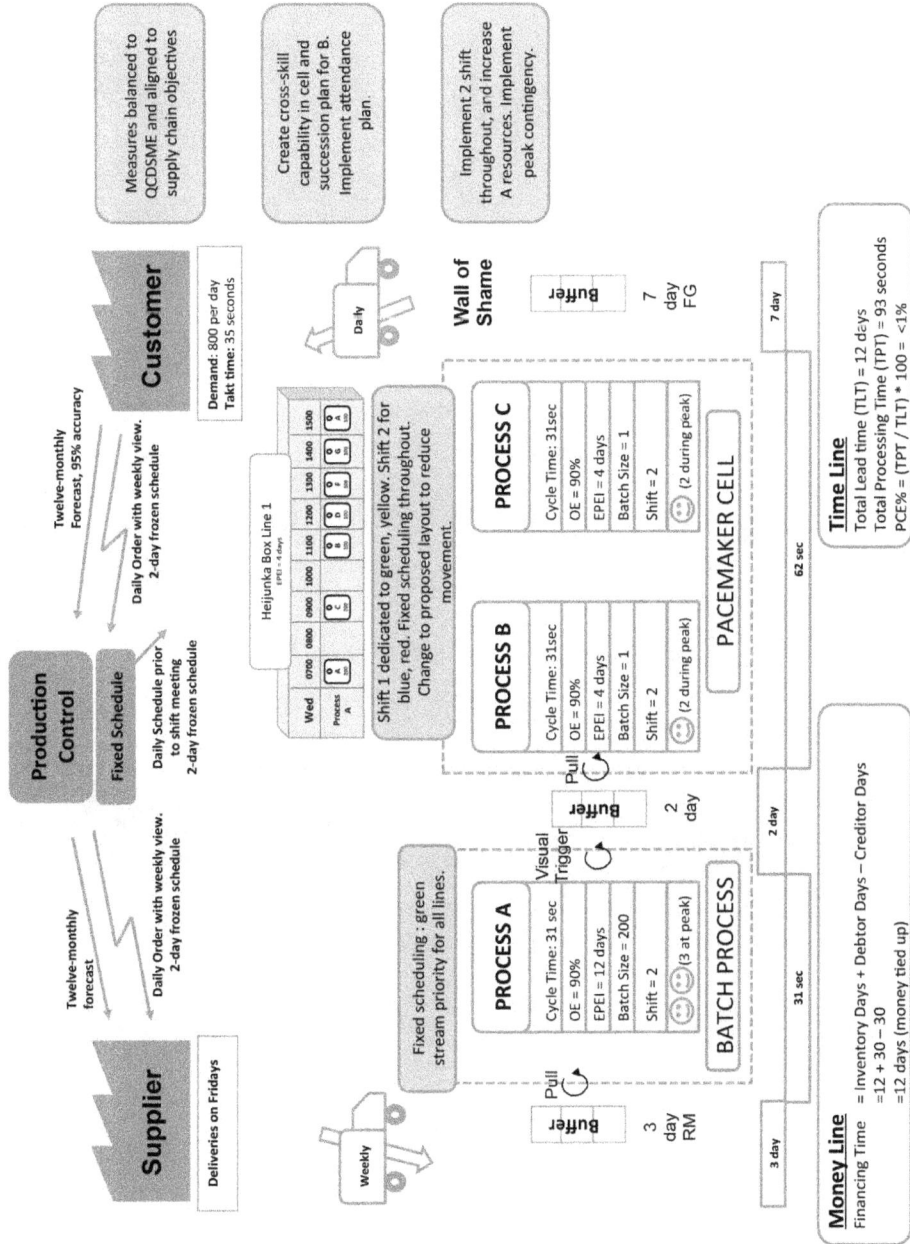

Figure 3.83

CLUSTERING OF MUDA, MURA AND MURI

Example

MONEY FLOW

- **MUDA** Paying key creditors sooner than contract specifies
- **MUDA** Significant customer pay late consistently

PEOPLE FLOW

- **MURA / MUDA** People not available to finish job on night shift
- **MUDA** People not always available at the constraint (B)
- **MURI / MURA** Always fixing the same problems - no time for problem solving

INFORMATION FLOW

- **MURA / MUDA** Schedule inaccuracy – making what is not needed
- **MUDA** Front line works off outdated information from the customer
- **MURA / MUDA** No available standards to show what good should look like
- **MUDA** No means to see performance to plan
- **MUDA** Cannot see relationship between standard work and TAKT

PHYSICAL FLOW

- **MUDA / MURA** Pace / value stream uncontrolled
- **MUDA** Excessive inventory clogging flow
- **MURA / MUDA** EPEI not aligned to customer requirement
- **MUDA / MURA** OE at constraint is good but A and C affect constraint performance
- **MUDA** 980 transport steps between departments to complete value stream
- **MURA** Constraint loaded at 95% capacity
- **MUDA** Long set-up times and large batching at Process B
- **MUDA** Effective cycle time cannot meet TAKT at B
- **MUDA** Constraint at Process B not protected from starvation
- **MURA** Variation in methods between employees
- **MUDA** Producing more than the customer needs
- **MUDA / MURI** Work released exceeds capacity
- **MUDA / MURI / MURA** Uncontrolled batch size at constraint
- **MUDA / MURA** High downtime at constraint
- **MUDA** Piles of quarantined product after Process C
- **MURI** Overtime or not delivering the answer to changes in demand
- **MUDA** Slow movers get in the way of fast movers
- **MURA** High variation in forecast accuracy
- **MUDA** Unnecessary steps to get the work complete

Mark off the muda, mura and muri that have been addressed so far.

Table 3.24

✓ FOR YOU TO TRY

- Improve money flow to achieve the vision by focusing on aspects such as:

  - Throughput improvement

  - Inventory reduction

  - Operational expense reduction

  - Linking projects to financial benefits.

- Update the Future State Map and the money line.

- Cross off the muda, mura and muri that have been addressed.

DEVELOP THE FUTURE STATE
EXECUTION LOGIC

🅠 WHAT IS THIS?

The success of the implementation will depend highly on how well the execution is planned. Unfortunately this is not as simple as just listing the actions and checking with responsible people when they will have time to implement them – there is a logic to the implementation that will need to be designed. For example, a level of flow is required to implement pull, and a level of stability is required to implement flow, so the sequence and timing of these steps must be thought through.

Like with most things, there is also a balance to be achieved. Find a healthy mix between results in the short term, and achieving the Future State Vision in the long term, with sufficient progress in between.

🅠 WHY IS THIS HELPFUL?

- Implementation logic drives the correct sequence of activities to achieve the Future State Vision.

- Expectation is clear, progress can be tracked and obstacles removed systematically.

- A consistent understanding and alignment to the plan is developed.

🅠 HOW TO DO IT

Develop the Execution Matrix

The example provided in table 3.25 is a good framework by which to structure your implementation logic. Remember that your North Star and Future State Vision should all align and start to come together. Developing the matrix first helps to categorise the improvement actions into flows as well as sequence. This will simplify the decision making around timing, sequence and expectations in the road map and project plan.

Example

FUTURE STATE EXECUTION MATRIX

	PHYSICAL FLOW	INFORMATION FLOW	PEOPLE FLOW	TIMING	VALUE STREAM IMPROVEMENT GOALS
BASIC STABILITY	Performance Improvement to TAKT Waste Elimination OE Improvement Quality Variation Demand Management Standardised Work Product Design	Performance Measures Plan Changes Information Provision and Quality	Constraint Skills Availability People Availability	6 Months	Improve Future Cycle Time to 31 seconds Increase OE at Process A to 90%; B to 90%; C to 90% Reduce Failure Demand by 50% Reduce Unplanned Changes by 70% Develop 2x2 Skills at Constraint Reduce Debtors Days to 30 Improve OTIF to 80%
FLOW	Continuous Flow Principles Strategic Buffers Material Flow	TAKT Image Information Synchronisation	People Flexibility Volume Flexibility Shift Flow	12 months	Reduce Lead Time to 12 Days Improve Processing Time to 96 seconds Improve total Stock Turns to 24 Develop 2x2 Skills in All Areas Implement 2-shift Throughout Improve OTIF to 90%
LEVEL PULL	Pace Regulation Connect to Demand	Visualise Physical Flow (Heijunka Box)		24 months	Reduce Lead Time to 8 Days Achieve EPEI = 4 days Improve OTIF to 98% Improve Total Stock Turns to 48

Table 3.25

✅ FOR YOU TO TRY

- Review the outcomes from the Future State mapping activities.

- Discuss the applicability of sequence and timing in the execution – for example, which activities must take place before others can be achieved?

- Complete the Future State Execution Matrix to show the sequence and logic behind the Future State achievement as well as the broad timings.

4 BASIC CASH LOSS EVALUATION
LINK IMPROVEMENT TO THE BOTTOM LINE

❓ WHAT IS THIS?

Driving an improvement strategy is not easy. Cutting through the hesitation, reservation and cynicism requires tremendous determination but if you present a solid business case for change very few will contest the motivation put forward. Leaders and stakeholders will have good questions – acknowledge this and prepare answers that will stimulate support and urgency for the work to be done. Common questions to start thinking about include:

- o How do we reduce costs and get the benefit to flow into profit?
- o How do we ensure the improvement focus will yield a financial benefit?
- o How can we improve leadership buy-in to initiate improvement activities?
- o How can we release the necessary funds to support the improvement drive?

It is possible to reduce costs, it is possible to focus efforts to bottom line impact and it is possible to motivate support from leaders and their budgets. This requires a thorough understanding of what drives cost in the business and where reasonable opportunities lie.

Don't be fooled though. Operational Excellence is not only about cost reduction but we are obligated to shareholders and customers to provide more value through the better use of existing resources. If this is done in a data-driven, responsible and mutually beneficial manner, it will assist in moving the organisation to new heights of performance and pave the way for further growth. If customer loyalty and focus on the long-term goals remains key, cost reduction can take place effectively with real long-term benefit to the company, environment, shareholders, customers and employees.

The Basic Cash Loss Evaluation is designed to give insight into the areas that will leverage the most impact to the business. It is emphasised that this is a basic evaluation, as there are scores of books covering this topic alone, but it should be seen as a complimentary view to the Best Practice and Value Stream Evaluations, and not a stand-alone tool. Combining what you have learned from the evaluations performed up until now, you will be armed with a well-rounded interpretation that will intelligently inform your improvement strategy.

The evaluation begins with a better understanding of the goals of a commercial business and what drives cost. Thereafter, you evaluate significant contributors to the cost drivers and establish a list of the business levers to be tackled. A summary reflecting the current condition and focus is completed, after which you will gain consensus on the target condition to be achieved.

A Motivation for Cost Reduction

Steven Bragg, author of Cost Reduction Analysis (Bragg, M, 2010, Cost Reduction Analysis) explains how it requires significantly more revenue generation than cost reduction to achieve the same percentage profit improvement and by eliminating unnecessary costs responsibly, a company can compound gains that keep piling up into the future. Instead of entrenching the best practice of ongoing costs reductions, companies often resort to organisation-wide cuts in a crisis. Good, responsible cost reduction strategies in contrast align with the North Star objectives and form part of the improvement cycle.

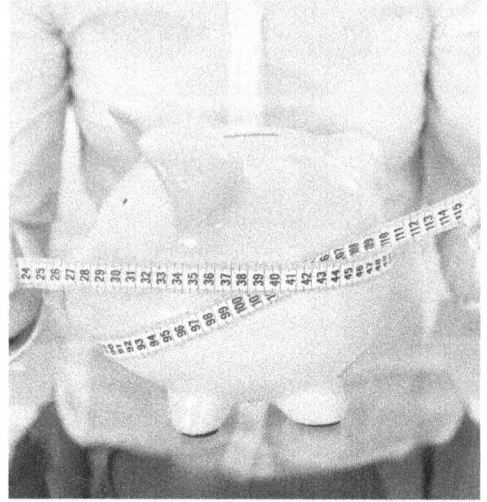

Cost reduction may also not be an option. It could be a prerequisite for survival in the following instances:

- Lost revenue: price reductions driven by the market create a need for cost reduction. Automotive industry suppliers in South Africa are constantly under pressure to reduce their prices triggering formal cost reduction strategies every year.

- Fixed costs: high investment in fixed costs means the need to utilise expensive capacity effectively is critical. Industry slow-down can be weathered if cost reduction has prepared the company ahead of time. The company left exposed and unable to sell the capacity could very well close their doors.

- Incremental creep: where there is no focus on cost reduction, costs naturally increase. This could be influenced by inflation, processes changes, increasing employee entitlements or a general complacency for cost in the organisation.

- Complexity: excessive layers of management requiring more levels of control and reporting, means leaders are disconnected from the heart of the operations. Often this results in precious time being spent on unnecessary activities that do not add value.

Cost reduction is therefore the easiest and most certain way to increase profits and enhance cash flow in the short term and can be a critical driver of long term growth. Furthermore it is within the control of the business, whereas revenue creation can be influenced by factors beyond your control.

Equipped with a robust method for identifying cost reduction opportunities, using the right measures and executing strategy for reinvestment, companies can realise significant benefits over time.

When Cost Reduction Fails

No doubt cost reduction has also been branded with a bad name. The worst form of cost reduction is a blanket approach in crisis-mode, where management enforce an across-the-board percentage cut. This is reactive in nature and invariably destroys value in the following ways:

- Operations are cut to the bone to the extent where service levels to internal and external customers are affected.

- Managers respond by padding budgets to compensate for future cuts, leading to unnecessary costs and fund allocations.

- Good people move on to greener pastures leaving behind a skills gap.

- Long-term-growth activities are also cut – for example, employee development and investment. The short term benefit creates a long term sacrifice.

Cost reduction is often misdirected and aimed purely at the lower-level employees. The organisation requires support from all staff to achieve true cost reduction strategies and this is best achieved when staff can see the same, if not more, effort being applied in the higher levels of the organisation. Improvement pain is best shared.

Finally, an investment may not necessaily align with strategic needs but has strong internal support from an individual. Staying focused on the North Star objectives is critical to filter out non-critical, cost driving activities (Bragg, 2010).

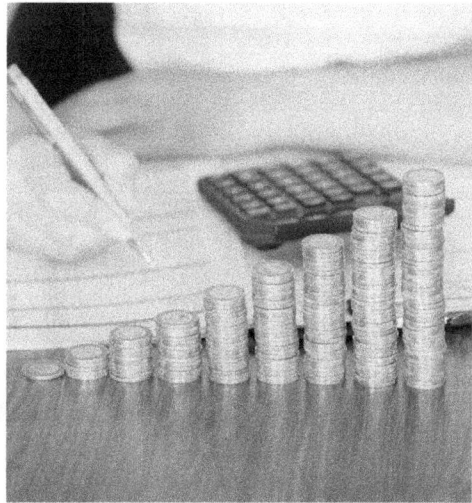

? WHY IS THIS HELPFUL?

- Business levers are understood and exploited.

- Improvement effort is more focused, data-driven and designed to yield financial results.

- Buy-in for the improvement strategy is more likely.

- KPIs for cost reduction are more focused.

- A system's-thinking approach improves the functional integration towards improvement.

- Justification for investment is made possible.

- A link is established between the business objectives and initiatives identified.

❓ HOW TO DO IT

Step 1: Gather a Team

The team involved with the previous evaluations would most likely be the same group to handle the Cash Loss Evaluation. Representation from the financial department is mandatory because they will be able to provide support in getting accurate financial figures and verifying the conclusions made from the data.

Step 2: Clarify the Goal

The Voice of the Business and in some cases the Voice of the Customer will specifically refer to cost-saving objectives and should tangibly express the expectations of 'how much cost reduction?'. Refer to the exercises completed in Chapter 1 and table 4.1 as an input to this step and update table 4.2 with specific goals and objectives for cost reduction.

Business Goals	Business Objectives	Key Initiatives
Reduce Working Capital by 18%	Reduce Inventory Holding by R20m	**?**
	Reduce Cash-to-Cash Cycle to 45 Days	
	Reduce Operating Expenditure by 25%	Example

Table 4.1

The analysis must align to these cost reduction objectives and we will use this as our starting point and sanity check for the sections that follow.

TIPS

Perhaps the goals and objectives are not as clear cut as they should be. If you find yourself in this position, cost reduction can also be focused by:

- Channelling improvements to areas important to future growth.

- Eliminating unprofitable business lines first to focus attention to retained lines.

- Focusing attention to the bottleneck process first and maximising throughput from there.

- Cleaning up reporting to expose costs and their locations more easily (Bragg, 2010).

COST REDUCTION GOALS	Business Objectives	Business Goal

Table 4.2

Step 3: Understand the Cost Drivers

A cost driver is described as a business activity that causes a cost to be incurred. For the purpose of this evaluation, consider cost drivers to be the key expenses influencing the management accounts.

This exercise centres around identifying costs that have the greatest impact on the cost reduction objectives and subsequently the greatest impact on the business goals. This is often not well understood and employees may not have a firm grip on the relationship between cost drivers and the business objectives.

It is recommended a financial representative facilitate a session to guide the team through the various cost drivers behind each objective (figure 4.1).

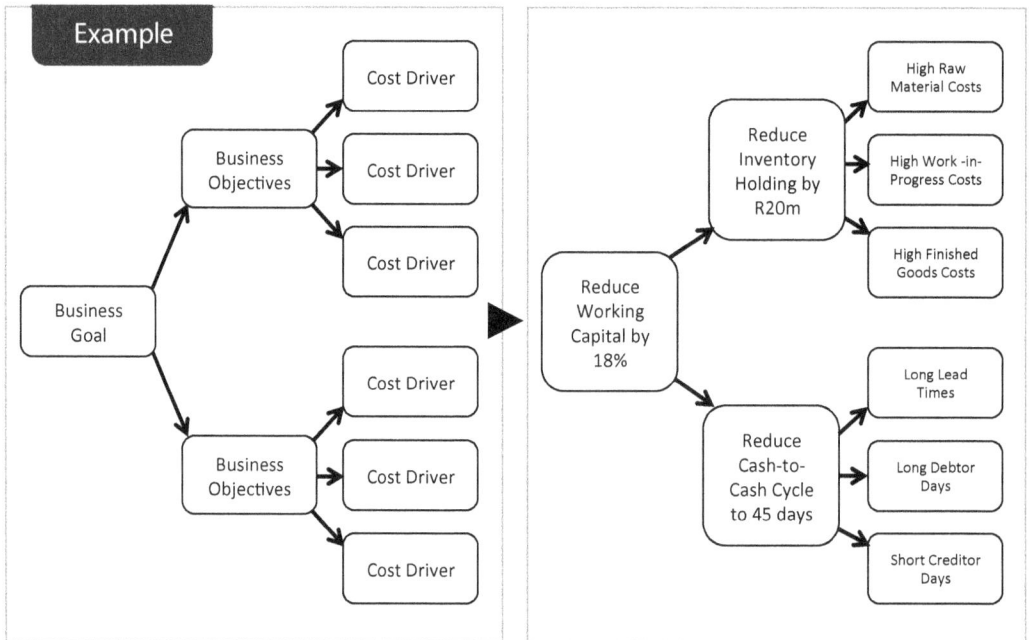

Figure 4.1

Update table 4.3 to show the cost drivers for each of the cost reduction objectives.

COST REDUCTION GOALS

Business Goal	Business Objectives	Cost Drivers

Evaluate each business objective and list the contributing cost drivers that significantly influence this cost.

Table 4.3

This evaluation is a data-driven activity and quite analytical in nature. It will require digging into information and conducting initial problem solving. Depending on how readily available information is in your organisation, this could lead to 'analysis paralysis'.

We recommend you strike a happy balance between enough accurate information to make a decision and not too much information that the team is unable to see the wood for the trees. The intention is to understand the current situation, place a stake in the ground and interpret where the benefit is most to be had.

CAUTION

Beware of
Analysis Paralysis

An experienced facilitator will be able to guide the group and help maintain the balance.

Step: 4 Summarise Cost Drivers and Categories into a Spreadsheet

It is best to develop this analysis in a spreadsheet to assist with formulas, sorting, hiding and visualising data into graph formats. This will also make updating and tracking far easier.

○ Refer to the results of the Value Stream Evaluation for cost reduction opportunities identified.

○ Review the guidelines provided in figure 4.2 and table 4.4 to stimulate further ideas for cost reduction and typical categories to consider.

○ List all relevant cost drivers to the business goals and objectives in a spreadsheet (table 4.5) and add your own description of what this is.

○ Determine the category of loss this falls under to better understand the impact of the cost driver (table 4.5). They generally fall into one or more of the categories indicated and this provides a view of what the cost driver is most likely to influence.

It is important to remember that the guideline in table 4.4 will prompt ideas but your financial representative must provide support in how the costs are described and calculated. Be aware of possible duplications and double counting as it must represent bottom line change.

Possible Loss Categories

Example

Lost Sales Opportunity	Lost Inventory	Lost Available Time
Lost Labour Time	Lost Material	Lost Money Flow

Cost Drivers

Wrong Investments	Transportation Waste	High Overtime
Poor Capacity Utilisation	Poor Constraint Management	High Procurement Costs
Poor First-Pass Yield	Absenteeism and Poor Leave Cover	Poor Water Management
Poor Roll-Through Yield	Product or Service Line Complexity	Lack of Equipment and System Standardisation
Inaccurate Bills of Material	High Employee Turnover	Lost Contracts
Unprofitable Products or Services	Long Cash-to-Cash Cycle	Poor Maintenance Management
Poor Inventory Management	Expediting	Unprofitable Customers
High Product or Service Cost	Unnecessary Contractor Costs	Unnecessary Training Costs
Poor Energy Usage	Speed losses	Wrong Manning Levels
Unnecessary Temporary Labour	Unnecessary Material Usage	Unnecessary Processes
Breakdowns and Idle Time	Emissions Waste	Bio-Diversity Waste

Figure 4.2

COST DRIVER GUIDELINE

Cost Driver	Quick Description	Category Examples
Wrong Investment	Investing in projects that are not aligned to strategic intents.	Lost Money Flow
Poor Capacity Utilisation	Overall Effectiveness (OE) directly impacts the utilisation of available capacity and is the combined effect of availability, quality and performance. Refer to Chapter 3 for more information on OE.	Lost Material, Labour, Available Time or Sales Opportunity
Poor First-Pass Yield	In manufacturing, this relates to scrapped and reworked product. In service, this relates to rework and backtracking of work because it was not right the first time. This could form part of OE and impact lost sales opportunity if the lost product could have been sold.	Lost Material or Labour
Poor Roll-Through Yield	The product of the first-pass yields. It represents the system yield once work has passed through all stations.	Lost Material, Labour or Sales Opportunity
Inaccurate Bills of Material	Errors in the bill of materials resulting in incorrect purchasing and levels of inventory.	Lost Inventory or Money Flow
Unprofitable Products or Services	Products or services that cannot be reduced in cost and that should be removed from the product or service offering altogether. Often these cause an unnecessary complexity in the process and increases in inventory or marketing literature. Refer to the Glenday Sieve in Chapter 3.	Lost Money Flow
Poor Inventory Management	Poor inventory practices or overproduction resulting in shortages and excessive stocks.	Lost Inventory, Available Time or Money Flow
High Product or Service Cost	Particular products or services that, by design, are expensive to deliver and result in lost sales. These products and services have the potential for improved design that reduces the cost to supply.	Lost Sales Opportunity
Poor Energy Usage	Excessive consumption of electricity and fuels.	Lost Money Flow
Unnecessary Temporary Labour	Use of temporary labour where opportunity for improved manning and utilisation is possible.	Lost Money Flow
Breakdowns and Idle Time	Lost time on equipment or systems due to stoppages, breakdowns or waiting times. This could form part of OE and impact lost sales opportunity if the time could have been used for saleable goods or services.	Lost Available Time
Transportation Waste	Excessive transportation to move people, documents, materials, supplies and finished goods.	Lost Money Flow
Poor Constraint Management	Not managing the utilisation and expense of the constraint effectively for optimum throughput at lowest cost.	Lost Sales Opportunity

Table 4.4

COST DRIVER GUIDELINE CONTINUED.../

Cost Driver	Quick Description	Category Examples
Absenteeism and Poor Leave Cover	Lost labour availability due to excessive absenteeism levels in comparison with industry standard. Poor leave planning resulting in labour shortages and imbalances. If labour affects the capacity utilisation of the constraint or throughput, this could also impact lost sales opportunity.	Lost Labour
Product or Service Line Complexity	When production or service volumes are scattered across a variety of products or services resulting in no economies of repetition and a negative impact to flow.	Lost Available Time or Sales Opportunity
High Employee Turnover	High turnover of staff due to morale, poor retention strategies or employment instability.	Lost Labour
Long Cash-to-Cash Cycle (Inventory, Debtors and Creditors)	Long lead times from the start to the end of the process that affects the time to receive cash in hand.	Lost Money Flow or Sales Opportunity
Expediting	Extra cost to expedite a service or product that has become urgent. Could include labour to address, freight costs, delays to other work priorities and crisis management.	Lost Money Flow
Unnecessary Contractor Costs	Utilising contractors where it is avoidable.	Lost Money Flow
Speed Losses	Lost speed of processing as a result of design changes to equipment, lack of training, staff instability, process and people variations. This could form part of OE and impact lost sales opportunity if the performance could be improved and used to produce saleable goods or services.	Lost Available Time or Labour
Unnecessary Material Usage	Using only virgin material during processing and not capitalising on recycling, remanufacturing or reusing. Losing material unnecessarily during processing.	Lost Material, Lost Money Flow
Emissions Waste	Emissions that cause pollution and could incur fines. Unnecessary loss of steam.	Lost Money Flow
High Overtime	Excessive overtime to compensate for lost time created by waste. This could also influence performance where overburdening employees results in lower productivity and increased errors.	Lost Labour, Money Flow or Material
High Procurement Costs	Inefficiency in procurement processes, too many suppliers, poor supplier relations and management, lack of total cost Best Practice, poor focus on procurement information and rationalising spend. Long procurement lead times could also result in lost sales opportunity.	Lost Money Flow
Poor Water Management	Excessive use and discharge of contaminated water both from offices and production.	Lost Money Flow

COST DRIVER GUIDELINE CONTINUED.../

Cost Driver	Quick Description	Category Examples
Lack of Equipment and System Standardisation	For equipment, non-standard specifications results in excessive spare part costs, the skills required to maintain and the time to repair. Non-standard systems results in the potential for stand-alone systems influencing additional steps in the processes and inaccuracy in information.	Lost Available Time or Money Flow
Lost Contracts	Customers who have stopped buying from the company and have switched their purchases elsewhere.	Lost Sales Opportunity
Poor Maintenance Management	Haphazard maintenance activities resulting in unplanned downtime. Reactive rather than proactive.	Lost Available Time
Unprofitable Customers	Expending efforts on customers who produce small overall sales volumes or low margins.	Lost Labour
Unnecessary Training Costs	Investing in training that is not aligned to strategic intents or facilitating training that does not yield the desired results.	Lost Money Flow
Wrong Manning Levels	Unbalanced labour allocations to demand requirements, shortages or poor flexibility and excessive labour.	Lost Labour, Lost Money Flow
Unnecessary Processes	Processes in the Value Stream that add no value and should be eliminated. This could also refer to unnecessary quality standards in place that create expenses but no value to the customer.	Lost Labour
Bio-Diversity Waste	Destruction of the environment to make way for 'progress' or overharvesting of natural resources. In the context of cost analysis this will directly affect capital investment in unnecessary structures and excessive cost associated with using virgin resources.	Lost Money Flow

2014 CASH LOSS SPREADSHEET		Example
Cost Driver	**Quick Description**	**Category**
Poor Roll-Through Yield (RTY)	Rework and backtracking of work. RTY = 35%	Lost Labour
Lost Customers	12 Customers moved to alternative suppliers	Lost Sales Opportunity
Long Cash-to-Cash Cycle	Long financing time (Inventory Days + Debtor Days – Creditor Days)	Lost Money Flow
Update your cost drivers and categories on a spreadsheet.		

Table 4.5

Step 5: Evaluate Data Requirements and Accountability

For each cost driver listed, data needs to be gathered to establish the Current State of this cost (table 4.6). Typically, an annualised figure is used if the information is available and the objective is to have one common language in which to compare the various losses identified so they may be sorted, prioritised and dealt with.

- Agree for each cost who will be responsible for finding the annual loss figure.

- Establish what information will be used to source this and assumptions for the costing.

- Ensure the financial representative in the team is in agreement and willing to sign each cost off as validated once complete.

- Update the spreadsheet (table 4.6).

| 2014 CASH LOSS SPREADSHEET | | | | Example |
Cost Driver	Quick Description	Category	How Quantified	By Whom
Poor Roll-Through Yield (RTY)	Rework and backtracking of work. RTY = 35%	Lost Labour	RTY from Value Stream Map. Calculate additional labour time required to address backtracking at average rate of R180 per hour.	Jenny
Lost Customers	12 Customers moved to alternative suppliers	Lost Sales Opportunity	Value of total lost business per annum from 12 Customers.	Vusi
Long Cash-to-Cash Cycle	Long financing time (Inventory Days + Debtor Days – Creditor Days)	Lost Money Flow	Lead time translated to financing cost: cost to finance the process until cash received is currently 79 days. Separate cost of debtor days.	Emma

Make a note of how each loss is to be quantified in terms of cash lost per annum, indicating all assumptions.
Ensure one person is accountable to source each cost and that the financial representative verifies each one before proceeding.

Table 4.6

Quantifying losses can be a tedious exercise and we provide pointers in the sections that follow to assist you. The intention is not to try and quantify everything but to expand on those cost drivers with significant impact on the business goals and objectives. Refer to the cost drivers relevant to your spreadsheet, and update table 4.6 where required:

Wrong Investments

In some cases, the plan to allocate CAPEX (Capital Expenditure) to a particular project may be deferred, allocated to the correct focus or avoided altogether. This is not about cutting out CAPEX altogether as investment is critical to growth but about ensuring it is used for the right projects, at the right time and is linked to the right strategic intents.

Develop a table to list and evaluate current or allocated investment cash (table 4.7).

CAPEX EVALUATION					Example
CAPEX Project	Cost	ROI	Implementation Time Frame	Strategic Link	Reason to Defer, Keep or Eliminate
Warehouse Expansion Project	R3.4m	5 Years	12 months	None	**Defer:** achieve reduced stock holding targets first and reduce bio-diversity waste.
New Equipment at Process X	R800K	2 Years	3 months	Raise capacity of line X	**Eliminate:** investigate raising current OE of 47% to 75% over 12 months.
Expand Sales Office	R1.2m	1 Year	4 months	Develop sales team for new line	**Keep:** recruitment drive to build sales team of 16 personnel, located at head office.
Cash Made Available	R4.2m				

Table 4.7

Customise the headings to suit but having completed the Value Stream Map, it may be possible to defer or eliminate some investments through the smarter use of existing resources.

Poor Capacity Utilisation

To guard against overestimating costs, it is recommended that this be calculated only at the bottleneck or constraint process (refer to Chapter 3 for descriptions of bottlenecks and constraints). It is then possible to quantify the loss in terms of the additional throughput that could be achieved if the OE is improved. It is important, that you consider the demand for this product or service as well. Improving OE beyond the needs of the market will not create additional throughput, and will not yield additional revenue. Figure 4.3 illustrates the breakdown of OE which was covered in Chapter 3.

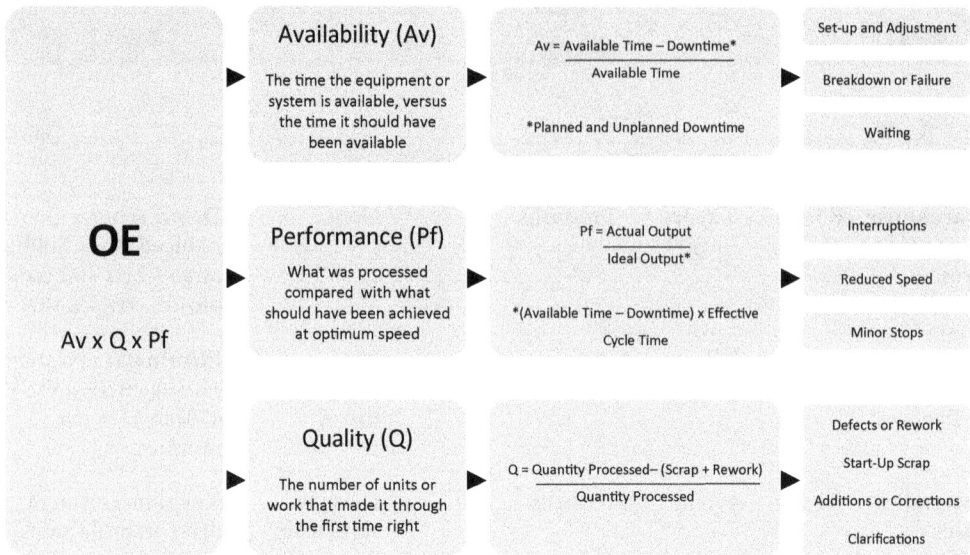

Figure 4.3

To quantify, evaluate the OE trend for the past 12 months and establish the best performance achieved over that time. Compare the best performance to the average OE performance for the 12-month period and calculate the difference in throughput between the two figures. If this information is not available, consider developing new measurement systems to start tracking the performance at the bottleneck or constraint.

In figure 4.4 the best performance of 73 percent was achieved in February and the average OE for the year was 65 percent.

Reviewing the throughput for this period, it will be possible to evaluate how much additional throughput would be achieved, through an increase in OE by 8 percent.

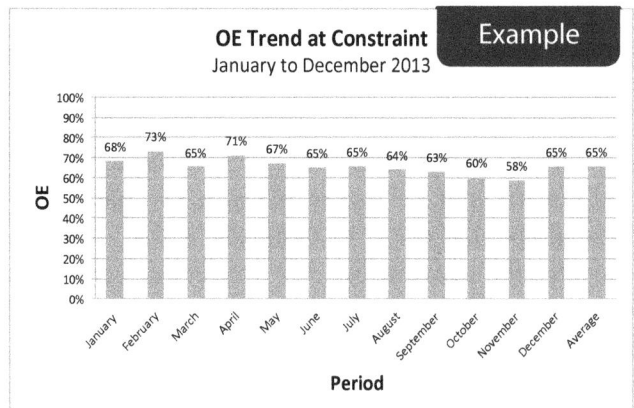

Figure 4.4

This can be a very telling calculation (see figure 4.5).

> **Example**
>
> Throughput at 65 percent = 120 000 units per month
> Throughput at 73 percent = 129 000 units per month (demand exists)
> 9 000 additional units at R56.00 gross profit per unit = R504 000 per month
> Loss of R5 544 000 gross pofit per annum due to low OE (using 11 months per annum)

Figure 4.5

With the involvement from sales and finance, establish what could have been sold if the OE improved to its best, achievable performance and calculate the lost sales opportunity (using gross profit). Remember, you are looking for the impact if the OE improved to its best performance, consistently.

For most industries an OE of 100 percent is not possible, so ensure the conclusion is reasonable. Be aware also, that OE is a complex measure made up of many variables, so improvement is usually possible through the right practices and problem solving – too low an estimate should also be avoided.

Other costs that could be considered for this calculation include:

- o Overtime worked to compensate for losses and achieve demand.
- o Temporary labour used to compensate for losses and achieve demand.
- o Cost of lost material as a result of poor quality.

Poor First-Pass or Roll-Through Yield

Yield directly affects the utilisation of available capacity and material cost, first introduced in Chapter 3. Figure 4.6 demonstrates the impact of lost yield along the process flow and the net effect on throughput. Although 100 units started out at 'Process A' only 37 made it out 'Process D' resulting in a 37 percent roll-through yield. If this variation was exposed in the Value Stream map and a future condition was agreed to, you can use the Future State value for your spreadsheet when setting the target condition.

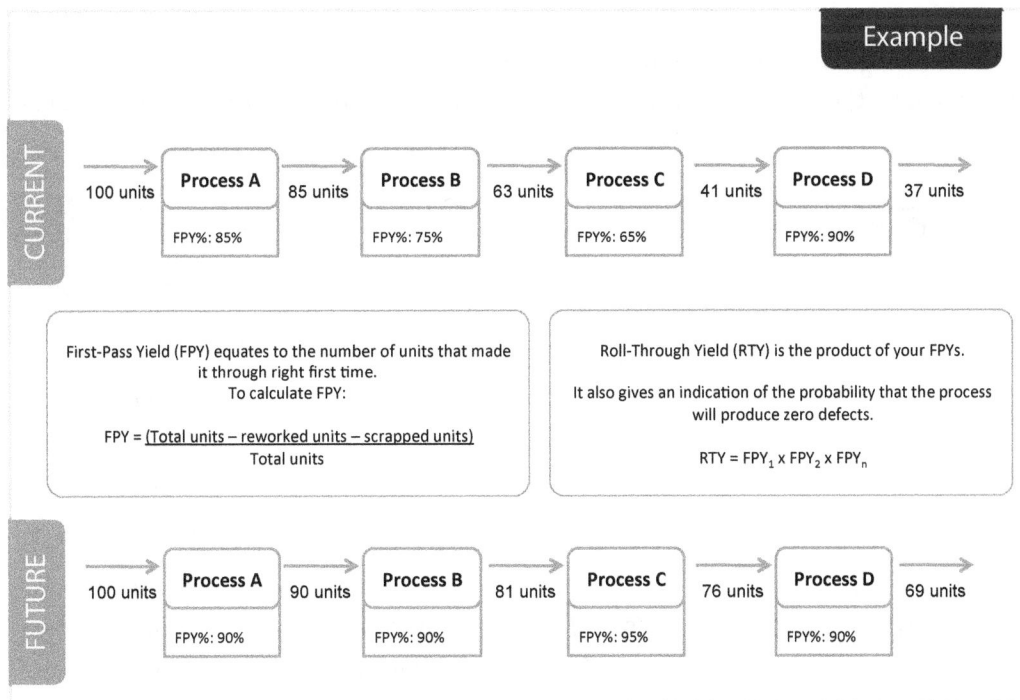

Figure 4.6

If the information is available, evaluate how many hours are spent reworking or repeating the work every month for 12 months. Using an hourly rate provided by the finance department, calculate the cost of this time. Where applicable, also include the cost of the material used to replace the scrapped item or to rework the item. Do not double-count with the OE quantification but if OE has not been used, consider the lost sales opportunity that may have occurred.

Inaccurate Bills of Material

A bill of material is the record of materials to build a product. To quantify the impact of inaccurate bills of materials, it is recommend that an audit be done to establish which bills are outdated or wrong. Taking the results from the audit, investigate the impact on stock levels for this error – for example:

o If a bill indicates one more component than is actually required, this may be triggering the ordering system to overstock an item not required. Establish the cost of this excess, as well as the associated carrying costs. Carrying costs include the costs of inventory, capital, space, insurance, labour, depreciation and so on. The financial representative will be able to provide a carrying cost relevant to your business.

o If a bill is missing a component, then this would result in frequent shortages, possible penalties for late delivery, expediting costs, substitution costs and so on. Worst case, it could be a lost sale or customer.

Unprofitable Products or Services

Evaluate the gross margin contribution per product offering and establish what to investigate further. In table 4.8 products or services resulting in negative or low gross margins are identified (see product offering 'E').

Example Product Offering	Volume Per Annum	Gross Margin per Unit	Gross Margin Total
A	15000	R 17.00	R 255 000.00
B	12000	R 22.00	R 264 000.00
C	10000	R 27.00	R 270 000.00
D	8800	R 8.00	R 70 400.00
E	7200	R -7.00	R -50 400.00
F	6200	R 15.00	R 93 000.00
G	5500	R 20.00	R 110 000.00
H	4300	R 8.00	R 34 400.00

Table 4.8

The real effect to the bottom line created by withdrawing a product or service must be proved before proceeding. In table 4.9, the impact to the bottom line is evaluated to determine whether removing product A is a smart move or not, based on its impact to the total margin achieved (Bragg, 2010):

Example	Product A	Product B	Product C	Totals
Units Sold	1 500	3 500	10 000	15 000
Price Per Unit	R8.00	R12.00	R15.00	
Variable Cost Per Unit	R3.00	R5.00	R6.00	
Overhead Allocation	R6.66	R6.66	R6.66	
Gross Margin Per Product	-R1.66	R0.34	R2.34	
Gross Margin Total	-R2 490	R1 190	R23 400	R22 100

Table 4.9

From table 4.9 it looks feasible to remove Product A because it makes a loss for the company but in this case, the overheads would be equally spread over two products if one was removed. See table 4.10 for the real impact of this removal:

Example	Product B	Product C	Totals
Units Sold	3 500	10 000	13 500
Price Per Unit	R12.00	R15.00	
Variable Cost Per Unit	R5.00	R6.00	
Overhead Allocation	R7.41	R7.41	
Gross Margin Per Product	-R0.41	R1.59	
Gross Margin Total	-R1 435	R15 900	R14 465

Table 4.10

Removing Product A would result in lower total margins (from R22100 down to R14465) and a negative impact to the bottom line because the fixed cost does not go away when the product is removed. In many cases, a product should be removed only when its price is lower than its variable cost (Bragg, 2010).

Going back to the Glenday Sieve Analysis created in Chapter 3, you learned to categorise the products and services in the various streams and highlight which offerings are contributing well to the revenue and margins (green streams), and which are not (red streams). It was very useful in evaluating Value Stream flow and opportunities for economies of repetition.

If you considered volume only in the Glenday Sieve Analysis, take the analysis further and include the margin contribution per offering as well as the sales revenue, to highlight possible areas for investigation (figure 4.7):

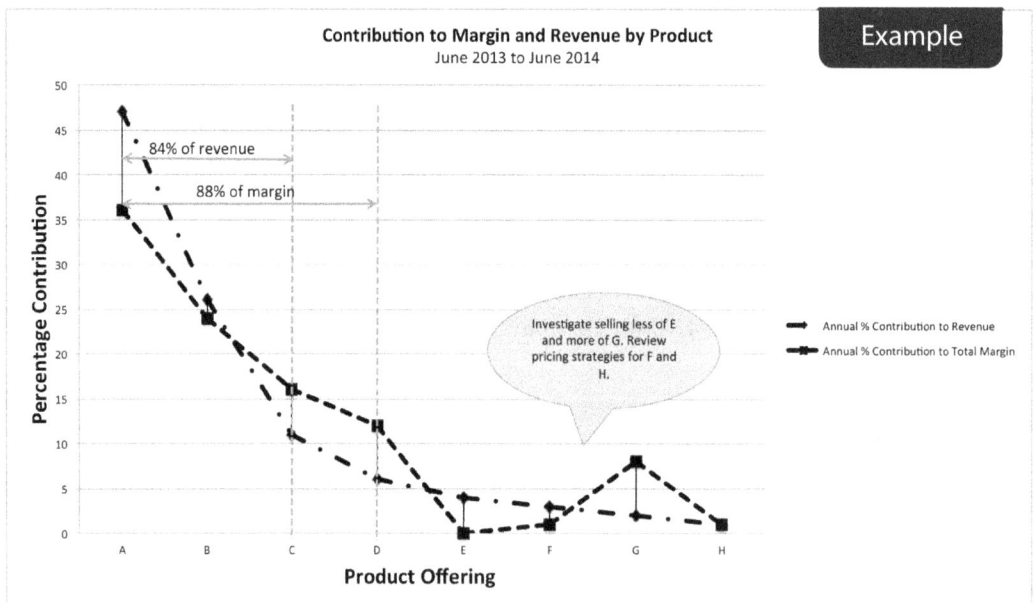

Figure 4.7

There are various ways you could present this data. A graph (figure 4.7) may tell you all you need to know about unprofitable products or services. Alternatively you may want to categorise them further, using the same approach taken in the Customer Mix Matrix (see the section on Unprofitable Customers). In the case of an unprofitable offering, methods of quantifying this cost may include (Bragg, 2010):

- ○ Excess inventory: the working capital required for the cost of the inventory, carrying costs and cost of obsolescence.

- ○ Engineering: the labour time to create designs, update bill of materials and routing.

- ○ Marketing activities: there may be unique literature pertaining to this particular product or service and the associated costs. Marketing and advertising costs could also be evaluated.

- ○ Product or service cost: the overhead cost to provide the offering.

- ○ Training costs: specific training provided to employees to process, service or manage these offerings.

- ○ Warranty costs: some products may have considerable warranty costs that could be eliminated by removing the product.

Deciding which products should be withdrawn from the marketplace is done through consensus. A particular product or service may be clearly unprofitable but perhaps this is supplied to a customer who purchases large quantities of other offerings or it is necessary to offer this product or service to prevent competitors entering the market. It may make strategic sense to keep taking the hit on profit, for the sake of large margin contribution elsewhere – just be sure this is the case. There may also be cancellation costs or exit costs to be taken into account when withdrawing an offering.

During this exercise, you may identify offerings with low contribution to margin and revenue. If it is not feasible to withdraw these products then other decisions as discussed in the Glenday Sieve Analysis may be necessary – for example, charge more for them, increase their volumes, ensure they do not interrupt green stream items, offer customers an upgraded option and so on.

Poor Inventory Management

This view in the Cash Loss Analysis cannot replace the detailed inventory analysis required to understand current systems and possible changes, and it is recommended this also be considered. However, at this point you should be able to identify and quantify obvious losses influencing the inventory holding from the Value Stream map and inventory data, forcing cash to be tied up unnecessarily.

Not all inventory is necessary to produce throughput to realise revenue and its value is constantly declining, therefore keeping inventory as low as possible and in the right places, without damaging customer service

levels, is critical. In the Value Stream mapping exercise, you may have highlighted the following:

○ Long lead times, which directly influence the inventory levels needed to fill orders.

○ Management policies, such as batch sizes, which also influence consumption of raw materials, build up of work-in-progress and possible build-up of finished goods.

○ Strategic inventory – for example, the location of strategic buffers to protect constraints rather than inventory piles allowed to accumulate at random. This could also include a strategy to hold higher levels of materials early-on in the process rather than further downstream where significant costs have been incurred.

○ Forecast accuracy, which has a direct impact on the ability of procurement to have the right stocks at the right place in the right time and for production to convert.

○ Work released into the system, greater than the capacity to process, would also over-consume raw materials, prompt early ordering and create 'process constipation' or work-in-progress.

○ Lack of information flow influencing the ability to plan and flow the right products through the system in time for consumption by the customer.

To quantify the findings, and allocate a number to excess stock, the following approach can be used:

○ Create a spreadsheet listing all stock items under evaluation.

○ Categorise each stock item according to its usage:

- A-items are constantly in use and should be kept well in stock.

- B-items are moderate frequency and low stock should be held.

- C-items are hardly in use and no stock should be kept but it should be ordered when required.

○ Compare the ABC categorisation with what is actually held in stock on average. Those items overstocked should be added up and included in the Cash Loss Analysis under 'over-stocking'. You may find reviewing the mid-month stock holding to be more representative or determine your own suitable method. Typical types of inventory include:

- Raw material, work in progress, finished goods

- Excess or obsolete, non-returnable stock

- Excess or obsolete, returnable stock

- Consumable stock

- Maintenance spares.

○ Include carrying costs in the calculation (insurance, warehouse space, interest charges and staff costs and so on).

Based on what you have learned from the Value Stream mapping exercise, estimate how much of the inventory is unnecessary and avoidable, and establish the value of the loss (cost price of materials, not selling price).

High Product or Service Cost

Some products or services may have been designed with little ongoing evaluation done on the true needs of the customer. If reviewed and eliminated, this would have a direct impact on the product or service cost and in some cases, increased saleability – for example:

○ Processes that add no value to the product or service such as excessive quality reviews that were identified in the Value Stream Map.

○ Specifications tighter than required by the customer.

○ Too much durability or reliability has been built in.

○ Unnecessary features that do not affect the majority of customers' purchasing decisions.

○ Finding opportunities where parts can be shared with other products, creating the benefit of higher volume components.

○ Redesigning to use fewer parts or to simplify the manufacturing process.

○ Long design-cycle times could be increasing costs to launch new products or services.

○ Processing techniques could be producing excessive scrap or rework.

○ Gaining lower product or service costs by increasing volumes, and gaining from the economies of labour efficiency, standardisation, task specialisation, equipment utilisation.

The above suggestions must be met with careful consideration. Any changes to processes, specifications, durability, reliability, features and designs must keep the customer satisfaction as top priority at all times and must not be 'improved' at the expense of the customer. Furthermore, the true cost reduction is to be verified to ensure a change has not resulted in an increase in costs. Involving design, finance and sales will help to understand the true impact on:

○ Overhead costs

○ Quality costs

○ Component costs

○ Procurement costs

○ Increased sales opportunity resulting from lower cost.

For example, if the sales team has done its research and concluded that if it targeted a market price of R100, it would be able to capture an additional annual revenue of R6 million and a margin contribution of R1 million. The target cost would therefore look as follows (table 4.11):

TARGET COST TO CAPTURE ADDITIONAL REVENUE	Example
Target Market Price	R100
Target Margin %	30%
Target Margin	R30
Target Cost	R70
Current Cost	R120
Cost Reduction Goal	R50

Table 4.11

With a definitive goal in hand, the team evaluates various aspects of the product and process, and concludes the R50 goal can be achieved by:

○ Using a new material that will reduce the cost by R22.

○ Removing unnecessary features not required by this market, reducing the cost by R16.

○ Eliminating the secondary quality test, not required by this market, reducing by a further R7.

○ Using an existing line with excess capacity and combining two processes to reduce the cost by R5.

The team deduces that the above cost reductions will not lower customer satisfaction and the changes will remain unnoticed, however, the cost benefit now provides the opportunity to capture a new market. This additional revenue generation is included in the analysis whereby the opportunity cost of not pursuing the action becomes the loss value.

Poor Energy Usage

Energy waste can come in various forms, resulting in a negative impact to both the organisation's environmental footprint and associated costs. Typically, energy usage is observed in the consumption of electricity and fuels to power electronics, heating, machinery, lighting, HVAC and so on, and can be quanitifed by examining monthly bills to understand the financial impact. In some industries this is better managed through awareness campaigns, scheduling of high energy-consuming activities during non-peak periods or even something as simple as improving insulation to reduce heat loss.

An effective way to understand the contributing factors to energy loss is through Green Value Stream Mapping discussed in PLANET because until you have a clear understanding of where energy is being consumed, in what quantity, and at what cost, it is difficult to estimate target reductions. In the meantime, review the accounts relating to energy consumption and consider a conservative estimate to include in the cash loss analysis. This can be refined once further energy audits have been formally conducted.

Unnecessary Temporary Labour

This type of labour is frequently used to buffer demand patterns over a cycle and can be a necessary evil in very specific circumstances. Conversely, the habit of throwing labour at every problem is a common addiction and may be a loss worth scrutinising:

○ Evaluate the trend in temporary labour costs over the past three years to establish if the trend is increasing or declining.

○ Evaluate the reasons behind using temporary labour – for example, absenteeism, increased pressure on the line, lack of skill, a wave of new orders and an increase in reworking activities.

○ Compare the temporary labour cost to the budget (if one is in place) and the cash loss per annum.

○ Having conducted the Value Stream mapping and an evaluation of capacity utilisation (OE), consider what would constitute an acceptable budget, if at all, and agree on the possible cost reduction opportunities from improvements identified in the processes.

Breakdowns and Idle Time

Waiting time in a process unless there is no demand is a waste, but be cautious that this is not over-estimated. The safest way to calculate the value of waiting time, is to measure it and quantify it at the bottleneck or constraint operation, as only an improvement here will yield additional throughput. Assuming there is demand for the product or service, calculate the additional throughput that would be achieved and the resulting gross profit that would be realised if the waiting time was reduced.

Waiting time can also be quantified through the use of excessive labour time to compensate for the waiting. If this occurs in several processes, then the value of this time can be estimated. Be sure to separate normal working time from overtime when quantifying in this way. Depending on your labour structure, the normal time improvement may not yield a bottom line change, unless it is through the use of temporary labour, which can be reduced. This may already have been handled in OE.

Transportation Waste

Are you in the business of making parts, providing service or are you in the transport business? If transport is not the core offering, ensure it is also not one of the greatest cost drivers.

Transportation waste refers to any excessive transportation to move people, materials, documents, supplies and finished goods in order to satisfy customers. This will be further discussed in PLANET but at this point, we recommend you quantify costs associated with the internal and external variable travel costs within the business – for example:

- Costs to transport between processes or sites (relating to forklift, trucks and company cars)
- Costs related to bringing in parts, materials, tools and supplies
- Costs related to deliveries to customers
- Incoming and outgoing freight bills
- Incoming and outgoing expenses from offices (mail, couriers and company drivers)
- Business travel costs.

Poor Constraint Management

A loss at the constraint or bottleneck is a loss to the system and insufficient focus on constraint management can lead to unnecessary losses that could be avoided.

Constraint management was discussed in Chapter 3, whereby it was recommended that OE be evaluated at the constraint to establish current losses and possible improvements, resulting in bottom line impact. Bottom line impact is possible only if the reduction of these losses results in increased throughput in the products or services from which you are able to sell and generate income.

If there is no demand, or if the available capacity is used for unneeded offerings, this will not result in a real cost saving or additional cash in the bank. In this case, at best it may help in reducing unnecessary labour costs. See Overall Effectiveness for quantification tips.

Absenteeism and Poor Leave Cover

Employees should not be permitted to cash-in on their sick days as this encourages them to show up sick and infect others, instead of using sick days to recover.

Good planning, however, around leave and absenteeism can reduce unnecessary and avoidable losses that impact the ability to achieve throughput.

This may already have been accounted for in OE (lost time as a result of labour unavailability or lost yield due to quality problems) but if not, this is an opportunity to gauge how much time or quality is being lost as a result of people availability. Focus your attention to the constraint and evaluate the losses, then quantify this financially in terms of the additional throughput that could have been achieved in a demand-hungry market.

Putting contingencies in place to create flexibility and address absenteeism when it occurs or conducting balanced leave planning to ensure critical skills are not absent at the same time, can go a long way in reducing these costs. Various options to deal with availability were discussed in Chapter 3.

Product or Service Line Complexity

Simplicity breeds efficiency. The more variety of work that moves through a line or department, the more complexity creeps in. The more complexity, the more people have to chop and change between thought processes and physical actions. With so many changes, and a lack of rhythm, employees lose productivity that could be created through economies of repetition. Because they are unable to take advantage of the benefits of repetition, the learning curve reduces the ability to perform at their best.

The Glenday Sieve Analysis completed in Chapter 3 helped evaluate the level of complexity in the business. If processes focused on a relatively small number of offerings, there would be a quicker accumulation of learning and costs would drop accordingly. Cost are expected to decline anywhere between 10 and 30 percent for every doubling of cumulative output (Evans and Lindsay, 1996). How we present this variety to the employees is therefore important.

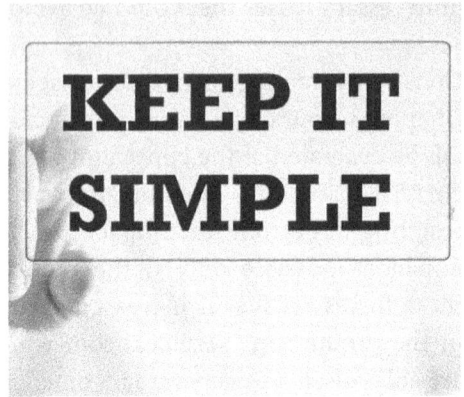

Points to consider when devising ways of reducing complexity:

○ Never fall into the trap of increasing batch sizes to reduce complexity. The calculation of batching is based on several factors, including available capacity, changeover times, scheduling constraints, hygiene and quality factors, and Operational Excellence encourages flexibility to customer needs. If increased batch sizes means this flexibility is compromised, and the impact to the customer is negative, the batch logic should be better understood before proceeding.

○ Complexity can be reduced by 'grouping' products or services in a way that encourages repetition, without impacting the overall mix but maximising performance through repetition. This economy of repetition is the key to achieving the learning curve advantage and the resulting cost effectiveness. Refer to the outcomes and interpretation of the Glenday Sieve Analysis in Chapter 3 for ideas.

The financial impact of complexity can be quantified in a variety of ways and will depend on the direction the improvement in the Value Stream takes:

○ How many unplanned changes take place over a period of time and what is the value of the time lost? If that lost time was reduced, what additional orders could be fulfilled and how much revenue could be generated?

○ What is the impact of unplanned changes on quality? What is the value of this in terms of time or material? If unplanned changes are reduced, how would quality costs be impacted?

○ If the Glenday Sieve helped expose opportunities to reduce batch sizes, what would be the impact on lead times and inventory levels? What is the value of this in terms of order delivery and inventory cost?

High Employee Turnover

Employee turnover will vary from industry to industry and it is worth first establishing what is normal before making any decisions – for example:

- In the fast-food industry, turnover is notoriously high on average.
- In a local market depressed by recession, turnover is generally quite low.
- In a market where skills are hard to come by, and are specifically head-hunted, the turnover may be higher in some segments.

Evaluate the costs associated with the excess in turnover – for example, if your company experiences an 8 percent employee turnover when your industry norm is 4 percent, then establish the losses associated with the 4 percent. Losses could include:

- Induction training costs linked to number of people attending
- Recruitment agency fees
- Lost productivity as a result of new employees on the job (challenging to quantify but the performance element in OE is directly affected by this)
- Lost productivity because of unavailability of labour (consider the impact on the constraint process and resulting loss of business)
- Benefits pay-outs every time an employee leaves.

Long Cash-to-Cash Cycle

The money line in the Value Stream map (Chapter 3) can help add more depth to this analysis. The Cash-to-Cash Cycle refers to the financing time and associated costs until cash is received from the customer.

Financing Time = Inventory Days + Debtor Days – Creditor Days

Improving the Cash-to-Cash cycle can be tackled from three angles if you evaluate the formula for financing time:

- Reduce the lead time from the time an order is triggered until the product or service is in the hands of the customer
- Optimise on debtor days
- Optimise on creditor days.

Investigate the following to get a view of the elements affecting cash conversion time:

- Late payment from debtors
- Late invoicing to customers
- Excessive time to deposit cheques
- Credit policies and limits currently in place for customers and adherence thereto
- Long queues resulting in long lead times until payment
- Long processing times and high inventory levels (raw material, work-in-progress, finished goods, consumables, spares)
- Early payments to creditors or late payments resulting in interest charges
- Payment plans to creditors (partial payments) and extended creditor terms.

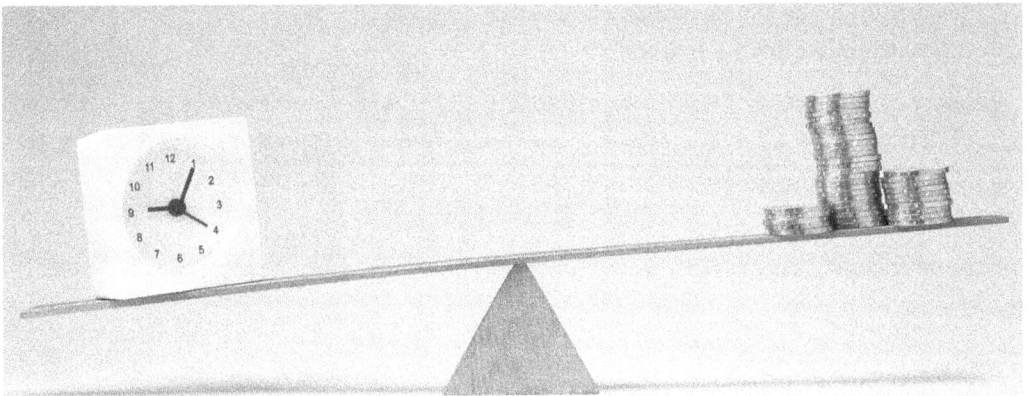

Quantifying the costs may include:

- Bad debt costs
- Overdraft costs and interest charges
- Labour costs associated with long lead times to process product or service
- Excessive inventory costs (this could be in excess of target or based on the evaluations made in the Future State Map)
- Lost sales opportunity as a result of long lead times to deliver.

Expediting

Tolerating ongoing expediting of product or service causes distress in processes through a spiral of disruption. An urgent order will be bumped up in the process, generating a snow-ball effect up and down the line, not dissimilar to figure 4.8 depicting the vicious circle below (Glenday, 2007):

Typically, consequential costs resulting from expediting include:

○ Overtime costs to meet the deadline, or to compensate for other offerings left in the lurch

○ Freight or courier costs to move information or parts quickly

○ Shortages and late deliveries on other offerings as a result of the priority order

○ Additional changeovers and lost availability, impacting less throughput

○ The labour time of the expeditor, which could be better used for value-adding work elsewhere (this may not be a bottom line saving as the time would be spent elsewhere).

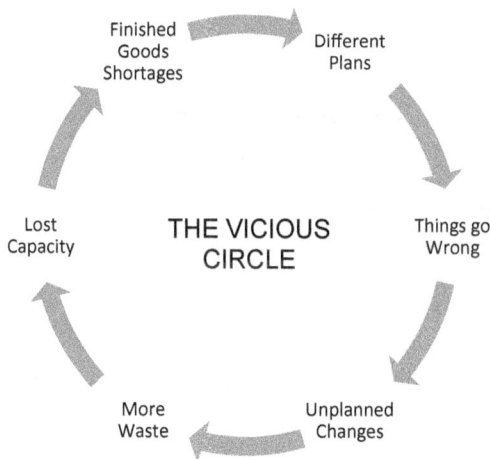

Figure 4.8

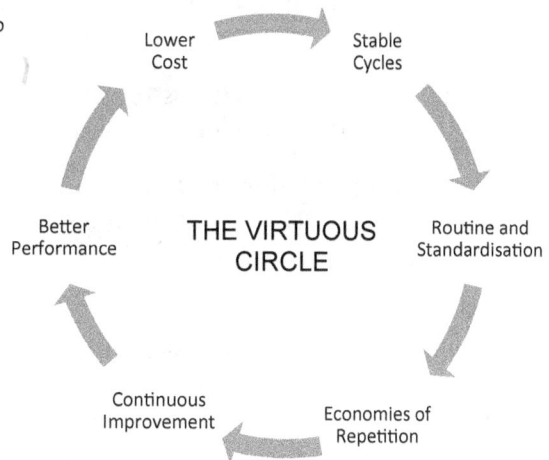

Figure 4.9

Through analysis and interpretation completed using the Glenday Sieve and Value Stream map, it will be possible to quantify potential reductions realised through a stable cycle where efficiency can flourish.

The result is the adapted virtuous cycle in figure 4.9 (Glenday, 2007).

Unnecessary Contractor Costs

In some cases, contractors assist in reducing costs in the business, where there is a short-term need for the particular skill or to cope with a spike in demand. In other cases, however, these can be unnecessary or avoidable through improved planning, improved systems or problem solving to reduce the need for the contractor.

Evaluate the contractor expenses in the cost accounts and establish possible opportunities for reduction, which will not negatively impact service to the customer. Removing this additional capacity must be coupled with an improvement that builds the internal capacity to deliver the same or a better service. There may be exit costs associated with this arrangement.

Speed Losses

Speed loss refers to the rate at which the employee is performing compared with the standard times expected and can be influenced through a variety of sources:

- Inexperienced employees or lack of skills evident in the cycle times and throughput performance by the particular individual.

- Modified equipment that no longer runs at the same speed as previously achieved, or for which it was designed.

- Using incorrect materials that the equipment was not designed to use, resulting in slower speeds than previously achieved. Quality may also be impacted.

- Using incorrect or bastardised systems that can no longer deliver the performance required.

- Using the incorrect settings on equipment leading to a reduction in throughput compared with the original standard.

- Frequent interruptions and minor stops affecting the routine and flow of work for the employee. This is evident in a reduction in throughput versus the plan, and possible quality problems.

Use the performance (Pf) formula of OE to establish the current state and any evidence of speed loss. Compare your findings with previous performance or estimate what portion can be improved through focused projects.

Unnecessary Material Usage

In manufacturing, materials (including those used for cleaning, maintenance and ablution) form a significant part of costs associated with supply-chain activities. From an environmental perspective, how materials are comsumed and disposed of are critical elements of the environmental mark left, which will be further discussed in PLANET. If 100 percent of the materials consumed are in their virgin state, this may be an opportunity to capitalise on recycling, remanufacturing or reusing. Material yield also presents an opportunity in how well material is being processed when comparing inputs to outputs, and whether or not there is material waste that could be avoided.

In service or knowledge worker environments, where paper usage is high, it may be possible to make better use of materials procured and reduce virgin consumption. Cleaning and ablution materials may also be relevant.

To quantify the loss incurred, discuss the following and agree on a suitable way to assign the financial value. Check the product design and material specifications. Are the correct quantities of material being put into the making of the product? If too much is going in – incorrect measurement, spillage, overdosing and human error – what is the value of this loss?

o Review the product design and evaluate if less material could be utilised while maintaining acceptable quality standards.

o Measure the input material used in the process to the output material. Compare this with the standard yield and evaluate if there is any avoidable wastage or yield loss.

o Compare the product with the competitor's product. Are they using less material? Can you do the same without compromising on customer value? Ask the customer.

o Review the costs of cleaning, maintenance and ablution materials and look for signs of overuse.

o Evaluate the use of paper and printing:

  - Can both sides be printed on?

  - Can print layouts be made to use less paper?

  - Can electronic formats replace hard copies?

  - Should more awareness be created around paper printing?

  - Is paper recycled?

  - Is paper reused?

Emissions Waste

Depending on what industry you are in, emissions can take many forms, such as gas, effluent, compounds and toxins released from ovens, smelters, welding, burning of fuel, HVAC (heating, ventilation and air conditioning) systems and so on.

Emissions are under scrutiny as they cause pollution and it is important to consider the source, the amount and the type of pollution that is emitted when producing a product or service. A detailed analysis of emissions is covered in PLANET but at this stage, it is sufficient to search for anything obvious being vented or discharged into the air, and to establish whether or not this is avoidable altogether or at best could be reduced. Examples include steam losses, excessive fuel burning and emissions from equipment exhausts. The following will prompt the team to investigate this form of waste further:

o Consider whether machines or equipment are operating to standard and if correct quantities of materials are being used.

o Is the company exposed to fines that can be avoided?

o Take a closer look at the processes – have alternatives been explored that will reduce emissions waste and associated costs?

o Could air drying replace oven baking?

o Could cure times be shortened without compromising quality or safety?

o Could temperature adjustment be explored as a means to release less emissions?

It is advised to evaluate what other companies or competitors have managed to achieve with emissions waste when deciding on possible areas and targets for cost reduction. Try source a subject matter expert in the company to assist in establishing the opportunity, or enlist the support of an external environmental auditor.

Estimate an approximate target for reduction, which could be reconciled when Green Value Stream mapping is complete and provides more accurate analysis.

High Overtime

Overtime can be a deliberate strategy, if to maintain the operation of a constraint or bottleneck, where the lost throughput cost outweighs the overtime costs.

It could be used periodically to buffer spikes in demand that do not warrant a permanent increase in labour or if machine capacity is insufficient during normal working hours. However, consistent overtime or misuse can be rife in a company and it is worth digging into when it results in extra cost and fatigue. Overtime is commonly used to compensate for avoidable losses, which can be reversed if the causes are tackled in a structured way, and problem solved until performance has improved:

- Evaluate the overtime costs per annum and trends for the past three years.

- Understand the reasons behind the overtime decisions.

- Much of the work conducted until this point has given a good indication of where capacity is being utilised ineffectively or how losses have impacted on the ability of the processes to perform to standard. Consider how overtime could be improved by addressing these problems. If you have been able to quantify a reduction in losses, you will also be able to improve the utilisation of manpower. How will this affect the overtime costs?

- It is not uncommon for employees to become dependent on overtime. This should be exposed when evaluating causes, but will also need to be handled diplomatically to preserve relationships and morale.

High Procurement Costs

There is significant cost associated with the procurement process itself, and streamlining here usually yields significant cost savings. If this has been the focus of your Value Stream mapping, then consider quantifying the following losses from the exercise:

- The impact of long procurement lead times on customer service and delivery achievement. This could result in lost sales or penalty costs.

- Additional labour costs to compensate for Value Stream wastes.

- Inaccuracies in the process resulting in unnecessary purchases.

- Complex processes encouraging 'every man for himself' buying patterns.

Key areas for cost reduction include supplier consolidation strategies to reduce procurement costs and the management of spend (Bragg, 2010):

Supplier Consolidation:

If the procurement process has already been streamlined, cost reduction may lie in the consolidation of suppliers. By concentrating purchases to a smaller number of suppliers, the higher purchasing volume could assist with negotiations for price reductions, rebates, discounts and consignment usage. This requires the development of a supplier-rating system. If the supplier is rated low, warned and no improvement results, the supplier is placed on a 'no-buy' list. Good performers are rewarded with increased orders or ongoing contracts.

Through this process, poor performers are highlighted. These suppliers often offer excellent prices but as a result of late delivery or bad quality, the cost of doing business with them far outweighs this advantage. The financial benefit of eliminating these suppliers could include eliminating receiving inspections (labour cost), product returns (inventory that cannot produce throughput) and the time to process credits.

To help achieve focus, it is recommended that the bottom 10 percent of suppliers be reviewed over time and that the poor performers be removed one by one.

For the purpose of the Cash Loss Analysis, consider the total acquisition cost rather than just the product or service cost before making a decision to consolidate:

- List price, less any rebates or discounts
- Freight cost to ship
- Packaging cost
- Tooling costs
- Set-up costs at the supplier
- Warranty details

- Inventory holding at supplier to buffer against long lead times
- Payment terms
- Currency used
- Performance levels and financial status also play a role.

Spend Management:

This can be quite an intense analysis and may require a dedicated team and a sensei to gain the full benefit to be had. However, the potential cost savings can offset the effort if properly managed. The generic process to improve spend management involves the phases in figure 4.10:

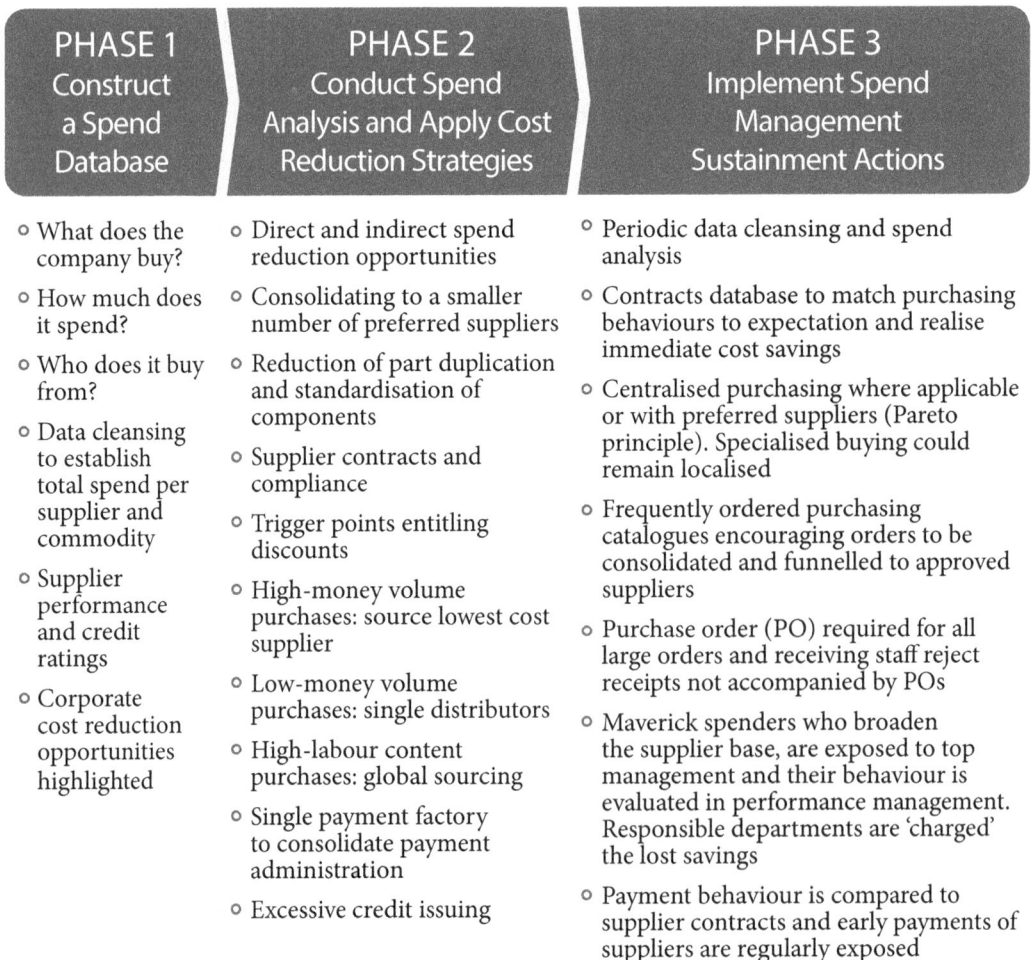

PHASE 1 Construct a Spend Database	PHASE 2 Conduct Spend Analysis and Apply Cost Reduction Strategies	PHASE 3 Implement Spend Management Sustainment Actions
○ What does the company buy?	○ Direct and indirect spend reduction opportunities	○ Periodic data cleansing and spend analysis
○ How much does it spend?	○ Consolidating to a smaller number of preferred suppliers	○ Contracts database to match purchasing behaviours to expectation and realise immediate cost savings
○ Who does it buy from?	○ Reduction of part duplication and standardisation of components	○ Centralised purchasing where applicable or with preferred suppliers (Pareto principle). Specialised buying could remain localised
○ Data cleansing to establish total spend per supplier and commodity	○ Supplier contracts and compliance	
	○ Trigger points entitling discounts	○ Frequently ordered purchasing catalogues encouraging orders to be consolidated and funnelled to approved suppliers
○ Supplier performance and credit ratings	○ High-money volume purchases: source lowest cost supplier	○ Purchase order (PO) required for all large orders and receiving staff reject receipts not accompanied by POs
○ Corporate cost reduction opportunities highlighted	○ Low-money volume purchases: single distributors	○ Maverick spenders who broaden the supplier base, are exposed to top management and their behaviour is evaluated in performance management. Responsible departments are 'charged' the lost savings
	○ High-labour content purchases: global sourcing	
	○ Single payment factory to consolidate payment administration	○ Payment behaviour is compared to supplier contracts and early payments of suppliers are regularly exposed
	○ Excessive credit issuing	

Figure 4.10

Poor Water Management

Water is fast becoming a scarce resource that will continue to rise in cost. Responsible companies have established methods for reducing usage and the levels of toxicity and have also found ways to harvest water and reuse it where possible. This topic will be further explored in PLANET as it has direct impact on the environmental footprint.

Check the water bills to establish the total cost of water consumption and conduct a 'quick and dirty' evaluation of what consumption should be. Propose obvious waste that needs to be adressed:

○ What are the biggest consumers of water in the business?

○ Are there examples of unnecessary waste, such taps left to run, leaks, drips, old and inefficient fixtures, inefficient spinkler systems or any place where water is dispensed unnecessarily?

○ What process, system or equipment changes could improve consumption efficiency?

Estimate an approximate target for reduction, which could be reconciled when Green Value Stream mapping is complete and provides more accurate analysis.

Lack of Equipment and System Standardisation

Standardisation of equipment, machines and systems has the advantage of simplifying operations, training, spares and maintenance tasks. Several enterprises that have grown over the years organically boast a multitude of varieties in their systems or equipment, which can have far-reaching impacts to costs. Evaluate the following and then discuss ways to simplify:

○ Costs associated with additional training needs and providers

○ Differences in maintenance costs between options

○ Additional cost of spares and holding costs

○ Impact on labour time to facilitate more complex maintenance tasks.

Lost Customers or Contracts

Evaluate how many customer or contracts have been lost per annum for the past three years and the value of the business they brought to the company (gross margin contribution). Understand the reasons for having lost the customers or contracts and include in the Cash Loss Analysis.

Maintenance Planning and Management

Inappropriate planning for maintenance of equipment, systems or machines may result in inefficient use of time and a reactive culture. This in turn could lead to overtime, unnecessary losses in availability and spares costs. By shifting to a preventive approach where maintenance is planned into the schedule, this could have a direct impact on these costs.

Again, priority must be given to the constraint or bottleneck in a market with available demand. Consider the following when establishing the costs:

- Maintenance spend versus budget (also evaluate how realistic the budget is in facilitating availability)
- Overtime to attend to crisis or badly planned maintenance activities
- Cost of spares versus budget and whether or not critical spares are catered for and managed by a formal system to ensure availability, and if not, the cost of that unavailability.

Unprofitable Customers

The sales and operations team may be spending time on customers who account for very little of the volume or margins. This could have a spill-over effect on processing departments who experience unplanned changes in work priorities for this category of customer, instead of concentrating on high-volume, green stream priorities. It is recommended you sort the customer base by annual contribution in margin (table 4.12).

Customer	Annual Volumes (units)	Annual Revenue	Annual Percentage of Revenue	Annual Contribution to Margin	Annual Contribution to Total Margin (%)	Cumulative Annual Margin (%)
A	150 000	R27 000 000	47%	R4 050 000	38.5%	38%
B	60 000	R15 000 000	26%	R2 700 000	27.5%	64%
C	20 000	R6 000 000	11%	R1 080 000	10.3%	74%
D	3 000	R1 365 000	2%	R887 250	8.4%	83%
E	2 000	R1 040 000	2%	R676 000	6.4%	89%
F	10 000	R2 800 000	5%	R504 000	4.8%	94%
G	5 000	R2 300 000	4%	R345 000	3.3%	97%
H	4 000	R1 880 000	3%	R282 000	2.7%	100%
TOTALS	**254 000**	**R 57 385 000**	**100%**	**R10 524 250**	**100%**	

CUSTOMER CONTRIBUTION TO MARGIN JUNE 2013 TO JUNE 2014 — Example

Table 4.12

Now that the customers have been sorted by the contribution they make, set customised rules around how the customers will be categorised using table 4.13 as a guideline. Consider what would constitute a high revenue or high margin customer, as setting these rules will determine how you interpret the results and what decisions are made around customer contribution versus effort to manage and sustain. Table 4.13 provides an example of rules used to differentiate customer categories:

CUSTOMER CONTRIBUTION CATEGORIES — Example

Type	Margin	Revenue
Type 1: High margin, low revenue	>8%	<R2m
Type 2: High margin, high revenue	>8%	>R2.5m
Type 3: Low margin, low revenue	<8%	<R2.5m
Type 4: Low margin, high revenue	<8%	>R2.5m

Table 4.13

Using the rules set in table 4.13 and the values from table 4.12, position customers on the Customer-Mix Matrix (figure 4.11) to visually depict which customers fall under which type:

1) High margin, low revenue customers

2) High margin, high revenue customers

3) Low margin, low revenue customers

4) Low margin, high revenue customers

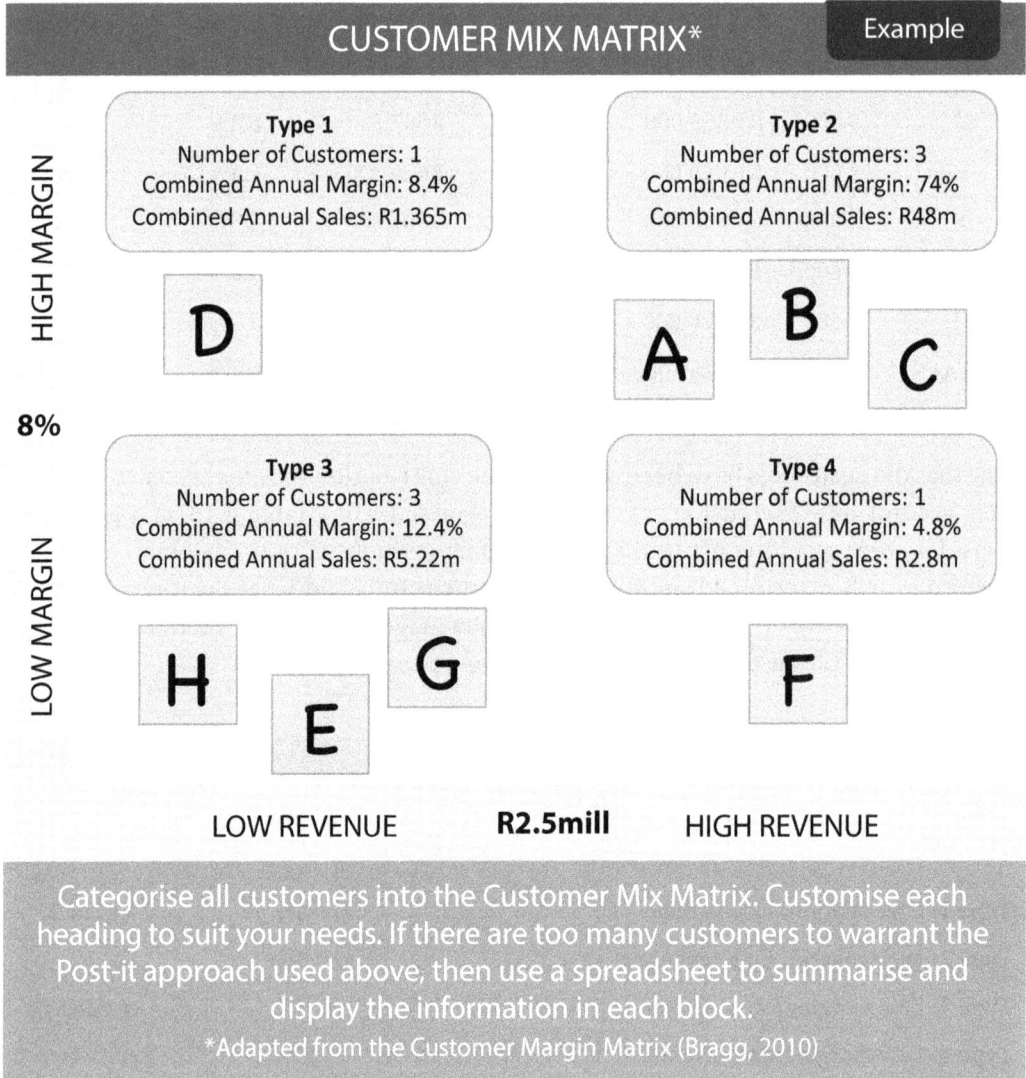

CUSTOMER MIX MATRIX*   Example

HIGH MARGIN

Type 1
Number of Customers: 1
Combined Annual Margin: 8.4%
Combined Annual Sales: R1.365m

D

Type 2
Number of Customers: 3
Combined Annual Margin: 74%
Combined Annual Sales: R48m

A   B   C

8%

LOW MARGIN

Type 3
Number of Customers: 3
Combined Annual Margin: 12.4%
Combined Annual Sales: R5.22m

H   G
  E

Type 4
Number of Customers: 1
Combined Annual Margin: 4.8%
Combined Annual Sales: R2.8m

F

LOW REVENUE   **R2.5mill**   HIGH REVENUE

Categorise all customers into the Customer Mix Matrix. Customise each heading to suit your needs. If there are too many customers to warrant the Post-it approach used above, then use a spreadsheet to summarise and display the information in each block.
*Adapted from the Customer Margin Matrix (Bragg, 2010)

Figure 4.11

The X-axis refers to the annual revenue contribution per customer and the Y-axis refers to the margin contribution per customer. This exercise could also be done using volume rather than revenue if it makes more sense to the interpretation. The interpretation of figure 4.11 requires careful consideration, and assuming the rules set have categorised the customers properly, you should be able to make decisions around some of the findings.

The highest volume and most profitable customers are to be found in the top right quadrant, and the low revenue but still high margin customers sit in the top left quadrant. These are the company's most important customers as they contribute the bulk towards margin (almost 83 percent of its margin comes from Type 1 and Type 2).

The Type 3 customer usually requires tremendous sales effort (and production effort) in exchange for low margins, and it may be possible that these customers should be terminated. There are of course exceptions to consider – for example, strategically, this customer could become important, but often this is not the case. Another factor worth considering is whether these customers are disrupting higher throughput and margin-generating products or services, in which case, this is further grounds for expulsion.

Type 4 customers should be targeted to raise their profile to the Type 2 category, which could be achieved by raising prices or adjust the product or service mix sold to them (Bragg, 2010).

Unnecessary Training Costs

Figure 4.12 illustrates that training is just a cost unless the return on investment is sought and the desired result from the training is achieved (Brinkerhof, 2010).

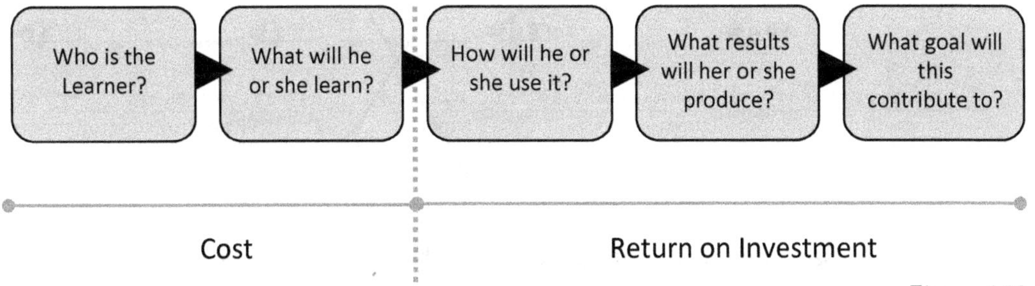

Figure 4.12

The scrap rate of training in some segments averages at 85 percent (figure 4.13) because the above steps are not followed through, and it is recommended that previous training be evaluated in this way to establish an estimated 'scrap rate'.

Looking forward at planned training and the associated costs, evaluate the cost planned and estimate the scrap rate cost (Brinkerhof, 2010). Unless the transition to the future in figure 4.13 is achieved, this will just remain a deficit in the Cash Loss Analysis. This topic is discussed further in Part II.

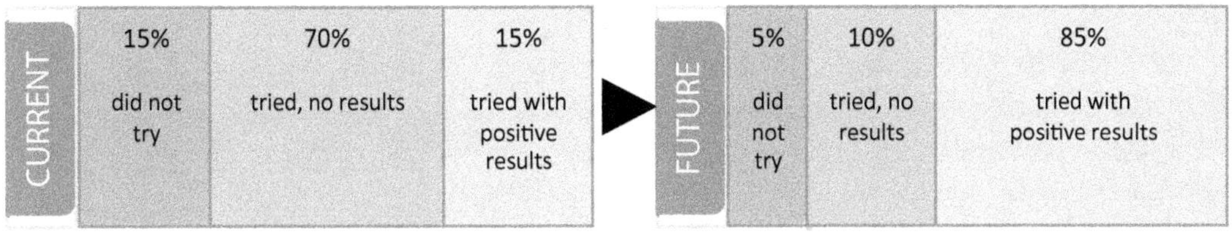

Figure 4.13

Wrong Manning Levels

This avoidable waste can come in various forms:

○ The correct total manning levels exist but the wrong allocation of staff to the various processes occurs (causing excess in some areas and shortages in others). An improvement in this would not necessarily yield an improvement in normal labour cost but could be quantified by reducing the lost time caused by shortages or the reduction of unnecessary overtime.

○ Manning shortage resulting in lost time or quality issues and the associated costs.

○ Manning excesses resulting in 'built-in-fat' in the process and unproductive use of time. This could be quantified through labour savings.

Unnecessary Processes

During the Value Stream mapping exercise, you may have identified processes that could be combined, simplified or eliminated altogether (figure 4.14):

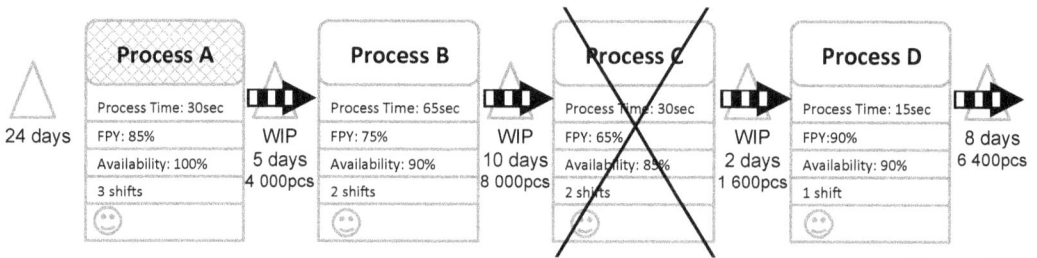

Figure 4.14

Variable costs associated with this process can be included in the spreadsheet. If employees are allocated to another process, then no bottom line impact will result but if planned recruitment, temporary labour and overtime can be impacted by these changes, this can be included.

TIPS

Remember the 'sanity check' to ensure you have not double-counted the same saving in two different losses.

Bio-Diversity Waste

Bio-diversity waste refers to the destruction of the environment to make way for 'progress'. It could also concern the harvesting of natural resources that are not being regenerated. It has dire effects on the environment and will be discussed further in PLANET.

This waste is often overlooked in circumstances where expansion and available land seems more accessible than making improvements that could render this need unnecessary.

For example, there is a Capex approval to expand a warehouse to make more space available. Land is to be cleared, trees removed and a structure erected to expand the storage facility. There have been no efforts to evaluate forecasting accuracies, excessive lead times, batch-logic and the resultant stock levels first, to determine if stock reduction is possible prior to expansion strategies. This could be a project that should be deferred until further investigation has been conducted.

Evaluate future expansion projects and the possibility to defer:

- If expansion is required to make more space available, evaluate the root cause driving this need before approving.

- Can 5S activities improve space utilisation (removing unneeded or obsolete items or storing items more efficiently).

- Can improved layouts reduce the need for expansion?

- Are facilities underutilised at other sites that could be used instead of expanding?

- Can vertical expansion through mezzanine floors or similar systems take advantage of existing structures?

If a project is identified that could be avoided, the value of the project is included in the spreadsheet.

Step 6: Update Cash Loss Analysis and Visualise

Having gathered the necessary data, conclude and update the loss values in the spreadsheet and sort the values from highest to lowest (table 4.14). Transfer the data into a graphic representation (figure 4.15).

CASH LOSS SPREADSHEET (JUNE 2014)

Example

Cost Driver	Quick Description	Category	How Quantified	By Whom	Current Loss per Annum
Lost Customers	12 customers moved to alternative suppliers	Lost Sales Opportunity	Value of total lost business per annum from 12 Customers.	Vusi	R1 800 000
Long Cash-to-cash Cycle	Long financing time (Inventory Days + Debtor Days – Creditor Days)	Lost Money Flow	Lead time translated to financing cost: cost to finance the process until cash received is currently 79 days. Separate cost of debtor days.	Emma	R1 200 000
Poor Roll Through Yield (RTY)	Rework and backtracking of work. RTY = 35%	Lost Labour	RTY from Value Stream Map. Calculate additional labour time required to address backtracking at average rate of R180 per hour.	Jenny	R880 000
High Procurement Costs	Three different suppliers used for standard consumables	Lost Money Flow	Lost opportunity for discounts for bulk and variation in total cost of acquisition.	James	R460 000
High Expediting Losses	Excessive expediting of work to meet deadlines	Lost Money Flow	Courier costs for urgent documentation.	Benson	R345 000
Poor Water Management	Groundwater consumed per annum	Lost Money Flow	Evaluation of water bill and proportion that cleaning processes contributes to this. This project will be pursued due to green business objectives driving improvement.	Kim	R255 000

Total Loss per Annum   R4 940 000

Update the loss values for each line and sort from highest to lowest by value.

Table 4.14

CASH LOSS CURRENT STATE SUMMARY

Unecessary Cash Losses – June 2013 to June 2014

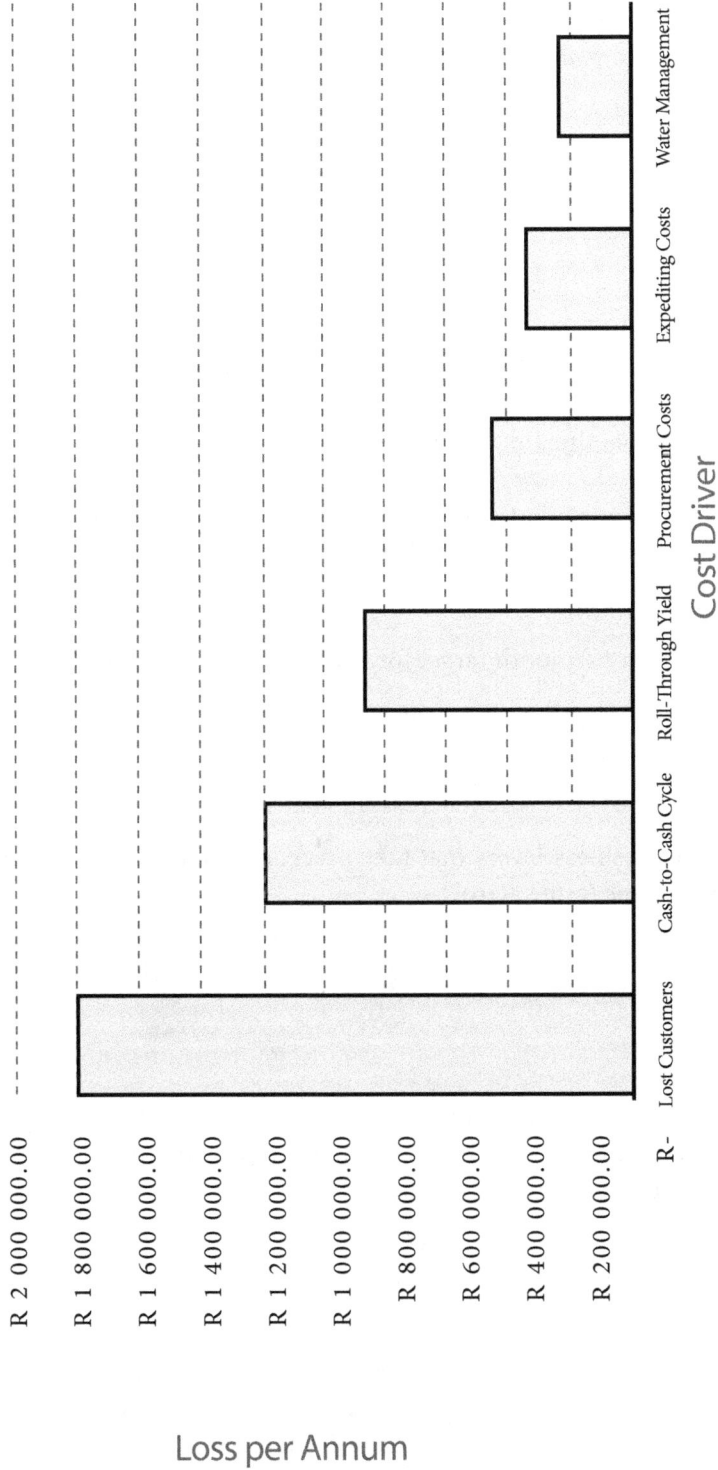

Represent the results in graph format.

Figure 4.15

281

Step 7: Identify the Business Levers

'Give me a lever long enough and a fulcrum on which to place it, and I shall move the world'

Archimedes, Greek mathematician and inventor.

It would be wonderful to address all losses found and take advantage of every opportunity immediately. Unfortunately, this is often neither practical nor possible and it makes good business sense to find those losses that if solved, would have the greatest impact to the bottom line, in the shortest possible time and the least amount of effort.

As such, it is recommended you review each loss, assign a target for reduction, and finish with a prioritisation exercise that will assist you in identifying the greatest leverage points.

- Set a minimum 12-month target for loss reduction (table 4.15).
- Develop your own Prioritisation Matrix with a rating system that matches the business priorities (table 4.16).
- Evaluate each loss and rate it across the matrix (table 4.16).
- Identify the business levers that take precedence and yield the greatest benefit in the shortest time (table 4.16).

TIPS

- If you find too many projects are resulting in the same rating, then review your factors and weighting. Sometimes improving the description will help the team better rate each item.

- Using the prioritisation tool works well when you need to gain buy-in for tackling the loss projects in the order they are chosen.

- In your own example, there may be many more losses than we have shown in the example. This means you will be able to visualise the order far easier than just selecting the losses that are the highest, but not necessarily the greatest leverage.

CASH LOSS SPREADSHEET (JUNE 2014)

Example

Cost Driver	Quick Description	Category	How Quantified	By Whom	Current Loss per Annum	Target Saving per Annum
Lost Customers	12 customers moved to alternative suppliers	Lost Sales Opportunity	Value of total lost business per annum from 12 Customers.	Vusi	R1 800 000	R1 800 000 (100% reduction)
Long Cash-to-cash Cycle	Long financing time (Inventory Days + Debtor Days − Creditor Days)	Lost Money Flow	Lead time translated to financing cost: cost to finance the process until cash received is currently 79 days. Separate cost of debtor days.	Emma	R1 200 000	R360 000 (30% reduction)
Poor Roll Through Yield (RTY)	Rework and backtracking of work. RTY = 35%	Lost Labour	RTY from Value Stream Map. Calculate additional labour time required to address backtracking at average rate of R180 per hour.	Jenny	R880 000	R528 000 (60% reduction)
High Procurement Costs	Three different suppliers used for standard consumables	Lost Money Flow	Lost opportunity for discounts for bulk and variation in total cost of acquisition.	James	R460 000	R460 000 (100% reduction)
High Expediting Losses	Excessive expediting of work to meet deadlines	Lost Money Flow	Courier costs for urgent documentation.	Benson	R345 000	R172 500 (50% reduction)
Poor Water Management	Groundwater consumed per annum	Lost Money Flow	Evaluation of water bill and proportion that cleaning processes contributes to this. This project will be pursued due to green business objectives driving improvement.	Kim	R255 000	R76 500 (30% reduction)
				Total Loss per Annum	**R4 940 000**	**R3 397 000**

Set a 12-month target for loss reduction, based on what is reasonable and challenging.

Table 4.15

PRIORITISATION MATRIX

Example

Factor	Bottom Line Impact	Link to Voice of the Customer	Link to Strategy and Objectives	Cost to Implement	Resources Needed to Address	Impact on Other Categories	Complexity to Implement	Time to Implement (months)	Measurable Results	Total Score as per Weighting	Business Lever Priority
Weighting	35%	10%	10%	5%	5%	5%	10%	15%	5%	Multiply each rating by its weight.	
Rating = 5	High	High	High Level	Zero	Very Few	High	Easy	<3 mths	Measurable	Add up the weighted ratings for each cost	
Rating = 3	Med	Med	Dept Level	Med	Moderate	Med	Moderate	3-6 mths	Difficult		
Rating = 1	Low	Low	Floor Level	High	Many	Low	Very Difficult	>6 mths	Intangible		
Lost Customers	5	5	5	5	3	3	5	3	5	4.5	1
Cash-to-Cash Cycle	1	5	5	1	1	5	3	1	5	2.4	6
Roll Through Yield (RTY)	3	5	5	1	1	3	1	1	5	2.8	3
Procurement Costs	1	1	5	5	5	1	5	5	5	3	2
Expediting Losses	1	1	5	3	3	5	3	3	5	2.5	5
Water Management	1	5	5	3	5	1	5	1	5	2.7	4

Rate each loss and assign a weighting. Set a priority for focus.

Table 4.16

Step 8: Summarise Results and Focus Areas

Visualise the results from the Cash Loss Analysis in such a way as to show the direct connection to the business goals and objectives (figure 4.16). If applicable you can expand this view to include the Voice of the Customer.

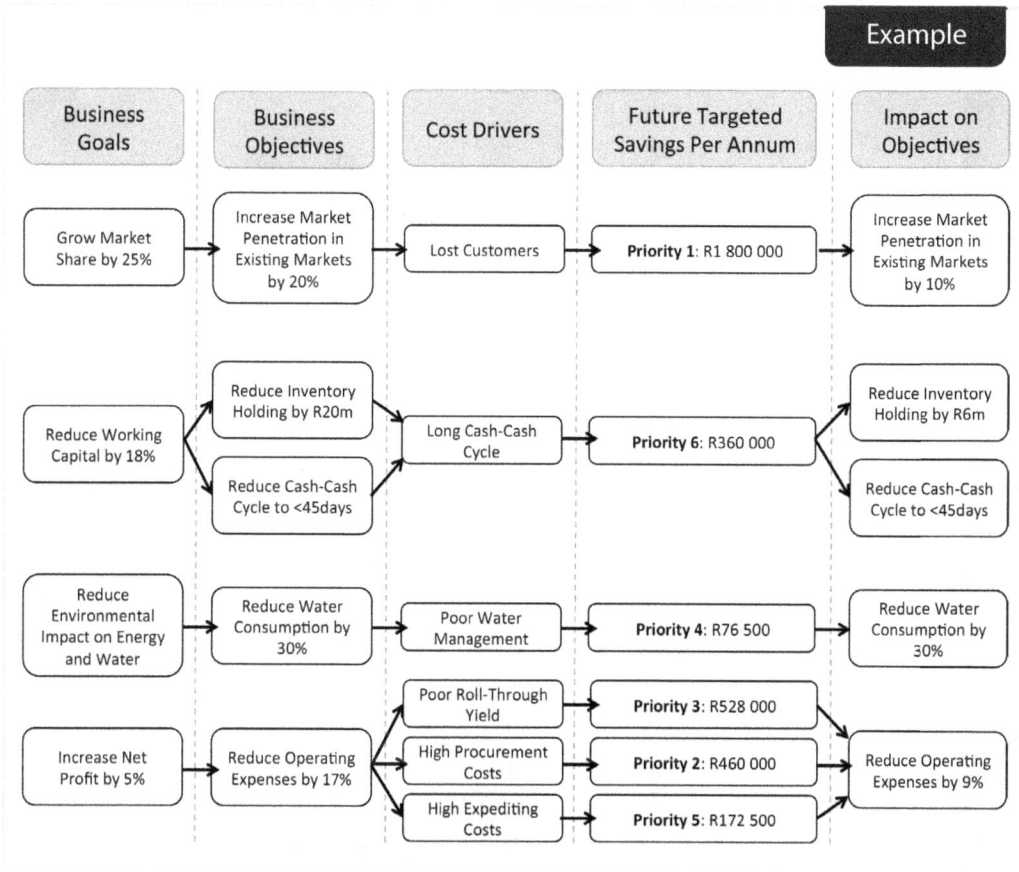

Figure 4.16

The diagram will at a glance expose any losses not directly impacting the strategic intents, and those where more work is required – for example, only a selection of the objectives defined in the Voice of the Business are impacted by the Cash Loss Evaluation. This could generate a second round of analysis to close the gaps. It also provides a basis for consensus on which efforts will be pursued.

Step 9: Summarise Target Condition

Much of the legwork has been done to understand the current state and future condition from a cost-reduction perspective, and it is good practice to now summarise the results into a graph format that can be shared (figure 4.17). This will become the guiding star for improvement projects and form the basis of the measurement system within each individual initiative (covered in PROBLEM SOLVING).

Example

2014 CASH LOSS SUMMARY – CURRENT STATE VS TARGET CONDITION

Current Losses Tackled

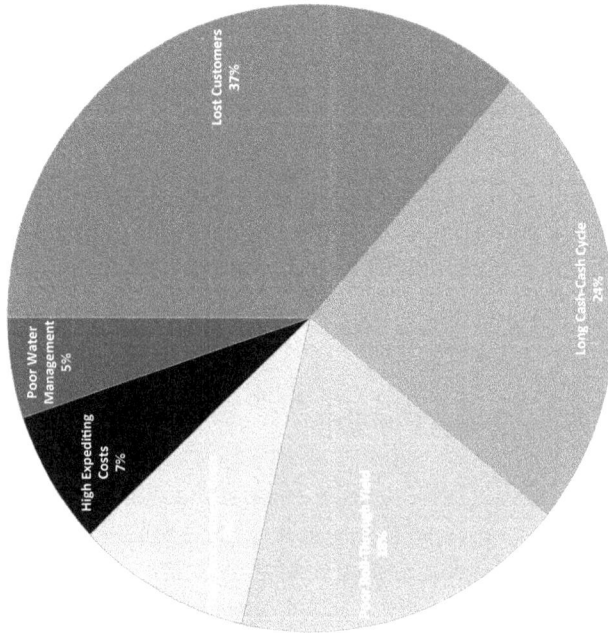

Current Loss Values per Annum

Target Loss Values per Annum at June 2015

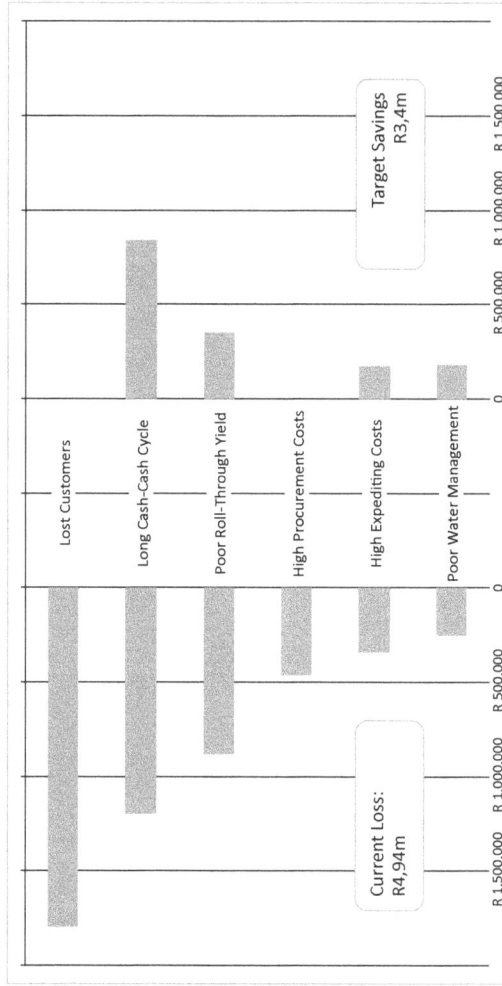

Select your own graph formats and capture the current state and target condition for cost reduction.

Figure 4.17

✓ FOR YOU TO TRY

○ Get together a team and ensure the finance department assigns a representative for the duration of the evaluation.

○ Capture the business goals and objectives for cost reduction to set the scene for the right focus areas.

○ Establish the cost drivers significantly influencing the objectives for cost reduction.

○ Create a spreadsheet to:

- Summarise the cost drivers

- Categorise them

- Agree on how costs will be gathered and with what assumptions.

○ Assign accountability and go get the data.

○ Update the spreadsheet and sort the loss values from highest to lowest.

○ Create a graph to represent the results.

○ Debate, and set a 12-month target for each cost-driver reduction, keeping it reasonable and fact-based.

○ Use the Prioritisation Matrix and identify the business levers that will make the most difference, realistically, to the bottom line.

○ Draw a Cash Loss Flow Diagram to show the link from goals through to the targets set.

○ Ensure the finance representative has verified the results.

○ Summarise the current and target condition, visually.

5 CONSOLIDATION
INTEGRATED FUTURE STATE ROADMAP

❓ WHAT IS THIS?

You are now in a position to bring it all together. The facts have been gathered, findings summarised and you should have an excellent idea of what problem you are trying to solve from each of the evaluations and the key initiatives required to do this.

The objective is to take the results from each of the preceding sections and merge them into a common approach for improvement. It is called the Integrated Future State Road Map, because it includes a holistic view of what needs to be done to raise the performance of the business to levels of excellence, and it clarifies the route to take. Figure 5.1 describes the thought process you will undertake:

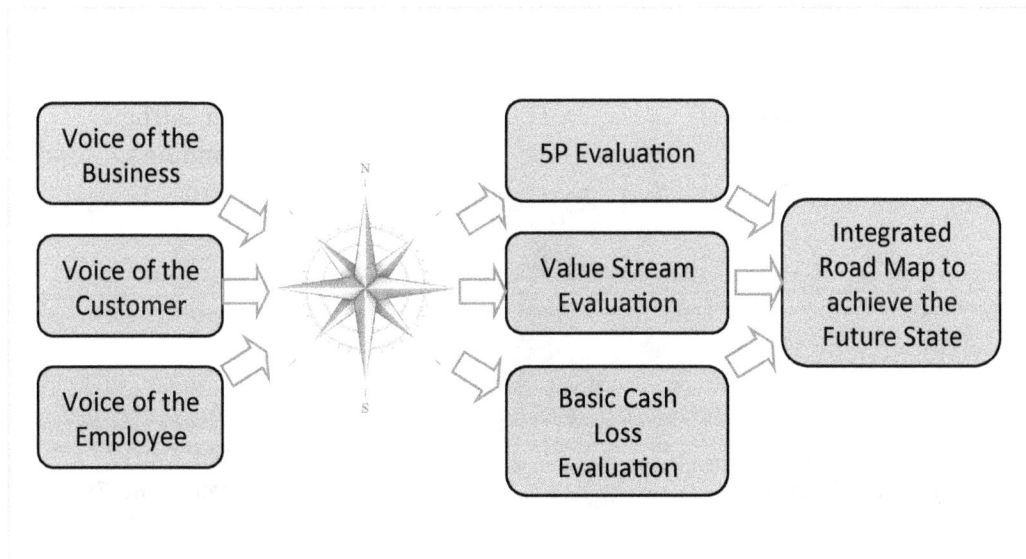

Figure 5.1

❓ WHY IS THIS HELPFUL?

- ○ All evaluations are consolidated into an all-inclusive, strategic view.

- ○ Initiatives are brought together under one umbrella to achieve a common goal for Operational Excellence.

- ○ A clear road map describes the critical milestones and expected results, and this can be tracked to show progress to plan.

- ○ The purpose and goals of improvement initiatives are clarified and ready for communication.

? HOW TO DO IT

Step 1: Clarify the Problem to be Solved

Refer to the North Star created in Chapter 1 and agree on the time period to which it will refer. Update and simplify each improvement area with your additional findings, the current performance and the target condition (figure 5.2):

NORTH STAR
2-Year Target Condition

Example

Reduce lead times
from 49 days to
fewer than 12 days

N

Improve Climate
Survey score from
2.19 to 3

Reduce customer
complaints from
15 per annum to
zero

W — — E

Improve 5P score
from level 1.4 to
level 3

Reduce Cash-to-
Cash Cycle from 79
days to fewer than
45 days

S

Reduce cash losses
from R4.940m per annum
to R1.543m per annum

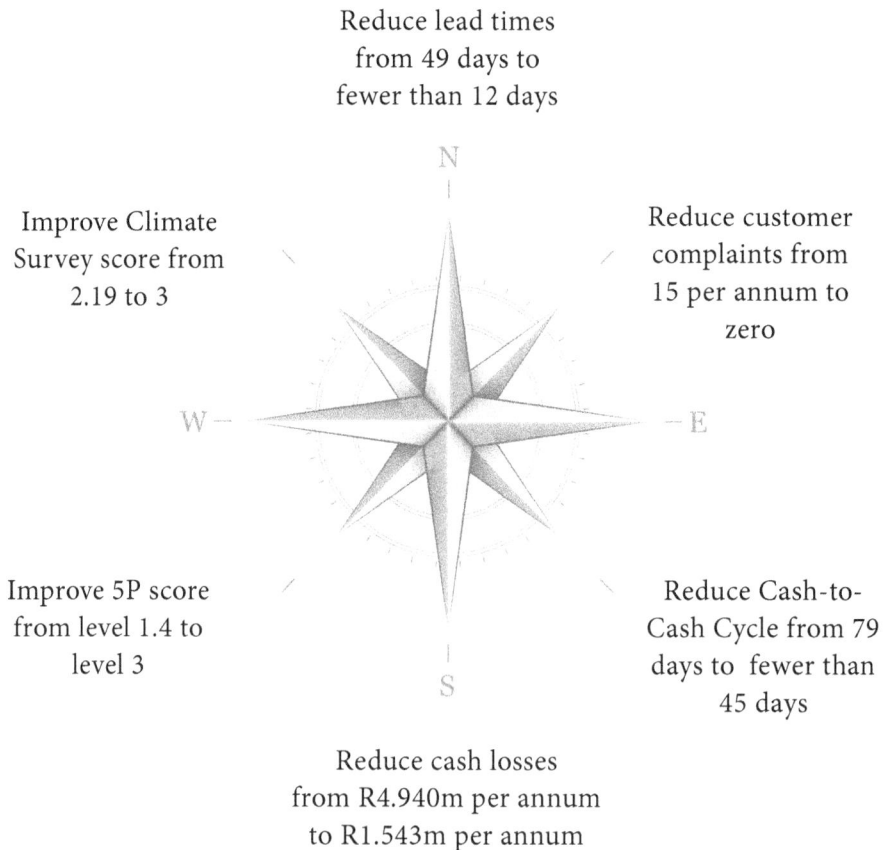

Clean-up and update the North Star with the Improvement Areas,
depicting Current to Target Performance and the respective time
period. Keep it simple and focused.

Figure 5.2

Step 2: Add the Key Initiatives

Based on what you have learned throughout the diagnostic and the ideas listed, expand each improvement area into its key initiatives (figure 5.3):

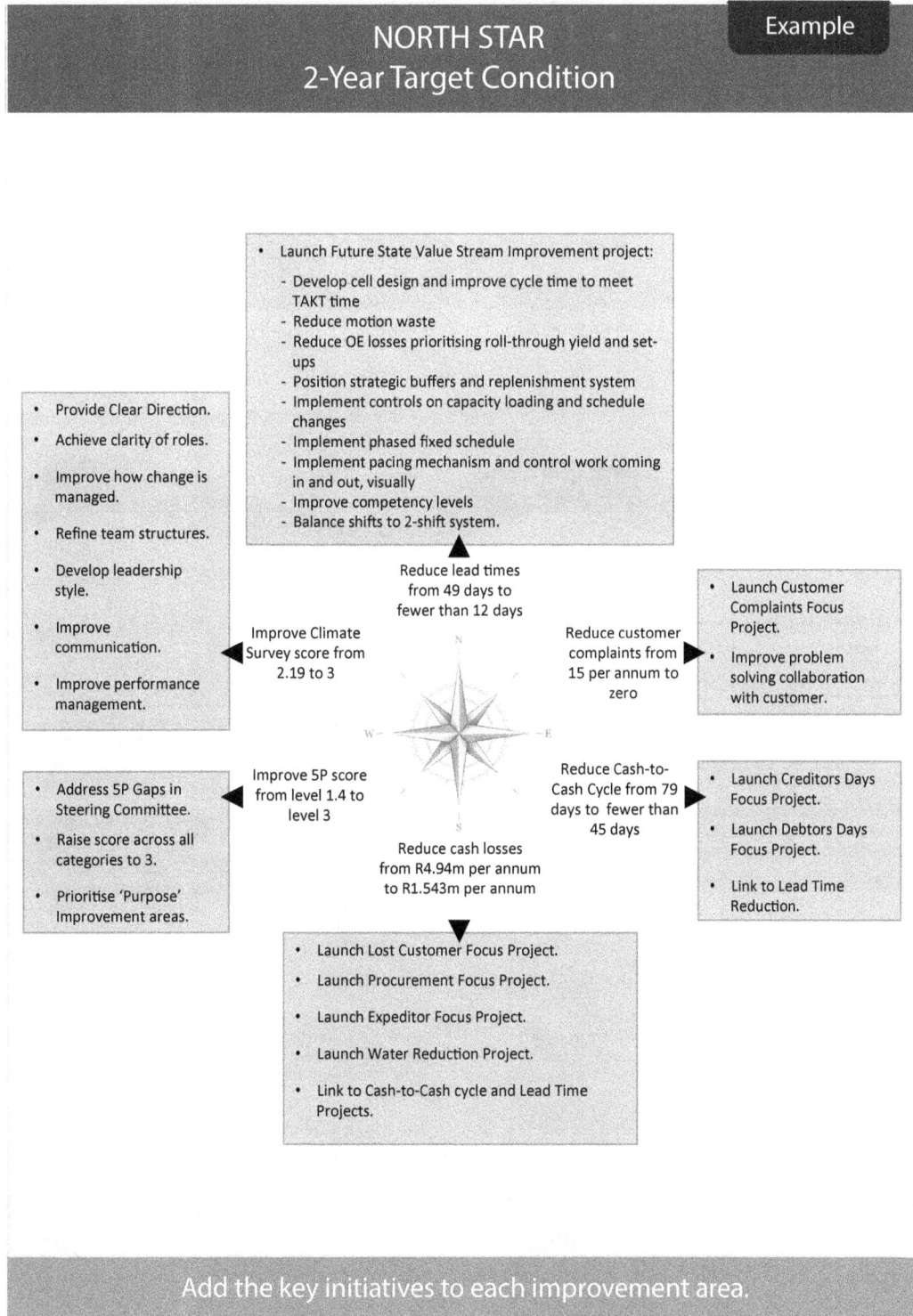

NORTH STAR
2-Year Target Condition

Example

- Launch Future State Value Stream Improvement project:
  - Develop cell design and improve cycle time to meet TAKT time
  - Reduce motion waste
  - Reduce OE losses prioritising roll-through yield and set-ups
  - Position strategic buffers and replenishment system
  - Implement controls on capacity loading and schedule changes
  - Implement phased fixed schedule
  - Implement pacing mechanism and control work coming in and out, visually
  - Improve competency levels
  - Balance shifts to 2-shift system.

- Provide Clear Direction.
- Achieve clarity of roles.
- Improve how change is managed.
- Refine team structures.
- Develop leadership style.
- Improve communication.
- Improve performance management.

Reduce lead times from 49 days to fewer than 12 days

Improve Climate Survey score from 2.19 to 3

Reduce customer complaints from 15 per annum to zero

- Launch Customer Complaints Focus Project.
- Improve problem solving collaboration with customer.

- Address 5P Gaps in Steering Committee.
- Raise score across all categories to 3.
- Prioritise 'Purpose' Improvement areas.

Improve 5P score from level 1.4 to level 3

Reduce cash losses from R4.94m per annum to R1.543m per annum

Reduce Cash-to-Cash Cycle from 79 days to fewer than 45 days

- Launch Creditors Days Focus Project.
- Launch Debtors Days Focus Project.
- Link to Lead Time Reduction.

- Launch Lost Customer Focus Project.
- Launch Procurement Focus Project.
- Launch Expeditor Focus Project.
- Launch Water Reduction Project.
- Link to Cash-to-Cash cycle and Lead Time Projects.

Add the key initiatives to each improvement area.

Figure 5.3

Step 3: Develop High-Level Road Map

A visual depiction of the road the company is taking to move forward is a good communication and focus tool that can be shared with the employees and leaders alike. It is critical that this be updated regularly to prove the leadership team is on the pulse of the improvement drive and that the clear link to strategy is preserved.

This is just an expansion from step two, but is often used as a large display in an area where most employees will be able to view it. This can be further exploited to show performance to plan as well and graphs indicating performance in the selected measures.

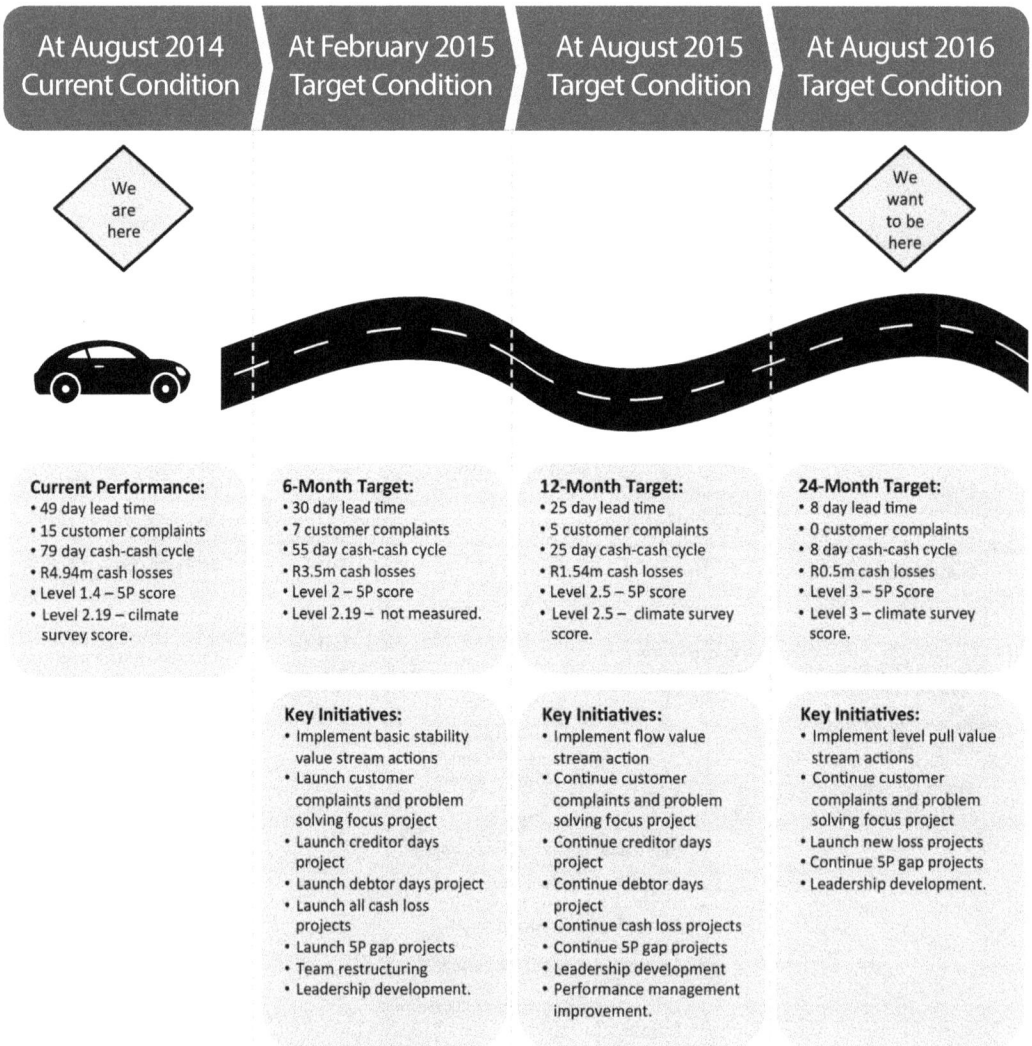

At August 2014 Current Condition	At February 2015 Target Condition	At August 2015 Target Condition	At August 2016 Target Condition

We are here

We want to be here

Current Performance:
- 49 day lead time
- 15 customer complaints
- 79 day cash-cash cycle
- R4.94m cash losses
- Level 1.4 – 5P score
- Level 2.19 – cilmate survey score.

6-Month Target:
- 30 day lead time
- 7 customer complaints
- 55 day cash-cash cycle
- R3.5m cash losses
- Level 2 – 5P score
- Level 2.19 – not measured.

12-Month Target:
- 25 day lead time
- 5 customer complaints
- 25 day cash-cash cycle
- R1.54m cash losses
- Level 2.5 – 5P score
- Level 2.5 – climate survey score.

24-Month Target:
- 8 day lead time
- 0 customer complaints
- 8 day cash-cash cycle
- R0.5m cash losses
- Level 3 – 5P Score
- Level 3 – climate survey score.

Key Initiatives:
- Implement basic stability value stream actions
- Launch customer complaints and problem solving focus project
- Launch creditor days project
- Launch debtor days project
- Launch all cash loss projects
- Launch 5P gap projects
- Team restructuring
- Leadership development.

Key Initiatives:
- Implement flow value stream action
- Continue customer complaints and problem solving focus project
- Continue creditor days project
- Continue debtor days project
- Continue cash loss projects
- Continue 5P gap projects
- Leadership development
- Performance management improvement.

Key Initiatives:
- Implement level pull value stream actions
- Continue customer complaints and problem solving focus project
- Launch new loss projects
- Continue 5P gap projects
- Leadership development.

Figure 5.4

It is recommended that before the road map is displayed, a staff briefing take place to properly facilitate the understanding and engagement. This is covered in the Part II, which includes the change management required for successful buy-in.

✔ FOR YOU TO TRY

- ○ Using the results and learnings from each of the evaluations, update the North Star improvement areas. Include the current and target conditions, keeping it simple and focused.

- ○ Expand the North Star view to show the key intiatives that will be launched to address each improvement area.

- ○ Discuss the best way to visually display the intentions to the rest of the company, and develop a High-Level Road Map that clearly shows the milestones to be achieved for each period and the key initiatives to help the company do this.

- ○ Develop the Change Management Strategy prior to displaying the road map (See Part II).

FUTURE STATE IMPROVEMENT INDICATORS

❓ WHAT IS THIS?

Tracking the progress periodically will ensure the desired results are in fact achieved, the improvements are well focused and that they are making good time. It also influences the behaviour of those involved as if they know how their input is to be measured, they understand how to act in a way that compliments this.

In Chapter 2 the Operational Excellence Matrix was introduced which provides a good high-level view of the state of Best Practice in the organisation in relation to the North Star objectives. You established a Best Practice score for each of the 5Ps and plotted the result vertically onto the x-axis stipulating a 'stake-in-the-ground' indicator for the Current State. You then included a target condition for Best Practice for agreed time frames. It is now necessary to shift attention to the y-axis to provide a view for performance in the improvement strategy by plotting a horizontal indicator for current and target performance representing a selection of indicators. The matrix will then be carried through to the Change Plan as an outcome of the Improvement Strategy (covered in Part II). Figure 5.5 reveals the product of completing both axes:

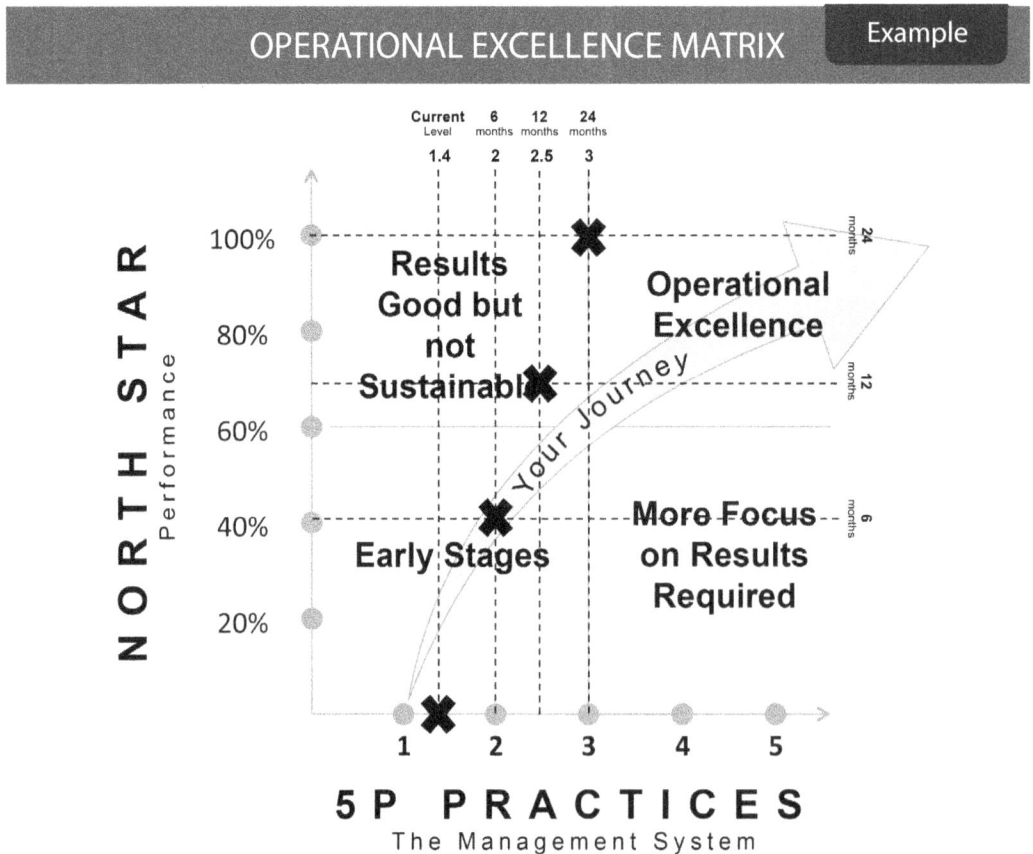

Figure 5.5

Once both axes are drawn, you make an 'X' at each period's intersection and interpret the position of the 'X' as follows:

'Early Stages' Quadrant

- Several practices that make up the management system are either not in place or at a basic level of implementation. Habits that drive Best Practice are undeveloped.

- Initiatives identified to steer change towards the North Star have just begun and either performance has not yet progressed or results are not yet evident.

'Results Good but not Sustainable' Quadrant

- Measured impact on the North Star objectives is noticeable. Performance has improved in the areas that matter.

- There is little focus on people development and the formation of the right habits that make up a system for continuous improvement.

- An individual or small group actively manage and drive performance in the North Star objectives, but the systems to sustain the gains are not yet established. If the focus of the individual or small group shifts elsewhere or they are no longer with the company, performance declines in their absence and employees deem the improvement effort unsuccessful.

'More Focus on Results Required' Quadrant

- Significant energy has been devoted to developing competency in Best Practice both on the front-lines and in the leadership ranks.

- Systems have been developed and implemented to support the 5P practices and regulate the behaviours that sustain improvement.

- Inadequate change in the North Star objectives or incorrectly focused improvement is evident.

- Employees are not convinced that the improvement strategy is deriving a benefit.

'Operational Excellence' Quadrant

- The organisation is mature in its Best Practice implementation. Habits and systems that drive continuous improvement are at an advanced stage of execution and this is evident in value derived for the customer or business.

- Initiatives pursued result in a critical mass of change and this is reflected in the results of the North Star objectives.

- Performance survives beyond the current leadership team.

- The organisation is a benchmark in its sector and is sustainable in the current market.

The matrix is dynamic and as explained in Chapter 1 exhibits characteristics not unlike the North Star used in navigation, whereby it changes over time. As such, expect the matrix to shift backwards each time the Future State becomes the new Current State, and the North Star target condition is tightened. The matrix is also unique to your business and its strategy and what is sustainable in today's market may be uncompetitive to tomorrow's market.

With the Operational Excellence Matrix providing a dynamic, high-level view for change, a next level of indicator is required to give depth to the actual changes required. This selection of metrics shows more detail than in the North Star, matrix and road map, by breaking down each improvement area and offering specific guidance to those accountable. See table 5.1 for a sample expansion of one improvement area:

FUTURE STATE BOX SCORE						Example		
IMPROVEMENT AREA	INDICATOR	CURRENT STATE BASELINE	6-MONTH TARGET	12-MONTH TARGET	24-MONTH TARGET	ACTUAL RESULT REVIEW 1	ACTUAL RESULT REVIEW 2	ACTUAL RESULT REVIEW...n
REDUCE LEAD TIME FROM 49 DAYS TO FEWER THAN 12 DAYS	Average OE	66%	86%	Sustain	Sustain			
	Distance travelled	980 steps	400 steps	10 steps	Sustain			
	Process B effective cycle time	64 sec	31 sec	Sustain	Sustain			
	Failure demand	22%	11%	Sustain	Sustain			
	Unplanned schedule changes	10 per week	3 per week	Sustain	Sustain			
	Multi-skilling	1x1 at Process B	2x2 at Process B	2x2 all areas	Sustain			
	On time in full (OTIF)	77%	86%	90%	98%			
	Total processing time	140 sec	120 sec	93 sec	Sustain			
	Stock turns	18	20	24	48			
	Number of shifts	Mixed	Mixed	2 shift	2 shift			
	Every Product Every Interval	18 days	18 days	10 days	4 days			

Table 5.1

? WHY IS THIS HELPFUL?

○ A stake in the ground marks the baseline and the target condition is clear.

○ The success of the implementation is tracked against expected results.

○ The relationship between the objectives, indicators and activities is clear.

○ The relationship between performance and Best Practice is clear.

○ A behaviour of focus and accountability is formed.

○ Employees have something against which to gauge their actions, which in turn allows them to make adjustments when necessary.

? HOW TO DO IT

Step 1: Calculate Expected Progess to North Star Objectives

Develop a table of high-level indicators that will be used to plot the y-axis on the Operational Excellence Matrix (table 5.2):

○ List the baseline measurement, and interim targets for each period under consideration.

○ Include review phases to show actual performance to expected outcome.

○ Calculate the percentage achievement expected at each review interval, for every indicator.

○ Calculate the average percentage progress expected at each review interval.

Step 2: Complete the Operational Excellence Matrix

Update your own matrix developed in Chapter 2 with the results of the calculation as illustrated in figure 5.5:

○ Plot the y-axis onto the matrix to show the performance expectations at each review interval by drawing a horizontal line through the percentage progress expected.

○ Where the horizontal and vertical line meet for each review interval, mark the position on the matrix to show the overall expectation per review interval.

PERCENTAGE PROGRESS TO NORTH STAR AT AUGUST 2014 — Example

IMPROVEMENT AREA	INDICATOR	CURRENT STATE BASELINE	6-MONTH TARGET	12-MONTH TARGET	24-MONTH TARGET	ACTUAL RESULT REVIEW 1	ACTUAL RESULT REVIEW 2	ACTUAL RESULT REVIEW...n
REDUCE LEAD TIME	Lead time from raw material to customer delivery	49 days	30 days	25 days	8 days			
	% Achievement	0%	46%	59%	100%			
REDUCE CUSTOMER COMPLAINTS	Number of complaints documented in non-conformance reports	15	7	5	0			
	% Achievement	0%	53%	67%	100%			
REDUCE CASH-CASH CYCLE	Financing time consisting of inventory, debtor and credit days	79	55	25	8			
	% Achievement	0%	34%	76%	100%			
REDUCE CASH LOSSES	Bottom line cash losses identified in the Cash Loss Evaluation	R4.94m	R3.5m	R1.54m	R0.5m			
	% Achievement	0%	32%	77%	100%			
AVERAGE PROGRESS		0%	41%	69%	100%			

Table 5.2

Step 3: Develop Future State Box Score

Based on the improvement goals set in the North Star, which indicators will best track the detailed progress and align with the overall business objectives? These indicators would be used by the improvement team to ensure each action results in a change to this score. The box score is also designed to show progress over time that can be tracked and easily reviewed at set frequencies (table 5.3).

TIPS

Select SMART targets when developing Future State expectations. This will help to align and meet the overall goals for each improvement area:

S	SPECIFIC, SIGNIFICANT, STRETCHING
M	MEASURABLE, MEANINGFUL, MOTIVATIONAL
A	AGREED UPON, ATTAINABLE, ACHIEVABLE, ACCEPTABLE, ACTION-ORIENTED
R	REALISTIC, RELEVANT, REASONABLE, REWARDING, RESULTS-ORIENTED
T	TIME-BASED, TIMELY, TANGIBLE, TRACKABLE

FUTURE STATE BOX SCORE

IMPROVEMENT AREA	INDICATOR	CURRENT STATE BASELINE	6-MONTH TARGET	12-MONTH TARGET	24-MONTH TARGET	ACTUAL RESULT REVIEW 1	ACTUAL RESULT REVIEW 2	ACTUAL RESULT REVIEW..n

Develop detailed indicators for each improvement area in the North Star and customise the time intervals. Capture the baseline and SMART target conditions for each period.

Table 5.3

FOR YOU TO TRY

- Develop a table to show the expected progress for North Star performance by each time interval.

- Refer to the Operational Excellence Matrix created in Chapter 2 and plot the results onto the y-axis.

- Mark the intersection between the x- and y-axis plots for each review period to show the progression to Operational Excellence.

- Expand each improvement area into its detailed indicators and baseline performance.

- Insert the interim target conditions necessary to achieve the overall goal of that improvement area, keeping to the SMART principles for goal setting.

- Complete for every improvement area listed in the North Star.

A HIGH-LEVEL FUTURE STATE PLAN

❓ WHAT IS THIS?

The success of your implementation will depend on how well the execution is planned. Project leaders and team members need a plan from which to work that shows with absolute certainty what needs to change and what business impact is expected. Having put all the effort into designing a Future State Road Map and box score is reason enough to ensure this next phase is handled well.

Unfortunately this is not as simple as just listing the actions and checking with responsible people when they will have time to implement them – the execution logic must be followed as well as a method for engagement (covered in Part II). It also will not contain all the detailed actions necessary to execute the change with, as a substantial amount of problem solving still needs to be performed to define what exactly will be done to tackle root causes. It is a high-level representation of all the decisions that have been made as a result of the evaluations conducted.

It is advised to find a simple approach and to remember the tool is not as important as the thought process sitting behind it. Engage the support of a sensei where required.

❓ WHY IS THIS HELPFUL?

- ○ 'What, who, when, where and how' for the implementation is clear.
- ○ A visual depiction of the short, medium and long-term plan is made available.
- ○ Implementation logic is presented to support the Future State Vision.
- ○ Expectation is clear, progress can be tracked and obstacles removed systematically.
- ○ A consistent understanding and alignment to the plan is developed.

❓ HOW TO DO IT

Develop the High-Level Plan

Using table 5.4 as a guideline, develop a plan that lists all the high-level activities required to achieve the Future State, for each of the improvement areas. Be sure to emphasise the impact to the business for each action.

Example

HIGH-LEVEL PLAN

EXECUTING THE FUTURE STATE

6-MONTH FOCUS

NORTH STAR IMPROVEMENT FOCUS	NO.	ACTION	EXPECTED IMPACT ON METRICS	IMPROVEMENT TYPE	RESPONSIBLE	INVOLVED	DATE	TIMING SEPT	OCT	NOV	DEC	JAN	FEB	PLAN	PROGRESS DO 20%	50%	100%	CHECK	ADJUST
REDUCE LEAD TIME FROM 49 DAYS TO < 12 DAYS	1	IMPROVE PERFORMANCE TO TAKT THROUGH CELL DESIGN AND WASTE ELIMINATION	IMPROVE A,B AND C CYCLE TIME TO MEET 31 SECONDS CONSISTENTLY AND TOTAL PROCESSING TIME FROM 140 TO 120 SECONDS.	KAIZEN	John	Jerry, Mary	10 Jan												
	2	REDUCE MOTION BETWEEN DEPARTMENTS (SEE PROPOSED LAYOUT)	REDUCE MOTION FROM 980 STEPS TO 400 STEPS.	PROJECT	Cyril	Amanda, Clive	25 Feb												
	3	REDUCE OE LOSSES FOR PROCESS A, B AND C PRIORITISE ROLL-THROUGH YIELD PERFORMANCE AND SET-UP TIME REDUCTION	IMPROVE AVERAGE OE FROM 66% TO 86%.	KAIZEN	Billy	Jack, Olivia	31 Jan												
	4	POSITION STRATEGIC BUFFERS AND PHASE 1 REPLENISHMENT SYSTEM	REDUCE VALUE STREAM INVENTORY FROM 49 DAYS TO 30 DAYS. 10% REDUCTION IN LOST TIME AT CONSTRAINT.	KAIZEN	Philip	Bob, Sandra, Themba	15 Feb												
	5	IMPLEMENT CAPACITY LOADING POLICY AND PHASE 1 FIXED SCHEDULE	CAPACITY OF CONSTRAINT LOADED TO 85% AND 95% ACHIEVEMENT OF PREVENTIVE MAINTENANCE SCHEDULE.	KAIZEN	Sandra	Bob, Themba	25 Feb												
	6	IMPROVE CONSTRAINT SKILLS	IMPROVE SKILLS FROM ONE PER SHIFT TO 2 RESOURCES PER SHIFT.	PROJECT	Sid	Stacy, Jane	30 Sep												

Link to North Star

Specific, measureable action

Measurable targets

Clear responsibility

Workload of actions levelled to ensure overall loading reasonable

Show whether this is a project or would require a 5-day kaizen event

Clear target dates

Visual tracking of progress

Table 5.4

✔ FOR YOU TO TRY

○ Review the actions from each part of the diagnostic.

○ Develop a high-level plan detailing:

- The link to the North Star

- Actions and expected results on tangible measures

- Improvement type (kaizen event or project)

- Responsibility and support structures

- Timing and workload levelling

- Progress tracking.

○ Ensure the responsible parties have been involved in the process and that agreement is reached on the plan before proceeding.

AN INTRODUCTION TO THE PDCA CYCLE

❓ WHAT IS THIS?

Although the PDCA Cycle is covered in more detail in Part III of this book and PROBLEM SOLVING, it is recommended that each of the projects and kaizen events be implemented according to the principles of plan, do, check and adjust (PDCA) to assure the quality of the implementation and achievement of expected results.

A common failing in implementation is rushing to get things implemented, without reflecting along the way. A lot of hard work takes place to implement but the team could become disillusioned when the effort put in is not yielding the right outcomes. Alarm and then apathy sets in when the implementation does not achieve the expected result. The team then slowly slips back to old performance levels. This can be extremely demotivating for the team, but the good news is, that it can be avoided.

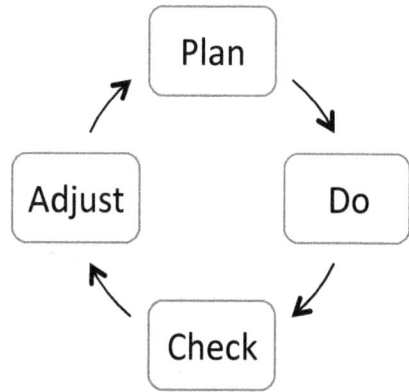

Plan → Do → Check → Adjust → (cycle)

Up until this point, the diagnostic of the Current State, the development of the Future State Road Map and the high-level plan, have all formed part of the 'plan' phase. It is quite possible that many of the projects identified still require further analysis as to the true root causes and it is critical that this be recognised and implementation not proceed unless actions are based on sound analysis. Having said this, there will also be actions that can proceed immediately as the root causes are already clear and further analysis would just paralyse the progress. The bird's-eye view logic behind PDCA is shown in figure 5.6 to illustrate the thought process (Liker, 2006):

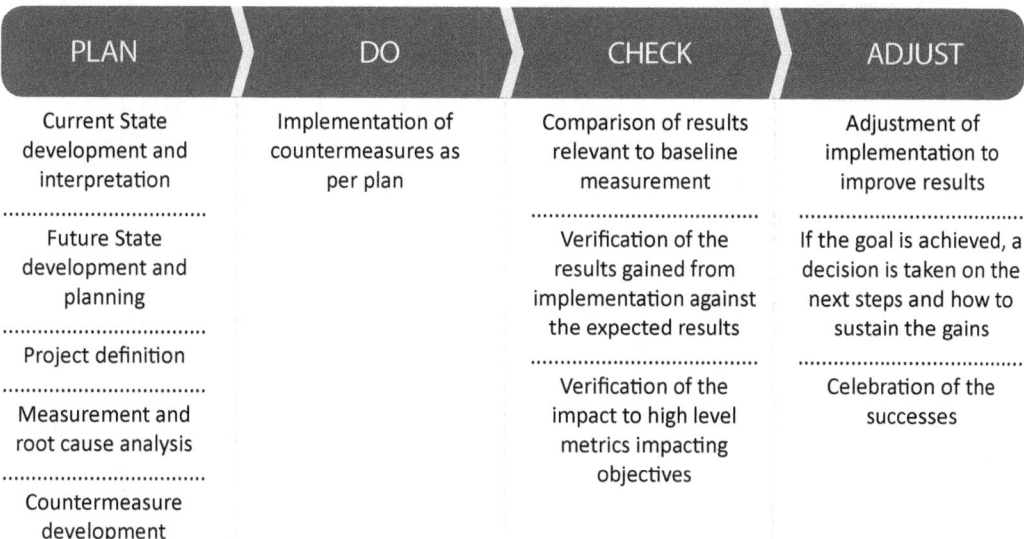

PLAN	DO	CHECK	ADJUST
Current State development and interpretation	Implementation of countermeasures as per plan	Comparison of results relevant to baseline measurement	Adjustment of implementation to improve results
Future State development and planning		Verification of the results gained from implementation against the expected results	If the goal is achieved, a decision is taken on the next steps and how to sustain the gains
Project definition		Verification of the impact to high level metrics impacting objectives	Celebration of the successes
Measurement and root cause analysis			
Countermeasure development			

Figure 5.6

? WHY IS THIS HELPFUL?

o It encourages a thought process that guides projects through all the necessary steps to achieve sustained improvement.

o Clear project definition and root cause analysis are expected prior to implementation.

o Verification of the implementation to assure quality of execution and results is assured.

o Alignment to overall objectives and improvement metrics is preserved.

? HOW TO DO IT

Step 1: Develop Problem-Solving Skills

This step is beyond the scope of this book and it is recommended that the PROBLEM SOLVING book be referred to. Ensuring the team members are able to successfully apply problem-solving logic to their projects will encourage the right steps to be followed and the right criteria to be met throughout.

Step 2: Track Implementation Progress According to PDCA

Include the PDCA cycle in the tracking of the project implementation. The example in table 5.5 demonstrates this approach and provided the team members understand what each phase means it will be possible to properly evaluate their projects:

HIGH-LEVEL PLAN
EXECUTING THE FUTURE STATE
6-MONTH FOCUS

Show progress through each cycle of PDCA

NORTH STAR IMPROVEMENT FOCUS	NO.	ACTION	EXPECTED IMPACT ON METRICS	IMPROVEMENT TYPE	RESPONSIBLE	INVOLVED	DATE	TIMING						PROGRESS					
								SEPT	OCT	NOV	DEC	JAN	FEB	PLAN	20%	50%	100%	CHECK	ADJUST
REDUCE LEAD TIME FROM 49 DAYS TO < 12 DAYS	1	IMPROVE PERFORMANCE TO TAKT THROUGH CELL DESIGN AND WASTE ELIMINATION	IMPROVE A,B AND C CYCLE TIME TO MEET 31 SECONDS CONSISTENTLY AND TOTAL PROCESSING TIME FROM 140 TO 120 SECONDS.	KAIZEN	John	Jerry, Mary	10 Jan												
	2	REDUCE MOTION BETWEEN DEPARTMENTS (SEE PROPOSED LAYOUT)	REDUCE MOTION FROM 980 STEPS TO 400 STEPS.	PROJECT	Cyril	Amanda, Clive	25 Feb												
	3	REDUCE OE LOSSES FOR PROCESS A, B AND C PRIORITISE ROLL-THROUGH YIELD PERFORMANCE AND SET-UP TIME REDUCTION	IMPROVE AVERAGE OE FROM 66% TO 86%.	KAIZEN	Billy	Jack, Olivia	31 Jan												
	4	POSITION STRATEGIC BUFFERS AND PHASE 1 REPLENISHMENT SYSTEM	REDUCE VALUE STREAM INVENTORY FROM 49 DAYS TO 30 DAYS. 10% REDUCTION IN LOST TIME AT CONSTRAINT.	KAIZEN	Philip	Bob, Sandra, Themba	15 Feb												
	5	IMPLEMENT CAPACITY LOADING POLICY AND PHASE 1 FIXED SCHEDULE	CAPACITY OF CONSTRAINT LOADED TO 85% AND 95% ACHIEVEMENT OF PREVENTIVE MAINTENANCE SCHEDULE.	KAIZEN	Sandra	Bob, Themba	25 Feb												
	6	IMPROVE CONSTRAINT SKILLS	IMPROVE SKILLS FROM ONE PER SHIFT TO 2 RESOURCES PER SHIFT.	PROJECT	Sid	Stacy, Jane	30 Sep												

Table 5.5

✅ FOR YOU TO TRY

- Develop the necessary problem-solving skills with the implementation team, and a clear understanding of PDCA.

- Implement PDCA tracking in the high-level plan and evaluate progress according to these principles.

- Coach team members to reflect and learn through the PDCA cycle to ensure the implementation achieves and sustains the required results.

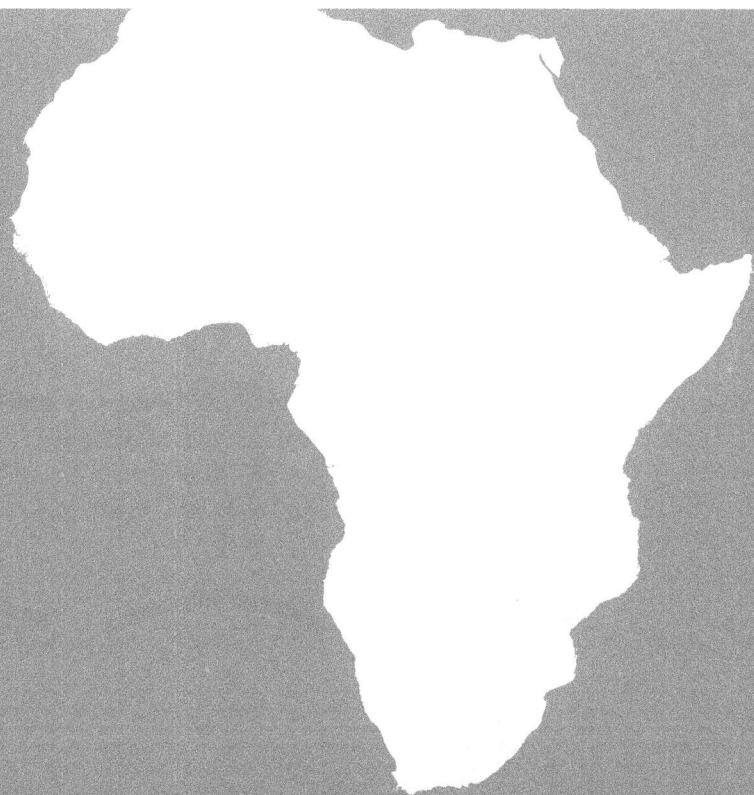

PART II
DEVELOP A CHANGE PLAN

A Clear, Compelling Plan to Raise Performance

CHANGE PLAN LEARNING ROADMAP

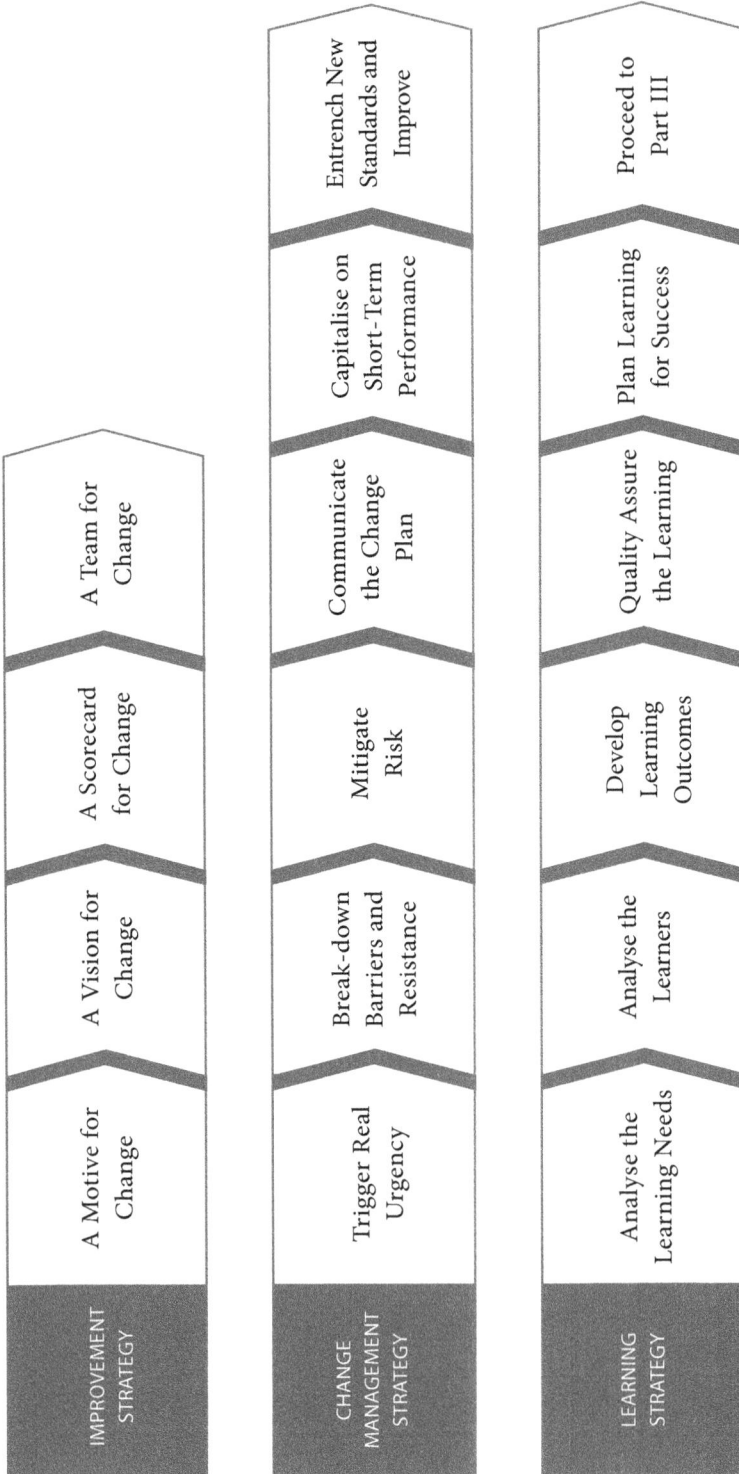

IMPROVEMENT STRATEGY

A Motive for Change → A Vision for Change → A Scorecard for Change → A Team for Change

CHANGE MANAGEMENT STRATEGY

Trigger Real Urgency → Break-down Barriers and Resistance → Mitigate Risk → Communicate the Change Plan → Capitalise on Short-Term Performance → Entrench New Standards and Improve

LEARNING STRATEGY

Analyse the Learning Needs → Analyse the Learners → Develop Learning Outcomes → Quality Assure the Learning → Plan Learning for Success → Proceed to Part III

6 IMPROVEMENT STRATEGY
FUNDAMENTALS TO DRIVE FOCUS

❓ WHAT IS THIS?

If employees were to ask you 'what is this change all about?', you need to answer them with a clear and concise explanation. You want to be sure everyone is singing from the same song book, so that when any member of the leadership team is asked this same question, there is consistency and credibility in the answer. Formally documenting the Improvement Strategy and the fundamental elements that drive focus helps articulate a message to answer these inevitable questions:

- What is the change?
- What has triggered us to do it?
- What benefit are we expecting to get out of it?
- Who is going to support us?

Leadership consensus on these answers lays a solid foundation for the change management process and success of the understanding, and therefore the execution.

❓ WHY IS THIS HELPFUL?

- Clarity and constancy of purpose is documented.
- Summarising the Improvement Strategy will bring together all the work conducted in the diagnostic and present it in a quick-reference book.
- The process and expected results are clear.
- A guiding coalition to lead the change is initiated.
- Personal accountability is established for the implementation and its success.
- The leadership team has faith in the plan it is expected to execute.

❓ HOW TO DO IT

Step 1: Establish a Motive for Change

Some people thoroughly enjoy change and see it as a necessary part of life and development. However, it is often a significant proportion that sees change as an uncomfortable, needless complication to an already jam-packed schedule. So depending on the current climate in your business and the scale of the improvement initiative, you may experience some trouble in getting people on board and fully committed.

Most people need to understand the reason for doing things, they need to believe in those reasons and they are unlikely to follow a new path blindly, especially if there have been any prior bad experiences making them approach with caution. It is very challenging to mobilise employees to share in the change vision if there is no burning need for change or an attitude of 'if it ain't broke, why try fix it?' prevails. Dissolving this complacency requires a thorough understanding of what must change, a solid plan to get there and a good understanding of what makes people tick.

Having completed the diagnostic in PART I, the business case for change was clarified. The North Star was refined, and the current performance and true potential exposed. The need for the diagnostic may have been prompted by competition pressure, market shifts, cost pressures and legislative changes, which in themselves help reveal the motive for change. The outcome of this is Clear Direction and a good grasp of the critical success factors to move from where you are to where you need to be — illustrated in the example road map we discussed earlier in Chapter 5.

The leadership team needs to collectively agree on the 'motive for change', so that a common approach takes form and becomes the key message communicated to the rest of the organisation. Use the example provided in table 6.1 to guide your thought-process and document your own 'motive for change' in table 6.2:

A MOTIVE FOR CHANGE 2014   Example

WHY ARE WE DOING THIS?

- To grow market share by 25% we need to become a more responsible company that provides quicker, fault-free service.

- To maintain shareholder interest and be price competitive, we need to do more with less cost.

- 12 Customers moved to alternative suppliers to the value of R1.8m per annum – fix and prevent!

WHICH INITIATIVES HAVE BEEN IDENTIFIED?

- Value Stream Improvement Project
- Customer Complaints Focus Project and Problem Solving Collaboration
- Creditor and Debtor Improvement Projects
- Lost Customer Focus Project
- Procurement Focus Project
- Expeditor Focus Project
- Water Reduction Project
- 5P Gap Reduction
- Climate Survey Gap Reduction

WHICH AREAS ARE TO BE INVOLVED?

- Procurement
- Quality
- Finance
- Health, Safety, Environment
- OpEx

- Human Resources
- Manufacturing and Operations
- Warehouse
- Planning
- Sales

HOW WILL THE SUCCESS OF THE INITIATIVES BE MEASURED?

- Lead time from raw material to customer delivery
- Number of customer complaints
- Financing time
- Cash Losses
- 5P Best Practice Score
- Climate Survey Score

Table 6.1

A MOTIVE FOR CHANGE

WHY ARE WE DOING THIS?

WHICH INITIATIVES HAVE BEEN IDENTIFIED?

WHICH AREAS ARE TO BE INVOLVED?

HOW WILL THE SUCCESS OF THE INITIATIVES BE MEASURED?

Discuss amongst the senior leadership team and gain consensus on the questions in table 6.2. Use the diagnostic results as the input.

Table 6.2

Step 2: Clarify the Vision for Change

The development of the Future State Vision was covered in PART I to give direction and purpose to the development of the Value Stream. In the context of the Change Plan, it is important to present this to the company as a shared vision for the change initiative, showing the clear direction the organisation is striving towards. Take a moment to review it with a fresh pair of eyes and document it with any revisions in the Change Plan:

FUTURE STATE IMPROVEMENT VISION   **Example**

In two years' time, we aim to be the African leader in protecting our customers against unforeseen circumstances. As the leader in Africa, we will:

- Outshine our competition in our ability to turnaround claims, first time right.
- Develop and challenge our employees to be the best in the industry.
- Satisfy our stakeholders through improved profitability.

We will achieve this, by:

- Achieving velocity in all critical processes.
- Developing skilled problem solvers throughout the organisation to address customer problems.
- Reducing the environmental footprint to preserve the planet for future generations.
- Focusing on the reduction of unnecessary cash losses.
- Raising the performance of our people practices.
- Improving the climate for change and growth.

We will know we have achieved our vision, when:

- Market share has grown by 25 percent.
- Working capital is down by 18 percent.
- Water and energy consumption is down by 30 percent.
- We have achieved a consistent year-on-year growth in net profit of 5 percent.
- Problems are solved daily, at the lowest level in the organisation, using a scientific method.
- Employee retention has improved by 80 percent.

Step 3: Develop a Scorecard for Change and Cascade to the Front-line

Having the right indicators in place provides focus and direction to those responsible for the roll-out. In this section, we emphasise the flow of indicators from the top-level goals and objectives, right down to the team-level metrics, to ensure the focus is properly cascaded to each level. There is also an expansion in this step from purely improvement-driven metrics, to a balanced view inclusive of metrics to drive morale, safety and environment, if this has not already been done. The diagram illustrated in figure 6.1 is a summary of the process you followed and completed in PART I and how this flow now cascades to the next level of operations.

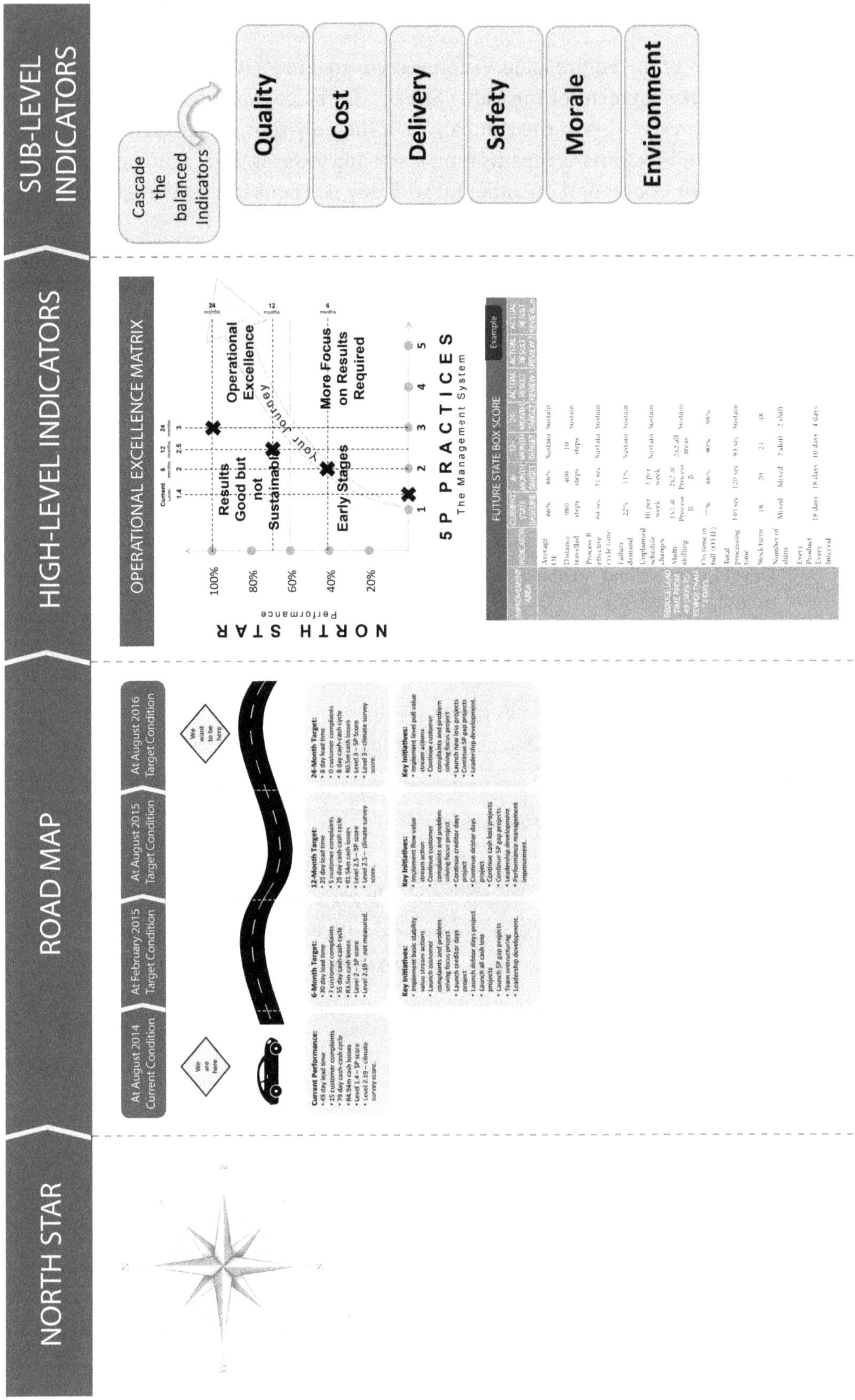

NORTH STAR

ROAD MAP

| At August 2014 Current Condition | At February 2015 Target Condition | At August 2015 Target Condition | At August 2016 Target Condition |

We are here

We want to be here

Current Performance:
- 49 day lead time
- 15 customer complaints
- 79 day cash-cash cycle
- R4.94m cash losses
- Level 1.4 – 5P score
- Level 2.19 – climate survey score.

6-Month Target:
- 30 day lead time
- 7 customer complaints
- 55 day cash-cash cycle
- R3.5m cash losses
- Level 2 – 5P score
- Level 2.19 – not measured.

Key Initiatives:
- Implement basic stability value stream action
- Launch customer complaints and problem solving focus project
- Launch condition days project
- Launch debtor days project
- Launch all cash loss projects
- Launch 5P gap projects
- Team restructuring
- Leadership development.

12-Month Target:
- 25 day lead time
- 5 customer complaints
- 25 day cash-cash cycle
- R1.94m cash losses
- Level 2.5 – 5P score
- Level 2.5 – Climate survey score.

Key Initiatives:
- Implement flow value stream action
- Continue customer complaints and problem solving focus project
- Continue condition days project
- Continue debtor days project
- Continue cash loss projects
- Continue 5P gap projects
- Leadership development
- Performance management improvement.

24-Month Target:
- 8 day lead time
- 0 customer complaints
- 8 day cash-cash cycle
- R0.5m cash losses
- Level 3 – 5P score
- Level 3 – Climate survey score.

Key Initiatives:
- Implement level pull value stream action
- Continue customer complaints and problem solving focus project
- Launch new loss projects
- Continue 5P gap projects
- Leadership development.

HIGH-LEVEL INDICATORS

NORTH STAR Performance

OPERATIONAL EXCELLENCE MATRIX

Operational Excellence

Results Good but not Sustainable

Your Journey

More Focus on Results Required

Early Stages

5 P PRACTICES
The Management System

FUTURE STATE BOX SCORE

SUB-LEVEL INDICATORS

Cascade the balanced Indicators

Quality

Cost

Delivery

Safety

Morale

Environment

Figure 6.1

To improve the balance of metrics across a spread of categories, it is recommended each indicator be classed under the headings in figure 6.2 (QCDSME). A selection of indicators is provided to help you see under which category they would generally sit – but bear in mind that some examples may fall under more than one heading.

This balance exposes the risk for improvement in one metric to the detriment of another – for example, if there is a strong push for speed but at the detriment of quality, cost or morale, then this would be made obvious and you can act on improving the balance.

Example

Quality	Not Right First Time, First Time Through, Defect Rate, Roll-Through Yield
Cost	Overtime, Consumables, Cost of Bad Quality, Cost of Lost Time
Delivery	On Time In Full, Delivery Schedule Achievement, Actual versus Planned
Safety	Number of Near Misses, Accident Rate, Audit Score
Morale	Training Assessment Scores, 5S Score, Attendance, Meeting Punctuality
Environment	Actual versus Planned for Water Consumption, Emissions, Energy Usage, Percentage Waste Recycled, Percentage Hazardous Waste

Figure 6.2

If the indicators from the North Star are categorised, the balance would look as presented in table 6.3:

NORTH STAR IMPROVEMENT INDICATORS	Example
CATEGORY	**METRIC**
Quality	Customer Complaints, Roll-Through Yield
Cost	Cash-to-Cash Cycle, Cash Loss Value
Delivery	Lead Time
Safety	(no indicator in place – consider including)
Morale	5P Assessment Score, Climate Survey Score
Environment	Water Consumption

Table 6.3

With the North Star indicators visualised develop the metrics that will regulate behaviour through the ranks in QCDSME and align with the improvement focus areas previously identified. In this way it is possible to drive the correct behaviours through measurement and at a later stage this can be extended to performance management and incentive systems for exceptional performance. Once the metrics have been improved and are ready for execution, proper engagement tactics can be agreed to before rolling out, to ensure the stakeholders are properly onboard. Review the example provided in table 6.4 and develop your own version in table 6.5 to cascade the indicators through the levels:

CATEGORISE AND CASCADE THE INDICATORS			Example
CATEGORY	NORTH STAR INDICATORS	DEPARTMENTAL LEVEL INDICATORS	TEAM LEVEL INDICATORS
Quality	Customer Complaints, Roll-Through Yield	First Pass Yield	First Pass Yield
Cost	Cash-to-Cash Cycle, Cash Loss Value	Work In Progress	Batch Size
Delivery	Lead Time	On Time In Full; Lead Time; Unplanned Changes	Actual versus Plan; Constraint Set-Up Time
Safety	Company Safety Audit Score	Department Safety Audit Score	Team Safety Audit Score
Morale	5P Assessment Score, Climate Survey Score	Attendance; Employee turnover	Attendance; Cell 5S Audit;
Environment	Water Consumption	Area Water Consumption	Cell Water Consumption

Table 6.4

TIPS

- o Do they meet SMART principles?
- o Do they align to the North Star?
- o Have the metrics been discussed with relevant stakeholders?
- o Are there fewer than ten metrics?
- o Are the metrics non-financial?
- o Do they make sense to the stakeholders?
- o Can they be measured frequently?
- o Are they within the team's control?
- o Will they drive the right behaviour that aligns to the values of the business?

SCORECARD FOR CHANGE

NORTH STAR INDICATORS

CATEGORY	INDICATOR	CURRENT	TARGET 1	TARGET 2	TARGET 3
Quality					
Cost					
Delivery					
Safety					
Morale					
Environment					

Capture the North Star indicators under their respective categories and identify any gaps that require attention.

DEPARTMENTAL INDICATORS

CATEGORY	INDICATOR	CURRENT	TARGET 1	TARGET 2	TARGET 3
Quality					
Cost					
Delivery					
Safety					
Morale					
Environment					

Cascade the North Star indicators to each of the departments and use the metric tips to check them. Complete one table for each department and remember to include the stakeholders before finalising.

TEAM INDICATORS

CATEGORY	INDICATOR	CURRENT	TARGET 1	TARGET 2	TARGET 3
Quality					
Cost					
Delivery					
Safety					
Morale					
Environment					

Cascade the departmental metrics to each of the front-line teams, and use the metric tips to check them. Complete one table for each team and remember to include the stakeholders before finalising

Table 6.5

Step 4: Form a Guiding Team for Change

Unfortunately the desire and a plan to improve is not enough to make it happen. You need people and they need to be doing very specific activities, which move the organisation closer to the goals. Designing the implementation structure will go a long way to ensure the right people are involved, doing the right things and in the right way. In PART III how to get these structures following through on the right activities through excellent execution practices will be discussed. The basic implementation structure in figure 6.3 is advised but this can be customised to suit your business and particular Change Plan:

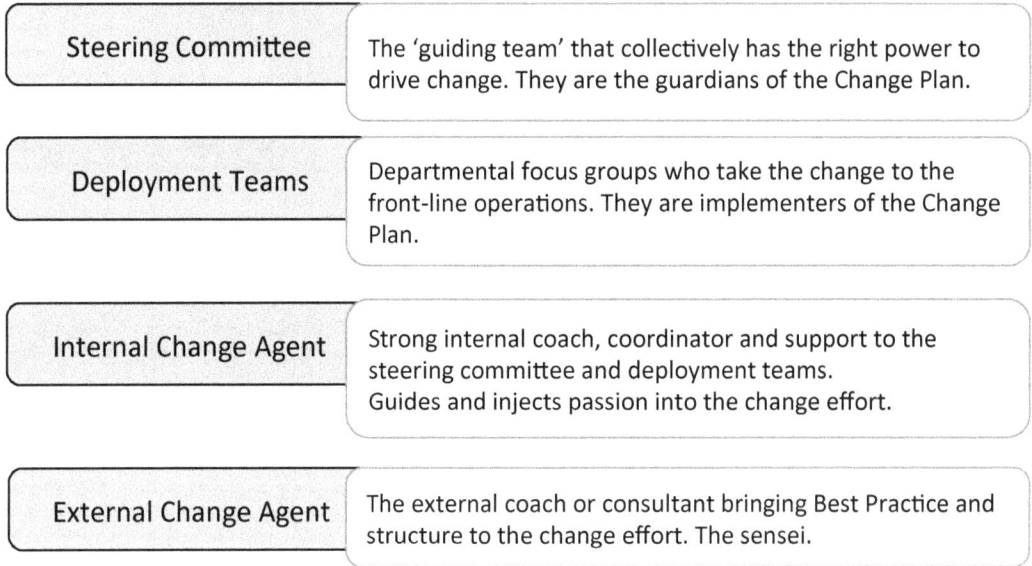

Steering Committee	The 'guiding team' that collectively has the right power to drive change. They are the guardians of the Change Plan.
Deployment Teams	Departmental focus groups who take the change to the front-line operations. They are implementers of the Change Plan.
Internal Change Agent	Strong internal coach, coordinator and support to the steering committee and deployment teams. Guides and injects passion into the change effort.
External Change Agent	The external coach or consultant bringing Best Practice and structure to the change effort. The sensei.

Figure 6.3

Selecting the Steering Committee

Using the following as a guideline (Kotter, 2002) identify the steering committee (steercom) members that collectively exhibit the following characteristics and update table 6.6:

○ A good mix of skills

○ The leadership capacity to create the vision, motivate and drive change

○ Organisational credibility and network in the organisation

○ Relevant knowledge to empower people and remove obstacles to change

○ Formal authority and the managerial skills associated with planning and organizing to facilitate short-term performance gains that trigger interest.

The following roles are recommended:

- ○ Chairperson:
  Sets the scene, ensures quorum, pulls the team together and leads the meetings according to a strict agenda.

- ○ Administrator:
  Captures decisions and actions and sends out administrative communications.

- ○ Deployment leaders:
  Leads the change effort in his or her respective area of control.

- ○ Internal change agent:
  Coaches, coordinates and supports the steering committee and deployment teams.

- ○ External change agent:
  The role is defined as per the service level agreement. This typically entails keeping the change effort 'honest' and providing the theory, benchmarks, methodology and coaching to support the process from conception to successful execution.

STEERING COMMITTEE		
NAME	POSITION	ROLE
		Chairperson
		Administrator
		Internal Change Agent

Together with the leadership team complete table 6.6 to establish formal structures to guide and take accountability for the change effort. Ensure each member is fully aware of his or her involvement and responsibilities.

Table 6.6

Consider the nature of the implementation planned and which stakeholders should be directly involved in the physical roll-out. This could be departmentally or Value-Stream focused relevant to the changes required. Consider the following suggestions when deciding on the members of the deployment team:

○ The area leader identified in the steering committee leads this team

○ Critical stakeholders responsible for implementing actions are pulled together

○ Sufficient skill and knowledge of the operations is required.

There may be more than one deployment team – for example representing each function or department. Complete one for each, as required.

DEPLOYMENT TEAM		
NAME	POSITION	ROLE
		Deployment Leader
		Administrator
		Team Member
		Team Member
		Team Member
		Team Member
		Team Member
		Team Member
		Team Member

Together with the leadership team complete table 6.7 to establish formal structures to implement the change at functional level. There may be more than one deployment team. Ensure each member is fully aware of his or her involvement and responsibilities.

Table 6.7

It will be necessary to have regular communication, planning and problem solving meetings to drive the Change Plan. Change efforts can very quickly get a bad name if meetings are not efficient, to the point and facilitate the change well. The moment members feel it is a waste of time or not achieving the objective, participation will weaken and absenteeism will kick in. Setting up a formal structure for the above team/s is therefore essential to ensure they meet and communicate regarding the Change Plan and discuss the correct elements. To assure the integrity of the change process, rigid frequency of the meetings must be agreed to, as well as the agenda that will guide the discussions and activities of the groups. Consider the following when designing the meeting structures:

o The steercom should meet every one to two months. The frequency can increase in the early stages if this is deemed necessary. Preferably for one to two hours at a time.

o The deployment team should meet every one to two weeks preferably for one hour at a time.

MEETING PLANNING						
MEETING TYPE	WHO TO ATTEND	REQUIREMENTS FOR QUORUM	PURPOSE OF MEETING	HOW OFTEN TO MEET	HOW LONG TO MEET FOR	WHO IS RESPONSIBLE
Steercom Meeting						
Deployment Team Meeting						
External Support Meeting						

Complete table 6.8 to prompt the implementation structure to meet regularly and address the needs of the Change Plan. Gemba walks prior to the meeting are recommended to safeguard against this just being a boardroom exercise.

Table 6.8

With the meeting structures set up, meeting agendas are now designed to guide the purpose and objectives for each meeting (table 6.9):

STEERCOM AGENDA

FREQUENCY: 3rd Tuesday of every month at 2pm

DURATION: 2 hours (plus 20 minutes gemba walk beforehand)

CHAIRPERSON: John Kottrel

ATTENDEES: Bill Ramos (Ops); Jane Mecer (Quality); Mark Jones (Supply
                    Chain); Brian Vilakazi (Fin); Seth Mhlangu (Opex); Estelle
                    Jackson (Hr)

PURPOSE: Evaluate progress to date, define next steps and remove
                    obstacles

NO.	AGENDA ITEM	DURATION	RESPONSIBLE
1	Welcome and attendance		JK
2	Gemba walk (meet at warehouse)	20 min	JK
3	Actions from last meeting	40 min	JK
4	Target vs actual review: North Star Indicators	10 min	JK
5	Deployment team feedback for each improvement area in A3 Format	40 min	All deployment leaders: BR; JM; MJ; BV; EJ
6	Obstacles and support needs	10 min	JK
7	New risks	5 min	ALL
8	Internal change agent feedback	10 min	SM
9	Update new actions	5 min	SM
10	Next meeting and close		

Develop a Steercom agenda to suit the North Star focus areas and
the goals of the Change Plan.

Table 6.9

DEPLOYMENT TEAM AGENDA

Example

FREQUENCY:	Every Tuesday at 9am
DURATION:	60 minutes (including gemba walk)
CHAIRPERSON:	Bill Ramos (Ops Director)
ATTENDEES:	John Ndlovu; Aiden Labuschagne; Philip Molape; Sandra Jones; Sid Marshall
PURPOSE:	Evaluate progress to date, define next steps and remove obstacles

NO.	AGENDA ITEM	DURATION	RESPONSIBLE
1	Welcome and attendance		BR
2	Gemba walk (meet at line 2)	15 min	BR
3	Actions from last meeting	5 min	ALL
4	Indicator tracking and trigger	10 min	AL
5	Project team feedback	20 min	JN; AL; PM; SJ; SM
6	Items for escalation to steercom/feedback	5 min	ALL
7	Update new actions	5 min	SM
8	Next meeting and close		

Develop a generic deployment-team agenda to suit the North Star focus areas and the goals of the Change Plan.

Table 6.10

TIPS

Meetings can become a negative part of anyone's day if not planned and run well. It is important to snap out of the bad habit of allowing meetings to lose their way, as good meetings are critical to the functioning of any business. Whether the meeting is for problem solving, communication, planning or other, there are a few generic points to check that your meetings are in fact effective, and efficient.

- Have an agenda and a purpose. Make it available ahead of time so that people can plan and know what to expect.

- Start on time. End on time.

- Take attendance, and deal with poor attendance as soon as possible.

- Someone must lead the meeting and keep it well aligned with the agenda and the timings.

- Factor in a minute or two at the beginning to encourage social interaction. Objectives for the meeting must be met, but developing relationships is also important. Thereafter, keep it structured and focused.

- Encourage participation from all members so that you achieve the input of many rather than the opinion of one.

- Encourage a culture of 'taking the blame' rather than 'shifting the blame'. When someone rightly takes the blame for something, they inevitably take on the responsibility as well, and promoting this behaviour is much better than pointing fingers.

- Sharing credit is as important as the point above, and meetings are an excellent place to do this.

- Develop rules for cancelling standing meetings – for example if the quorum is not met, postpone the meeting and if appropriate escalate the poor attendance.

- Be specific about action items, responsibility and timings. Make sure a good system is used to capture them (white board, or worst case minutes) and that they are written well enough to understand them the next time you look at them. Never allow the responsible person to be 'everyone' and certainly don't encourage timings to say 'asap'. Be precise.

- For lengthy meetings, allow time for breaks. This will reduce fidgeting and distraction.

✓ FOR YOU TO TRY

○ Together with the leadership team complete the templates provided for:

- The Motive for Change

- The Vision for Change

- The Scorecard for Change.

○ Identify key individuals using the guidelines provided who will form the steercom and deployment teams to take ownership for the Change Plan and its execution.

○ Structure necessary meetings so that it is clear as to who must attend, the purpose, requirements for quorum, frequency, duration and responsibilities.

○ Develop structured, focused agendas to keep meetings on track and effective.

○ Summarise each template into your own Change Plan that can be bound into a reference book.

○ Complete the whole of Part II before sharing the outcomes with the employees.

7 CHANGE MANAGEMENT STRATEGY
FIRST HEARTS THEN HEADS

❓ WHAT IS THIS?

There is one thing we can be certain of: change will always be a part of our lives, both personally and professionally. How leaders manage and adjust to suit the change will directly influence how employees feel about the transformation and in the long run, whether the objectives are supported or not. Designing a strategy that proactively deals with change and provides processes in which to structure it more effectively is invaluable. Subsequently, linking this to the values of the organisation adds integrity to the process. The following section details a thought-process by which to plan change (Kotter, 2002):

○ The section kicks-off with a discussion around complacency and how to progress employees from a mental state of 'all is good, let's not rock the boat by changing anything' to a realisation that 'we have to do something about the problems and opportunities, now!' This is central to change success and may require somewhat creative methods to get the change juices flowing to trigger real urgency amongst the troops.

○ Change efforts do not always run smoothly, and we highlight the reality of opposition and appropriate ways to expose and deal with it. Manoeuvring to elicit good responses from stakeholders will prepare the leadership and change agents for what is sure to be a bumpy ride ahead. Having a plan to cope with this will go a long way in convincing 'the resistence' that leaders are serious about following through on the Change Plan.

○ The company that is well prepared for potential risks is in a better position to prevent failure or possible derailment in the improvement drive. Potential risks are raised and proposed responses prepared priming leadership with a 'heads up' when change goes wrong.

○ Unclogging communication channels will help to overcome festering mistrust or confusion around the change effort. Developing a formal communication plan will make it easier for the leadership team to send out clear, regular, credible and sincere messages that cultivate heart-felt buy-in.

○ Employees may not be convinced the change will yield real benefit. If they believe this is just someone's hobby-horse, a 'smell of the week' or the latest fad, they will be unlikely to give it any genuine support – and who can blame them? It is necessary to prove the effort is worth the outcome by deliberately creating wins early-on in the process to assist employees see and feel the potential, and to persuade them that all the talk actually has substance.

○ It is inspiring to witness real change for the better take place in a business but it is equally demoralising to watch it slip back to how it used to be. This means taking a strong stance on sustaining the change through a scientific method (PDCA), relentless leadership, discipline for the Management System and ensuring employees perform in new ways – despite their 'love for tradition'.

❓ WHY IS THIS HELPFUL?

○ A common approach to dealing with the realities of change are captured and a delivery mechanism for constancy of purpose from the leadership team is made possible.

○ Individuals and the impact change will have on them are considered and dealt with. Resistance is exposed and dealt with.

○ Potential risks are dealt with before they create a mode of failure or throw the initiative into crisis.

○ Employees are well informed and feel part of the change through good communication.

○ Short-term gains stimulate motivation and a desire to proceed.

○ The Management System to sustain the gains is set in motion.

❓ HOW TO DO IT

Step 1: Trigger Real Urgency

This is a good time to mention that 'change has a heart'. John Kotter teaches us that 'people change what they do less because they are given analysis that shifts their thinking than because they are shown the truth that influences their feelings' (Kotter, 2002: p1).

He further explains that we have to help them 'see' by creating compelling, eye-catching, dramatic situations that visualise the reality. Only showing employees the results of a diagnostic is really just showing them unconvincing analysis. We use the diagnostic in PART I to make informed decisions and provide direction but this will not win their hearts. It takes concerted effort to take employees along for the change and often unconventional methods to shock them into a restless mode are needed to break the complacency.

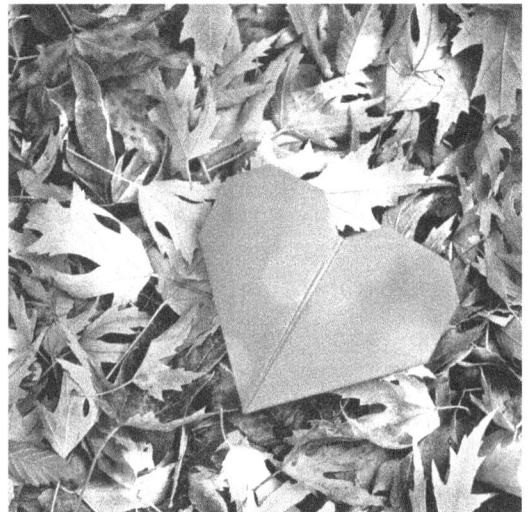

For instance, find a compelling way to show how money is being lost in the business. One company piled their scrap in the middle of the factory and placed a sign on it to show the money value being lost everyday. Another put up a banner to demonstrate the losses incurred from using a variety of suppliers for the same item. A third filmed an angry customer to show the impact of his frustration with poor product design.

Review the feedback documented from the Voice of your Customer and the North Star objectives in PART I and brainstorm an elaborate way to address complacency in the business and trigger an urgency for change. Remember to maintain respect for people and aim to achieve the goal of helping them to see, feel and then change. Ultimately, you want them to start itching to make a difference. Here are a few pointers to generate questions and devise means to stimulate people to want to change (Kotter, 2002):

- Can you show people something that is direct, exists and affects the business, such as an unhappy customer?

- Can you create something new that will highlight the problem, such as displays.

- Can you do something indirectly? Like helping a leader to see how he sets a negative example for his team and how they act as a result.

- How can you visually depict the results from the diagnostic to make it easy for people to understand the results and the key points of interest – all the while not falling into the trap of uninspiring analysis. Perhaps building onto the road map could work here.

- Keep it simple, cheap and respectful.

Kotter explains that there are different types of urgency. False urgency occurs when employees busy themselves with many activities, none of which contribute to the North Star. True urgency occurs when peoples' daily, weekly and monthly activities progress towards the North Star with great gusto and heart-felt determination.

Discuss options to mobilise your employees to achieve real urgency and trigger them to want to make a difference to the change effort. Capture your ideas and a plan to execute it with in table 7.1.

A PLAN TO TRIGGER URGENCY				
Area of Complacency	Trigger	Expected Result	Responsible Person	Timing

Based on the results from the diagnostic in PART I, discuss areas in which the business is complacent. Brainstorm elaborate methods amongst the steerom to tackle complacency and drive behaviour towards real urgency.

Table 7.1

Step 2: Break-down Barriers and Resistance

Gaining cooperation from those impacted by the change will certainly pave the way for a more successful execution but this will not happen by chance. It is necessary to spend time identifying and evaluating the various types of stakeholders, pre-empting their reactions, proactively planning to address this and incrementally winning over their support.

○ To begin, identify all the stakeholders that will be influenced by the work about to be done (figure 7.1). Initiatives have been identified through the Best Practice, Value Stream and Basic Cash Loss Evaluation, summarised in the Future State Road Map. Who will be impacted by these initiatives and how will they be affected?

○ Next, prioritise them into a matrix according to the level of power they hold and amount of interest they will show in the change effort (figure 7.2). Use the guideline provided.

○ Finally capture their expected reactions into the Stakeholder Analysis (table 7.3) and discuss how the leadership team should respond accordingly.

STAKEHOLDER LIST   Example

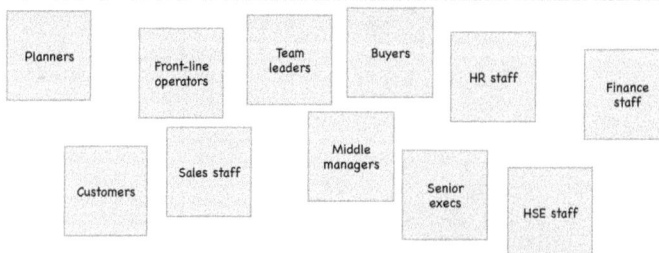

List all the stakeholders that will be directly or indirectly influenced by the change as shown in figure 7.1.

Figure 7.1

You may have quite a list of stakeholders but they will not all be handled in the same way. Some stakeholders will be significantly impacted, some will be able to exert great influence and others may not even be too interested. The Stakeholder Matrix in figure 7.2 will help narrow down your focus:

STAKEHOLDER MATRIX

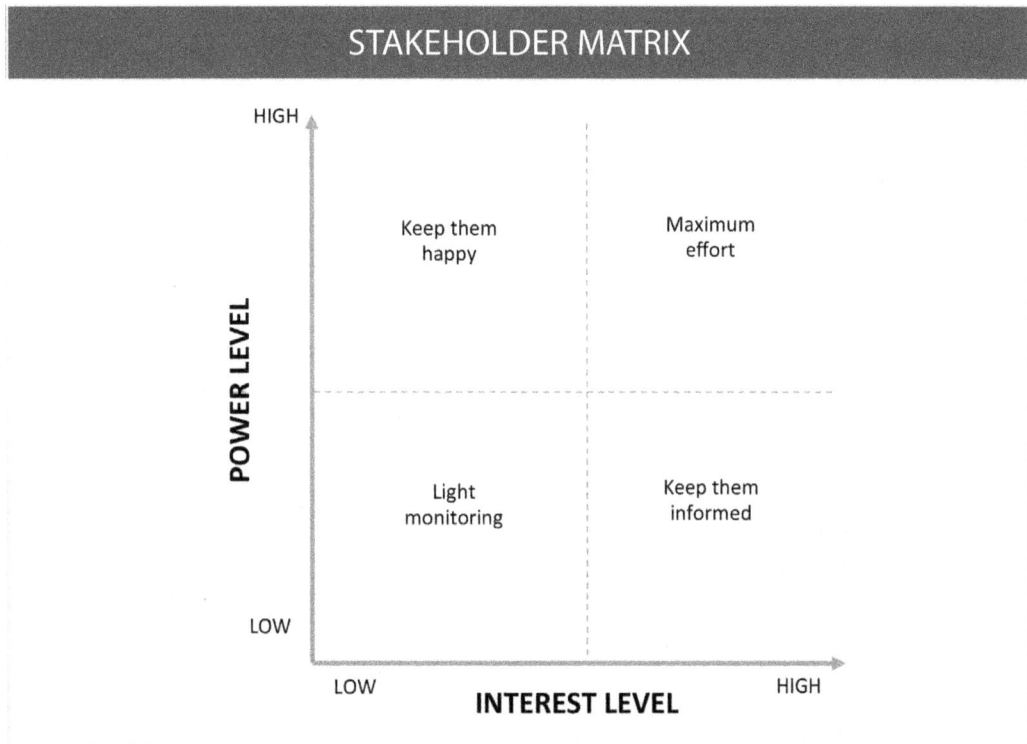

Figure 7.2

Position your stakeholders on the matrix in figure 7.2 using the following guideline:	
High Power, High Interest	Fully engage with this group and make the greatest efforts with them.
High Power, Low Interest	Put enough work in with this group to keep them satisfied but not so much that they become bored with the message.
Low Power, High Interest	Keep them adequately informed, and talk to them to ensure that no major issues are arising. This group can often be very helpful with the detail.
Low Power, Low Interest	Monitor this group but do not bore them with excessive communication.

When completing the Stakeholder Analysis in table 7.3, consider the results of the Climate Survey conducted in PART I, as well as what the stakeholders are saying. If needed, conduct informal interviews to gauge the views and perceptions of some of the key stakeholders to include in the findings. Discuss amongst the steering committee what policy changes may be required to successfully facilitate the improvement strategy, as this may reveal responses from staff that will need to be effectively dealt with. Table 7.2 lists possible decisions that may be worth thinking about at this point (Mann, 2005):

POLICY DECISIONS TO CONSIDER		
Policy Area	How Can this Support Operational Excellence?	Potential Obstacles to Consider
Job Rotation	Rotation mitigates the risk of repetitive stress injuries. It results in a cross-skilled workforce where employees can step in when needed. Having more eyes on each job increases the chances for seeing improvement opportunities.	This must be a policy applied to all or it is not enforceable. When initiated, not all may be able to succeed at each job in the rotation pattern.
Layoff or Retrenchment	Even though lean thinking as an element of Operational Excellence will result in elimination of some work, nobody should lose employment as a result. The long-term goal must be to preserve jobs. Layoffs do occur when conditions change in the market but it is not an opportunity to cut costs when waste has been removed. How excess capacity will be used must be clear –marketing and additional revenue streams, continuous improvement activities, transference to areas where skills are required and reduced overtime or variable staff spend.	Is the organisation willing to temporarily absorb employees made surplus through improvements? If not, then participation and co-operation will not be sustained.
Job Classification and Grades	Operational Excellence works best with a flexible, cross-skilled workforce. Specialised knowledge is now contained in standardised work, previously complex jobs have been redesigned to support flow. The number of classifications and jobs has been simplified.	Many employees will be proud of the grade or classification they have achieved over years of work. They will see consolidation as a loss. The organisation needs to be willing to realise and address this.
Pay	Work may be restructured into smaller elements, rotation is in place, job grades and classifications have been consolidated. The pay system will need to align with these changes.	Reducing the distinctions in pay may end up reducing the pay of some employees.
Staggered Start Times	To facilitate processing what is needed, when it is needed, start times may need to be reviewed.	Changing start times can be surprisingly emotional. Support to employees during this period of adjustment should be considered.
Staggered Break Times	To facilitate processing what is needed, when it is needed, break times may need to be reviewed.	Some employees have managed their own break time and enforcing rigidity to support flow will require adjustment.

Table 7.2

STAKEHOLDER ANALYSIS

Category	Stakeholder	How will the change affect them?	Will their reaction be positive or negative? Why?	If their reaction is negative, what could help to increase their support?	If it is not likely that support can be won, how will this be managed?	What support will they require from the leadership team?
High power, high interest						
High power, low interest						
Low power, high interest						
Low power, low interest						

Do not guess the answers, speak to the key stakeholders and ask for their feedback on the questions above. You can also use the feedback from the Climate Survey as an input.

Table 7.3

Step 3: Mitigate Risk

A risk is an uncertain event that, if occurs, could have a negative impact on the change effort. There will most likely be several risks associated with implementing the proposed changes and a formal plan to lessen the impact will transform them into opportunities for building mutual respect.

'Denial is a common tactic that substitutes deliberate ignorance for thoughtful planning.'

Charles Tremper

Use the following guidelines to prepare a Risk Response Plan (table 7.4) to reduce the probability of failure:

- List the possible risks the steercom anticipates.
- Determine the probability of the risk – how likely it is to happen?
- Determine the severity of the impact if it were to happen.
- Establish what can be done to mitigate or reduce the probability.
- Brainstorm possibilities to reduce the impact.
- Assign accountability to each risk.

Once a Risk Response Plan is developed, it is the responsibility of the steercom to ensure the actions identified are actioned. Of course, risks will pop-up along the way and it is therefore recommended that this remain a dynamic plan, where new risks and responses are added each time they are surfaced.

This will go a long way in putting sceptics' minds at ease, and growing support for the change effort, assuming the risks raised are effectively dealt with.

RISK RESPONSE PLAN

Potential Risk	Probability of Occurring (Percentage)	Severity of Impact (High, Medium, Low)	How to Reduce Probability	How to Reduce Impact	Agreed Actions	Who	When

Refer to the Stakeholder Analysis (table 7.3) and interview a selection of stakeholders to gather opinions on possible risks. Brainstorm all possible risks with the steercom and complete the Risk Response Plan (table 7.4).

Table 7.4

Step 4: Communicate the Change Plan

Communication planning is the art and science of reaching a target audience. It explains how to convey the right message, from the right communicator, to the right audience, through the right channel, at the right time.

The impact of good consultation and open communication channels in a change effort cannot be overstated. Getting the right message out and aligning this with leadership behaviour can help deliver improved employee engagement and participation. These are critical ingredients when you need to make real improvement happen.

Various forms of communication will be used, but the typicals examples include:

- ○ Providing upfront communication about the improvement drive.

- ○ Allowing employees the opportunity to raise their concerns, and let issues be dealt with.

- ○ Ensuring ongoing communication throughout the process to keep employees up to date and well informed.

- ○ Advertising progress to plan, and give recognition where it is due.

- ○ Repeating the cycle everytime the diagnostic is redone (the old Future State becomes the new Current State) and the associated Change Plan is revised.

Various communication channels can be explored to suit the objectives – for example:

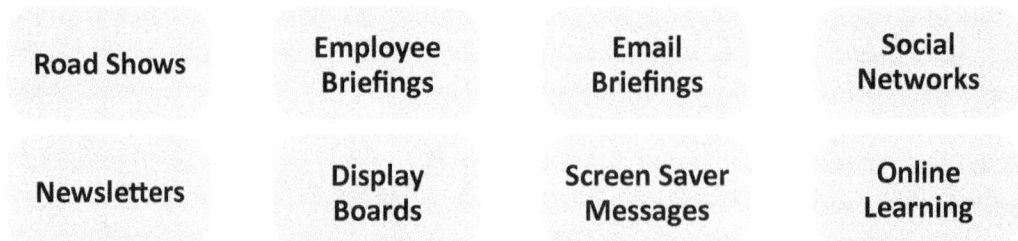

Road Shows	Employee Briefings	Email Briefings	Social Networks
Newsletters	Display Boards	Screen Saver Messages	Online Learning

Refer to the findings from the Climate Survey (table 1.3), Stakeholder Analysis (table 7.3) and Risk Response Plan (table 7.4) to use as inputs for the Communication Plan (table 7.5) and assist in addressing some of the issues already revealed. Accountability for each communication medium must be clear to ensure the plan is rigorously followed through and updated from time to time with the latest needs.

COMMUNICATION PLAN

WHY Outcome Desired	WHAT Key Message	WHO Target Audience	HOW Communication Vehicle	WHEN Timing and Frequency	BY WHOM Responsible Person

Brainstorm a communication approach amongst the steercom to help facilitate buy-in and employee engagement. Update the Communication Plan (table 7.5) with the decisions.

Table 7.5

Step 5: Capitalise on Short-Term Performance

'In successful change efforts, empowered people create short-term wins – victories that nourish faith in the change effort, emotionally reward the hard workers, keep the critics at bay, and build momentum. Without sufficient wins that are visible, timely, unambiguous, and meaningful to others, change efforts inevitably run into serious problems.'

(Kotter 2002: p125)

The path to employee buy-in is smoother when benefits can be seen up-front. As an improvement initiative first launches, it is difficult to gain support as very little change has actually taken place. By strategically and deliberately focusing on short-term gains in the change process, sceptics can see positive transformation and support is prompted – especially if the benefit is experienced personally! This applies equally to the leadership team and rest of the employees in the business.

In PART I, initiatives were identified to drive the goals of the North Star. It was possible to prioritise these initiatives based on the all-round benefit they brought to the business – for example, through the use of the Prioritisation Matrix in the Basic Cash Loss Evaluation which detailed what could be managed in the short and medium term (table 7.6):

PRIORITISATION MATRIX											Example
Factor	Bottom Line Impact	Link to Voice of the Customer	Link to Strategy and Objectives	Cost to Implement	Resources Needed to Address	Impact on Other Categories	Complexity to Implement	Time to Implement (months)	Measurable Results	Total Score as per Weighting	Business Lever Priority
Weighting	35%	10%	10%	5%	5%	5%	10%	15%	5%	Multiply each rating by its weight.	
Rating = 5	High	High	High Level	Zero	Very Few	High	Easy	<3 mths	Measurable		
Rating = 3	Med	Med	Dept Level	Med	Moderate	Med	Moderate	3-6 mths	Difficult	Add up the weighted	
Rating = 1	Low	Low	Floor Level	High	Many	Low	Very Difficult	>6 mths	Intangible	ratings for each cost	
Lost Customers	5	5	5	5	3	3	5	3	5	4.5	1
Cash-to-Cash Cycle	1	5	5	1	1	5	3	1	5	2.4	6
Roll Through Yield (RTY)	3	5	5	1	1	3	1	1	5	2.8	3
Procurement Costs	1	1	5	5	5	1	5	5	5	3	2
Expediting Losses	1	1	5	3	3	5	3	3	5	2.5	5
Water Management	1	5	5	3	5	1	5	1	5	2.7	4

Rate each loss and assign a weighting. Set a priority for focus.

Table 7.6

Refer to the results from PART I and discuss amongst the steercom which initiatives will yield benefits in the short-term and how will this be leveraged to gain additional support. Consider allocating some of the savings to resolve issues close to the hearts of staff, and update table 7.7 with your decisions.

SHORT-TERM PERFORMANCE

Initiative Identified	Business Benefit	Customer Benefit	Employee Benefit	Time to Implement	Leverage Point to Yield Employee Buy-In	Responsible Person

Refer to PART I and identify short-term wins that can help stimulate buy-in and motivate employees. Include in table 7.7 and update your Communication Plan (table 7.5) with any new items that will require 'advertising'.

Table 7.7

Step 6: Entrench New Standards and Improve

Although in the early stages of the change effort, think ahead to when momentum does kick in and results start to emerge. The first part to making change stick is maintaining this momentum. This means you need to discourage the sigh of relief coupled with the remark 'shew...we finally did it, now we can relax', and keep the pressure on. In the beginning of PART II it was noted that complacency is a strong stumbling block to change and keeping your foot on the gas is important. The plan created to trigger real urgency (table 7.1) will assist in this regard.

A second part, and often neglected enabler of successful change, is the Management System. This is the framework of processes, policies and procedures used in concert to achieve a set of goals. Good intentions and a handful of improvement tools are an adequate start but will not result in sustainability of new performance. However, the Management System, and how it all fits together, will.

In Chapter 2 you plotted the results of your 5P assessment on the Operational Excellence Matrix. This provided a stake-in-the-ground measurement of the maturity in your operations and a view of the gaps to be closed. It was discussed how performance in the North Star objectives can only be sustained if the Management System backs it up with a set of habits that entrenches new practices. With this new, best method for Operational Excellence standardised and sustained in the system, you have a baseline from which to launch your next level of change. The ongoing development and refinement of your Management System will therefore entrench the worthy changes into the very fabric of your organisation.

In conclusion, the design of the Management System will support the good habits that preserve what has been achieved, some of which are summarised as follow:

- Keep finding ways to build efficiency into people's work. Get employees into the habit of making time for improvement by asking, 'Is this adding value or just adding to the noise?' Of course, this starts with the leadership team and cascades down. Look at leader standard work and make it part of the system (Leader Standard Work is covered in PEOPLE).

- Get the steercom into the habit of constantly looking for new ways to keep the urgency alive. One way is to be cautious of developing rigid, long-term plans that do not cater for flexibility along the way. Yes, it is important to keep focused on the North Star, but conditions do change, progress is made and keeping up the momentum may require interim adjustments to activities in order to meet the long term goals (see PART III).

- Encourage employees by rewarding successes, but then discuss with them new levels of performance that can be achieved next. Emphasise that the improvement strategy is a never-ending journey that strives for continuous improvement. It is not a once-off act of brilliance never to be seen again.

- Keep showing the employees the successes, advertise and communicate the achievements and always give credit to the team involved.

- Continue to update the Risk Response Plan at every steercom meeting and improve the Communication Plan accordingly.

- Discourage the tapering off of steercom and deployment team meetings. If these groups lose momentum, the rest of the employees will be sure to follow. Often it is necessary to revisit agendas, timing and objectives to check for relevance and focus. Ensure there are no disruptive changes to the team members that can also cause a loss of drive.

✅ FOR YOU TO TRY

○ Get the leadership together and complete each template provided in this section:

- Discuss the level of complacency in the business and what areas the employees will need help with. Develop recommendations to trigger a sense of urgency for change.

- Evaluate the stakeholders impacted by the change and their possible reactions. Brainstorm how to grow their support and alleviate barriers to success.

- Evaluate possible risks and the responses required by the steercom to increase the success rate of the improvement initiative.

- Discuss how to convey credible and relevant messages to the employees to meet communication objectives and encourage buy-in and participation. Design suitable vehicles to deliver the communication.

- Fast-track short-term performance gains to diffuse cynicism, pessimism and scepticism. Leverage employee engagement by linking gains to resolving issues close to their hearts.

- Develop the Management System for Operational Excellence to acquire behaviours that will drive a culture of improvement, sustainment and new target conditions.

○ Update the High-Level Future State Plan prepared in Chapter 5 with additional actions identified.

○ Summarise each template into your own Change Plan that can be bound into a reference book.

8 LEARNING STRATEGY
ALIGN LEARNING TO THE NORTH STAR

❓ WHAT IS THIS?

Learning and development plays a major role in the success of connecting people with process, and although this section does not aim to replace the overall learning strategy or training model, it can give critical input to ensure the training selected to close the skills gap, is both relevant and results-driven in the change effort. Hopefully training is not seen as the first cost driver to be cut in cost-reduction strategies. If training brings real business benefit, it should receive the support and longevity it deserves.

Of course, training costs time, money and in many cases, productivity, so putting some thought into how it will be dealt with, will motivate for its place in the roll-out plan. Figure 8.1 adds incentive for the sections that follow as it represents the proportion of training that actually yields the desired results – which is a shocking realisation in view of the investments made (Brinkerhof, 2010):

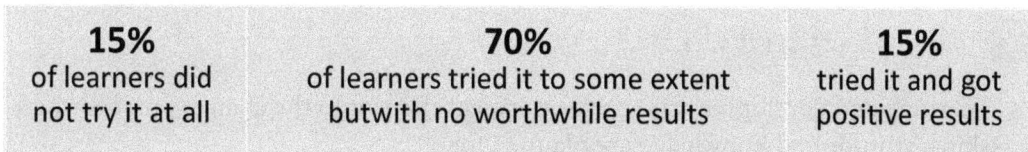

15%	**70%**	**15%**
of learners did not try it at all	of learners tried it to some extent butwith no worthwhile results	tried it and got positive results

Figure 8.1

Further to this study, a training failure mode analysis was conducted on why 85 percent of training generally does not deliver expected results, and the following reasons were established and detailed as in figure 8.2 (Brinkerhof, 2010):

BEFORE	DURING	AFTER — Example
○ Senior leaders did not see how the training could help the business and failed to support it. ○ Managers of trainees did not understand how the training would benefit them or their goals. ○ Managers did not encourage trainees to participate.	○ The training facilitators did a poor job. ○ The material was not relevant to the trainees. ○ The trainees were not capable of learning the content. ○ The training materials were poorly organised. ○ The sessions were scheduled at inconvenient times.	○ Managers did not hold trainees accountable for applying the learning. ○ The incentives for continuing to follow existing procedures were still attractive. ○ The measurement and feedback systems were not sufficient to track new behaviours. ○ Trainees did not get good coaching in how best to use the new behaviours. ○ Managers were pressured to keep top-line revenues up and told trainees to just focus on doing things the way they used to.

Figure 8.2

The study shows that most of the issues are in fact coming from the 'before' and 'after' phases, and the best part, is that this is avoidable! The intention of this section is to shift the expected high scrap rate from 85 percent down to 5 percent by ensuring that the above failures are pre-empted and dealt with as follows:

- Establish the learning needs emerging from PART I. Capture the needs and the expected outcomes to ensure that the training selected is relevant and will produce the right results for the investment.

- Thereafter, analyse the proposed audience to understand the prerequisite knowledge and skill to ensure the training is adequately targeting them. Culture, learning styles and background, amongst other things, will influence the training design and methodology.

- Capturing the learning outcomes follows and will provide direction and substance to the training and development techniques, as well as a basis for assessing competence.

- Formally devising a system to quality assure the learning and warrant success.

- Finally, establish practical checks that can be done pre and post training interventions to ensure the chances of failure are reduced.

❓ WHY IS THIS HELPFUL?

- Learning and development is seen as a critical element to the change process where skills, attitude and knowledge are planned for.

- There will be reduction in training 'scrap rates' and improved return on investment.

- The link between the North Star and training is clarified.

- Leaders can encourage employees to participate and learn with meaning.

- Accountability for results is made possible.

❓ HOW TO DO IT

Step 1: Conduct a Learning Needs Analysis

This analysis helps clarify what training is required, for whom, and for what purpose. At this stage, there should be a good idea of the obvious learning needs to get the initiatives off the ground and achieve the objectives set in the North Star. Review the example in figure 8.3 showing the link between the North Star and learning needs, and with input from the steercom, complete the Learning Needs Analysis template provided in table 8.1.

Example

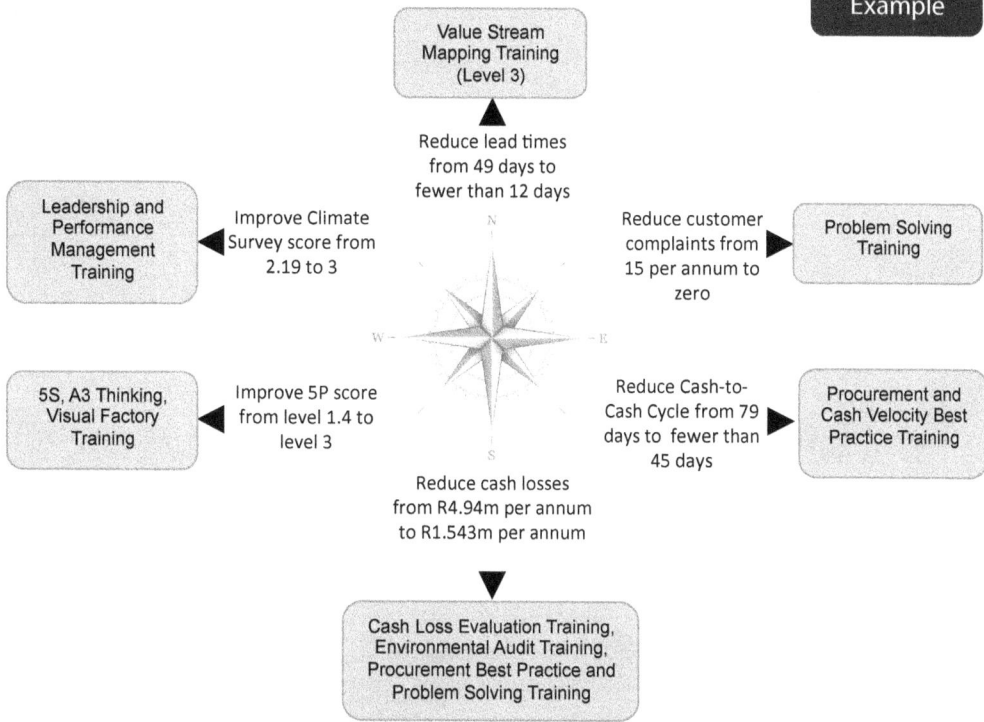

Figure 8.3

LEARNING NEEDS ANALYSIS

Improvement Area from the North Star	Training Type Required	Skill, Attitude, Knowledge to be Learned	Target Audience	Expected Results from Training	Responsible Person

Refer to the North Star and diagnostic results and brainstorm training required to prepare the staff for improved performance. Update as further progress is made during the execution and additional training is identified.

Table 8.1

Step 2: Complete the Learner Analysis

To ensure training closes the skills gap effectively, it is important to understand a little more about the learners. This will help to select the right service provider for the job and deliver training that achieve learner participation. This is especially important where there is diversity in the workforce with regards to skill, age, experience, culture, learning styles, background, values and beliefs, and where the choice of methodology will be critical to their successful application of the learning to achieve results. The company human resources specialist will be able to provide guidance, but here are some pointers to think about (Ford, 1999):

o Be mindful that not everyone can be taught to do everything and the learner is not a blank canvas waiting to be coloured in. Learners are at different levels in their knowledge, absorb at different rates and in different ways. True learning takes place when the participation of the learner has been achieved. Theory alone is no longer the primary source of engagement.

o Running masses of people through generic training, whether or not they need it or can apply it, is not the goal. This is sometimes referred to as 'sending them through the sausage machine'. Decision makers must ensure training is customised as much as is practical, to ensure the training does not just take the form of the sausage factory analogy but truly focuses on the learning needs and desirable outcomes for each individual. This may sound like more work and a less-efficient approach, but when dealing with such high scrap rates in training, it is necessary to look at learning with a fresh

o We observe three typical learning styles in people.

- A few enjoy learning by listening, and are easily drawn into discussions and 'war stories'. They are skilled at listening and absorbing information this way.

- The majority of learners out there are visual creatures, which means they love to watch videos, see demonstrations or see first-hand how it all works. They are good at observing and then absorbing the learning.

- The last group enjoys hands-on learning and physically interacting with the content in order to learn it.

o It is therefore good practice to cater for each learning type within the training design so that everyone will have a chance to participate in a way that works for them.

○ Adult learning is another factor to consider. Adults appreciate self-direction and being in control of their own learning, and it is worthwhile thinking about how they will best learn and produce the results you are looking for. Allow participants to share experiences. because acknowledgment of prior learning is appreciated by adults. Where new learning contradicts experience, the facilitator must handle this with care and guide the learner to slowly undo old habits before mastering new ones. Adults prefer learning what they can use immediately and associate relevance to on-the-job application. Finally, adults commonly absorb learning better when there is a change in their lives and coupling this with the the sense of urgency discussed in Chapter 7, can be helpful.

○ To cater for various needs and styles, good training designs should take note of the following:

- A little theory that guides the quality of what is to be learned.

- Some experiential learning to help drill and practice what has been learned.

- Exercises done individually that help self-discovery.

- Group exercises that stimulate learning from others.

○ When evaluating your learners, you want to understand the following elements about them:

- What do they already know?

- Are they beginners or experts because mixing the two in one session can be a challenge or an advantage to think about.

- What is their attitude towards learning about Operational Excellence?

- What would motivate them to learn?

- Do they have the basic skills to learn what is being proposed or are there concerns around their numeracy or literacy skills?

- Are there any cultural and diversity considerations to take into account?

In Table 8.2 you will find a simple exercise to help in understanding the target audience better. If you believe more information is required, consider involving the human resource specialist to conduct a more formal analysis through focus groups or interviews. A useful tip, is to involve some of the target audience in the training design or bring in subject matter experts to assist. Try keep it simple but remember that the objective is to ensure that what is being trained is designed with the North Star in mind and is capable of appealing to a diverse group of learners. Complete your own Learner Analysis provided in table 8.3.

Example

TRAINING TYPE	TARGET AUDIENCE	LEARNER ANALYSIS						
		CURRENT SKILL LEVEL None, Basic, Intermediate, Advanced	ATTITUDE Is a positive or negative attitude towards this training expected, and why?	LANGUAGE Style of language preferred	MOTIVATION Will learners value what they are taught and see how it will improve their work?	CONFIDENCE How confident will learners be to succeed in their training?	COMMENTS How to leverage the training with this audience to produce results
	3 Managers	Intermediate	Positive	Formal	Yes	High	Invite to present at team leader training.
	8 Team Leaders	None	Negative – time constraints and concerns about what the training will mean to workload.	Less formal, in English, but with option of translation.	No – change management must address this because they are not yet familiar with the process. Share the motive for change.	Medium to low and strong facilitator and good instructional design required to address this.	Involve a selection of team leaders in the initial stages of design to understand the methods that will work best for this audience. Ensure feedback from first session used to improved roll-out sessions.
VALUE STREAM MAPPING	2 Change Agents	Intermediate	Positive	Formal	Yes	High	Invite to present at team leader training.

Table 8.2

LEARNER ANALYSIS

TRAINING TYPE	TARGET AUDIENCE	CURRENT SKILL LEVEL	ATTITUDE	LANGUAGE	MOTIVATION	CONFIDENCE	COMMENTS
		None, Basic, Intermediate, Advanced	Is a positive or negative attitude towards this training expected, and why?	Style of language preferred	Will learners value what they are taught and see how it will improve their work?	How confident will learners be to succeed in their training?	How to leverage the training with this audience to produce results

Table 8.3

Step 3: Define the Learning

To shape the content of the training, give it clarity and focus, it is suggested that the learning outcomes for each training type be developed. This will ensure the design of the training meets these objectives and creates measurable objectives to assess the competence from. Provided it has been designed with the North Star in mind, it will drive the learning towards the right results. A learning outcome is best described as (Ford, 1999):

- A clear statement of purpose for the training.
- A specific outcome to be achieved by the training.
- A change in behaviour by the learner.
- A description of what tasks, principles, procedures and concepts need to be learned.

Once these are clearly documented, evaluate the ability of the service provider to meet these needs. To illustrate the technical development techniques, a learning outcome should at a minimum include the following components:

- A statement of the target behaviour in the form of an imperative verb – for example, 'Demonstrate the ability to identify wastes in the process and categorise for elimination'. This is action-oriented and measurable.
- A statement of the standards the learner will achieve once he or she has mastered the learning outcome.

Use verbs such as 'identify', 'demonstrate', 'define', 'solve', 'explain' and 'apply' rather than verbs such as 'know', 'understand', 'become familiar with', 'perceive', 'be aware of', and 'think about' to keep it clear, concise and to the point. To sequence them properly, start off with preknowledge required, then move to principles, application and finally to the strategic results expected. See table 8.4 to guide this preparation.

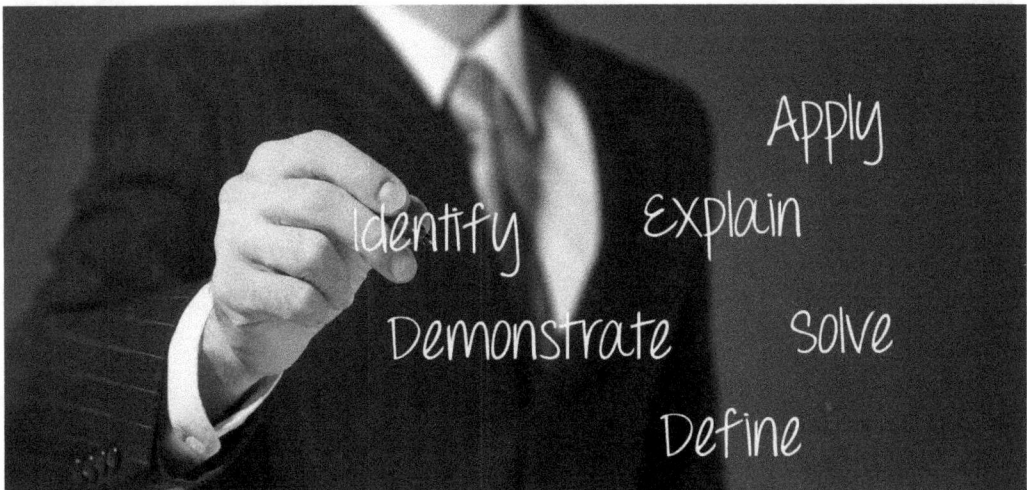

LEARNING OUTCOMES

Training Type	Pre-requisite Knowledge	Principles and Theory Learning Outcomes	Application and Job Performance Learning Outcomes	Results Learning Outcomes	Comments

For each of the training types, develop the learning outcomes to ensure the objectives and design of the training meets the needs of the North Star.

Table 8.4

Step 4: Quality Assure the Learning

Checking the training is effective is as important as planning and delivering the intervention. Too often the training is conducted, with great feedback after the event but the application that was talked about when the training was motivated for, never quite realised. The trick is not to sigh with relief when the training is done and staff schedules are going back to normal but to be vigilant that the process is not yet complete until the results are singing. Think about the PDCA cycle discussed in PART I and apply it to the training process:

PLAN your training intervention → **DO** the training → **CHECK** it worked to plan → **ADJUST** take corrective action

Again, the learning and development department will have processes to evaluate this but the top three we recommend at design stage are as follows (Ford, 1999):

o Determine how the training is to be evaluated – both learning and behavioural change (see table 8.5, 8.6 and 8.7)

o Determine how the business results will be evaluated (see table 8.5, 8.6 and 8.7)

o Develop a system to monitor delivery and results, with a feedback and corrective action loop (see table 8.5).

EVALUATION OF LEARNING			Example
Evaluation Area	**Evaluation Criteria**	**Examples**	**Recommendation**
Learner Satisfaction	How will the learner's satisfaction of the training be evaluated?	Participant survey; one-on-one session	Revise material based on common feedback received
Learning Evaluation	How will the skill and knowledge of the learner be evaluated?	Assessment aligned to learning outcomes	Evaluate results and provide recommendations
Behavioural Evaluation	How will change in job behaviour be evaluated?	Leader survey; on-the-job evaluation	Institute custom coaching before recommendations
Business Results Evaluation	How will the contribution of the new skills to the overall objectives and business results be evaluated?	KPIs; performance reviews	Institute custom coaching before recommendations
Delivery Feedback and Correction	How will you know if the training is not working, and what response will be triggered?	Measurement system and accountability process	Institute custom coaching before recommendations
Review the current system of evaluation and discuss how the quality of training and focus on results will be assured.			

Table 8.5

SAMPLE PARTICIPANT SURVEY*   Example

LEARNING INTERVENTION:

FACILITATOR:

DATE:

INSTRUCTIONS:

Read through each of the questions and mark the statement that best describes your experience with the training intervention.

TRAINING PREPARATION	Strongly Agree	Agree	Neither	Disagree	Strongly Disagree
1 I was well informed as to why I needed to attend the training and how it will contribute to the goals of the department.	☐	☐	☐	☐	☐
2 I received good communication about the date, time, location and information about the training.	☐	☐	☐	☐	☐
3 The timing of the training was well scheduled and I was given sufficient time to plan my attendance.	☐	☐	☐	☐	☐
4 My manager or leader is supportive of the training.	☐	☐	☐	☐	☐
5 I had the required knowledge to attend this training.	☐	☐	☐	☐	☐

ADDITIONAL COMMENTS:

FACILITY EVALUATION	Strongly Agree	Agree	Neither	Disagree	Strongly Disagree
1 The facilities and equipment were favourable for learning.	☐	☐	☐	☐	☐
2 All refreshments were adequate for the training	☐	☐	☐	☐	☐

ADDITIONAL COMMENTS:

Table 8.6

TRAINING CONTENT	Strongly Agree	Agree	Neither	Disagree	Strongly Disagree
1 The learning outcomes were well explained and I clearly understood the objectives of the training.	☐	☐	☐	☐	☐
2 The training met all of the learning outcomes.	☐	☐	☐	☐	☐
3 The practical examples and activities used in the training illustrated the theory well.	☐	☐	☐	☐	☐

ADDITIONAL COMMENTS:

TRAINING DESIGN	Strongly Agree	Agree	Neither	Disagree	Strongly Disagree
1 The methods used to deliver the training were effective and helped me learn the content well.	☐	☐	☐	☐	☐
2 The training material was well suited to our company with relevant examples to my department.	☐	☐	☐	☐	☐
3 The training material is useful to me and I will be able to refer to it in the future.	☐	☐	☐	☐	☐
4 I was given sufficient time to grasp the key concepts and principles and to ask questions.	☐	☐	☐	☐	☐

ADDITIONAL COMMENTS:

FACILITATOR EVALUATION	Strongly Agree	Agree	Neither	Disagree	Strongly Disagree
1 The facilitator was well prepared and maintained the punctuality of the training.	☐	☐	☐	☐	☐
2 The facilitator's presentation was well structured and easy to follow.	☐	☐	☐	☐	☐
3 The facilitator created a positive atmosphere.	☐	☐	☐	☐	☐
4 The facilitator was knowledgeable about the subject presented.	☐	☐	☐	☐	☐
5 Overall, I was satisfied with the facilitator.	☐	☐	☐	☐	☐

ADDITIONAL COMMENTS:

TRAINING APPLICATION	Strongly Agree	Agree	Neither	Disagree	Strongly Disagree
1 My knowledge and skill in the subject have increased as a result of the training.	☐	☐	☐	☐	☐
2 I can apply what I have learned to my work.	☐	☐	☐	☐	☐
3 If I apply the learning to my work, I believe I can make a positive impact to the business objectives of our company.	☐	☐	☐	☐	☐
4 Overall, I believe this training has been a valuable investment of my time.	☐	☐	☐	☐	☐
5 I would recommend this training to other members in my department or within the company.	☐	☐	☐	☐	☐

ADDITIONAL COMMENTS:

OVERALL IMPRESSIONS

What did you like best about the training?

What did you like least about the training?

What would you like to see included or removed from the training?

What additional comments or suggestions would you like to make?

We value your input and will ensure your feedback is used to improve the quality of our training.

* Adapted from the Sample Participant Reaction Survey (Ford, 1999).

Example

SAMPLE BEHAVIOUR CHANGE SURVEY**

LEARNING INTERVENTION:

DEPARTMENT:

DATE:

NUMBER OF PARTICIPANTS WHO ATTENDED THE
TRAINING IN YOUR DEPARTMENT:

INSTRUCTIONS:

As the manager of the learners, read through each of the questions and mark the statement that best describes your satisfaction with
the training provided . Ensure you choose only one answer.

GENERAL IMPRESSIONS

		Very Satisfied	Somewhat Satisfied	Neutral	Somewhat Dissatisfied	Very Dissatisfied
1	How would you rate the overall satisfaction with the training your employees received?	☐	☐	☐	☐	☐
2	What was your employee's personal productivity before they participated in the training?	Very High ☐	Better than Average ☐	Average ☐	Worse than Average ☐	Very Low ☐
3	What was your employee's personal productivity after completing the training?	Very High ☐	Better than Average ☐	Average ☐	Worse than Average ☐	Very Low ☐

ADDITIONAL COMMENTS:

Table 8.7

SKILLS DEVELOPMENT

For each skill listed below, estimate the current skill level of your employees, how often they use this skill and how important this skill is in achieving targets.

Skill Learned	Current Skill Level (5 to 1)	Frequency of Use (5 to 1)	Importance to Job (5 to 1)	Additional Comments
	5 - High 4 - Good 3 - Average 2 - Low 1 - Poor	5 - Always 4 - Often 3 - Sometimes 2 - Infrequent 1 - Never	5 - Very Important 4 - Somewhat Important 3 - Neutral 2 - Somewhat Unimportant 1 - Very Unimportant	

1. ....

2. ....

3. ....

4. ....

5. ....

TRAINING SUPPORT

Please check all the ways you support training in your department:

☐ You personally coach your employees to improve the application of the training. Please specify how often this occurs:............................

☐ You have allocated a coach to support the employees in applying their training. Please specify how often the coach supports:............................

☐ Peers are formally coaching each other. Please specify how often this occurs:............................

☐ Your performance measurement system indicates the impact of training and this triggers support to the learner.

☐ You conduct on-the-job training.

☐ You provide job aids such as visual guides and one-point lessons directly related to the training provided.

☐ Other, please specify:

_____

_____

_____

ADDITIONAL COMMENTS:

TRAINING EFFECTIVENESS

Support Activity	Very Effective	Somewhat Effective	Neutral	Somewhat Ineffective	Very Ineffective
You personally coach your employees to improve the application of the training	☐	☐	☐	☐	☐
You have allocated a coach to support the employees in applying their training	☐	☐	☐	☐	☐
Peers are formally coaching each other	☐	☐	☐	☐	☐
Your performance measurement system indicates the impact of training and this triggers support to the learner	☐	☐	☐	☐	☐
You conduct on-the-job training	☐	☐	☐	☐	☐
You provide job aids	☐	☐	☐	☐	☐
Other (please list):	☐	☐	☐	☐	☐
_____	☐	☐	☐	☐	☐
_____	☐	☐	☐	☐	☐

TRAINING EFFECTIVENESS CONTINUED

Has the learning delivered the change in results expected?

What barriers or obstacles (if any) have made it difficult for your employees to apply their newly learned skills?

What enablers or motivators help employees apply their newly learned skills?

What changes to the training your employees underwent will help them to perform better?

What changes to the preplanning of the training will help prepare or facilitate the training more effectively?

What changes to the post-planning of the training will help the effectiveness of the training to deliver the results?

What additional support do you require to be able to provide the necessary support to your employees in applying their training?

ADDITIONAL COMMENTS:

We value your input and will ensure your feedback is used to improve the quality and application of the training.

★★Adapted from the Training Behaviour Survey (Ford, 1999).

Step 5: Plan Learning for Success

In the overview to this section we drew attention to the fact that up to 85 percent of training does not yield the expected outcomes. We then described the types of failures expected due to poor pre-planning, poor in-session planning, and poor after-planning.

There are a few basic checks that can be done to increase the chances of success (table 8.8). We describe them in more detail below, but use the check list on the following page to ensure all the necessary factors have been taken into account. Customise with your own examples to make it fit for purpose.

Senior Management to Buy-in and Support Learning and Development

Employees quickly sense when top management is not behind their learning. The learning and development department plays a strong role in aligning learning outcomes to business requirements, and achieving this means leaders will be in a position to motivate employees to participate and deliver the results. This will provide substance to the leader's motivation.

Subsequently, if managers of those learners fail to see how the training will help achieve goals, they will inevitably see training as a drain on resources and may even sabotage learning efforts. The remedy is to ensure managers are involved and well informed of the expectations, and what their role in motivating their own staff is. In addition to this, they need to be involved throughout the learning process, so that support is offered to employees still finding their feet with new skills. Managers and leaders may be expected to coach and guide employees in the proper use of the training and achievement of results. In PEOPLE we will discuss how it is every leader's role to develop employees.

Employees to be Held Accountable for the Application of Training

Once the learners have been assessed as competent in the training, how are they being held accountable for achieving the expected results as depicted in the Learning Needs Analysis? Do their managers actively follow up on the progress to check if the application is yielding the change in business results? This is an ongoing process.

Measurement and Feedback Systems to Monitor and Control

The learning outcomes defined earlier in this section are a good place to start in assessing the learner's change in behaviour as a result of the training. What mechanisms are in place to evaluate the actual application of training and what triggers additional support to the learner to help them in achieving the goals? If performance has not improved, is a coach allocated to provide assistance?

BASIC PLANNING CHECK-LIST

PLANNING PHASE	CHECK POINT	CHECK RESULT YES OR NO
Before Training Intervention	Training has been well designed in accordance with the Learning Needs Analysis, Learner Analysis and learning outcomes documented. The leadership team has faith that the training design will support the business results expected from the learners.	☐
	Senior leaders understand how the training will support the achievement of business goals and convey this message to the managers and employees.	☐
	Managers of learners understand how the training will help to achieve their goals and motivate their employees to participate and excel.	☐
	Learners are well informed of the reasons for the training, the logistics arrangements, their involvement and expected results.	☐
	Sessions have been scheduled at convenient times conducive to encouraging good attendance and participation.	☐
After Training Intervention	Measurement and feedback mechanisms are in place to assess learner competence and check that the application meets the expected outcomes.	☐
	Coaches have been allocated to support learners that are still developing their skills to standard and to yield results.	☐
	Managers hold learners accountable for the application of the learning and evaluate the achievement of the outcomes identified. Managers coach learners where applicable.	☐

Use the checklist provided to note the basic planning required to reduce training failure. Include your own checks where applicable.

Table 8.8

✔ FOR YOU TO TRY

- Ensure you have involved a human resource representative when tackling this section. Bear in mind this will not replace the company learning strategy, only provide valuable input to it.

- Refer to the North Star and the results from PART I, and agree amongst the steercom on the learning needs to achieve the objectives set.

- Evaluate the target audience and analyse the elements that will influence the ability of the training to practically meet the varying needs of learners.

- Develop learning outcomes to establish focus and structure for the training to meet business needs.

- Discuss how training effectiveness to yield results is to be evaluated. Develop systems to check, provide feedback and adjust to meet quality standards required.

- Use the Basic Planning Checklist to sanity-check pre and post training activities, and ensure avoidable training failures are pre-empted and improved upon. The outcome must be to reduce the scrap rate of training, deliver results and facilitate return on investment.

- Summarise each template into your own Change Plan that can be bound into a reference book.

- Print the Change Plan and issue as a reference booklet to every member of the steercom. There may be additional recipients identified by the organisation, but ensure the issue is coupled with a proper briefing to explain the purpose and content.

- Update the Change Plan every year to reflect achievements or changes in focus areas.

PART III
DEPLOY THE CHANGE PLAN

Channel Activities towards Effective Execution

DEPLOYMENT LEARNING ROADMAP

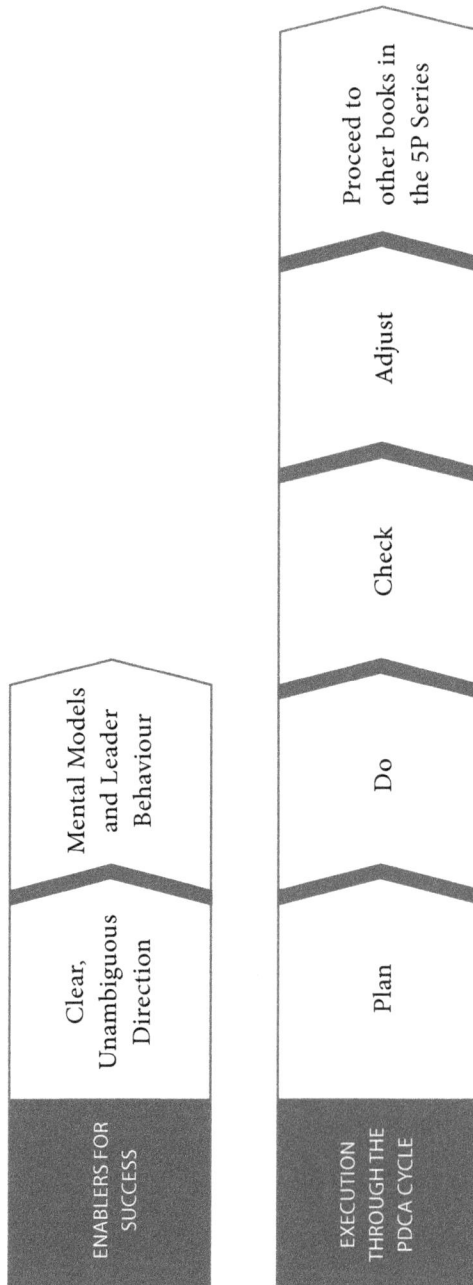

ENABLERS FOR SUCCESS

Clear, Unambiguous Direction → Mental Models and Leader Behaviour

EXECUTION THROUGH THE PDCA CYCLE

Plan → Do → Check → Adjust → Proceed to other books in the 5P Series

9 ENABLERS FOR SUCCESS
A SOLID FOUNDATION FOR EXECUTION

❓ WHAT IS THIS?

Enablers are core business capabilities that allow an organisation to advance towards the North Star. Without them clearing the way, progress may stagnate at the first sight of barriers or worse, the change effort may never quite get off the ground. These are important fundamentals to design into an execution system to get the right things done, by the right people, in the correct way.

The enablers covered in this section have been partly introduced in PART II. However, illustrating the connection between these enablers and deploying the Change Plan is helpful when putting the ideas into practice. The outcome we want is an execution model that will make all the decisions and plans captured in the Change Plan become a reality. Although a fair amount of work has already been done to enable change, two more aspects are explored before proceeding.

You will begin by reviewing the elements of Clear Direction that have been developed and establishing a readiness for execution. The development of the North Star was tackled early-on in PART I, with incremental improvements along the way until it was used to formulate the Change Plan. It is helpful to reflect on this message, confirm its content and then simplify before carrying it through the levels. The original sentiment is to be preserved, even when communicated through a variety of media, but in a way that builds confidence in the message.

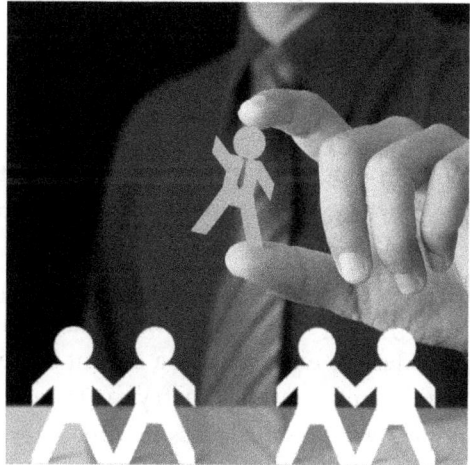

The second enabler relates to the implementation of the Management System described in Part I and II which imposes the need for a mature leadership style to support the changing habits. The buck stops at leadership – the behaviour of the leaders will power a persuasive message through the levels and these behaviours need to echo the core intentions of the Change Plan. The mental models that may currently be in place and manipulating the improvement culture are discussed, and the future models needed to accomplish the goals in the Change Plan are targeted.

? WHY IS THIS HELPFUL?

○ A view of what will enable or hinder deployment is underlined and critical success factors are subsequently considered before designing the execution model.

○ Constancy of purpose is reinforced through an unambiguous strategy ready for execution.

○ Awareness of how the leader state-of-mind cultivates the improvement culture is initiated and specific actions to address the leadership culture.

? HOW TO DO IT

Step 1: Confirm Understanding of the Strategy

You have done the work. PART I and PART II is complete, and you have progressed through the relevant steps to arrive at a set of essential elements that collectively make up the life force for Clear Direction. These include:

○ The all-encompassing North Star indicating the goals for change and learning needs

○ A High-Level Road Map detailing key initiatives, sequence and timing

○ Future State Improvement Indicators regulating performance to the goals

○ A High-Level Future State Plan illustrating the key activities to achieve the goals with.

With this in hand, the final stretch is to take all the work and simplify it into a message worth sharing. Employees do not need to go through the level of detail you have to play their part. You went through the pain of rummaging through the issues and ideas to emerge with a decent understanding of the problem you are trying to solve and the respective plan to address it with. They only need the 'soccer highlights' and just the relevant parts – so this is where you put your troops on a 'need-to-know' basis providing them with what they need to execute change, and nothing more.

It takes tremendous insight to capture an Improvement Strategy on one page, and this will become your final test before rolling out. Evaluate if you are ready to take the plunge to execution by completing table 9.1. If any one of these points is not marked as complete (ticked) then refer back to Part I and II as needed to close the gap before moving through deployment.

CLEAR DIRECTION QUICK CHECK

CHECK POINT	CHECK RESULT YES OR NO

WHERE ARE YOU NOW? WHERE ARE YOU GOING?

A formal diagnostic has been conducted to establish current performance to required performance. Gaps to close are clear and the target condition is defined.

☐

WHAT STEPS WILL YOU TAKE AND WHEN?

The North Star shows the key improvement areas and objectives, and this has been linked to a Future State Road Map that details the key initiatives, their sequence and timing to be tackled.

☐

HOW WILL YOU CHECK YOURSELVES?

A means of checking, performance to plan has been established through key indicators defined for each relevant level as well as desired targets.

☐

HOW WELL HAVE YOU DEVELOPED YOUR IMPROVEMENT MESSAGE?

The Improvement Strategy, Change Management Strategy and Learning Strategy have been developed and captured into a Change Plan. The leadership team supports the plan and understands its role in driving the message through the organisation.

☐

HOW WELL DO YOU UNDERSTAND YOUR IMPROVEMENT STRATEGY?

The Improvement Strategy is ready to be simplified and captured on one page, showing the background, Current State, Future State, execution logic, milestones, indicators and follow-up approach.

☐

Use the checklist in Table 9.1 to evaluate how ready you are for execution. Any check points marked with a cross must first be addressed before moving forward.

Table 9.1

Step 2: Check the Mental Models in Play

A mental model can be described as our personal, contextualised understanding of how things work and is influenced by the sum of our experiences and who we are as individuals. In the context of Operational Excellence, how leaders think plays a significant role and undoubtedly sets the scene for how the rest of the organisation thinks and acts. In fact, 80 percent of your workforce behaviour is determined by how the leader thinks and acts. Another hard hitting fact, is that 70 percent of business transformations do not achieve the results they aimed for. This is largely as a result of the way transformations are designed and the role and behaviour of involved management (Aernoudts, 2010).

> *'It's a person's assumptions about how the world works, based on their experience, upbringing and temperament. Mental models are the glasses we all wear, which filter and often distort reality. Until we accept the fact that the constraint is between our ears, nothing will change.'*

> *(Pascal, 2006: p19)*

Tools are certainly key and make up part of the Management System as illustrated in the 5P Evaluation, but the way the leaders think underlies these tools and will make or break the deployment of a well-thought-out improvement strategy. To avoid early derailment of the change effort, consider what current mental models exist in the organisation, and how they should be developed to result in the right behaviours. There are two extreme leadership styles that dominate the work environment:

Collaborative Leadership where the leader becomes the teacher but provides solid direction and structure without boxing in the employee:

- ○ 'Follow me and let's figure this out together'
- ○ 'I value your opinion'
- ○ 'What do you think?'

In this style, leaders teach by asking questions, commonly referred to as the Socratic Method.

Autocratic Leadership where the leader tells the employee what to do, depriving them of the ability to think and taking on a responsibility they should own:

- ○ 'Clock-in but leave your brain at the door'
- ○ 'Don't think, just do as I say'
- ○ 'Don't ask questions, I know where we're going'.

In this style, leaders command and control employees.

Complete the quick evaluation in Table 9.2 to test the predominant leadership style.

MENTAL MODELS QUICK CHECK

COLLABORATIVE LEADERSHIP	AUTOCRATIC LEADERSHIP
☐ Leaders are clear on the direction the organisation is taking and the implications to their own area of control. Employees are emotionally involved in the vision of where the company and their respective areas are going.	Leaders do not provide clarity of purpose in the daily work of employees. Every day is focused on meeting the day's targets, with little view of the bigger picture and where the team is working towards. ☐
☐ Leaders actively seek ideas from subordinates by asking what they think and using leading questions. The leader plays the role of teacher.	Leaders predominantly dictate to employees and tell them what to do. ☐
☐ Leaders go out to the gemba daily to see for themselves the heart of the operations and where they can assist the team.	Leaders confine themselves to their offices and prefer to solve problems in the offices or meeting rooms. Problems generally come to them when someone knocks on the door. ☐
☐ Employees are provided with clear, concise, up-to-date and visual standards to help guide them in doing the right things, together.	Employees are uncertain about the current standards and rely on their own experience to get the job done to the best of their individual ability. ☐
☐ Employees are empowered to stop work and alert their leaders of problems that cannot be solved themselves.	Employees are focused on moving the work as fast as possible even if there are problems being passed on to the next process. ☐
☐ Employees and leaders actively strive to make problems visible and raise the alert when one is discovered.	Employees are reluctant to expose problems. Often the fear of more work or being disciplined by a leader is a strong deterent. ☐
☐ Everyone solves problems using the simplest of methods.	Specialists are trained in complex methods and expected to solve problems. ☐

Mark the statement that is more commonly found in your organisation, most of the time amongst most of the leaders. Which style is more predominant at senior leadership and at middle management?

Table 9.2

There are scenarios where both the collaborative and autocratic leadership style are required, and the skilled leader is able to adjust according to the situation – for example, in a crisis, a leader will invariably err towards an autocratic style to focus the team and contain the situation, but the skilled leader will switch to a more participative, collaborative style to initiative growth and improvement once the crisis has stabilised. If your organisation is predominantly autocratic, to enable successful deployment of the Change Plan, a strategy may be required to move the leaders from a traditional to more forward-thinking mental model. You may already have covered this in PART II but table 9.3 lists additional points to consider:

DEALING WITH MENTAL MODELS*

POSSIBLE CONSTRAINT	EXAMPLE	POSSIBLE COUNTERMEASURE
THE LEADER AS A PERSON	The current mental model of the leader based on experience, character and upbringing influences a more traditional leadership style. To date, the leader's current role and behaviour has worked well and the need for change is not understood. The leader protects status quo. There is uncertainty about the new role they are expected to perform. The leader is concerned about a loss of power and how he or she will cope in the changing environment.	Create awareness around the traditional leadership style, what is positive and worked in the past and possible short comings. This needs to be handled with respect for experience and past successes. Be clear about the need for the new model and link it with the sense of urgency defined in PART II. Provide clarity, learning and development to the leader on his or her changing role, what the expectations will be and how this aims to grow the role rather than diminish it.
OPERATIONAL EXCELLENCE	Operational Excellence can be complex to understand. How all the parts make up the whole can be confusing to leaders until they have fully understood what it has to offer as an integrated system, and their role in it. Operational Excellence places tension on an existing system, exposes problems and prompts responses. Some leaders may see it as an unnecessary complication to an already busy day.	Provide leaders with the learning and development to help them see the integrated system of Operational Excellence, and how the parts fit together in concert to achieve the business purpose. Coach them to take it step by step, and 'learn to see' how the system unfolds. Help leaders understand that tension is a necessary evil for exposing problems. There are no quick fixes only structured ways to see problems and eliminate root causes. They need to be allowed time to do this.
LEADERSHIP TRAINING AND DEVELOPMENT IN OPERATIONAL EXCELLENCE	Learning has traditionally been focused on only understanding tools and the system's-thinking approach has been ignored. 'One-hit-wonder' training has been delivered, in the hope that necessary skills are now installed successfully. Although classroom training is invaluable, it has been treated as a stand-alone means of learning and development. No PDCA on the training has been initiated and used to ensure the desired results have been attained.	Allow sufficient time to plan and properly design the learning material and outcomes. Ensure the training aligns perfectly to the Improvement Strategy and not just with service provider standard offerings. The Improvement Strategy and subsequent Change Plan will dictate what should be included and the changes in systems and behaviours required as a result. Engage a learning and development process to ensure PDCA is adequately addressed. Refer to the Learning Strategy in PART II.

*Adapted from a presentation given by René Arnoudts at the Lean Summit Africa 2010

Table 9.3

KEY AREAS TO BE ADDRESSED DEPLOYMENT ENABLERS		
DEPLOYMENT ENABLER	IMPROVEMENT FINDINGS	SHORT, MEDIUM, OR LONG-TERM FOCUS
CLEAR DIRECTION		
MENTAL MODELS		
GENERAL		
Capture any findings for each deployment enabler and include a comment to show if it is a short, medium or long-term focus for the business: Short: <6 months Medium: 6 to 12 months Long: >12 months Update the High–Level Plan, Risk Reponse Plan, Learning Strategy and Communication Plan accordingly.		

Table 9.4

✅ FOR YOU TO TRY

○ Confirm the Improvement Strategy is fully understood and complete the Clear Direction Quick Check to identify any outstanding items still required before execution begins.

○ Using the Mental Models Quick Check, assess the predominant leadership style present at senior and middle management level. Discuss the appropriate style needed to facilitate the Change Plan, and agree on possible countermeasures to address the constraints.

○ Capture the key actions derived from each of the above activities and update the High-Level Future State Plan and Change Plan where applicable.

10 EXECUTION THROUGH PDCA
A SCIENTIFIC MODEL FOR SUCCESS

❓ WHAT IS THIS?

The topic of PDCA was introduced briefly in PART I, relating to improvement projects and the thought process followed to successfully implement for sustainability.

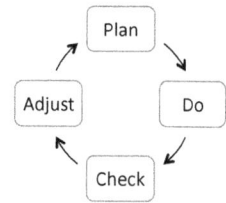

PDCA is, however, a much broader concept that can be applied to just about any change. In the context of executing the Improvement Strategy, it is extremely helpful in ensuring the right thinking and follow through take place to achieve the set goals. The following diagram in figure 10.1 describes the meaning behind each of the PDCA phases in the cycle:

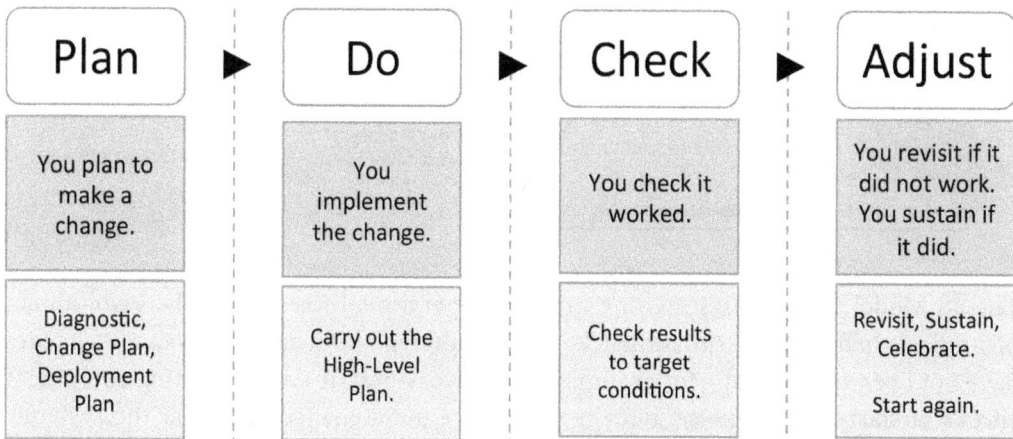

Plan	Do	Check	Adjust
You plan to make a change.	You implement the change.	You check it worked.	You revisit if it did not work. You sustain if it did.
Diagnostic, Change Plan, Deployment Plan	Carry out the High-Level Plan.	Check results to target conditions.	Revisit, Sustain, Celebrate. Start again.

Figure 10.1

Using the mental model of PDCA in execution, provides a structured, scientific approach to carrying out the plans that have been developed so far. It is considered a foundation for strategy deployment and encourages the thinking and action amongst leaders that guarantees the work carried out every day is aligned to the bigger picture. Figure 10.2 illustrates the effect of using PDCA for execution on performance:

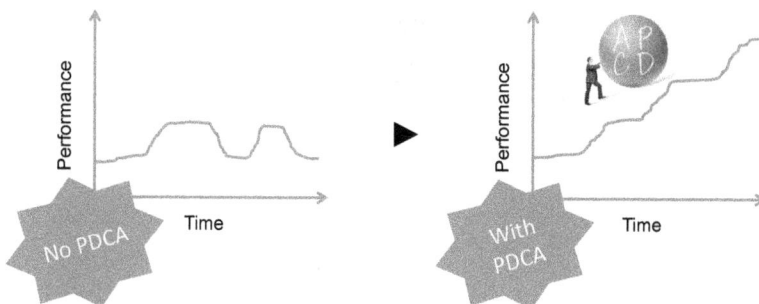

Figure 10.2

An Introduction to the 3S Model

It is particularly useful to view an organisation in terms of three disctinct levels of operations and the 5P books in the series will refer back to this model for each topic covered. The model divides the organisation into the strategic, systemic and situational levels, presented as the pyramid structure in figure 10.3 (Faull, 1998). It demonstrates how each level has its own focus, and how this translates into key activities each respective level is responsible for. During the diagnostic phase of PART I you may have experienced examples of overlap between the levels and this could affect the organisations ability to transition to a collaborate environment – for example – middle managers take on a responsibility the front-line levels should own.

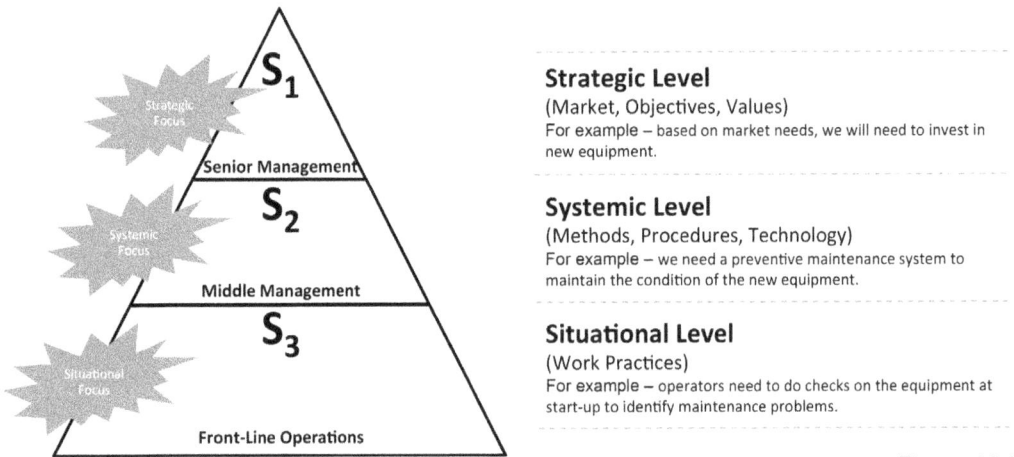

Strategic Level
(Market, Objectives, Values)
For example – based on market needs, we will need to invest in new equipment.

Systemic Level
(Methods, Procedures, Technology)
For example – we need a preventive maintenance system to maintain the condition of the new equipment.

Situational Level
(Work Practices)
For example – operators need to do checks on the equipment at start-up to identify maintenance problems.

Figure 10.3

The 3S Model also exposes missing links. In Operational Excellence, the sustainment of improvements at the situational level will falter if the necessary system's changes have not been considered – for example – if the work practice of conducting equipment checks at start-up is in place, but the preventive maintenance system at the systemic level is defective, the performance of the equipment will decline resulting in possible lost time. Furthermore if incorrect investment took place at the strategic level, the effects will be evident at the situational level. This means that every significant change made in the operations should be seen at each level in the structure to be truly effective.

Returning to the principles of PDCA in executing the Improvement Strategy you can apply the 3S Model to structure this more effectively. Using the mental model of PDCA is a great start, but William Deming (father of the quality revolution) teaches us to see PDCA as nested cycles and not in isolation. PDCA cycles should therefore be promoted through each level, to ensure proper execution throughout the organisation as shown in figure 10.4.

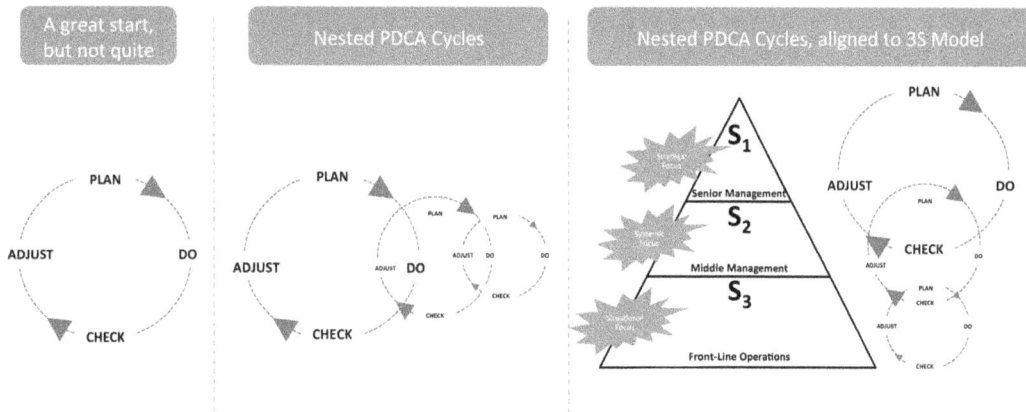

Figure 10.4

In the context of strategy execution the 3S Model helps you visualise the process of cascading high-level initiatives through the ranks to the front-line, and establishing clear feedback loops (figure 10.5).

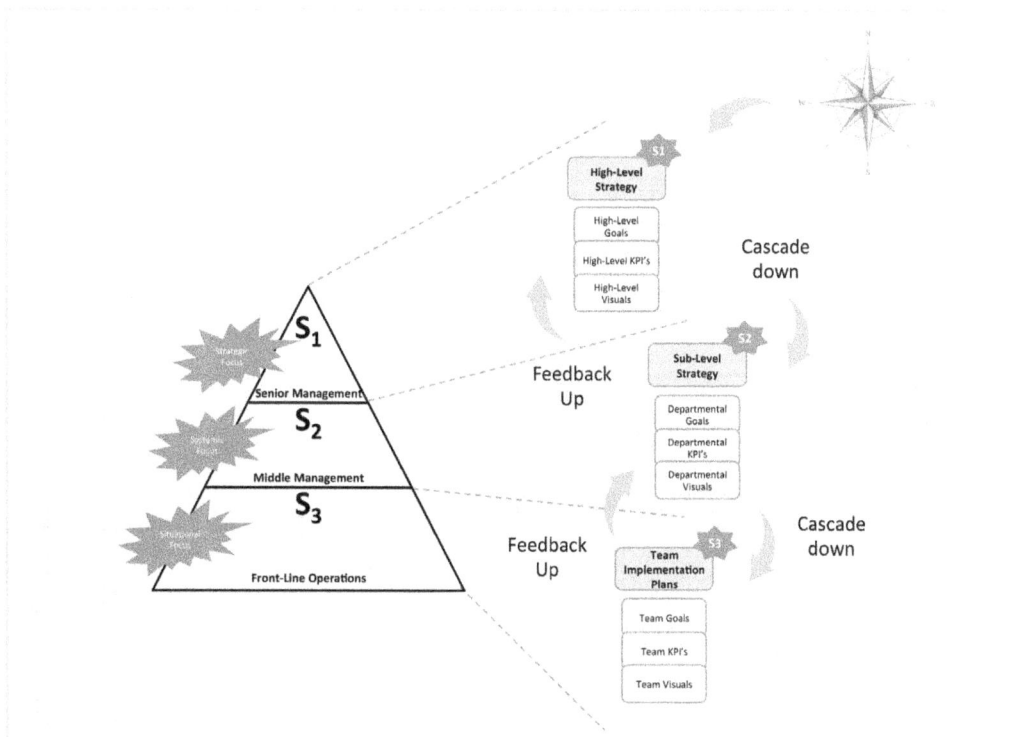

Figure 10.5

An Introduction to the A3 Summary for Strategy

To illustrate the PDCA cycle in a simple way, and give leaders a logical, visual process to follow, we make use of the A3 Strategy Summary. This is effectively capturing each of the PDCA phases onto one A3 page, so that everyone can view the issues and progress through the same lens. Equipped with the one-pager, owners of the page can use it to structure the progression through PDCA and use the tool for reviews and feedback sessions. See the example provided in figure 10.6 (Pascal, 2006):

Example

A3 THEME:
High Level Improvement Strategy

FOCUS:
Quality, Cost, Delivery, Safety, Morale, Environment

DEPARTMENT:
Exco Team

DATE:
Aug 2014 to Aug 2015

Performance, Gaps and Targets

This is where you highlight the results achieved from last year and the targets going forward for three to five years.

Use colour coding and visuals with as few words as possible.

Reflection on Previous Years' Activities

Assess each of the activities set for last year and indicate what worked and what did not work.

Include any learning points.

Justification for this Year's Activities

What needs to be done in the coming year and why?

How will these changes create benefits?

Milestones for this Year

Insert the Future State High-Level Plan showing the major milestones to be accomplished.

Include a means of tracking the goals to see if the desired results are being achieved.

This plan will summarise the key areas that will be actively worked on to achieve the goals for improvement.

Who, what, where, when and how is answered here.

Follow Up

How will progress be checked?

What barriers will need to be removed?

SIGNATURES:

AUTHOR:

VERSION:

Figure 10.6

A Process to Deploy the Change Plan with

The process begins by capturing the PLAN into an A3 Strategy Summary. Most of the work has already been done but the details will be simplified into the A3 format.

Thereafter, you will look at tackling the DO phase. This involves cascading the high-level activities to next-level departments and creating sub-level A3s to help maintain the right focus across disciplines. We also look at typical reactions that take place during this phase and how to address them.

The next phase considers the CHECK process and how to make abnormalities obvious so that they may be dealt with to achieve the goals set. Various levels of checks required and review cycles are discussed.

Finally, the outcome of the CHECK phase is reviewed and evolved into the ADJUST phase, and typical problem-solving activities that will come into play at this point. Deviations from target are addressed and where targets are accomplished, rigorous sustainment actions are developed. Problem solving and the support structures needed are briefly discussed.

❓ WHY IS THIS HELPFUL?

- The PDCA mental model for execution develops a community of 'scientists' (Pascal, 2006).

- Activities and changes are aligned to the overall goals for improvement and help employees remain focused on the priorities.

- A structure for executing the plan and achieving the desired results is created.

- Leaders develop confidence in the improvement strategy as they see the results materialise.

- Simple, visual methods make the process transparent and understandable.

❓ HOW TO DO IT

Step 1: PLAN

You are now at a point where you have grasped the current situation by completing the Diagnostic (PART I) and developed the Change Plan (PART II) that focuses attention to the few critical items that will make a difference. How the success is to be measured is clear and a compelling plan for change is ready to deploy. So, much of the work for the PLAN phase is complete, and this section aims to add the finishing touches to make it ready for PDCA execution. The PLAN tells you where you are going, how to get there and whether you are on or off course at any point in time. This provides the opportunity to expose problems and make abnormalities in the execution process visible so that leaders can respond and keep the ship sailing towards its North Star.

'If you can't express your plan on one page,
you probably don't understand it. Less is more.'

(Pascal, 2006: p10)

Your PLAN is put to the test when you take it through the A3 Thinking Process and have to capture the key elements into the A3 Strategy Summary. The thought process is as shown in figure 10.7:

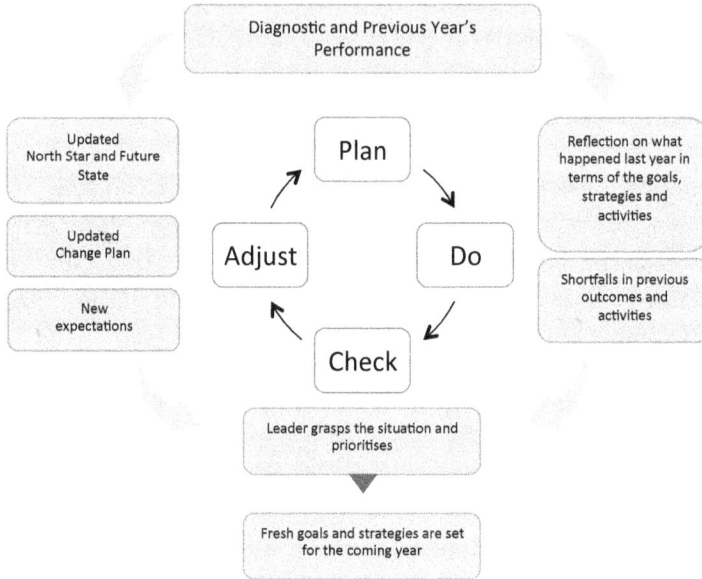

Figure 10.7

Where do you focus now?

At this point you are still dealing with the High-Level Improvement Strategy and will complete the PLAN phase for this. It is called the High-Level Strategy for Improvement because later you will expand these into Sub-Level Strategies for Improvement at departmental level as depicted in figure 10.8:

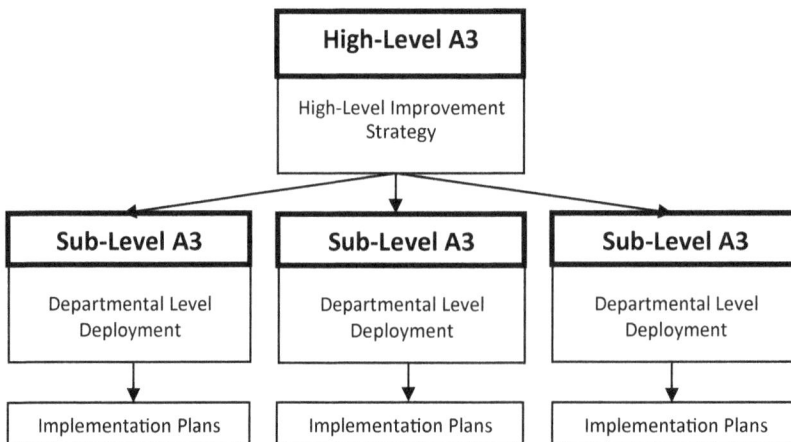

Figure 10.8

How to encourage cross-functional ownership

It is important that the process undertaken discourages silo mentality and promotes the various disciplines to take a cross-functional view of the PLAN. The High-Level Strategy at this stage is broad, and achieving the buy-in and direct involvement from each leader will lead to better consensus and improved focus. Refer to the Change Plan and update the Deployment Leaders where applicable and now assign them specific improvement areas to be responsible for as shown in table 10.1:

DEPLOYMENT LEADER ASSIGNMENTS	Example
Lead Time	Bill Ramos, Operations Director
Customer Satisfaction	Jane Mecer, Quality Director
Cash Velocity	Mark Jones, Supply Chain Director
Cash Loss	Brian Vilakazi, Financial Director
Best Practice	Seth Mhlangu, OpEx Director
Employee Satisfaction	Estelle Jackson, Human Resources Director
Strategy Deployment	John Kottrel, Managing Director

Table 10.1

This will create 'chief scientists', who become dedicated to ensuring PDCA in their area of assigned focus. They will then guide the process in developing the Sub-Level strategies and implementation plans to achieve the High-Level Strategy. Select your deployment leaders and complete table 10.2, considering the following:

- Who is the right deployment leader for each improvement area?

- What obstacles can the leader expect to meet and how will they be supported? Update the Risk Response Plan if applicable.

- What skills will the leaders need to be provided with? Update the Learning Strategy if applicable.

DEPLOYMENT LEADER ASSIGNMENTS			
Improvement Area	Who	Position	Steercom Role (if applicable)

Refer to Change Plan and discuss which deployment leaders will be assigned to each improvement area. The individual must understand his or her role in the process and agree to take on the responsibility going forward.

Table 10.2

How to develop the High-Level A3 Strategy template

You will work through each step systematically to develop the A3, and the sequence will look as follows (figure 10.9):

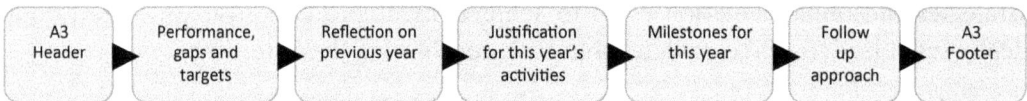

Figure 10.9

Keep it short, sweet and to the point all the time remembering that the purpose of the tool is to capture the essence of the strategy on one page and serve as a review and reflection instrument going forward. Using the North Star and Road Map created in the Diagnostic (PART I) and Change Plan (PART II), refer to the example provided in figure 10.10 and 10.11 and develop your own A3 Strategy Summary.

Example

A3 THEME:
High Level Improvement Strategy

FOCUS:
Quality, Cost, Delivery, Safety, Morale, Environment

DEPARTMENT:
Exco Team

DATE:
Aug 2014 to Aug 2015

Performance, Gaps and Targets

At August 2014
Current Condition

Current Performance:
- 49 day lead time
- 15 customer complaints
- 79 day cash-cash cycle
- R4.94m cash losses
- Level 1.4 – 5P score
- Level 2.19 – climate survey score.

At February 2015
Target Condition

6-Month Target:
- 30 day lead time
- 7 customer complaints
- 55 day cash-cash cycle
- R3.5m cash losses
- Level 2.5 – 5P score
- Level 2.19 – not measured.

At August 2015
Target Condition

12-Month Target:
- 25 day lead time
- 5 customer complaints
- 25 day cash-cash cycle
- R1.54m cash losses
- Level 2.5 – 5P Score
- Level 2.5 – climate survey score.

At August 2016
Target Condition

24-Month Target:
- 8 day lead time
- 0 customer complaints
- 8 day cash-cash cycle
- R0.5m cash losses
- Level 3 – 5P Score
- Level 3 – climate survey score.

Reflection on Previous Years' Activities

Activity	Rating	Key Results / Issues
Reduce customer complaints from 25 to 10 pa	YELLOW	Progress but missed target. Focus changed mid-year due to QMS implementation.
Reduce RM, WIP and FG inventory to reduce leadtime by 20%	RED	Not achieved. No clear accountability and fire fighting hindered progress.
Reduce procurement costs to R250kpa	YELLOW	Reduced from R50k to R460K and experienced problems with consolidation.
Reduce quality losses to R900kpa	GREEN	Achieved and sustained. New targets required.

Justification for this Year's Activities

Results from Voice of the Business, Customer and Employee have been consolidated to form the North Star, which represents the key focus areas and initiatives to be tackled. This will ensure the right focus in achieving the business goals for increased market growth, reduced working capital and increased net profit

- Grow market share
- Reduce working capital
- Increase net profit
- Reduce lead time
- Reduce Customer Complaints
- Reduce Cash-to-Cash Cycle
- Reduce Cash Loss
- Raise 5P Score
- Raise Climate Score

Milestones for this Year

HIGH-LEVEL PLAN
EXECUTING THE FUTURE STATE

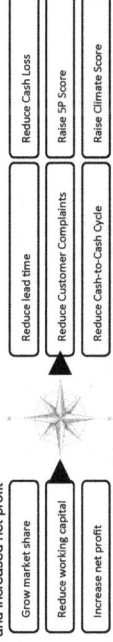

Follow Up

Each activity will be tracked according to the PDCA completion and progress in the Future State Box Score at the monthly steercom meeting. The high-level metrics will be updated to reflect the overall result. The MD will personally assist in addressing barriers to success raised.

The Operational Excellence Matrix will be reviewed every six months.

SIGNATURES:

AUTHOR: John Kottrel   **VERSION:** Rev 0

Figure 10.10

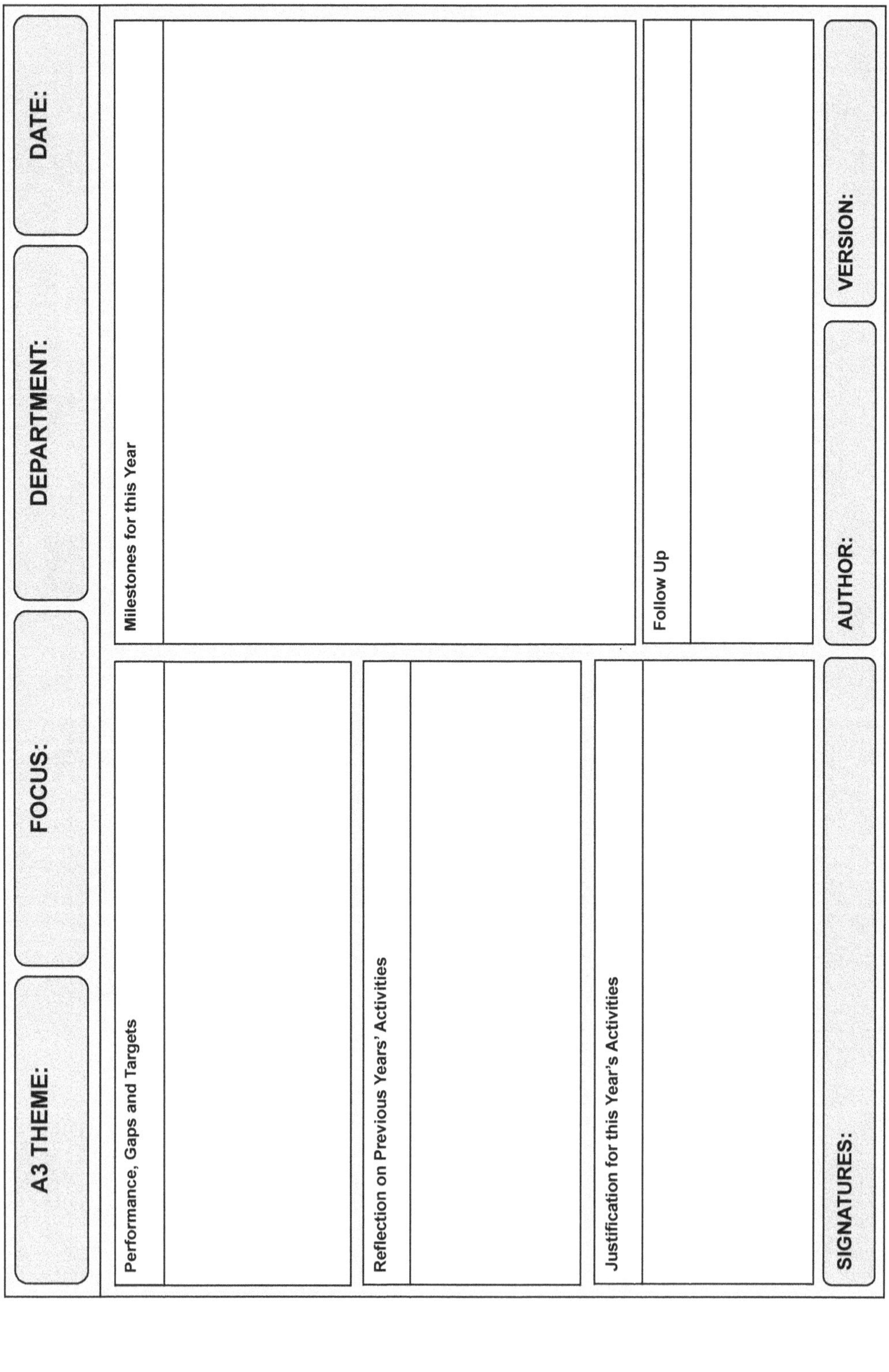

A3 THEME:	FOCUS:	DEPARTMENT:	DATE:

Performance, Gaps and Targets

Milestones for this Year

Reflection on Previous Years' Activities

Justification for this Year's Activities

Follow Up

SIGNATURES:	AUTHOR:	VERSION:

Figure 10.11

Step 2: DO

All leaders have a dual role in the work they are expected to do every day. The first part is to handle the routine work that takes up a large chunk of the day. The second part is to do improvement work to ensure gradual changes are made to improve the business.

Helping leaders take the PLAN developed in the preceding section, and turn it into real action is the next challenge. The High-Level A3 Strategy Summary does not go into detail as to how these goals are to be met, so there is some extra effort required by the leaders to develop the next-level tactics for improvement. This may require referring to the Diagnostic (PART I) for details, doing additional Value Stream Maps or using principles of problem solving but essentially, they need to answer the question of what holds them back from achieving these goals and what do they need to DO to make them happen.

Another point to remember at this stage, is that doing things without actually understanding what you are doing is a waste in itself. It is important that deployment leaders not just be told in an autocratic way how to deploy the PLAN, but that they also reflect and discover for themselves how it should be done and develop their own corresponding A3s.

How will People React in this Phase?

You will probably experience a mixed-bag of reactions depending on the culture in the company and how well the change management has been handled around the improvement effort. Refer to the Risk Response and Communication Plan developed in the Change Plan (PART II), for indicators of how different stakeholders will react and how to address them. Three typical reactions occur during the DO phase (Pascal, 2006):

- ○ Supporters: 10 percent are generally supportive of the plan.
- ○ Watchers: 80 percent are generally pleased that the company is getting their act together, but are waiting to see what happens next.
- ○ Grumblers: 10 percent are generally against it.

Back the supporters as much as possible; stick religiously to the plan until the watchers are won over; and do not worry about the grumblers too much, as they probably will not change anyway.

Each of the deployment leaders can now refer to the Diagnostic and conduct their own activities to develop the departmental-level tactics. Refer to the example provided in figure 10.12 and complete the Sub-Level A3 Summary provided in figure 10.13 for each improvement area. If necessary, take it down one more level to team-level.

Example

A3 THEME:
Departmental Strategy

FOCUS:
Reduce Lead Time

DEPARTMENT:
Operations Department

DATE:
Aug 2014 to Aug 2015

Performance, Gaps and Targets

Average Lead Time vs Target
August 2013 to August 2014

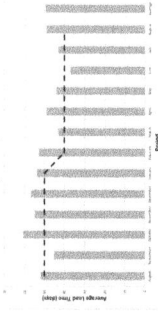

END AUGUST 2014 PERFORMANCE
Average lead time from raw material to customer delivery has varied between 37 and 61 days, around a mean of 49 days.

Reflection on Previous Years' Activities

Activity	Rating	Key Results / Issues
Reduce cycle time for every process to under 40sec	YELLOW	Too broad a goal. Constraint not known and improvements made in processes that did not assist in yielding more throughput.
Set policy around frequent changes in plan and freeze plan for 10 days	RED	Not achieved, reasons for plan changes were not explored and the solution therefore did not stick.
Improve layout to facilitate flow	GREEN	Achieved but benefits realised only once cycle times improvements are achieved

Justification for this Year's Activities

The diagnostic revealed the North Star focus and relevant initiatives to be tackled for 2014. Lead Time reduction is a critical contributor to Cash-to-Cash Cycles and improved customer service, as defined in the Voice of the Customer

- Improve Performance to TAKT
- Reduce Schedule Disruption
- Improve Constraint Performance
- Improve Constraint Skills
- Reduce Failure Demand
- Improve PCE%

Reduce lead time

Milestones for this Year

PROJECT PLAN
EXECUTING THE FUTURE STATE : REDUCE LEAD TIME
12 MONTH VIEW (SHOWING 6 MONTH FOCUS)

Follow Up

Each activity will be tracked according to the PDCA completion and progress in the Future State Box Score fortnightly, at the deployment team meeting. The high-level metrics will be updated monthly to reflect the overall result. Bill Ramos will personally assist in addressing barriers to success raised.

SIGNATURES:

AUTHOR: Bill Ramos

VERSION: Rev 0

Figure 10.12

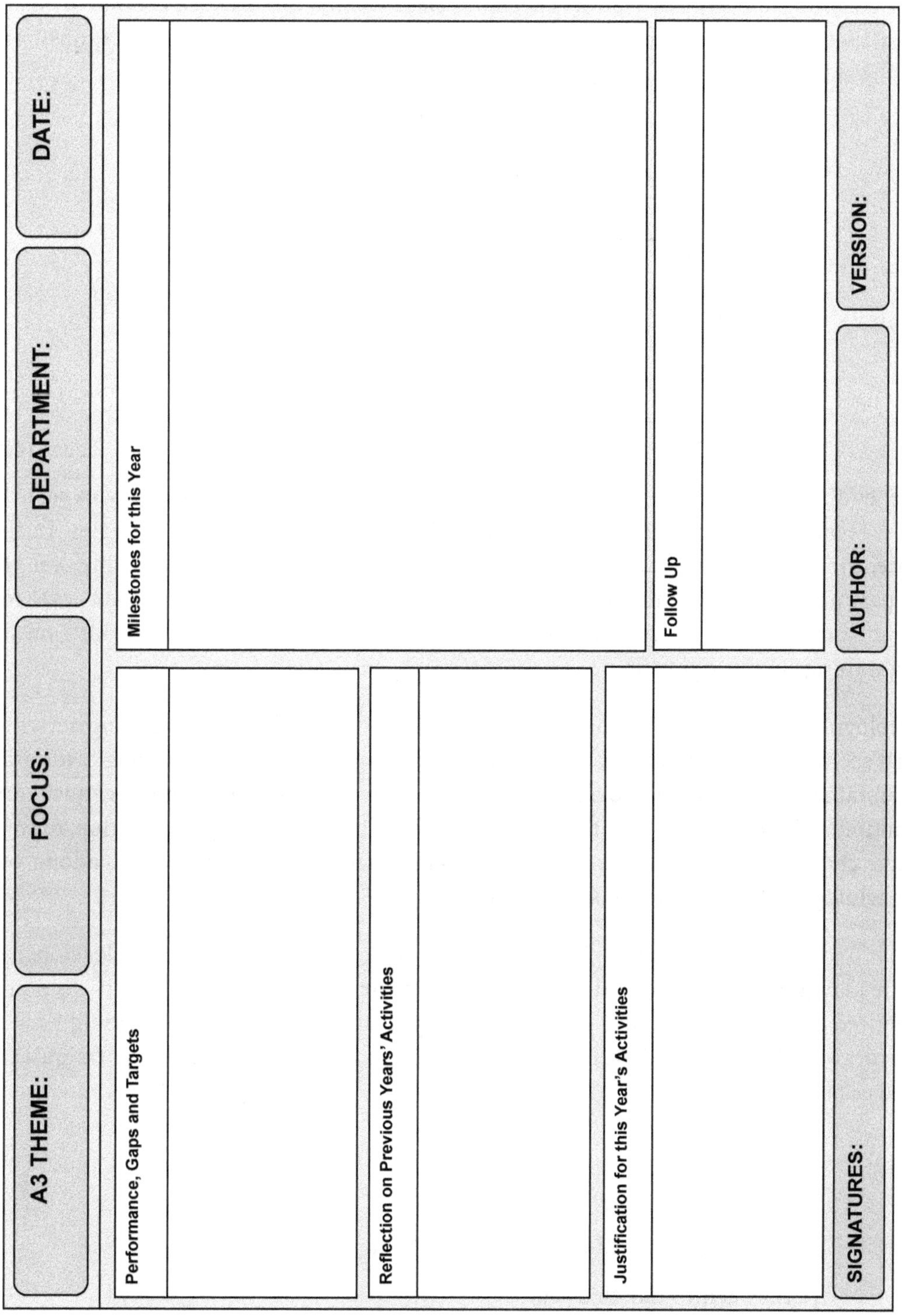

A3 THEME: **FOCUS:** **DEPARTMENT:** **DATE:**

Performance, Gaps and Targets

Milestones for this Year

Reflection on Previous Years' Activities

Justification for this Year's Activities

Follow Up

SIGNATURES: **AUTHOR:** **VERSION:**

Figure 10.13

Sanity Check and Maintaining Focus

The deployment leaders develop their Sub-Level A3 Strategy Summaries, which align perfectly to the High-Level Strategy. This is clear when a quick check is done to ensure all activities listed in the high-level plan are expanded to further detail and responsibility in the sub-level plan (figure 10.14).

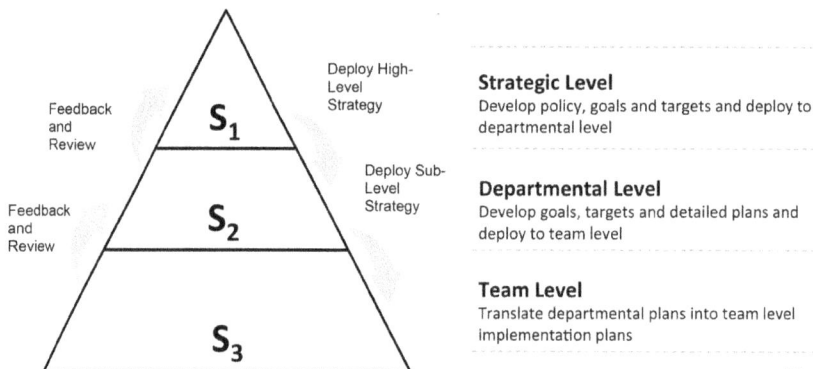

Figure 10.14

Depending on the learning strategy defined in the Change Plan, you may expect the next level to continue with A3 Thinking to develop their team-level strategies. In this case, the development will follow exactly the same process as with the high-level and departmental-level, but the necessary activities and changes required at team-level will be included. This is a powerful way to ensure the right employees are working on the right things in the right time.

Deployment leaders can become sidetracked and start including or chasing activities that seem urgent or are close to their hearts. It is important that the steering committee maintains the strategy deployment process, assists the group in staying on track, and continuously works towards the North Star. The initial phases of execution may be quite challenging, and ensuring the leaders are coached at this time will go a long way in helping achieve excellence in execution.

The first round of A3 Strategy Summaries may take quite a bit of time to develop. Not only may it be a new tool in the business, but ensuring the diagnostic detail is suitably reduced to one page will also have its challenges, and may even require going back to the drawing board. Stay determined because the next round of A3s will be far quicker, and easier to generate.

TIPS

o Do all the activities add up to the North Star?

o Are they achievable this year?

o Where there are schedule and loading conflicts, have they been adjusted?

Getting Started with DOING

Now that what needs doing is properly thought-through, understood and clearly documented, the hard work of getting the right things done commences. This actually falls between the 'deploying' part and the 'checking part' (Pacsal, 2006).

Depending on what you are trying to improve, you may start initiating a series of kaizens or projects, the details of which are covered in PROBLEM SOLVING.

To conclude the DO part of PDCA, the responsible people now actively follow through on the PLAN developed, and implement the actions. It is up to the deployment leaders to ensure that once the implementation starts, they are involved in removing barriers to success as they arise. Existing policies in place may deter employees from implementing and this is where we urge you to review the policy changes required on an ongoing basis at the steercom meeting and continue to update the Risk Response Plan.

This is the time to stay focused, rigorously work through the activities in the PLAN and strive to achieve the goals set. The next section will discuss the process of CHECK and how the progress can be evaluated and improved upon.

Step 3: CHECK

The PLAN has been developed and deployed to the applicable levels in the company, and some activities are starting to get done, putting the DO phase into full swing. Although some changes are already yielding results, a proper monitoring system to ensure the expected results are achieved is still needed. This section explores how to develop a robust CHECK process to monitor and assure progress. The process will look as shown in figure 10.15:

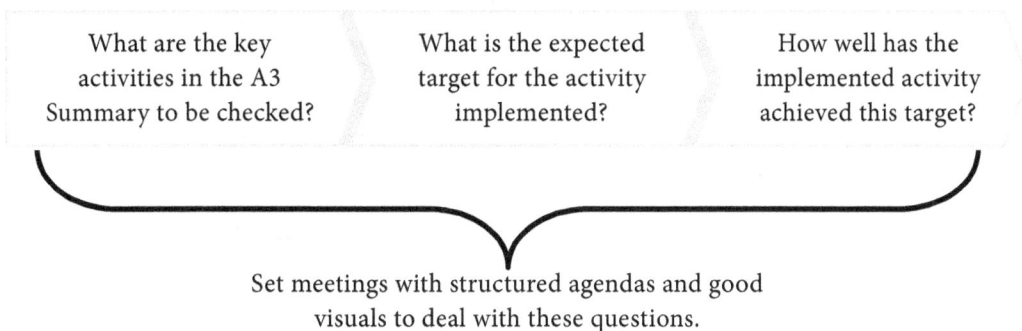

What are the key activities in the A3 Summary to be checked?	What is the expected target for the activity implemented?	How well has the implemented activity achieved this target?

Set meetings with structured agendas and good visuals to deal with these questions.

Figure 10.15

The objective is to make abnormalities and non-conformance to PLAN obvious so that action can be taken to get the activities back on-track and moving steadily towards the North Star. Typically, organisations are good at planning and doing but checking and adjusting falls short. This will result in a lack of execution and missed targets and cannot be bypassed.

The enablers and structures for the CHECK process have already been developed as part of the Change Plan, so this section will improve the focus and efficiency. The following depicts how these structures will be used (figure 10.16):

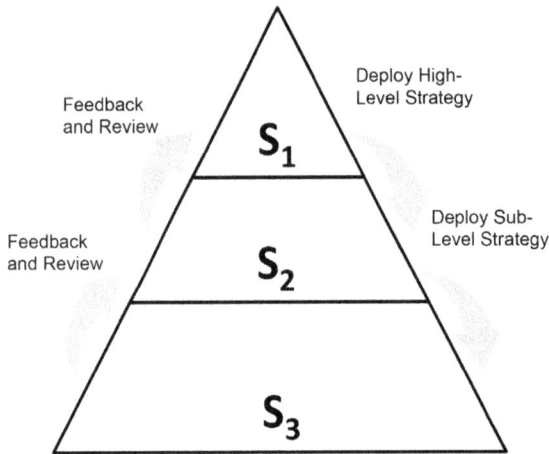

CHECK Processes

Feedback and Review

Deploy High-Level Strategy

S_1

Strategic Level
Review progress with High-Level A3 Strategy at steercom meeting. Conduct annual review.

Feedback and Review

Deploy Sub-Level Strategy

S_2

Departmental Level
Review progress with Sub-Level A3 Strategy at deployment team meeting.

S_3

Team Level
Review progress with team implementation plans at team meeting.

Figure 10.16

PDCA Review Cycles

The diagram in figure 10.17 shows that some reviews are done in the short term and some take a bigger picture view over the longer term. It is important to have both because keeping an eye on the details will get the right things done. However, if there are strategic issues affecting the company, some decisions may change the bigger picture, which will then need to filter down into the execution levels again. You could be focusing furiously on getting the implementation plans complete but the climate has changed, making these efforts null and void.

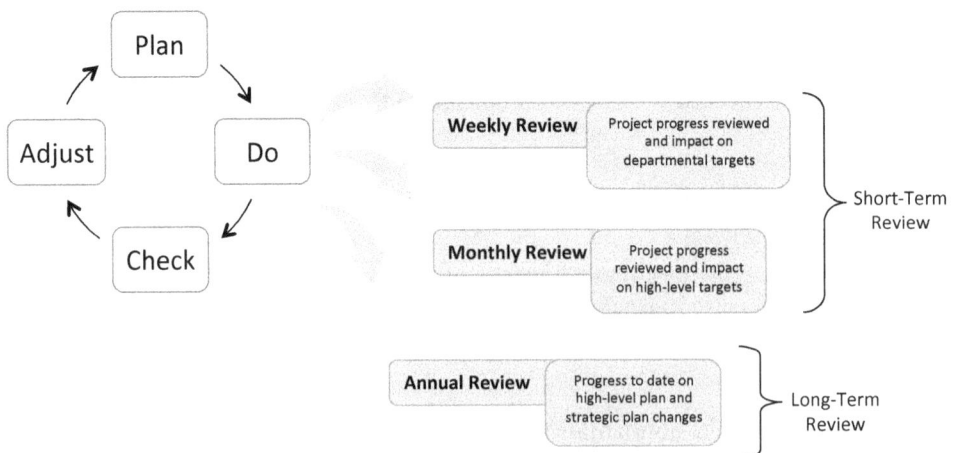

Plan

Adjust   Do

Check

Weekly Review | Project progress reviewed and impact on departmental targets

Monthly Review | Project progress reviewed and impact on high-level targets

Short-Term Review

Annual Review | Progress to date on high-level plan and strategic plan changes

Long-Term Review

Figure 10.17

Planning your review cycles up front and getting the routine into people's schedules is important. Typically, the short-term reviews work well with systemic level meetings and long-term reviews align to the financial cycle.

Short-Term PDCA Reviews

The monthly steercom meeting discussed in PART II is used to track and execute the High-Level A3 Strategy. It is important that this meeting provides the platform to check the actual performance of each activity listed in the A3 against the expected result and that the action plan coming out of this meeting, registers the decisions made.

Some organisations prefer to run this meeting weekly for the first month, after which it can fall into a more practical interval to meet (one to two months). This is to encourage upfront focus and assist leaders in adjusting to the new format. If required, each of these weekly meetings can be dedicated to one of the deployment leaders to present their progress to the steercom. Using the A3 format in the team feedback is a good standard to follow.

Similarly, the weekly deployment team meeting agenda serves the same purpose of checking on the execution of the Sub-Level A3 Strategy and maintaining focus amongst the team members. The results from this meeting will filter into the steercom meeting and the steercom will provide feedback into the deployment team meeting. Although the meeting is typically run weekly, over time, this may be changed to fortnightly once the participants are achieving good flow in the execution.

Moving to the next level of execution, daily team-level meetings are also aligned to meet the objectives of the overall strategy. Typically these meetings aim to include both daily routines and strategic issues. The team KPIs would have been determined in the Change Plan (PART II) but carefully aligned to the needs of the business and control of the team. Weekly feedback can be built into the team meeting in specific improvement projects underway that support the departmental level strategy. Alternatively, 'off-line' meetings every week can be dedicated to this purpose. Results from this meeting filter to the deployment team, and feedback is provided to the team meeting within a reasonable time period. Steercom and deployment team meeting agendas were discussed in Chapter 6, but see table 10.3 for an example of a team-level meeting agenda.

TEAM-LEVEL MEETING AGENDA   Example

FREQUENCY:	Every day at 7AM
DURATION:	15-20 minutes (gemba walk before meeting)
CHAIRPERSON:	Phillip Molape (Team Leader)
ATTENDEES:	Bob Viljoen; Sandra Jenkins; Themba Ngemntu; Stacey Lake; Cedric Anderson; Vusi Ntanzi
PURPOSE:	Evaluate past 24 hours, plan next 24 hours and remove obstacles

NO.	AGENDA ITEM	DURATION	RESPONSIBLE
1	Welcome and attendance		PM
2	Actions from last meeting	3 min	ALL
3	Previous 24 hour performance: KPI tracking and triggers: Target vs actual	7 min	BV
4	Next 24 hour plan	3 min	VN
5	Project team feedback (once per week): A3 one-pager	5 min	PM
6	Items for escalation to deployment team/ feedback	2 min	ALL

Develop a team-level agenda to suit the North Star focus areas and the goals of the Change Plan.

Table 10.3

More detail on creating the visual factory is provided in PROCESS and PEOPLE but at this point it is important to understand how PDCA needs to feature at each level of execution.

PDCA Meeting Preparation: Steercom and Deployment Team Meetings

To maintain momentum and enthusiasm in the PDCA meetings – for example, steercom and deployment team meetings – good organisation cannot be over-emphasised. No one enjoys a badly-organised or badly-run session. The following checklist in table 10.4 is designed to assist participants in preparing adequately to support the goals of the meeting:

MEETING CHECK-LIST		
PLANNING PHASE	CHECK POINT	CHECK RESULT YES OR NO
Before the Steercom or Deployment Meeting	Diaries and facilities are booked in advance and all participants have accepted. The chairperson personally contacts participants who have declined for an explanation.	☐
	Each participant has received the agenda and action items from the previous meeting.	☐
	The chairperson has planned which items will be evaluated on the gemba walk.	☐
	The chairperson has updated the KPI progress and has prepared questions for the relevant participants. Where applicable, participants have been asked to come prepared with specific feedback.	☐
	Each deployment or project leader has updated the Project Plan PDCA progress and prepared explanations on where targets have been missed or achieved, and further action to be taken. The visuals in the meeting room have been updated accordingly.	☐
	Each member has prepared possible risks and obstacles to be discussed.	☐
	The internal agent has prepared overall feedback and possible coaching topics for the group.	☐
After the Steercom or Deployment Meeting	The action board is updated and each participant is aware of his or her actions.	☐
	The Risk Response Plan is updated accordingly.	☐
	Each participant actively works on his or her actions until the next steercom meeting.	☐
Use the checklist provided to facilitate the PDCA process at the Steercom or Deployment Team Meeting. Include your own checks where needed.		

Table 10.4

Long-Term PDCA Reviews

The annual review takes a step back and reviews the progress for the year against the strategic plan. It is good practice to introduce a mid-year review using the same format so that no nasty surprises sneak up on the steercom at the last minute. As indicated earlier, this review usually coincides with the financial cycle and budgeting process.

Table 10.5 is an Annual Review Template that may be customised to suit your planning cycle:

A3 ANNUAL REVIEW	FOCUS AREA:		DEPARTMENT:			DATE:		
North Star Focus	North Star Target	Initiatives	Year To Date Results		Comments	Next Steps		
			Target	Actual				

SIGNATURES: AUTHOR: VERSION:

Table 10.5

Visual Dashboards that Promote PDCA

Creating visuals for the check process helps create an understanding of the improvement process being followed, each department's role in the strategy and triggers to encourage response. The design of this visual can take many forms and it is recommended that the steercom brainstorms a design and implements it before the first meeting takes place. Essentially, it should highlight the following:

- What are the hotspots or key areas of focus?
- What are we doing about them? What activities are on the go?
- What is the target?
- How are we actually performing to target?

Refer to figure 10.18 as a guideline and customise your own strategic-level board:

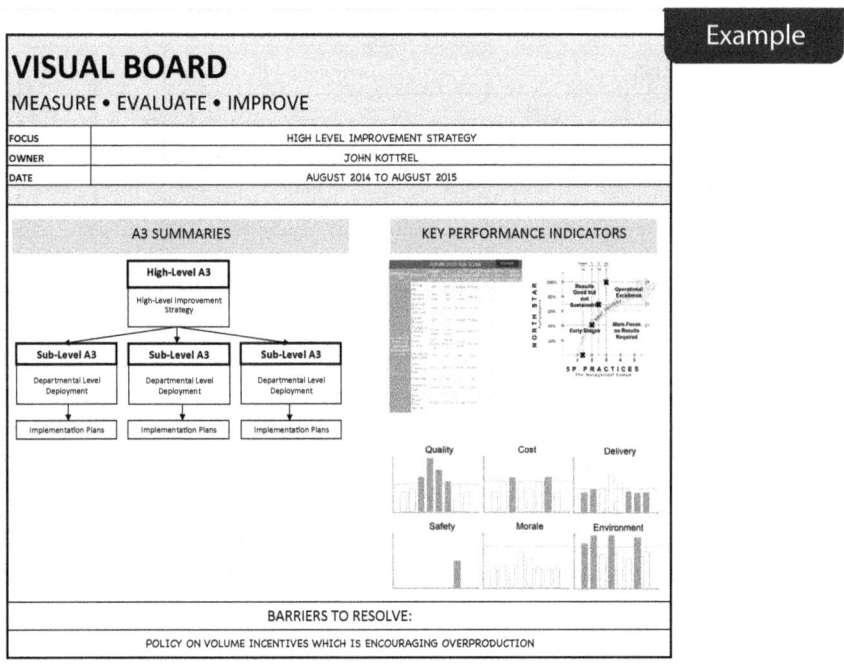

Figure 10.18

TIPS

Wherever possible, use colour to show at a glance the progress – for example, red = not achieved, yellow = in progress and green = achieved

Consider a visual action board to capture all decisions coming out of the meeting. This is a less cumbersome option to keeping minutes and has the psychological benefit that responsible people tend to action their items when they are displayed for all to see (figure 10.19):

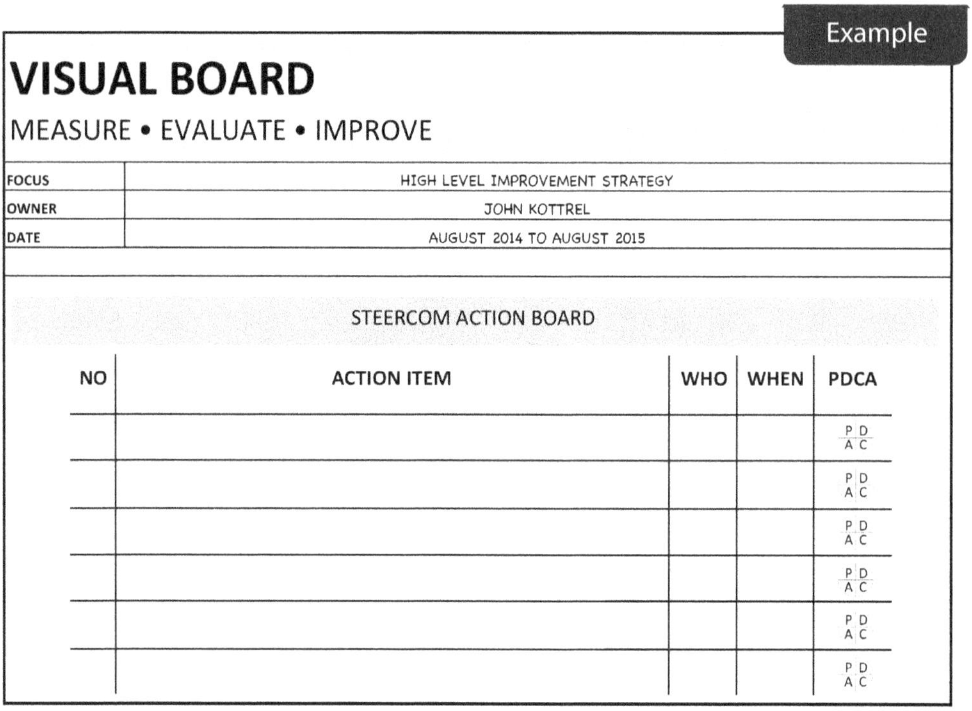
Example

VISUAL BOARD

MEASURE • EVALUATE • IMPROVE

FOCUS	HIGH LEVEL IMPROVEMENT STRATEGY
OWNER	JOHN KOTTREL
DATE	AUGUST 2014 TO AUGUST 2015

STEERCOM ACTION BOARD

NO	ACTION ITEM	WHO	WHEN	PDCA
				P D A C
				P D A C
				P D A C
				P D A C
				P D A C
				P D A C

Figure 10.19

Remember to write actions clearly, always assign only one name and a specific date. Avoid words such as 'everyone', 'team', 'a.s.a.p' and 'ongoing'.

If space allows, give each deployment leader his or her own display area to be able to show more detail pertaining to the improvement area – for example, KPIs, actions, Value Stream Maps, DMAIC steps (Define, Measure, Analyse, Improve, Control) and kaizen activities (covered in PROBLEM SOLVING). This board would then be used to provide feedback to the steercom and would also be used for the deployment team meeting. Try to implement a standard look for all the boards for easy interpretation and good-housekeeping practices. Refer to figure 10.20 for a systemic-level example and develop your own board design to suit.

Example

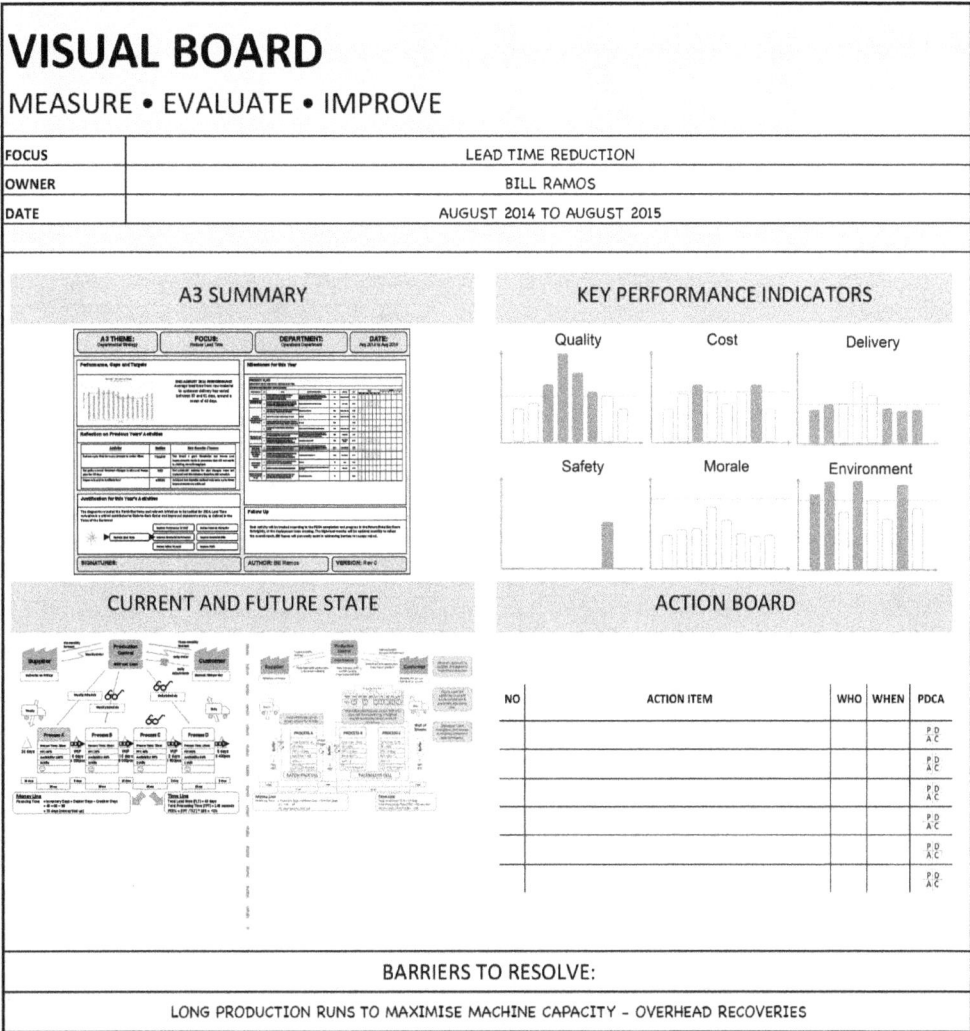

Figure 10.20

Team-level visual boards and hourly boards are covered in more detail in PROCESS and PEOPLE but remember that team activities also include both routine work and improvement work. The improvement focus and relevant KPIs coming from the A3 Strategies therefore directly influence the design of the board and team-meeting content, and should also be considered when designing the CHECK processes into the systems. See figure 10.21 for a situational-level example and develop your own board design to suit.

Example

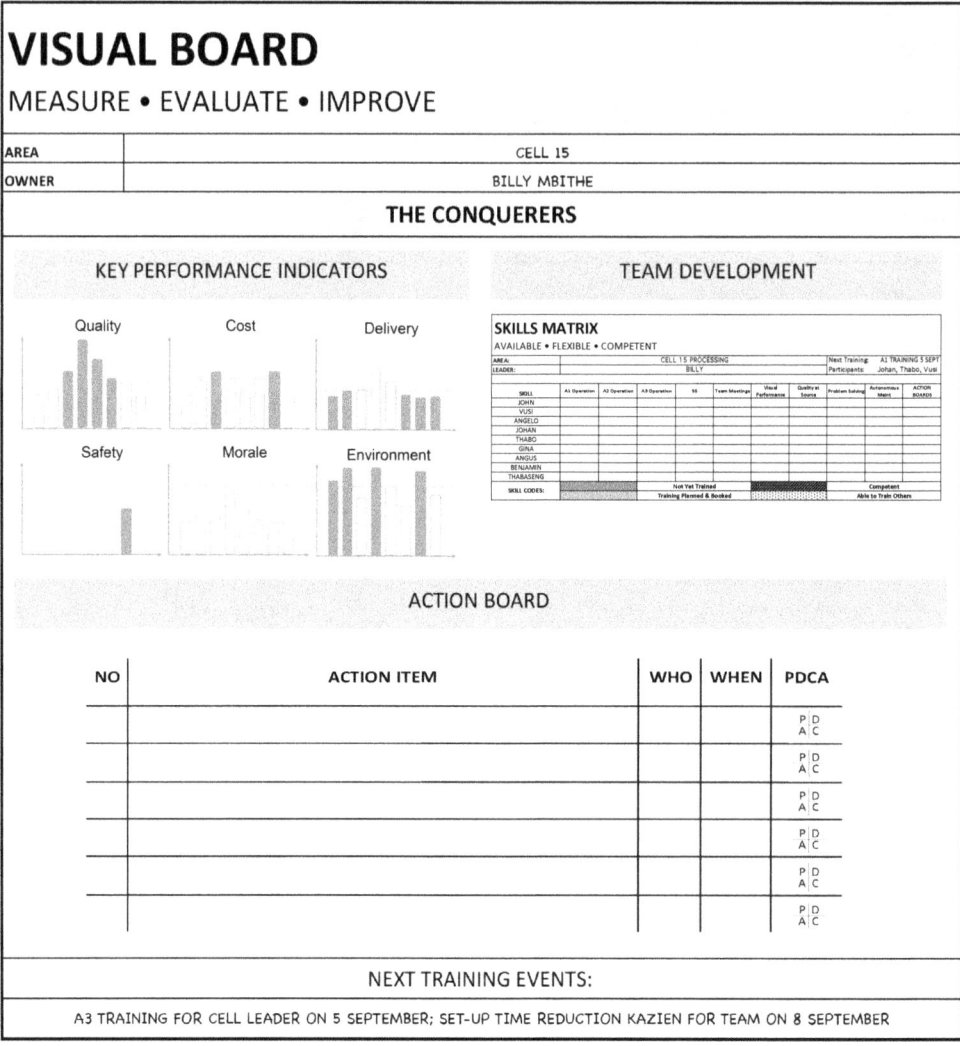

Figure 10.21

Build-in Exception Management

This is all about keeping focus on the hot spots rather than diluting attention to a range of activities. This has the knock-on effect of making meetings more efficient, allowing team members more time to deal with the important items and pinpointing what to problem solve.

In crisis mode, it is easy to get sidetracked from the North Star and realise, only when year-end results are looked at, how little was actually done about the improvement strategy. If this sounds familiar then exception management can make a big difference to execution in your organisation.

The CHECK process can be further developed to include exception management principles so that the right abnormalities are exposed and afforded the precious time of the team. Consider the following pointers:

○ Maintain a strict agenda for all PDCA meetings and ensure adherence to the topics at hand – for example, steercom meeting and deployment team meeting.

○ When a crisis occurs detracting the attention from the key focus areas, ensure the crisis is stabilised, root causes addressed and then 'business as usual on the A3 Strategies' is preserved thereafter.

○ Use visuals to prompt response to the right items – for example in figure 10.22, if a key performance metric drops below an agreed line (trigger line) three times in a row, this automatically prompts the need for a problem-solving activity and the deployment leader or project leader must present to the group on how the abnormality was effectively dealt with.

○ If a target (or interim target) is to be achieved by a particular date and the target is missed at that time, this triggers a response.

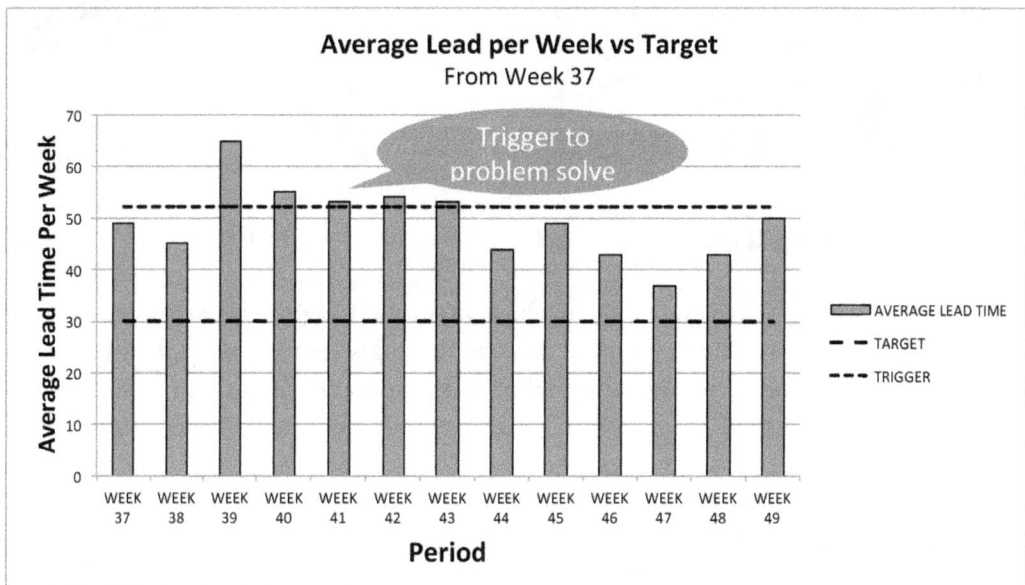

Figure 10.22

Growing an Atmosphere Conducive to CHECK

Think about the culture in your organisation. Is it an environment where individuals blame others when times are tough or is there a healthy culture where individuals take responsibility for problems and actively look to resolve them? Is the leadership style more collaborative where problems exposed are rewarded positively or is the leadership style more autocratic where employees are reluctant to bring problems forward? The quick check you conducted in Chapter 9 will help to answer some of these questions.

The CHECK phase of PDCA relies heavily on a culture where reporting mistakes is habitual and considered positive. The leadership team will need to follow through on the change management required to create this atmosphere. It will start in the review meetings.

Maintaining Healthy Tension

Tension may develop when the CHECK phase kicks in. Tough conversations will take place as leaders increase the pressure to achieve the goals set for the team. A common reaction to this tension is to lower the goal or relax the standard but you are cautioned against this (Pascal, 2006).

Assuming the structured process of conducting the Diagnostic (PART I), developing the Improvement Strategy and the improvement goals have been followed (PART II), goals set should be based on sound analysis and consensus. As such, these goals must remain intact. Falling into the trap of adjusting the goal, will foster a culture of denial. The best defense in this situation is to focus on problem-solving skills and increase the leadership support. Stay focused on the problem or behaviour and not the person.

Using the principles discussed above, refer to table 10.6 and agree on how the review cycles will be designed and implemented.

Review Cycle	Review Meeting	Purpose of Review	Chairperson and Participants	What key topics will be covered in the agenda?	What visuals will be used to create understanding and trigger response?	How will exception management be applied?
				CHECK REVIEW CYCLE DESIGN		
ANNUAL REVIEW	A3 ANNUAL REVIEW					
MONTHLY REVIEW	STEERCOM MEETING					
WEEKLY REVIEW	DEPLOYMENT TEAM MEETING					
	WEEKLY TEAM LEVEL MEETING REVIEW					

Discuss amongst the steercom how the PDCA Review Cycles will be designed and capture comments for each of the headings above.

Table 10.6

Step 4: ADJUST

The CHECK process is in place and ensuring what was planned is deployed in such a way as to achieve the expected result. It exposes problems as they arise and pinpoints successful actions requiring sustainment. As such, problem solving is a natural outcome from the CHECK process and a critical input to the ADJUST phase.

ADJUST is more than just a minor tweak, it is about leveraging the knowledge, skills, experience and innovation of employees to help gather the evidence and find suitable countermeasures to set the work back on course. The process looks as shown in figure 10.23 (Pascal, 2006):

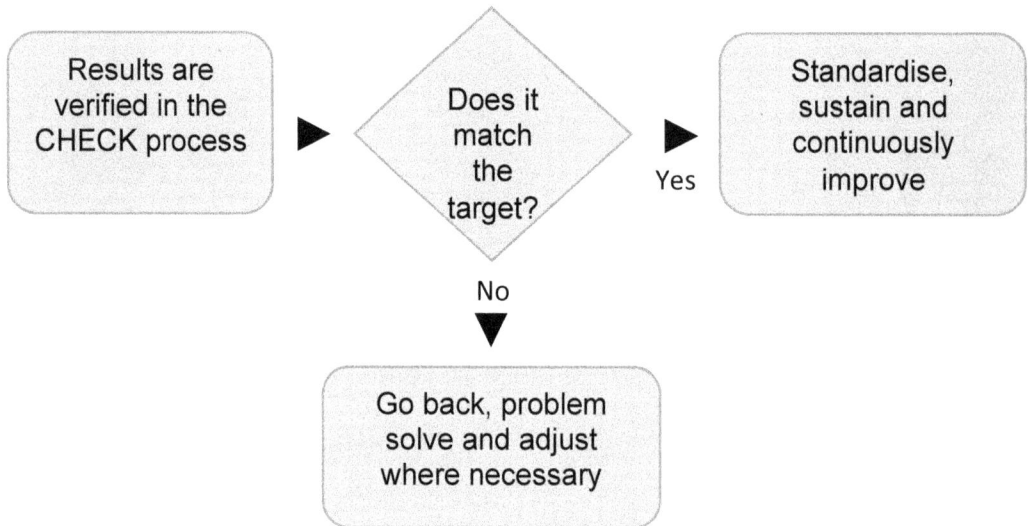

Figure 10.23

Where the result matches the target, standardisation and sustainment is triggered. Standardisation should encourage simple, easy-to-use visuals of how the work should be done. These could include training plans, poke-yokes (mistake-proofing), work instructions, trouble shooting and assessments, amongst other things. There is also no 'one best way' when determining countermeasures, so it is expected that over time, standards will be improved upon and adjusted to suit new methods of working. The principles of standardisation and sustainment are covered in more detail in the PROCESS and PROBLEM SOLVING books.

The trick to completing the ADJUST phase, is to create problem solvers at all levels in the organisation that can respond adequately when the result does not match the target. This develops the logical, thinking process needed to complete the strategy deployment process and go full circle back to PLAN.

In reality, if you analysed the types of problem that arise in the business, you will discover plenty low-hanging fruit, some system-level problems and a handful of strategic problems (figure 10.24). Of course, as you move up the levels, complexity increases and a higher level of authority and skill is required to resolve the problem.

In most cases, resolving the low-level problems, will reduce the problems filtering up through the ranks.

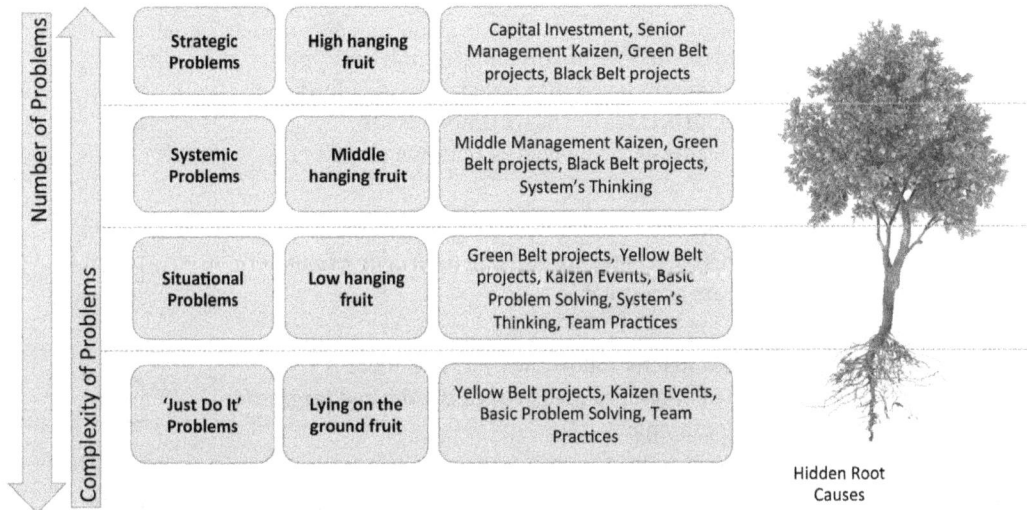

Number of Problems ↑ Complexity of Problems ↓			
Strategic Problems	High hanging fruit	Capital Investment, Senior Management Kaizen, Green Belt projects, Black Belt projects	
Systemic Problems	Middle hanging fruit	Middle Management Kaizen, Green Belt projects, Black Belt projects, System's Thinking	
Situational Problems	Low hanging fruit	Green Belt projects, Yellow Belt projects, Kaizen Events, Basic Problem Solving, System's Thinking, Team Practices	
'Just Do It' Problems	Lying on the ground fruit	Yellow Belt projects, Kaizen Events, Basic Problem Solving, Team Practices	Hidden Root Causes

Figure 10.24

Problem solvers therefore need to be developed to address each of these levels, using relevant tools suitable to the complexity of the problem. It is important not to use a 5kg hammer for a 2kg job so professional training on these techniques and sound coaching structures are highly recommended to set this practice in motion.

Problem solvers are not created by training alone. The support structure to create the right environment for problem solving is required for success. Support includes developing the infrastructure, creating standard approaches, strengthening standardisation and amending roles and responsibilities where applicable. This is covered in more detail in PROBLEM SOLVING.

Once the right skill level and environment for problem solving has been established, the quality of the ADJUST phase of PDCA will improve. The following checklist in table 10.7 will assist in evaluating the ADJUST phase – remember it will take time to create the right habits:

'ADJUST' CHECK-LIST

CHECK POINT	CHECK RESULT YES OR NO
A problem solving strategy specifies an approach to create both continuous improvement and breakthrough change, and this guides how targets are met.	☐
A problem solving model describes the methodology, tools and techniques to address the different levels of problem. It also defines the escalation and feedback processes to ensure problems are adequately addressed and leaders are involved in removing barriers.	☐
Each rank in the organisation has been trained according to the relevant skill required at their level and are suitable to the complexity of problem for which they are accountable.	☐
PDCA meetings and process strictly follow the cycle and there is immediate response to out-of-standard results until the desired target is achieved. Leaders set the example.	☐
A cultural mindset towards rapid-response to problems is developed and producing results.	☐
Adherence to PDCA and problem solving is rewarded in the company and employees are encouraged in a positive way to continue exposing and eliminating the issues.	☐
The response triggered when missed targets occur is process-driven and every level is performing this in a standard way.	☐
The skills level in dealing with problems is improving and the right level of person is assigned to the correct level of problem. More problems are being solved at the lower levels, allowing the leaders sufficient time to focus on more systemic and strategic problems.	☐
The time and effort to achieve activities specified in the A3 Summary is becoming shorter and more efficient.	☐
A culture of achieving PLAN is in place.	☐

Use the checklist provided to periodically assess the Current State of the ADJUST phase. The objective is to develop problem solvers at all levels, who follow-through on problems to sustainability.

Table 10.7

✅ FOR YOU TO TRY

- Discuss the PDCA Cycle amongst the steercom and agree on how this process will be used to execute the strategy.

- Evaluate the current cross-functional ownership for execution and discuss how this will be achieved going forward. Assign deployment leaders to each improvement area using the template provided.

- Refer to the findings from the diagnostic and the Change Plan, and develop the A3 High-Level Strategy Summary using the template provided or a variation thereof.

- Deployment Leaders are to cascade the High-Level Strategy to A3 Sub-Level Strategy Summaries and team-level implementation plans.

- Discuss the current review cycles taking place during the year and agree how the reviews will work going forward to ensure a PDCA mental model drives the execution progress.

- Develop the short-term review structures, update the meeting agendas and design appropriate visual displays to facilitate the PDCA Cycle.

- Develop the long-term review structures, update the meeting agendas and design appropriate visual displays to facilitate the PDCA Cycle.

- Agree on how the principles of exception management will be used to govern the efficiency of the execution and include the approach in the meeting structure.

- Evaluate the quality of the ADJUST phase periodically to assure the PDCA cycle is progressing through each step to sustainability.

WAY FORWARD

Congratulations! If you have followed the guidelines in *Clear Direction* then you are well on your way down the path to Operational Excellence. This is a good time to pause and reflect on the progress you have made so far, and to start thinking about your next steps.

The detailed analysis is complete and you have a plan to generate involvement and execute change. You have been enabled to:

- Define your North Star and the key initiatives that will guide you to your goals.
- Establish the Current State of your Best Practices and how well the management system is geared for the journey to Operational Excellence.
- Streamline your processes to deliver value with velocity.
- Source the levers that drive cost in your organisation, and link changes to the bottom-line.
- Consolidate your improvement strategy under one umbrella for change that tackles all the major value drivers.
- Effectively plan how you will enthuse and take people along with you on the journey, so that the Future State Vision becomes a reality.
- Set in motion a structured, robust means for driving change, so that all the hard work materializes into results for the Business, Customer and Employee.
- Construct a foundation for continuous improvement and respect for people.

In working through Purpose you would also have touched on elements of Process, People, Problem Solving and Planet which form the remainder of the 5P series. The next phase of the journey will involve pinpointing elements from each part of the model that will contribute to the initiatives identified in the North Star to enable successful execution of the High-Level Plan and ultimate achievement of the Future State Vision.

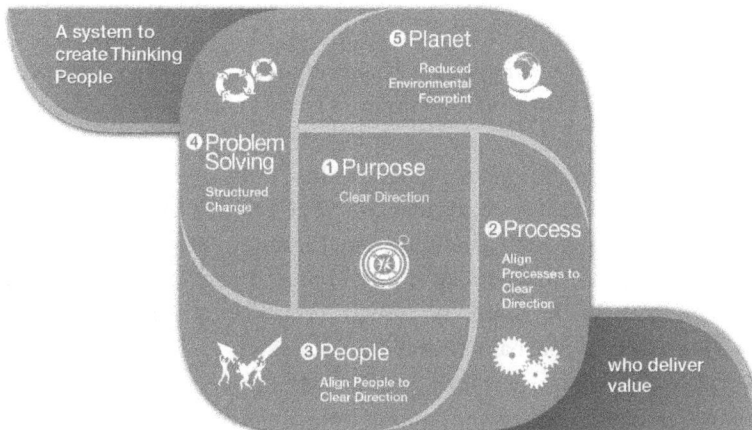

Ballé, M. & Ballé, F. (2009) *The Lean Manager.* Cambridge MA, The Lean Enterprise Institute

Bicheno, J. (2004) *The New Lean Toolbox.* Buckingham, PICSIE Books

Bicheno, J. & Catherwood, P. (2005) *Six Sigma and the Quality Toolbox.* Buckingham, PICSIE Books

Bossidy, L. & Charan, R. (2002) *Execution The Discipline of Getting Things Done.* London, Random House Business Books

Bragg, S. (2010) *Cost Reduction Analysis.* New Jersey, John Wiley & Sons Inc.

Brinkerhof, R. (2010) *L&D: Business Partner, not Order Taker.* Michigan, BTS

Dennis, P. (2009) *Getting the Right Things Done.* Cambridge MA, The Lean Enterprise Institute

Evans, J. & Lindsay, W. (1996) *The Management and Control of Quality.* New York, West Publishing Company

Faull, N. (1998) *Competitive Capabilities: A novel strategy for re-engineering.* Cape Town, Juta

Ford, D. (1999) *Bottom-Line Training.* Houston, Gulf Publishing Company

George, M., Rowlands, D., Price, M. & Maxey, J. (2005) *Lean Six Sigma Pocket Toolbook.* New York, McGraw-Hill

Glenday, I. (2007) *Breaking through to Flow.* Ross-on-Wye, Lean Enterprise Academy

Goldratt, E. & Cox, J. (2004) *The Goal.* Great Barrington, The North River Press Publishing Corporation

Grütter, A. (2010) *Introduction to Operations Management.* Cape Town, Pearsons

Harvard Business Review (2008) *Manufacturing Excellence at Toyota.* Boston, Harvard Business School Publishing

Hill, T. (2000) *Manufacturing Strategy: Text and Cases.* New York, McGraw-Hill

Hopp, W. & Spearman, W. (2000) *Factory Physics (2nd Edition).* New York, McGraw-Hill

Jackson, T. (2006) *Hoshin Kanri for the Lean Enterprise.* Boca Raton, CRC Press

Jacob, D., Bergland, S. & Cox, J. (2010) *Velocity.* New York, Free Press

Japan Management Association (1985) *Kanban Just-In-Time at Toyota.* Tokyo, Japan Management Association

Kotter, J. (2002) *The Heart of Change.* Boston, Harvard Business School Publishing

Liker, J. & Meier, D. (2006) *The Toyota Way Fieldbook.* New York, McGraw-Hill

Liker, J. & Hoseus, M. (2008) *Toyota Culture.* New York, McGraw-Hill

Mann, D. (2005) *Creating a Lean Culture.* New York, Productivity Press

Martichenko, R. & von Grabe, K. (2010) *Building a Lean Fulfillment Stream.* Cambridge MA, The Lean Enterprise Institute

Ohno, T. (1988) *Beyond Large Scale Production.* Portland, Productivity Inc.

Rother, M. & Shook, J. (1999) *Learning to See.* Cambridge MA, The Lean Enterprise Institute

Rother, M. & Harris, R. (2001) *Creating Continuous Flow.* Cambridge MA, The Lean Enterprise Institute

Rother, M. (2010) *Toyota Kata.* New York, McGraw-Hill

Shook, J. (2009) *Managing to Learn.* Cambridge MA, The Lean Enterprise Institute

Smally, A. (2004) *Creating Level Pull.* Brookline, The Lean Enterprise Institute

Sobek, D. & Smalley, A. (2008) *Understanding A3 Thinking.* Boca Raton, Productivity Press

Spearman, M., Woodruff, W. & Hopp, W. (1990) *CONWIP: A Pull Alternative to Kanban.* Cambridge MA, International Journal of Production Research

Wills, B. (2009) *Green Intentions.* New York, Productivity Press

Womack, J. & Jones, D. (2005) *Lean Solutions.* London, Simon & Schuster UK Ltd

INDEX TO TABLES

INDEX TO FIGURES

INDEX TO TOPICS

www.ingramcontent.com/pod-product-compliance
Lightning Source LLC
Chambersburg PA
CBHW080137220326
41598CB00032B/5089